FOXMAN
DELAWARE VALLEY
TORAH INSTITUTE

ISIDORE AND FANNIE FOXMAN ע״ה

Mesivta **BAIS DOVID**
of Cherry Hill

The rare event of *Bircas Hachammah*, masterfully elucidated in this volume we present to you, evokes the imagery and awareness of the wonders of *ma'ase b'reishis*- Almighty's creation of the world. One cannot help but contemplate the mysteries and intricacies, grandeur and majesty of our vast universe. And even as we do, we cannot escape the timeless questions of origin and purpose.

What preceded the universe? What blueprint did the Creator follow in crafting heaven and earth? In what merit is the miracle of creation continually renewed? What is the purpose of the seemingly random and perplexing events of world and human history?

Chazal, our sages, teach us that the answer to all of the above is one — *Torah*. Torah is the singular cosmic force that maintains the universe and defines its nature and purpose.

On the 14th of *Nissan*, Jewish communities far and wide will assemble to sanctify the name of Hashem and recite the blessing of *Bircas Hachammah*. Just days earlier, the 10th of *Nissan*, will mark the first *yahrtziet* of our beloved and revered Rebbe, Hagaon Rav A. Henoch Leibowitz of blessed memory. He lived his life for an ideal — simple yet profound. A Yeshiva, an academy of Torah study in the midst of a community, sustains and elevates all of its members and institutions.

Foxman Delaware Valley Torah Institute-Mesivta Bais Dovid is a center of Torah learning for young men in our communities. Its classes teach reverence for Torah's laws and observances as they inspire passion for its ideals and values. Its mission is not simply to impart Torah knowledge but to glorify its study. Graduation is not the completion of a program of studies but the beginning of a wholesome and meaningful life's journey, guided and inspired by Torah.

As much as the Torah study of our students fuels their own transformation, it influences every sphere of our communities' consciousness. It purifies our hearts and homes. It shapes our attitudes and ambitions. It strengthens our synagogues and communal institutions and reinforces our responsibilities to one another.

It is our prayer that the banner of Torah in our communities be raised ever [...] [...]ming of *Moshiach* speedily in our days.

[...] Institute/Mesivta Bais Dovid
February 15, 2009

DEDICATED BY

MR. STEPHEN FRANKEL

IN HONOR OF HIS WIFE

IRIS

MAY HASHEM GRANT HER GOOD HEALTH
AND MAY WE ENJOY TOGETHER
CONTINUED NACHAS FROM OUR CHILDREN

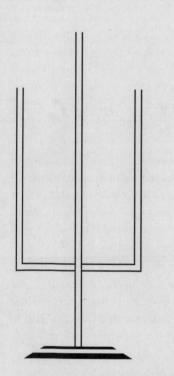

In memory of

Maurice M. Rothman ז"ל

and

Golde N. Rothman ע"ה

לחמו מלחמות ה'

*"who lived and fought
for Torah-true Judaism"*

Published through the courtesy of the
HENRY, BERTHA and EDWARD ROTHMAN FOUNDATION
Rochester N.Y. • Circleville, Ohio • Cleveland

Dedicated
to the
Memory
of

David Krupnick

and in
Honor
of

Marilyn Krupnick

SPONSORS

MR. AND MRS. SHERMAN FRAGER

∞∞∞

HEIMOWITZ LANGER LIBRARY

∞∞∞

MR. AND MRS. TED KOSLOFF

∞∞∞

MR. AND MRS. MARVIN RAAB

∞∞∞

MR. ALBERT STEIN

∞∞∞

MR. AND MRS. STANLEY SVED

ArtScroll Mesorah Series®

Rabbi Nosson Scherman / Rabbi Meir Zlotowitz

General Editors

BIRCAS HACHAMMAH

סדר ברכת החמה

Published by

Mesorah Publications, ltd

BIRCAS HACHAMMAH

BLESSING OF THE SUN — RENEWAL OF CREATION

A HALACHIC ANALYSIS AND ANTHOLOGY WITH
A NEW TRANSLATION AND COMMENTARY.

by Rabbi J. David Bleich

Overviews by Rabbi Nosson Scherman

FIRST EDITION
First Impression … December 1980
SECOND EDITION
Revised and Corrected
First Impression … February 1981
THIRD EDITION
Revised and Expanded
First Impression … January 2009
Second Impression … February 2009

Published and Distributed by
MESORAH PUBLICATIONS, LTD.
4401 Second Avenue / Brooklyn, N.Y 11232

Distributed in Europe by
LEHMANNS
Unit E, Viking Business Park
Rolling Mill Road
Jarow, Tyne & Wear, NE32 3DP
England

Distributed in Australia and New Zealand
by GOLDS WORLDS OF JUDAICA
3-13 William Street
Balaclava, Melbourne 3183
Victoria, Australia

Distributed in Israel by
SIFRIATI / A. GITLER — BOOKS
6 Hayarkon Street
Bnei Brak 51127

Distributed in South Africa by
KOLLEL BOOKSHOP
Ivy Common
105 William Road
Norwood 2192, Johannesburg, South Africa

ISBN 10: 0-89906-175-3 / ISBN 13: 978-0-89906-175-7 (hard cover)
ISBN 10: 0-89906-176-1 / ISBN 13: 978-0-89906-176-4 (paperback)

Typography by CompuScribe at ArtScroll Studios, Ltd.

Printed in the United States of America by Noble Book Press Corp.
Bound by Sefercraft, Quality Bookbinders, Ltd., Brooklyn N.Y. 11232

לע"נ
בתנו הדגולה חמדת לבנו
חיה גנעשא
זכרונה לברכה
אשת הרה"ג ר' שמואל חיים הכהן גורוויץ יבלחט"א

חכמות נשים בנתה ביתה והשאירה אחריה ברכה

ידידות משכנותיך אהבה ותורתך שעשועיה

הללה ה' בחייה זמרה לאלקיה בעודה

נקטפה בדמי ימיה ועלתה נשמתה

הטהורה השמימה שביעי של פסח תשס"ח

תהא נשמתה צרורה בצרור החיים

⋖§ Table of Contents

◆§ Preface

אַשְׁרֵי אִישׁ יָרֵא אֶת ה' בְּמִצְוֹתָיו חָפֵץ מְאֹד — *Happy is the man who fears* HASHEM, *who desires His mitzvos greatly* (*Psalms* 112:1). These words of the psalmist eloquently express the attitude of a Jew toward fulfillment of a *mitzvah*. Each *mitzvah* is treasured; each is a source of delight. The preciousness of each *mitzvah* and the joy attendant upon fulfillment of the divine command spurs the quest for proficiency in its observance.

Little wonder, then, that voluminous tomes have been written explaining the nature of individual *mitzvos* and the *halachos* surrounding their performance. *Bircas haChammah*, despite its relative simplicity and infrequency of occurrence, is no exception. Although, in essence, it is but the recitation of a brief *bircas hoda'ah* (blessing of thanksgiving) once every twenty-eight years, *Bircas haChammah* has received extensive treatment in rabbinic literature. Indeed, the rarity of its occurrence has served to magnify the rejoicing in its performance and to enhance the scholarly attention it has received. The present publication was undertaken as the fashioning of yet another link in the long chain of works of this genre. Since much of the information surrounding *Bircas haChammah* is not readily available, an attempt was made to perform the task in a comprehensive manner. Hopefully, the endeavor to be thorough has not involved undue sacrifice of clarity.

The task, undertaken at a late date, and involving use of sources that are relatively obscure, could not have been completed without the assistance of a number of individuals to whom the author is most grateful. Particular thanks are due to MISS FAIGIE ZYLBERMINC of the Oriental Division of the Library of Congress, who not only shared her remarkable bibliographic knowledge but also went far beyond the call of duty in making the resources of the Library of Congress available to me; to RABBI JACOB B. MANDELBAUM of the Mendel Gottesman Library of Yeshiva University, whose encyclopedic knowledge of *sefarim* was of inestimable value; to MRS. SARAH LEVY of the Mendel Gottesman Library, for her assistance and perseverance in securing needed volumes; to MR. E. KAHN, Librarian of Jews' College, London, for his efforts in locating various monographs dealing with *Bircas haChammah;* to the entire staff of the Oxford Centre for Postgraduate Jewish Studies, for their invaluable assistance; and to RABBI ABRAHAM GUBBAY and RABBI ABRAHAM SCHISCHA of London, who graciously made their personal libraries available to me.

For reasons of consistency the material in this volume conforms to the general style of the ArtScroll Mesorah Series. Matters of style, transliteration, rendering of Divine appellations, capitalization, etc., do not necessarily reflect the preference of the author. I wish to express my appreciation to the entire staff of MESORAH PUBLICATIONS for their unfailing cooperation, diligence, high standards of professionalism, graphic excellence and that rarity among publishers — speed! Special thanks are due to REB SHEAH BRANDER whose devoted efforts cannot be attributed solely to professional and artistic pride, but stem from a deep commitment *lehagdil Torah uleha'adirah.*

Both Mesorah Publications and the author wish to commend MR. AARON HEIMOWITZ as well as the Roshei Yeshiva and officers of the various CHOFETZ CHAIM YESHIVOS throughout the U.S.A. and the YESHIVA DAY SCHOOL OF SOUTH QUEENS, who have recognized that this publication presents an opportunity for dissemination of Torah knowledge. In undertaking to provide copies of this work to the many individuals associated with these institutions, they have encouraged Torah study in a meaningful manner.

My deep appreciation also to my brother-in-law, RABBI MORDECHAI OCHS, for his careful reading of the manuscript and his many valuable suggestions. My thanks as well both to him and to my esteemed friend, RABBI DOVID COHEN, for the pleasure and benefit of many conversations devoted to the *masa umatan shel halachah.* Finally, this work — as indeed everything I have been privileged to write — has benefited from the creative insight and collaborative effort of each and every member of my family.

J.D.B.

Channukah, 5741

ᵉ᷎§ Preface to the Revised and Expanded Edition

In the wake of publication of the first edition of *Bircas haChammah* in 5741 I received communications from a number of readers. I wish to express my thanks to each of them for their valued observations. In several instances the present edition has been modified to reflect their comments. Particular mention should be made of the detailed and erudite notes of the late MR. CHARLES ELKIN, of blessed memory, to whom I owe a special debt of gratitude.

The present edition has benefited from the insights of my son RABBI MOSHE BLEICH and is enhanced by the valuable calendrical charts that were prepared by MR. MOISHE MILLER, for whose diligence and suggestions I extend my thanks. My thanks also to MR. HERSHEL EDELSTEIN for his assistance in formulating the methods used for calculating the times of *Bircas haChammah* according to various authorities. The meticulous proofreading of my granddaughter HADASSAH GURWITZ has spared this work from many inadvertent errors. My appreciation also to the current staff of the Mendel Gottesman Library of Yeshiva University for their unflagging cooperation and dedication: to RABBI MOSHE SHAPIRO for going beyond the call of duty in identifying and locating sources on my behalf; to MR. ZALMAN ALPERT for sharing his expertise with regard to rabbinic journals in particular; and to MR. ZVI ERENYI for assistance in tracking arcane bibliograpic references. I would also like to thank RABBI MOSHE ROSENBLUM, RABBI AVROHOM YITZCHOK DEUTSCH, ELI KROEN, MRS. MINDY STERN, MRS. ESTHER FEIERSTEIN, MRS. TOBY GOLDZWEIG, MRS. SURY ENGLARD, REIZY KNOPFLER, DEVOIRY WEISBLUM and their colleagues on the staff of MESORAH PUBLICATIONS for their conscientious attention and unstinting efforts. Last but not least, my thanks to MR. MENDY HERZBERG who graciously shepherded this edition through the publication process.

The Hebrew material in the appendix is reprinted from my *BeNesivos haHalacha*, Vol. II (Hoboken, N.J., 5759), published by The Michael Scharf Publication Trust of Yeshiva University Press.

J.D.B.

Tishrei, 5769

⋖ The Overviews

Of Beginning and Purpose

Measurements from Sinai

An Overview –
Of Beginning and Purpose

וַיַּעַשׂ אֱלֹהִים אֶת שְׁנֵי הַמְּאֹרֹת הַגְּדֹלִים ... וַיְהִי
עֶרֶב וַיְהִי בֹקֶר יוֹם רְבִיעִי

And God made the two great luminaries ... and there was evening and there was morning, a fourth day (Genesis 1:16,19).

הָגוֹ סִיגִים מִכָּסֶף וַיֵּצֵא לַצֹּרֵף כֶּלִי. הָגוֹ רָשָׁע לִפְנֵי
מֶלֶךְ וְיִכּוֹן בַּצֶּדֶק כִּסְאוֹ

Remove dross from silver, a vessel can emerge for the refiner; when an evildoer is removed from the king, his throne is established in righteousness (Proverbs 25:4-5).

תָּנוּ רַבָּנָן: הָרוֹאֶה חַמָּה בִּתְקוּפָתָהּ ... אוֹמֵר בָּרוּךְ
עוֹשֶׂה בְרֵאשִׁית

Our Rabbis taught: He who sees the sun at its turning point [the point at which it was at the moment of its creation (Rashi)] ... should recite [the blessing] "Blessed ... Who makes creation" (Berachos 59b).

I. Heavenly Testimony

A Reminder

Tradition teaches that the sun's first appearance in the newly-created heaven is reckoned from Nissan, the month of Passover and springtime.

ON THE FOURTH DAY GOD CREATED THE SUN, and it began to function as the center of our solar system. After approximately 365¼ days, the sun would be at its original place in the sky and a new year would begin, in a cycle that still continues without change. Tradition teaches that the sun's first appearance in the newly-created heaven is reckoned from Nissan, the month of Passover and springtime. A quarter of a year later — after about 91 days, 7½ hours — the next season would begin and so on. If that very first year began on the eve of Wednesday, then the next one would start fifty-two weeks and a day and a quarter later, on a Thursday night.*

Every twenty-eight years the sun would begin its spring season on the eve of a Wednesday, at the same moment when it was emplaced in the cosmos. So in a sense, that rare Wednesday is an anniversary of sorts, a milestone that reminds man of the God Who created him, his sun, and his earth. It is a time for him to pause in his incessant quest to feed himself and conquer his surroundings, a time to look at the teeming heavens and squint at the fiery sun, to contemplate the vastness of space and the infinite God to Whom the heavens are merely a throne, to recognize anew that man matters no more in all this expanse than an electron on Everest — yet Man was proclaimed the master of all creation and given the task of subduing it, making it productive, and utilizing it to assist him in the service of God.

Not often do circumstances remind us that our attention was meant to be occupied by bigger things than the next customer, the next test, the next vacation, the next meal, the next election, the next set of statistics. Sometimes a great event occurs that cries out to us, "Insignificant *Homo sapiens*, stop your foolish preoccupation with yourself and the politics and economics of your neighbor. There is a Power greater than you. Your significance is measured solely by how well you serve Him. Ultimately, you are important only to the extent that you recognize your insignificance, strong only if you acknowledge your weakness, worthy of allegiance only if your only allegiance belongs to God." We do not exaggerate when we say that a person's worth may be judged according to how he reacts to such events.

---

* The calculations are far more complicated than this. The exact length of the years and seasons, and their halachic ramifications, are discussed in Chapter 2 of this book.

Does he let them shock him into an awareness that his best-laid plans are worthless unless they conform with God's will, or does he shrug his shoulders, gird his loins, and regroup for another attack on the impregnable?

Rejected Message

When the atom was split, it would have been a propitious moment for man to say, "I subjugate myself to the One Who created the atom and the human intelligence that unlocked it."

WHEN THE ATOM WAS SPLIT, EVERYONE STOOD awestruck at its unimaginable power and destructive force. The black mushroom cloud became a universal symbol of terror and danger. It would have been a propitious moment for man to say, "I subjugate myself to the One Who created the atom and the human intelligence that unlocked it." And what did man do? He turned his scientists loose on finding more efficient means of greater destruction and his diplomats loose on hiding such murderous activities with smoke screens that are, in their own way, more dangerous than what they conceal.

A spacecraft traveled a billion miles and sent back pictures of Saturn, pictures that confounded scientists and rendered untenable laws of planetary motion that had been considered inviolable. What a splendid opportunity for human genius to exclaim, "I have raised my eyes to the heights and perceived Who created all this!" And what did man do? He quickly submerged his astonishment in a welter of theories that would be honed into laws to be proclaimed unabashedly as the *new* wisdom that is as inviolable as the old used to be, and will remain so until the next time it must be scrapped and recycled.

This is not to suggest that scientists, statesmen, physicists, and astronomers should abandon their crafts. To the contrary — *let* them do their work, but let them do it with the realization that they are God's servants and that the ultimate law is His. If a phenomenon leads a person to this recognition, then it has served a lofty purpose. If not, then he has failed, just as a businessman fails if he purchases merchandise in the wrong style or for the wrong season. Opportunity knocked, but he opened the wrong door.

If a phenomenon leads a person to this recognition, then it has served a lofty purpose. If not, then he has failed. Opportunity knocked, but he opened the wrong door.

Every month the new moon reminds the Jew that creation is not static, and he recites a blessing to sanctify the phenomenon that testifies to God's mastery of the heavens. Every twenty-eight years on a Wednesday morning, the Jew sees the sun rising just as it did on the very first Wednesday, so he blesses God Who fashioned creation and maintains it. These phenomena bear witness to the God Who made them, but like all testimony they are of value only to those who see, listen, think, perceive. To the detective, fingerprints are evidence to be guarded and evaluated; to the janitor, they are smudges to be wiped away. To one person, a human being is sacred; to another he is a conglomeration of matter and electrical impulses that can perform useful tasks until it can be safely discarded. The prophet exclaims:

שְׂאוּ מָרוֹם עֵינֵיכֶם וּרְאוּ מִי בָרָא אֵלֶּה

Raise your eyes on high and see who created these (Isaiah 40:26).

To Isaiah, the spectacle of the heavens proves who created these; to the blind it is grist for computer mills.

To Isaiah, the spectacle of the heavens proves *who created these;* to the blind it is grist for computer mills.

II. Fashioning Vessels

Initiating Creation

The Midrash likens heaven and earth in the early stages of creation to two exquisitely engraved tables submerged in murky water.

THE MIDRASH (*BEREISHIS RABBAH* 10:2) LIKENS heaven and earth in the early stages of creation to two exquisitely engraved tables submerged in murky water. Because the tables are barely visible, their beauty is only vaguely suggested. As the water is drained, the onlooker becomes gradually aware that two treasures are emerging, until finally, they are revealed in all their magnificence. So too, heaven and earth. At the beginning, heaven and earth were created, but they were empty. *In the beginning of God's creating the heavens and the earth — when the earth was astonishingly empty, with darkness upon the surface of the deep ...* (Genesis 1:1-2). It was as if two magnificent vessels — heaven and earth — were enveloped in emptiness and confusion. Slowly, the universe as we know it took shape. Light, the sky, oceans and land, vegetation, the heavenly bodies ....

With each successive step in creation, another bit of murkiness was siphoned away until the universe was complete.

With each successive step in creation, another bit of murkiness was siphoned away until the universe was complete. The physical aspect of creation was done, and all that remained was to add the spiritual dimensions of rest and a recognition that God had created a perfectly balanced world. To do that, God made the Sabbath.

The "dross" of formlessness and lack of completion had been removed, with the result that the Divine Smith's perfect "vessel" had emerged into view.

נַעֲשׂוּ כֵּלִים! הֲדָא הוּא דִכְתִיב וַיְכֻלּוּ הַשָּׁמַיִם וְהָאָרֶץ

[Heaven and earth] had become finished vessels! This is indicated by the verse: "Thus the heaven and earth became vessels" [i.e., a play on the word וַיְכֻלּוּ *(literally, were finished), which is similar to* כְּלִי*, vessel] (Genesis 2:1).*

By likening the primeval heaven and earth to tables and describing the finished parts of the universe as vessels, the Sages of the Midrash have illuminated man's role on earth and how he is to use the gift of creation. Every week, the cycle of six days of labor climaxed by the Sabbath is repeated. Man's spiritual goals are clouded during the six days of labor. The turmoil of a busy society, the pressures of earning a livelihood, the cacophony of myriad conflicting activities camouflage the spiritual essence of man and the world he inhabits. Each week, every human being in his personal little world must emulate the deeds of the Creator in His world thousands of years ago. God acted to pick away at the confusion and sharpen the distinctions between dross and

Each week, every human being in his personal little world must emulate the deeds of the Creator in His world thousands of years ago.

essence. Every person must do the same each week with his own comparatively tiny quota of cares and possessions.

Which deeds are important, which are good, which are beneficial? What must he improve, what must he avoid, what must he acquire, what must he give? What can he do to enter the next Sabbath with his personal world a better place than it was last week? Then the Sabbath arrives, and if he has succeeded, each master of a miniature world will have made his own domain a better vessel with which to recognize and serve His Maker.

What can he do to enter the next Sabbath with his personal world a better place than it was last week?

Means to Perfection

If Israel accepts the Torah, you shall continue to exist, but if they do not, I will turn you back into the astonishing emptiness of primeval times.

HOW DOES ONE FIND THE WAY TO PERFECT HIS world? The Sages give us an insight: The Holy One, Blessed is He, made a condition with the works of creation: If Israel accepts the Torah, you shall continue to exist; but if they do not, I will turn you back into the astonishing emptiness of primeval times (*Shabbos* 88a, *Avodah Zarah* 3a). In the beginning, God removed the earth from its state of formlessness by filling it with accomplishment; in order for earth to endure, Israel had to accept the Torah. And having done so, we must hold fast to it, and mold creation according to the Torah's tenets. During the first six days of creation and during each succeeding week, the world seems to be composed of discrete disharmonious elements. Conflict and confusion are the rule. Lack of understanding and absence of clarity haunt people seeking meaning in their roles on earth. These are the products of lifestyles devoid of the soul imparted by the study, observance, and values of Torah.

Only Israel was charged with the responsibility of observing the Torah in its entirety. By using the Torah to chart his daily life and by shutting out the distractions of material existence with the coming of the Sabbath, the Jew maintains his even keel amid the maelstrom of daily life.

Life on earth hardly seems conducive to such a sublime goal.

Life on earth hardly seems conducive to such a sublime goal. How does one reconcile the Torah's dictates with international conflict over markets, resources, and power; personal struggles over jobs, influence, and neighborhoods; philosophical struggles over emotions, ideologies, and rights? How does one find the answers to the problems of a post-industrial society in a 33-century old revelation?

The questions represent a difficult test of faith.

The Sages teach that God used the Torah as a veritable blueprint of Creation. He was like a benevolent, all-powerful planner who decides what sort of society he would like to have and then builds a city — including industrial plants, commercial facilities, schools, shopping, and housing — so that all its elements will facilitate the achievement of his vision. God fashioned a universe in accord with the commandments and values of the Torah. Its principles contain the answers to all questions, provided, of course, that one has the intelligence to find them and the faith to accept them (*Sfas Emes*).

God's Partner

A person trying to live a useful life dares not be satisfied with minor accomplishments at the expense of major goals.

AN EFFORT CANNOT BE CONSIDERED SUCCESSFUL unless it accomplishes the task at hand. A surgeon called to treat acute appendicitis cannot rub his hands with satisfaction if he operated on an ingrown toenail instead. Similarly, a person trying to live a useful life dares not be satisfied with minor accomplishments at the expense of major goals. All his perspiration and concentration are wasted if he forsakes his soul for the sake of his prestige, or if he deludes himself into thinking that he has served his family well only by clothing, feeding, and housing them luxuriously. Filled though it may be with treasure and pomp, such a life is truly empty.

In this manner, *Ramban*, as understood *by Mei haShiloach*, understands the Sages' dictum that the world would revert to emptiness unless Israel accepted the Torah. It need not mean that creation will literally cease to exist, but it *does* mean that a world without Torah is empty and meaningless. Throughout history — and modern times are no exception — major segments of society have been rightly regarded as corrupt and worthless despite huge accumulations of resources and power. As the Sages put it, the wicked are regarded as dead even during their lifetimes. It is axiomatic to moral people that life must have a redeeming purpose, otherwise it has no valid reason to exist. Without the Torah and the holiness it infuses into physical existence, the universe remains as formless as it was at the first moment of creation — worse: then it had the potential to flourish, but if Israel were to refuse the Torah it would destroy even the hope for something better.

Without the Torah and the holiness it infuses into physical existence, the universe remains as formless as it was at the first moment of creation.

This is why the Sages say:

אָמַר רַב הַמְנוּנָא כָּל הַמִּתְפַּלֵּל בְּעֶרֶב שַׁבָּת וְאוֹמֵר
וַיְכֻלּוּ מַעֲלֶה עָלָיו הַכָּתוּב כְּאִלּוּ נַעֲשֶׂה שֻׁתָּף
לְהקב״ה בְּמַעֲשֵׂה בְרֵאשִׁית

R. Hamnuna said: Whoever prays on Sabbath eve and says [the paragraph beginning], "And [heaven and earth] were completed," is considered by Scripture as if he were a partner of the Holy One, Blessed is He, in the work of creation (Shabbos 119b).

God had no need for a world except as a vehicle for the fulfillment of the Torah. This concept is expressed by the transition from the workweek to the Sabbath. As we saw above, the completion of creation represents the idea that heaven and earth with all their fullness are nothing more or less than vessels with which to serve God. In this sense, God alone could not bring about the fulfillment of His plan, as it were, for it was His wish that man and man alone — of his own free will — should bring meaning to the universe by using it to serve God. When Israel accepts the Torah and its sons and daughters remain loyal to the Torah's concepts and dictates, the universe becomes saturated with purpose. Instead of a setting for the moral grafitti of consumption and conquest, it becomes a sounding board resounding with the

Instead of a setting for the moral grafitti of consumption and conquest, it becomes a sounding board resounding with the message of its Creator.

message of its Creator. Is not the one who accomplishes that worthy of being called God's partner? (*Mei haShiloach*).

III. Man's Declaration

The Heavens Declare

A S THE PSALMIST SINGS, הַשָּׁמַיִם מְסַפְּרִים כְּבוֹד אֵל וּמַעֲשֵׂה יָדָיו מַגִּיד הָרָקִיעַ, *The heavens declare the glory of God and the expanse of the sky tells of His handiwork* (*Psalms* 19:2). Most commentators agree that it is by their precise orbits, patterns, and constellations that the heavenly bodies declare the greatness of the One Who made them. They need not speak; their very existence and functioning tells more than can be distilled into words. Because the fulfillment of God's purpose depends on the deeds of man, however, even the heavenly bodies are affected by him, somehow, for better or worse. Man's good benefits even the farthest reaches of the universe; his evil harms it. Thus, they, too, testify to the role of man, God's "junior partner" in creation. That testimony is not apparent to us when we gaze in wonderment at the heavens, but God surely hears the message. Accordingly, the Psalmist is telling us that the heavens, the expanse of the sky, make two declarations: by their very existence *they declare* the glory of God Who created them, and by the degree of holiness imparted to them by Israel's study of Torah and performance of the commandments, they tell God how successful *His handiwork* — Israel, the bearer of man's mission — has been in serving Him.

It is by their precise orbits, patterns, and constellations that the heavenly bodies declare the greatness of the One Who made them.

This concept seems strange to us, of course, but it is closer to our experience than we imagine.

This concept seems strange to us, of course, but it is closer to our experience than we imagine. An acute, trained observer can sit in on a classroom, a workshop, an office, or a factory floor and form a good impression of its morale and general efficiency from what his five senses — and his sixth sense — tell him, and how his fund of experience and comprehension interpret the data he absorbs. Similarly, one who is spiritually attuned can feel the vibrations of a synagogue or study hall. In a like manner, the spiritual emanations of earth affect the message of the heavens in a way that is readily audible to the Supreme Listener (*R. Chaim Vital*).

His Oneness

One who is spiritually attuned can feel the vibrations of a synagogue or study hall.

Rabbi Moshe Chaim Luzzatto sets forth that mortal man can comprehend only one of God's essential characteristics.

THE DAILY MORNING AND EVENING PRAYERS REflect Israel's role as the driving force in the realization of creation's goal. In *Daas Tevunos*, Rabbi Moshe Chaim Luzzatto sets forth that mortal man can comprehend only one of God's essential characteristics. We cannot fathom such attributes as His intelligence, strength, and mercy, for such terms are of necessity relative. For example, if we are told that someone has extraordinary intelligence, we may imagine him as more brilliant than the greatest genius we know, wiser than the most sagacious counselor, quicker and with a greater store of knowledge than the town genius. By such means, we describe intelligence as best we can, but we are inevitably limited by our own experience. To say that someone has a "computer-like mind" meant much more in 2000 than it did in 1970; undoubtedly it will mean more in 2030 when an earlier generation's marvels are obsolete, but no such comparison can define God's intelligence in *absolute* terms. Such characterizations cannot delineate God's wisdom any more than one can compare the mind of the *Vilna Gaon* to that of a guppy. We lack the terms or the capacity to deal with God's wisdom in any meaningful way. The same is true of His might, goodness, justice, and any other trait we may choose. Only one thing are we capable of defining: יִחוּדוֹ, *His Oneness*.

By God's Oneness we mean that *everything*, without exception, emanates from Him and is an expression of His Will. Surely, we do not understand *why* He causes everything to happen, but we can acknowledge that even the most mystifying phenomena are caused by Him and cannot

We cannot define the limits of God's strength because it is infinite, but we can define His Oneness by saying simply, there is nothing save Him.

exist without Him. We cannot define the limits of God's strength because it is infinite, but we can define His Oneness by saying simply אֵין עוֹד מִלְבַדּוֹ, *there is nothing save Him.* Or as we express it in our prayers:

שְׁמַע יִשְׂרָאֵל ה׳ אֱלֹהֵינוּ ה׳ אֶחָד

Hear, O Israel, HASHEM is our God — HASHEM is the One and Only (Deut. 6:4).

In the blessings that precede the recitation of the *Shema*, particularly in the lengthier morning service, *Shacharis*, we declare that the creatures of heaven and earth sing God's praises. Just as the

Just as the heavenly bodies declare His glory ... so do all parts of creation by virtue of their obedience to His will.

heavenly bodies declare His glory by the precise and intricate manner in which they function, so do all parts of creation by virtue of their obedience to His will. The croaking frog, the buried and decaying vegetation ever so slowly becoming hydrocarbons, the erupting mountain, the scurrying ant — all "declare" His glory by being what He created them to be. On a level that is higher in degree, but not in kind, the angels sing *Holy, holy, holy ...* and arrange themselves before Him according to their ascending degrees of sanctity. This concept is contained in the first of the two blessings that introduce *Shema*.

All of these, however, from the bacterium to the seraph, are in a sense inferior to man — for they have no freedom of choice to do other than that for which they were created. But man *can* disobey. He can be seduced by the desire that whispers sweetly in his ear about the pleasure and profit of sin.

That man disdains the messages of his senses in favor of the dictates of his Maker is the greatest praise of all.

That man disdains the messages of his senses in favor of the dictates of his Maker is the greatest praise of all, for it represents conscious effort.

Every man has a role, but only one family earned the privilege of being God's chosen people. Abraham and his offspring, Israel, accepted the Torah, the instrument by means of which every mode of existence is exalted. So the blessing that directly precedes the *Shema* speaks of the love God showed Israel by choosing it to receive His Torah, the most profound expression of love in the history of the universe. בָּרוּךְ אַתָּה ה׳ הַבּוֹחֵר בְּעַמּוֹ יִשְׂרָאֵל בְּאַהֲבָה, *Blessed are You, HASHEM, Who chooses Israel with love.*

Then we proclaim the Oneness of God: *Hear O Israel ... (HaRav Moshe Eisenmann; see his Iyunim b'Tefillah).*

IV. Clear as the Sun

בָּרְבִיעִי הָיוּ אוֹמְרִים אֵל נְקָמוֹת ה׳ עַל שֵׁם שֶׁבָּרָא חַמָּה וּלְבָנָה וְעָתִיד לִפָּרַע מֵעוֹבְדֵיהֶם
On the fourth day [the Levites in the Temple] would recite, "HASHEM is a God of vengeance ..." (Psalm 94), because He created the sun and moon [on the fourth day] and He will exact vengeance from their worshipers (Rosh HaShanah 31a).

R' TZADDOK HAKOHEN (RESISEI LAYLAH) GIVES us a new insight into the vengeance God will exact at the end of days. Unlike all of human history when good and evil are confused for one another and false philosophies clothe the most heinous or worthless deeds in the cloak of virtue, the ultimate Redemption will bathe creation in a new light of truth and clarity. All masquerades will be stripped away. Good and evil will stand starkly separate and revealed for what they are.

The ultimate Redemption will bathe creation in a new light of truth and clarity.

Imagine what would happen if clever slogans and well-written claims could not embellish an inferior product. If no other consideration but quality were available, and the lack of quality could not be sugarcoated, how different the marketplace would be! Or if personality and rhetoric were removed from the political process in favor of an infallible test of integrity and ability, how transformed government

Imagine what would happen if clever slogans and well-written claims could not embellish an inferior product.

would be! Our freedom of choice is constantly compromised by facades that deceive us and by illusions we create ourselves. Only in such a climate can evil and falsehood exist, for they do not survive where their message has no acceptance.

The endurance of evil on the spiritual plane — sin — is quite similar. As long as man's desires vacillate, he provides existence to evil. Because his sins stem not from a conviction that sin is the proper course, but from rationalizations born of human desire or mistaken attitudes, he is not totally bad. Indeed, the evil within him is a necessary factor in the inner struggle that God wants man to wage and win. So even the basically good person is not perfect, and has not extinguished the evil within himself; therefore evil survives. If man could become vividly aware of the truth however, all that would change. Therefore, R. Shimon ben Lakish teaches:

Even the basically good person is not perfect, and has not extinguished the evil within himself; therefore evil survives.

אֵין גֵּיהִנּוֹם לָעוֹלָם הַבָּא אֶלָּא הקב"ה מוֹצִיא חַמָּה מִנַּרְתִּיקָהּ צַדִּיקִים מִתְרַפְּאִין בָּהּ וּרְשָׁעִים נִידוֹנִין בָּהּ

There will be no Gehinnom in the World to Come [i.e., life on earth after the resuscitation of the dead (Ran)]. Rather, the Holy One, Blessed is He, will remove the sun from its sheath, the righteous will be healed by it and the wicked will be punished by it (Nedarim 8b).

R. Tzaddok HaKohen explains that the "sun" symbolizes the clarity to distinguish the worthwhile from the worthless. When one has adequate light, he can take the kernels and discard the chaff. In the spiritual brilliance of the World to Come, man will know good from evil. Those who are basically decent and desirous of doing good, despite the many times they stumble and fall, will be healed of their blind vision, faltering step, and faulty perceptions. Clearly recognizing right from wrong — finally! — they will excise evil, with the result that it will no longer exist for them. But the sinners will be

When one has adequate light, he can take the kernels and discard the chaff. In the spiritual brilliance of the World to Come, man will know good from evil.

different. They had allowed themselves to be so deluded and corrupted that they no longer care to improve. They sin because they enjoy sin and truly believe in it. Their occasional twinge of pity or remorse is a personal aberration. Provided with the clear distinction between good and evil, they choose to sin. When they do so, they cannot survive, for unrelieved evil cannot live.

It is like a human body when the soul leaves it. We call it death, but in reality it is simply a case of holiness — the soul — departing from a material object — the body. Something that was meant to be a repository of sanctity cannot live when no sanctity is left. The Temple's physical destruction was inevitable once God's Presence had departed from it in reaction to Israel's sinfulness [see *Overview* to ArtScroll *Ezekiel*]; a Holy Temple without holiness is a contradiction in terms. And a Jew without at least a spark of good left in him cannot live. So when that illuminating, discriminating "sun" ultimately shines forth, good people will be healed of their myopia and bad people will be stripped of their claim to life.

When that "sun" ultimately shines forth, good people will be healed of their myopia and bad people will be stripped of their claim to life.

Sanctify Creation

AT EVERY MOMENT OF EVERY DAY, IT IS IN OUR "power" to sanctify all of creation, yet some moments are more propitious than others. When a new cycle begins we are reminded of the very first cycle, and we recall the reason for its creation. Every twenty-eight years the sun comes home to the moment at which God said, *"Let there be luminaries."* For us, whom the Divine wisdom made dependent on the sun for light, energy, and life, it is a moment when we are called upon to look beyond the mighty fireball and perceive the One Who placed it in the heavens, the One Who picked our galaxy out of millions, our sun out of billions, our planet out of the eight in this solar system, Abraham's family out of the three score and ten nations, and said, "I have chosen Israel to receive My Torah and use it to make of My universe what I longed for it to become."

It is a moment when we look at the physical sun and long for the sun of truth and clarity that will shine when the world is at peace and all humanity follows Israel to the zenith of spiritual accomplishment.

It is a moment when we gaze heavenward and declare: "Blessed are You HASHEM, our God, King of the universe, Who made the works of creation!"

✺§ An Overview —
Measurements from Sinai

THE TWENTY-EIGHT-YEAR CYCLE OF *BIRCAS haChammah* is based on the calculations of the Talmudic sage Shmuel. His view, however, is disputed by Rav Adda, whose opinion is adopted by the Talmud regarding other halachic matters. According to Rav Adda, the sun's cycles *never* bring it back to its original place on the eve of a Wednesday in Nissan. Astronomical calculations, too, do not agree with Shmuel's view. If so, the entire premise upon which *Bircas haChammah* is based is erroneous and, since the Talmud itself accepts Rav Adda's opinion, it seems strange that the Sages ordained a ritual and blessing based on a calculation that they themselves knew to be inaccurate. This difficulty has been raised by many of the classic commentators and is discussed fully in Chapter 2 of this book, with the sources and background. For that reason, it will not be dwelt upon in the Overview.

It seems strange that the Sages ordained a ritual and blessing based on a calculation that they themselves knew to be inaccurate.

Chazon Ish (Orach Chaim 138:4) resolves the difficulty by providing a new perspective on Shmuel's calculation, a perspective that goes beyond its application to *Bircas haChammah*. We offer his seminal view for the reader's benefit.

As part of his thesis, *Chazon Ish* offers an important explanation of the teachings of the Sages in cases where they are not found explicitly in the Torah, but nevertheless have the status of Torah Law. Sometimes their teaching was part of the direct, unbroken tradition from Moses. Sometimes the original tradition was forgotten and the Sages, by means of Divinely guided exegesis, were able to derive the forgotten law. As *Yerushalmi* puts it: "A subject to which the Sages dedicated themselves, they were privileged [to derive] just as it was given at Sinai."

Regarding Shmuel's calculation, the fact that it is not exact would be surprising or disturbing only if he and the Talmud that adopts it for *Bircas haChammah* intended it to be mathematically accurate. Astronomical exactitude, however, was not their purpose. It is illustrative that in areas such as the determination of intercalation (the insertion of a thirteenth month) and the examination of witnesses who testified to having seen the new moon, the Sages used a more involved calculation than the familiar one of Shmuel. A similar instance involves the formulas given in the Talmud to determine the circumference of a circle (*Eruvin* 13b) and the proportion of a circle's area to that of a square (*Succah* 8a). In both cases, the standard mathematical equations are based on the Greek symbol *pi*, which, as every schoolchild knows, is about $3\frac{1}{7}$. The Sages, however, base their rule-of-thumb formulas on *pi* equaling only *three*. The diagonal of a square is given by the Talmud as two-fifths more than a side (*Eruvin* 57a), but here, too, an exact mathematical calculation yields a slightly larger figure.

In all such cases, the Sages knew that the figures they used were not *exact*, but the figures *were* as close as was necessary for the task at hand. Like all measurements needed in the performance of *mitzvos* — like the age of *bar* or *bas mitzvah*, the amount of food to be eaten or wine drunk for the *Pesach Seder* and so on — these measurements were part of the Tradition transmitted to Moses at Sinai. God gave the *mitzvos* in order to purify His servants so they could properly accept His sovereignty, correctly perform His commandments, and comply with the revealed and hidden wisdom of the Torah as it is contained in the various precepts. To accomplish this purpose, the Divine scheme considered it important that the measurements be simple enough for even unsophisticated and unlearned people to perform the commandments. It is surely true that *pi* is equal to 3.141592 ... — and the decimal could be extended *ad infinitum*. To base all calculations on the exact fraction would assure accuracy, but it would also require an uncommon knowledge of mathematics and a degree of precision that would exclude large numbers of people. This was not the Torah's purpose.[1]

Shmuel's calculations of a year as exactly 365 ¼ days and each season as exactly 91 days and 7 ½ hours fall under the above category even though they are at variance with the more accurate figure of Rav Adda and that of modern-day astronomy. As such, the calculation of Shmuel, like that of Rav Adda, is a part of the Oral Law revealed to us by the Sages of the Talmud. For someone to say that Shmuel merely adopted the primitive — and erroneous — calculation that was in vogue in his day is to be the unwitting tool of the heretical inclination that makes it tempting and enjoyable to regard the Sages as lacking in knowledge.

The calculation of Shmuel, like that of Rav Adda, is a part of the Oral Law revealed to us by the Sages of the Talmud.

Calculations like Shmuel's are for *general* use in determining the times of the *mitzvos* to which they apply, but for matters that required more exact knowledge, such as the verification of testimony and decisions on when to add a thirteenth month of a year, the Sages had more exact figures. This reckoning was taught to those who had to know it. As the commentators put it: Shmuel's reckoning of

As the commentators put it: Shmuel's reckoning of the seasons was public and Rav Adda's was private.

---

1. Someone once asked the *Brisker Rav*, Rabbi Yitzchok Ze'ev Soloveitchik, whether the use of telescopes would be permitted to sight the new moon. If so, the time when the moon became visible would be advanced by several hours with the result that a Sanhedrin might occasionally be able to proclaim Rosh Chodesh (the New Month) at times when sighting with the naked eye could not be made soon enough. He replied that the minimum size of the emerging moon crescent that is required for Rosh Chodesh is the size that the *naked* eye can see. God based His measurement on the visual capacity of an ordinary human being. A crescent *so minute* that it can be observed only telescopically is too small to constitute the required New Moon. The concept is the same as that set forth by the *Chazon Ish:* The Torah was not given for laboratories and observatories; it is meant for all Israel and the measurements with which to perform the *mitzvos* are those that can readily be determined by the mass of people.

Tiferes Yisrael and *Aruch HaShulchan* make essentially the same point.

the seasons was public and Rav Adda's was private. Rav Adda's calculation is a practical one that does not fall under the category of Sinaitic tradition, nor can we be sure that it was the one used by the Sanhedrin, but we know that the Sages *did* have a more accurate reckoning than Shmuel's — perhaps it was Rav Adda's, perhaps some other one — and they used it where needed.

Rav Adda's calculation does not agree exactly with that of modern astronomy, but it was adequate for its time to assure proper investigation of witnesses. With the coming of the Messiah and the reestablishment of the Sanhedrin, the Sages will adopt whatever reckoning they deem useful to facilitate verification of testimony, for such astronomical calculations are not matters of unchanging Halachah, but are merely expedients to determine the accuracy of witnesses.

Such astronomical calculations are not matters of unchanging Halachah, but are merely expedients to determine the accuracy of witnesses.

Our generation, which is so exposed to the skepticism of those who cast aspersion on the wisdom of the Talmud, is fortunate indeed to have the benefit of modern-day sages like *Chazon Ish*. Indeed, there is hardly a better indication for us of the greatness of the Sages than the clear headedness and brilliance of their heirs. May the sun of Redemption quickly illuminate the truth so that all will recognize the One Who made the works of creation.

Nosson Scherman

19 Kislev, 5741
Revised
30 Sivan 5768

Chapter One

❧ The Purpose

שְׂאוּ מָרוֹם עֵינֵיכֶם וּרְאוּ מִי בָרָא אֵלֶּה הַמּוֹצִיא בְמִסְפָּר צְבָאָם
לְכֻלָּם בְּשֵׁם יִקְרָא מֵרֹב אוֹנִים וְאַמִּיץ כֹּחַ אִישׁ לֹא נֶעְדָּר

Lift up your eyes on high and see: who created these? He who brings out their host by number, calling them all by name; by the greatness of His might and because He is strong in power, not one is missing (Isaiah 40:26).

Lift up your eyes on high, exclaims the prophet, because when man does so in a thoughtful manner he may discern the answer to the most profound of questions: *Who created these?* The attentive star-gazer must perceive that it is God who created the awe-inspiring panorama of the universe. The overwhelming vastness of the firmament and the sheer number of stars testify to the existence of a Creator; the orderliness with which He "brings out" the heavenly hosts, each one assigned "by name" to a fixed place in the firmament, confirms His continued providential guardianship of the universe.

The psalmist gives praise לְעוֹשֵׂה הַשָּׁמַיִם בִּתְבוּנָה — *To Him who makes the heavens with wisdom* (Psalms 136:5). The term תְּבוּנָה does not connote knowledge of bare facts but refers to the understanding associated with relationships, entailments and inferences. In this verse the term שָׁמַיִם denotes the heavens together with all the heavenly bodies. R. Samson Raphael Hirsch draws attention to the fact that the position and orbit of each of these bodies is determined by its interaction with, and distance from, each of the other bodies. God established the laws of nature and created the universe in conformity with them. Had creation and positioning of the celestial bodies not taken into account the influence which each one of these heavenly bodies exerts upon every other body, the world would not long endure. It is this exhaustive and penetrating understanding of the ramifications of every aspect of the creation of the heavens that is reflected in the use of the word תְּבוּנָה in this context.

R. Samson Raphael Hirsch, in effect, points to fundamental principles of nature in order to deepen our appreciation of the grandeur of the Creator. Indeed, one need look no further than

Kepler's laws of planetary motion to formulate a teleological proof for the existence of a Deity. Planets move in continuous, fixed and predictable orbits. Kepler's laws serve to explain both the motion of these bodies and the stability of the planetary system. Kepler perceived that celestial bodies tend toward union. Sir Isaac Newton later showed that this phenomenon is none other than a manifestation of the force of gravity which is inherent in every body possessing mass. The planets, the earth and the sun do not fuse into one conglomerate mass because, by virtue of their positions relative to one another, opposing and conflicting forces are brought to bear on each of the celestial bodies. The result is a state of equilibrium. It must be remembered that the force of gravity depends directly upon two factors: 1) Gravitational force is a function of mass. The greater the mass of a body, the greater is its force of attraction. 2) Gravitational force is also contingent upon distance, since the force of gravity weakens geometrically in accordance with the distance between objects. It is then readily understood that the harmony and stability of the universe is a direct result of the mass of each individual celestial body as well as of its precise position in the solar system. Relatively small changes in the mass or in the location of the planetary bodies would long since have resulted in a cosmic cataclysm. This is averted only because the universe is the construct of the Creator who designed the celestial configurations with utmost precision. Indeed, in the concluding words of this passage in Isaiah, the prophet, referring to the celestial bodies, marvels מֵרֹב אוֹנִים וְאַמִּיץ כֹּחַ אִישׁ לֹא נֶעְדָּר — *by the greatness of His might and because He is strong in power, not one is missing.*

Much the same concept is expressed by Abarbanel in his elucidation of the verse וַיַּרְא אֱלֹהִים כִּי טוֹב — *And God saw that it was good (Genesis 1:18)*, as stated in reference to the work of the fourth day of creation. This expression of divine approval of the nature of the sun, the moon and the stars, declares Abarbanel, reflects a judgment concerning their relative size and position. Had the sun been made larger or smaller, or placed closer to or further from the earth, life as we know it could not exist. Abarbanel emphasizes that this is true not only of the sun and the moon but also of each of the stars. It is the extreme accuracy with which the relative mass and gravitational force of each of the celestial bodies was established by the Creator that makes possible the continued existence of the universe. It is because the heavens do indeed reflect such precision of design and phenomenal intelligence of structure that God assessed His handiwork at the close of the fourth day and determined, "It is good!"

The celestial bodies, their movements, orbits and configurations constitute an eloquent and forceful teleological proof for the existence of God. R. Bachya ibn Pakudah, *Chovos haLevavos, Sha'ar haBechinah*, chap. 2, cites the words of Isaiah: שְׂאוּ מָרוֹם עֵינֵיכֶם וּרְאוּ מִי בָרָא אֵלֶּה — *Lift up your eyes on high and see: who created these?* — not simply as a formulation of this proof for the existence of God but as a directive addressed to man, bidding him to reflect upon, and to become aware of, the lesson taught by the stars in the heavens.

The Gemara, *Shabbos* 75a, declares, "Any person who is capable of calculating the *tekufos* and *mazalos* but does not do so, of him Scripture says, *But they do not look upon the work of* HASHEM *and the work of His hands they do not see*" (*Isaiah* 5:12). The meaning of this dictum is quite clear. Astronomy provides eloquent testimony not only to the existence of a Creator, but also to the intricacy and precision of creation. Knowledge of what astronomers speak of as celestial mechanics is a key to perception of the omnipotence of God. Any person can memorize the theorem which teaches that the square of the hypotenuse of a right triangle is equal to the sum of the square of each of its sides. But the mathematician who has constructed the proof for this proposition knows that $a^2 + b^2$ *must* be equal to c^2. Both know the same fact. But the first knows it only as an external fact to be parroted without real comprehension, while, for the second, it is an irrefutable verity, an inalienable part of his own intellect. One who has not opened his mind to the dazzling experience of calculating *tekufos* and *mazalos* can know that the universe is ordered with utmost precision only impassionately, as an intellectual construct — an article of faith. One who has studied the *tekufos* and *mazalos* "sees" the works of God. His intellectual awareness is akin to sensory perception. He does not simply know in an abstract, detached manner, but experiences God as the omnipotent Creator.

◄§ Continuous Creation

Judaism teaches that God not only created the universe *ex nihilo* — out of nothing — but that וּבְטוּבוֹ מְחַדֵּשׁ בְּכָל יוֹם תָּמִיד מַעֲשֵׂה בְרֵאשִׁית, "in His goodness, He renews the work of creation each day continually." Rambam, in the first of his Thirteen Principles, affirms the truth of a principle of faith which, in philosophical terminology, is known as the doctrine of continuous creation or as the principle of constant conservation. This doctrine states that creation is a continuous, dynamic process rather than a single act that requires no repetition. It is not the case that the world exists solely by virtue of an act of creation that took place "in the beginning" and continues to remain in existence on the basis of that primordial act. Creation is not a phenomenon that occurs but once in an eternity. Rather, the act of creation must be repeated each and every moment throughout the ages; otherwise the universe would revert to nothingness. Existence is constantly infused into all created entities by the Creator. Thus, Rambam, *Hilchos Yesodei haTorah* 1:1, declares that not only did God bring everything that exists into being but, moreover, "All existing things of heaven and earth and what is between them do not exist other than through His true existence." Creation is an ongoing process of which God is the author.

There is no miracle greater than the continued existence of the natural order. Nature is nothing less than a continuum of miracles following one another in a patterned sequence. But, because of the recurring and predictable character of these phenomena, man becomes accustomed to their occurrence and hence insensitive to their miraculous quality. Overt miracles, which manifest themselves as an apparent suspension of the natural order, declares R. Meir Simchah haKohen of Dvinsk in his *Meshech Chochmah, Parshas Bechukosai,* are designed solely in order to arouse mankind to awareness that *all* events are the product of divine providence. Miracles serve to arouse man from complacency, to awaken in him the realization that just as the miraculous event is the result of divine intervention, so also are phenomena ordered by nature the product of providence.

"One who recites *Hallel* each day commits blasphemy," declares the Gemara, *Shabbos* 118b. Yet, at the same time, the Sages,

Berachos 4b, proclaim that one who recites *Tehillah leDavid,* the familiar *Ashrei* psalm, three times each day is assured of a share in the world-to-come. Both are hymns of praise to God. Why is indiscriminate singing of *Hallel* to be abjured, whereas ongoing repetition of *Ashrei* is deemed to be meritorious? The answer, declares *Meshech Chochmah,* lies in the fact that *Hallel* is replete with references to miraculous occurrences, while *Ashrei* is a poem of praise to God for man's continued existence and sustenance. One who is prompted to express thanksgiving solely for miracles in the belief that natural phenomena do not require a similar expression of gratitude commits blasphemy in impliedly denying that nature, subsequent to its original creation, no longer requires the ministrations of a Creator. Each recitation of *Ashrei* is a renewed acknowledgment of divine providence that is manifest in the phenomenon of continuous creation. Each day, each part of the day, and indeed each moment of existence, occasions its own hymn of praise. One who recites *Ashrei* thrice daily testifies to his belief in God's ongoing providence and thereby merits His providence in the next world as well as in this.

Man owes a continual debt of gratitude to the Creator and should feel prompted to declare his thanksgiving each moment. But familiarity and habituation breed complacence. We do not perceive the miracle of creation unfolding before our eyes every moment because we take it for granted.

The texts of our daily prayers are replete with references to God as the Creator of the universe and as the providential guardian of His people. These liturgical expressions, by their very number and repetition, serve to prevent us from losing sight of this fundamental fact of our existence. הַשָּׁמַיִם מְסַפְּרִים כְּבוֹד אֵל וּמַעֲשֵׂה יָדָיו מַגִּיד הָרָקִיעַ — *The heavens declare the glory of God; and the firmament tells the work of His hands (Psalms 19:2).* Man dare not allow himself to forget what it is that the heavens recount and the firmament tells. R. Bachya, *Sha'ar haBechinah,* chap. 6, explains that this is precisely what the psalmist seeks to convey to us when he proclaims in the very next verse: יוֹם לְיוֹם יַבִּיעַ אֹמֶר וְלַיְלָה לְּלַיְלָה יְחַוֶּה דָּעַת — *Day unto day utters speech and night unto night bespeaks knowledge.* Although the message is the same and the lesson identical, man must be attuned to perceive this truth anew each day.

◆§ An Evocative Blessing

Yet the repetition in prayer of our praise of God as Creator has a certain abstract quality. Unlike blessings upon partaking of food and the like, these professions of praise are not necessarily occasioned by any particular experience. They are designed primarily as reinforcement of intellectual awareness. Man does not express his thanks to God for each moment of creation in the way, for example, in which he thanks Him for each piece of bread. Indeed, were man required to do so, he would perforce be required to recite the blessing "who makes the work of creation" each time this verity is forgotten and again called to mind.

Since man's psychological and spiritual state is, in fact, such that his consciousness is not continuously aroused to perceive the miracle of creation, he is not called upon formally to bless God constantly as the Creator who continuously "makes the work of creation." However, on occasion, when observing phenomena that occur but rarely, man does perceive God in the act of creation. Since these occurrences are infrequent, man does not react jadedly with a sense of *déjà vu* but is — or should be — receptive to their cosmic import. Thus, for example, when sighting a meteor or witnessing lightning, man has the capacity for the psychological and emotional response that is required in order to praise God as the Creator of the universe with proper awareness, feeling and *kavannah*. For this reason the Sages ordained the blessing בָּרוּךְ אַתָּה ה' אֱלֹהֵינוּ מֶלֶךְ הָעוֹלָם עוֹשֶׂה מַעֲשֵׂה בְרֵאשִׁית — "Blessed are You, HASHEM our God, King of the universe, who makes the work of creation" on such occasions and on such occasions only.

The Sages ordained that the selfsame blessing be pronounced upon the sighting of the sun once every twenty-eight years. As will be explained later, this blessing is recited on the day on which the sun returns to the very spot in the heavens that it occupied relative to earth at the moment of its original creation when that event occurs on the day and hour identical to the day and hour of its original creation. At that moment the solar cycle reaches completion. The sun returns to its place in the firmament after completing the celestial journey for which it was created, only to begin the very same cycle anew. The process of "creation" thus begins once again. The blessing praising God on this occasion as עוֹשֶׂה מַעֲשֶׂה בְרֵאשִׁית, "He who makes the work of creation," is a paean to God, not simply as the Creator of the sun during the original six days of creation, but as the continuous Creator of the sun and its movements. Each solar cycle is a replica of the first; each moment the universe is recreated in the same form with which it was endowed at the beginning of creation.

It would seem that the blessing "who makes the work of creation" serves two distinct functions, varying in purpose in accordance with the occasion for which the blessing is ordained. The blessing is a *bircas hoda'ah,* a blessing of thanksgiving, and serves in that role when recited by one who witnesses falling stars or lightning. In this capacity the blessing is responsive in nature. Feelings of thanksgiving and gratitude well up within man and find expression in the act of praising God. The very same blessing recited upon sighting the sun once in twenty-eight years is certainly not a response to an observable phenomenon. The sun, after all, on the morning of Wednesday, April 8th, of every 28th year in the 20th and 21st centuries appears to the observer in a manner no different from its appearance on any other day. Left to his own devices and responses man would experience no distinctive emotion. But the uniqueness of the event demands of man that he pause and ponder the wondrous nature of creation, that he acknowledge God as the constant conservator of the universe. The blessing on this occasion, it would seem, is evocative rather than responsive. It is designed to arouse man from his lethargy, to force him to reflect upon this cosmic phenomenon, to summon him to contemplation. Marking yet another solar milestone in the calendar of eternity, the occasion calls out to man: *Lift up your eyes on high and see: who created these?*

Chapter Two

❧ The Calendar

In order properly to understand the nature of *Bircas haChammah* it is necessary to be familiar with some pertinent data concerning the Jewish calendar.

There are essentially three types of calendrical systems that men have fashioned to measure the passage of time. Each one has been adopted by various civilizations, frequently with variations of one type or another. The first system is based upon the motion of the sun. The solar year is the period of time in which the earth completes its orbit around the sun and encompasses a complete cycle of the four seasons. The present civil calendar of the Western world, which is borrowed from the Romans, is a solar calendar. The second system is based upon the revolution of the moon around the earth. One such period, known as a lunation, is a lunar month. Indeed, the very word "month" is derived from the word "moon."

It is, however, not possible to combine the two systems of calculating the passage of time by dividing the solar year into twelve lunar months or by declaring twelve lunar months to be equal in duration to one year in which a cycle of the solar seasons is complete. This is so because the length of a solar year is 365 days, 5 hours, 48 minutes and 46 seconds, while the length of a lunar month is 29 days, 12 hours, 44 minutes and 2.841 seconds. Thus, the solar year, i.e., the length of time it takes the earth to complete its orbit around the sun, exceeds twelve lunar months by about eleven days. In the course of but a few years the accumulated difference would become considerable and would have the effect of causing the beginning of each year to "wander" through the different seasons. The Moslem calendar is entirely lunar in nature, composed of twelve months of twenty-nine and thirty days in length, and does not at all follow the pattern of the solar year. Therefore, any given month of the Moslem calendar may, depending upon the year, fall during any of the solar seasons.

The third type of calendrical system is lunisolar. A calendar of this nature is not based upon either the lunar month or the solar year alone but reconciles the two in a "lunisolar" mode of calculation in which the months are reckoned according to the moon, while the years are calculated according to the sun. The Jewish calendar is lunisolar. This is mandated by the fact that the Torah repeatedly describes the festival of *Pesach* as occurring in *chodesh haAviv,* the month of spring, and commands: שָׁמוֹר — *watch* or *preserve* — *the month of Aviv and observe Pesach to HASHEM your God* (*Deuteronomy* 16:1). Were the Jewish year to be regulated on the basis of a simple lunar calendar, *Pesach* would occur some eleven days earlier in each successive solar year. The months of the year would therefore retrograde through the seasons with the result that the month of Nisan, and hence *Pesach,* would not regularly occur in the spring. Accordingly, the commandment *Preserve the month of Aviv* must be understood as mandating that the cycle of lunar months be adjusted parallel to the seasons of the solar year. The necessary adjustment is accomplished by intercalation, i.e., by adding an extra month in some years. Adar Sheni, the intercalary month[1] is added in seven out of every nineteen years. This nineteen-year cycle is called the *machzor katan,* the small cycle,[2] or *machzor halevanah,* the lunar cycle. Construction of a calendar providing for the addition of seven months in each nineteen-year cycle is based on the assumption that the mean lunation is 29 days, 12 hours, 44 minutes and $3\frac{1}{3}$ seconds[3] in duration, and that the mean solar year is 365 days, 5 hours, 55 minutes and $25\frac{25}{57}$ seconds long. Thus, a cycle of nineteen such solar years contains 6,939 days, 16 hours, 33 minutes and $3\frac{1}{3}$ seconds

---

1. Cf. Rashi, *Rosh HaShanah* 19b, who describes Adar Rishon as the intercalary month.

2. As distinct, as we shall see later, from the twenty-eight-year cycle of solar years, which is known as the *machzor gadol* or the great cycle.

3. In rabbinic literature the calculation is customarily given as 29 days, 12 hours and 793 *chalakim.* The hour is divided into 1080 parts; each part is called a *chelek.* Thus, a *chelek* is the equivalent of exactly $3\frac{1}{3}$ seconds. Accordingly, there are 18 *chalakim* to our minute, and 793 *chalakim* thus equal 44 minutes and $3\frac{1}{3}$ seconds.

R. Elijah, Gaon of Vilna, explains that the hour is divided into 1080 parts, rather than into some other number of divisions, because only division of the hour into 1080 parts enables the duration of the lunation to be expressed without use of a fraction (or more precisely, 1080 represents the smallest number of divisions that will achieve this purpose). This is readily apparent from the fact that 793 is a prime number, i.e., is not evenly divisible by any number other than one and itself. See *Kol Eliyahu, Rosh HaShanah* 25a. Cf., however, Rambam, *Hilchos Kiddush haChodesh* 6:2. See also E. Mahler, *Handbuch der Jüdischen Chronolgie* (Leipzig, 1916), p. 27 and W.M. Feldman, *Rabbinical Mathematics and Astronomy* (London, 1931), p. 101.

and equals exactly 235 lunations of the assumed duration.[4] Put somewhat differently, the 235 lunar months in the nineteen-year lunar cycle are precisely equal to nineteen solar years.

The findings of contemporary astronomy differ from these figures on two counts. It is now established that the length of the solar year is 365 days, 5 hours, 48 minutes and 46 seconds, which is approximately $6^2/_3$ minutes less than the 365 days, 5 hours, 55 minutes and $25^{25}/_{57}$ seconds which is assumed by the Jewish calendar.[5] Thus, the beginning of every Jewish year will advance forward from the true astronomical date at the rate of one day every 216 years. Hence, each date in the Jewish calendar occurs *later* in the solar year by one day every 216 years. Or, to put it in other words, the Jewish year is a bit too long and, as a result, the dates of the *Yomim Tovim* creep forward and occur progressively later in the solar year. In 100 lunar cycles, or 1900 years, there is a cumulative discrepancy of almost nine days.[6] Since our present calendar was promulgated by Hillel II in the year 4119 (358/59 C.E.), and has been in effect for a little less than 1650 years, the discrepancy over that period is less than eight full days.

The lunations, i.e., the length of the monthly lunar cycles, are established with much greater precision but, here too, there is a minor discrepancy. At present, the astronomical calculation of the lunation fixes the monthly cycle at 29 days, 12 hours, 44 minutes and 2.841 seconds, which is slightly less than the 29 days, 12 hours, 44 minutes and $3^1/_3$ seconds assumed by the Jewish

---

4. It is therefore necessary to add an extra month in seven out of every nineteen years. The sum of the months contained in seven leap years, each composed of thirteen months, is 91, which, when added to the sum of the months of twelve ordinary or common years, which is 144, yields a total of 235.

5. See *Jewish Encyclopedia,* III, 501, where the astronomical value is given as 48 minutes, 46.069 seconds. Since 55 minutes and $25^{25}/_{57}$ seconds equals 55 minutes, 25.439 seconds, the discrepancy is equal to 6 minutes, 39.37 seconds. Taking the astronomical value as 48 minutes, 46 seconds, the discrepancy is often expressed as 6 minutes $39^{25}/_{57}$ seconds. See *Encyclopedia Britannica,* thirteenth ed., IV, 1001.

6. Isidore Loeb, *Tables du Calendrier Juif* (Paris, 1886), p. 6, states that the nineteen-year cycle of the Jewish calendar exceeds the Gregorian by 2 hours, 8 minutes and 15.3 seconds. The difference over a period of 1900 years is then 8 days, 21 hours, 45 minutes and 5 seconds. See *Jewish Encyclopedia,* III, 500. More accurately, the nineteen-year cycle of Rav Adda exceeds Gregorian years by 1 hour, 58 minutes and $15^1/_3$ seconds. The cumulative difference over a period of 1900 years is thus 8 days, 14 hours, 48 minutes and $53^1/_3$ seconds.

calendar. The discrepancy between the reckoning of the lunar month in fixing the Jewish calendar, of which the lunar month is the basic unit, and the astronomical calculation is equal to one day in 14,000 years. This means that the discrepancy between the length of the lunar cycle assumed by the Jewish calendar and the astronomical calculation of the lunation is constantly growing, albeit infinitesimally.[7]

In actuality, the calculations upon which the Jewish calendar are based are extremely close approximations. Approximations are necessary in every calendrical system for the simple reason that the length of a month, or of a year, cannot simply be expressed as a given number of days because neither the revolution of the moon around the earth, nor that of the earth around the sun, is empirically fixed in a round number of days, hours, or even minutes. Necessarily, the result is an approximation of the number of days in a year or in a month, combined with periodic intercalations within a given cycle of years. The necessity of reconciling lunar months with solar years makes the task even more difficult. In light of these considerations, accuracy to within one day in 14,000 years in the calculation of lunar months and a discrepancy of only $6^2/_3$ minutes a year in reconciling the lunar calendar with the solar year is truly remarkable.[8]

However, as noted earlier, the dates of the Jewish calendar fall

---

7. The matter is further complicated by an additional factor that would seem to mitigate the discrepancy somewhat. It is believed that the acceleration of the mean lunar motion is constantly decreasing by a very small amount, that is, the moon travels at an increasingly slower rate of speed and, therefore the lunar month is constantly growing longer. That would result in a narrowing of the gap between future astronomical calculations of the lunation and the calculation of the lunar month assumed by the Jewish calendar.

However, the ostensive increase in the length of the lunar month is counterbalanced by the fact that the earth's rotational speed is decreasing even more significantly with the result that the length of the solar day is increasing. The slowing of the earth's rotation causes a loss of somewhat less than a second per year which translates as an increase in the length of a mean solar day. (It was for this reason that a leap second was added to the atomic clock on December 31, 2008.) Accordingly, when the length of the lunar month is expressed in terms of mean solar days, the increase in the length of the solar day will produce a decrease in the length of the mean lunar months. Hence, the discrepancy between the astronomical mean lunar month and the length of the lunar month assumed by the Jewish calendar will increase.

8. Dr. Hugo Mandelbaum has demonstrated that a true, repeating lunar-solar cycle occurs only every 689,472 years. This makes an absolute reconciliation of the lunar calendar with the solar year an impossibility. See "The Problem of *Molad Tohu,*" *Proceedings of the Association of Orthodox Jewish Scientists,* III-IV (1976), 80. See also Leo Levi, *Jewish Chrononomy* (Brooklyn, 1967), p. 8.

later and later in the solar year. *Pesach* is now celebrated approximately 4½ days later in the solar year than was the case 1,000 years ago. Eventually, according to this system of calculation, *Pesach* would, after many thousands of years, advance to a date in the middle of the summer.[9] However, the present calendrical system will not endure indefinitely. At the time of the Redemption, it will be supplanted by reintroduction of a system in which the day upon which *Rosh Chodesh* occurs and the intercalation of months will be determined on the basis of visual observation of the New Moon and mathematical calculation by the *Beth Din*. This, of course, must await the reinstitution of the Sanhedrin. But integral to the faith of the Jew is the belief that the Redemption will come, and with it the reinstitution of the original mode of sanctification of the New Moon, long before any discrepancy between the lunar month and the solar year becomes a matter of significant concern. In this sense, then, the very establishment of our present calendar by Hillel II reflects faith in the coming of the Messiah and, since the present calendar can be superseded only upon the reinstitution of the Sanhedrin, its very promulgation serves as a guarantee that the advent of the Messiah will not be unduly delayed.[10]

◄§ The Tekufos

There is one aspect of the Jewish calendrical system that is entirely solar in nature. The four seasons of the year depend upon the position of the sun *vis-à-vis* the earth. Each of these positions or "turnings" marks the beginning of a new season and is called a *tekufah* (from *lehakif,* "to go around" or make a circuit).

The sun, in its apparent motion around the earth, has four "turning points" or *tekufos* in the course of a year. At the beginning of spring and autumn when the sun appears at the equinoctial points and crosses the equator, it is spoken of as "turning" from one side of

9. Cf. the commentary of R. Ovadiah ben David in the published editions of Rambam, *Hilchos Kiddush haChodesh* 9:3.

10. Cf. the comments of *Bi'ur Halachah* 427:1. The *Tur* presents certain calendrical information that is disputed by *Pri Chadash. Bi'ur Halachah* indicates a number of corrections that must be made in the *Tur's* calendar until approximately the end of the next century and concludes, "We need not be overly concerned beyond because certainly at that time, and even much earlier, there will be the Redemption and we shall sanctify [the New Moon] on the basis of visual observation."

the celestial equator to the other. At the time of the solstices the sun is at its maximum distance or declination from the equator. The sun is at its maximum distance to the north of the equator at the time of the summer solstice and at its maximum distance to the south at the time of the winter solstice. Instead of progressively increasing its declination and traveling yet further away from the celestial equator, the sun "turns" and progressively decreases its declination as it approaches the celestial equator.

The *tekufah* of Nisan marks the vernal equinox or the beginning of spring; that of Tammuz marks the summer solstice; that of Tishrei marks the autumnal equinox; and that of Teves marks the winter solstice. The term *tekufah* is used not only for the beginning of the season, but also as the name of the entire season. Thus, the term *Tekufas Nisan* is used both as a reference to the vernal equinox and as a term for spring; *Tekufas Tishrei* is both a reference to the autumnal equinox and a term for autumn, etc.

Although the Jewish calendar is lunar in nature, the determination of the *tekufah,* a solar event, is of utmost importance. *Deuteronomy* 16:1 stipulates that *Pesach* must occur in the *chodesh haAviv,* in spring. Thus we find that the Gemara *Rosh HaShanah* 21a, reports, "Rav Huna bar Avin sent to Rava: When you see that *Tekufas Teves* extends until the 16th of Nisan,[11] make

---

11. Although *Pesach* occurs on the fifteenth of Nisan, and hence the calendar must be designed so that the equinox falls no later than the fourteenth of Nisan, Rav Huna advises that an intercalary month is mandatory only if the *tekufah* will otherwise occur on the fifteenth. This is so because were *Tekufas Teves* to extend only until the fifteenth of the month it would not be necessary to declare a leap year in order to assure the occurrence of *Tekufas Nisan* prior to *Pesach.* Under those circumstances, it would suffice to make Adar a thirty-day month rather than a month containing twenty-nine days. This would result in the occurrence of *Tekufas Nisan* one day earlier, i.e., on the fourteenth of Nisan. [It should, however, be noted that according to one opinion recorded in *Sanhedrin* 13a, *Tekufas Nisan* may occur as late as the sixteenth day of Nisan. Consistent with the statement of the Gemara, *Rosh HaShanah* 21a, Rambam, *Hilchos Kiddush haChodesh* 4:2, rejects that opinion in ruling that an intercalary month must be added if the *tekufah* occurs on the sixteenth of Nisan or later. According to information provided by Mr. Moishe Miller and Professor Irvin Bromberg, the *tekufah* of Rav Adda occurs on the sixteenth of Nisan approximately once in a century, but never after 11:00 A.M. At the time of Hillel II the *tekufah* occurred on the sixteenth of Nisan at 9:51 and 21.59 seconds A.M. in the year 4120. It will next occur on the sixteenth of Nisan at 9:47 and 11.58 seconds A.M. in the year 5773. In establishing our calendar, Hillel II seems to have accepted the view that *tekufas Nisan* may occur on the sixteenth of Nisan. If so, Rambam's ruling is puzzling as are the comments of Rashi, *Rosh HaShanah* 21a, s.v. *velo tachush.* See also *Masais Binyamin,* no. 101, who states both that our calendar is

that year a leap year... as is written *Preserve the month of Aviv.*"

The determination of the various *tekufos* is also important for two liturgical purposes, viz., for the determination of the date for the commencement of the *tal umatar* prayer for rain in the Diaspora and for the determination of the occasions on which *Bircas haChammah* is to be pronounced. The Gemara, *Ta'anis* 10a, states that the recitation of *tal umatar* begins on the 60th day of *Tekufas Tishrei*. It is understandable that the proper date for the recitation of prayers for rain be calculated according to the autumnal equinox since the rainy season is a function of solar events, as are all the seasons of the year. Hence, the Jewish calendar must provide some means for calculating the day on which the autumnal equinox, or *Tekufas Tishrei,* occurs. The relationship of *Bircas haChammah* to the *tekufah* will be shown later.

According to some authorities, there is one additional aspect of halachah that is associated with the *tekufos*. Rema, *Yoreh De'ah* 116:5, declares that it is the accepted practice not to drink water at the time of the *tekufah* because drinking water at the time of the *tekufah* is associated with danger. In explaining the source of this custom, an earlier authority, Avudraham, states that each of the *tekufos* is an occasion that is associated with a historical occurrence in which water changed to, or became mixed with, blood. The waters of Egypt turned to blood at the time of *Tekufas Nisan*. God commanded Moses and Aaron to speak to the stone and order it to give forth its water at the time of *Tekufas Tammuz*. Instead, they struck the rock and blood flowed from it; at that moment all the waters "were afflicted with blood." Abraham stood ready to sacrifice his son at the time of *Tekufas Tishrei;* at that moment a drop of blood fell from his knife and "spread into the waters." The daughter of Yiftach was sacrificed by her father at the time of *Tekufas Teves* and again on that occasion "all the waters turned to blood." Rema's ruling is accepted by many later

predicated upon the calculation of Rav Adda and that the *tekufah* must occur before the sixteenth of Nisan. *Yad Ramah, Sanhedrin* 13b, s.v. *veika dekashya,* recognized the problem and resolved it by interpreting the Gemara, *Rosh HaShanah* 21a, as ruling that the *tekufah* can occur any time until the conclusion of the sixteenth of Nisan. Rabbeinu Chananel, *ibid.,* states that the concern regarding the *tekufah* was germane only when the *omer* was sacrificed. *Me'iri, Sanhedrin* 13a, implies that the *halachah leMoshe miSinai* providing for introduction of a perpetual calendar also permits ignoring the *tekufah.* Cf. the endeavor of Rabbi David Heber to resolve the difficulty presented by Rambam and Rashi in his recently published *Sha'arei Zemanim* (Baltimore, 5768), no. 1, sec. 8. Cf. also R. Mordechai Schwimmer, *VaYichtov Mordechai* (Brooklyn, 5767), chap. 2.]

authorities. However, *Taz, Yoreh De'ah* 116:4, cites the remarks of Ibn Ezra who declared, " 'לֹא נַחַשׁ בְּיַעֲקֹב' — *there is no sorcery in Jacob*' (*Numbers* 23:23), rather, the 'early ones' stated these matters so that people may become infused with the fear of God and repent, so that God preserve them from [the vicissitudes of] the four seasons." According to Ibn Ezra, there is no actual danger in drinking water at the time of the *tekufah*.

How, then, is the *tekufah* to be determined? The Gemara, *Eruvin* 56a, records the statement of Shmuel to the effect that there are always 91 days and 7½ hours between each of the successive *tekufos*.[12] This calculation yields a solar year of exactly 365 days and 6 hours. This is precisely the length of the year in the Julian calendar. The year of the Julian calendar contains 365 days with an additional day added in February of every fourth year in order to account for the additional six hours of each solar year in excess of the 365 days of the ordinary calendar year. The solar year thus consists of 52 weeks and 1¼ days. Accordingly, each of the four

---

12. Quite apart from the question of the accuracy of the length of Shmuel's solar year as a whole, the astronomical seasons are, in point of fact, not of equal duration. This is so because the earth does not travel around the sun with equal speed throughout the year. During the winter (in the northern hemisphere), when the distance between the earth and the sun is smaller, the earth moves faster; during the summer, when the distance is greater, the earth moves more slowly. This astronomical fact was demonstrated by Johannes Kepler in what has come to be known as Kepler's second law of planetary motion. Kepler demonstrated that a planet travels faster while closer to the sun and at a slower speed when more distant from the sun. In formulating this law, Kepler rejected the Aristotelean astronomical theory that the planets travel with uniform speed.

There are approximately 92.84 days between the first day of spring and the first day of summer and 93.6 days between the first day of summer and the first day of autumn, but only 89.8 days between the first day of autumn and the first day of winter, and only 89.02 days between the first day of winter and the first day of spring. Shmuel's reckoning of each season as 91 days and 7½ hours represents a mean of the lengths of all four seasons. This was recognized and commented upon by so early a figure as the 14th-century scholar, R. Isaac Israeli, a disciple of the *Rosh*, in his classic work on the calendar, *Yesod Olam,* Sixth Treatise, chap. 11.

In an article appearing in the *Proceedings of the Association of Orthodox Jewish Scientists,* VI, (1980), p. 113, note 21, Charles Elkin points out:

> It is interesting to note that the modern Persian (Iranian) calendar, one of the world's most accurate solar calendars (though at some expense of simplicity), starts its year at the Vernal Equinox and counts its first six months at 31 days each so as to start its seventh month accurately on the day of the Autumnal Equinox 186 days later. The remaining months are then 30 days each. The result is that the first day of the first, fourth, seventh and tenth months in the Persian calendar falls correctly on the day of the spring and fall equinoxes and the winter and summer solstices.

tekufos moves forward in the week in each succeeding year by one day and six hours. According to this calculation, each *tekufah* will again occur on the same hour and the same day of the week as its first occurrence only once in twenty-eight years. Thus, as can readily be seen in the chart published in the appendix, pp. 207-209, in the last year of the previous 28-year cycle, 5741 (1981), *Tekufas Nisan* occurred on Tuesday evening, April 7, at 6:00 P.M. Twenty-eight years later, in the last year of the present 28-year cycle, 5769 (2009), *Tekufas Nisan* will again occur on Tuesday evening, April 7, at 6:00 P. M. Hence, Shmuel's 28-year solar cycle is called the *machzor gadol,* the great cycle, or the *machzor chammah,* the solar cycle. Similarly, in the Julian calendar the first day of the year will occur on the same day of the week every twenty-eight years with subsequent days of the various months corresponding to the same days of the week throughout the year, and the sequence of the days of the week on which the first of January will occur in subsequent years is repeated. The Julian calendar thus, in effect, replicates itself in cycles of 28 years. This period is known as the solar cycle or the cycle of the sun and is the equivalent of the *machzor gadol.*

However, in point of fact, the year of Shmuel, as well as the Julian year, are longer than the astronomical solar year (which is only 365 days, 5 hours, 48 minutes and 46 seconds in length) by 11 minutes and 14 seconds. This error amounts to approximately one day in every 128 years (or, more precisely, 23 hours, 57 minutes and 52 seconds).

This discrepancy led to the reformation of the Julian calendar which, at one time, was in use in all European countries. The Julian calendar was adopted in Rome in the year 46 B.C.E. When the Julian calendar was first introduced, the vernal equinox fell on the 25th day of March. By the year 1582 the equinox had retrograded to March 11th. In 1582 Pope Gregory XIII directed that ten days be suppressed or dropped from the calendar. This was accomplished by designating that October 5th, 1582 became October 15th.[13]

The dates October 5th through October 14th were simply

---

13. It is interesting to note that a detailed exposition of the calendrical innovation of Gregory XIII is presented by *Otzar Nechmad* in his commentary on the *Kuzari,* Fourth Treatise, sec. 29.

eliminated from the calendar for the year 1582. In this way the vernal equinox, which then would have occurred on March 11th, was shifted forward to March 21st. March 21st was selected by Gregory XIII as the date of the vernal equinox and the beginning of spring because the equinox fell on March 21st in the Julian calendar in the year 325, the year in which the Council of Nicaea was held. It was the Council of Nicaea which promulgated rules for setting the date of Easter so that it would occur after the equinox but would not coincide with the Jewish *Pesach*. It was disdain for Jews and Judaism that prompted purposive error and the suppression of historical reality in establishing the ecclesiastical calendar. At the time of Gregory XIII this policy was aptly portrayed in a popular epigram describing the promulgators of the church calendar as individuals who chose to be "wrong with the moon rather than right with the Jews."[14]

At first, the Gregorian calendar was accepted only in Spain, Portugal and parts of Italy, including, of course, Rome. Shortly afterwards, the Gregorian calendar was introduced in France and in the Catholic states of Germany. The Protestant states of Germany, however, did not accept the new calendar until the year 1700. The Gregorian calendar was introduced into Sweden and Denmark at about the same time. Great Britain and the American colonies adopted the new calendar only in 1752, in which year the dates September 3 through September 13 were eliminated, while Russia refused to change its calendar until well into the twentieth century. The Russian Orthodox Church to this very day continues to calculate its ecclesiastical calendar in accordance with the principles of the Julian calendar. In all of these countries sociological considerations led to persistence of inaccuracy and resistance to calendrical change.

When the Gregorian calendar was adopted, some leap year intercalations had to be omitted. This was necessary in order to prevent future recurrence of the same type of retrogression that the new calendar had been designed to correct. Since the Julian year exceeds the true solar year by one day in approximately every 128 years, or, more roughly, by three days every 400 years, Gregory

---

14. See T.H. Beirne, *Puzzles and Paradoxes* (London, 1965), p. 174.

ordered that the extra day of the leap year be omitted in all of the centenary years, except in those that were multiples of 400. Accordingly, in the Gregorian calendar, every year whose number is evenly divisible by four is a leap year, with the exception of the century years that are leap years only when divisible by four after omitting the last two zeros. Thus, the year 1600 was a leap year, while 1700, 1800, and 1900 were not, but the year 2,000 was a leap year.

This method of calculation is, of course, still somewhat inaccurate. The Gregorian calendar has 97 intercalations, or leap years, every 400 years. Four hundred years, therefore, contain 365 x 400 plus 97 days. Dividing the total by 400 yields a year equal in length to 365 days, 5 hours, 49 minutes and 12 seconds. This exceeds the true solar year (which is 365 days, 5 hours, 48 minutes and 46 seconds) by 26 seconds with the cumulative error being equal to one day every 3326 years.

◄§ Shmuel and Rav Adda

The Jewish calendar promulgated by Hillel II also provides for the correction of the discrepancy between the true solar year and the solar year based upon the calculations of Shmuel. Shmuel's *tekufos* of 91 days and 7½ hours were replaced by a more accurate calculation of the *tekufos*. The *tekufos* calculated in this manner are known as the *tekufos* of Rav Adda.[15] According to the reckoning of Rav Adda, the solar year equals $12^{7}/_{19}$ lunar months or 365 days, 5 hours, 55 minutes and $25^{25}/_{57}$ seconds (or, as given in *chalakim*, 5 hours, $997^{12}/_{19}$ *chalakim*). Remembering that nineteen lunar years (including the seven intercalated months of the seven leap years in each nineteen-year lunar cycle) are presumed to be equal to nineteen solar years, this figure may readily be derived by dividing the 235 lunations in the 19 years (each lunation reckoned at 29 days, 12 hours and 793 *chalakim*), which equal 6,939 days, 16 hours and 595 *chalakim*, by 19. Thus, for Rav Adda, the length of

---

15. The talmudic source of the *tekufah* of Rav Adda is unclear. See Hirsch Mendel Piniles, *Darkah shel Torah* (Vienna, 1861), pp. 147-150, who asserts that a statement of R. Yochanan found in the *Yerushalmi, Avodah Zarah* 1:2, is predicated upon acceptance of the *tekufah* of Rav Adda; see also Feldman, *Rabbinical Mathematics and Astronomy*, pp. 75 and 201-204, who elucidates this reference.

a solar year is exactly ¹⁄₁₉ of the 19-year lunisolar cycle. Rav Adda's solar year is shorter than that of Shmuel (which deviates from the true solar year by approximately 11 minutes and 14 seconds) by approximately 4½ minutes. Thus, the discrepancy between Rav Adda's solar year and the astronomical year is somewhat less than the discrepancy between Shmuel's solar year and the astronomical year, but is still some 6²⁄₃ minutes longer than the actual solar year. This corresponds to the discrepancy noted above between the Jewish year as promulgated by Hillel II and the length of the solar year as determined by astronomical calculations.

This does not mean that Shmuel must have been ignorant of Rav Adda's method of calculation. Despite acceptance of Hillel's calendar based upon the divergent calculations of Rav Adda, Shmuel is depicted in the Gemara, *Berachos* 58b, as being as familiar with the "paths of the sky" as he was with the alleys of his own city of Nehardea. It may be assumed that Shmuel adopted a simpler method of calculation in order to avoid the necessity of manipulating fractions. This is noted by so early an authority as R. Abraham Ibn Ezra who states in his *Sefer haIbbur*, p. 8, that the *tekufah* of Shmuel is not the true *tekufah* and moreover, that Shmuel knew his announced calculations to be imprecise. Nevertheless, Shmuel chose a close approximation because of the difficulty which most people have in working with fractions.[16] The same explanation is also advanced by the 17th-century Sephardic scholar, R. David Nieto, in his *Kuzari Sheni, Vikuach Chamishi*, no. 146.[17]

---

16. Ibn Ezra states, "*Tekufas Shmuel* ... is not the true *tekufah* and it is quite likely that Shmuel knew this. But he arranged [the calendar] in this manner ... because it is not within the capability of all men to understand fractions or fractions of fractions." See also the commentary of Ibn Ezra on *Exodus* 12:2. The identical observation is made by R. Isaac Israeli, *Yesod Olam, ma'amar* 4, chap. 1 and *Otzar Nechmad,* commentary on *Kuzari,* Part 4, sec. 29. See also *Teshuvos Masais Binyamin,* no. 101. It may be noted that in earlier times, astronomers also avoided use of fractions. Thus, Ptolemy, *Almagest* 1:10, writes that he used multiples of 60 in order to "avoid the embarrassment of fractions." See Elkin, p. 100.

This thesis is supported by Shmuel's construction of a calendar for only sixty years and the statement (*Rosh HaShanah* 20b) that he was capable of designing a calendar for a much longer period of time. This implies that Shmuel was aware of the necessity for adjustment. Otherwise, it would require no great acumen to design a perpetual calendar based upon a year of precisely 365¼ days. Cf. Elkin, *loc. cit.* Cf., however, R. Betzalel haKohen of Vilna, *Reishis Bikkurim* (Jerusalem, 5729), introduction, pp. 113ff. and 147ff., as well as R. Shlomo haKohen of Vilna, *Atzei Beroshim,* no. 60.

17. See also *Teshuvos Poras Yosef, Orach Chaim,* no. 4.

Shmuel's calculations are also discussed in another source from which a somewhat different resolution of this question may be gleaned. R. Isaac Israeli, a disciple of the *Rosh,* in his work on the calendar, *Yesod Olam,* Fourth Treatise, chap. 15, explains that the astronomical calculations that are necessary to establish the calendar were described by the Sages as the *sod ha'ibbur,* the "secret" or "mystery" of intercalation, because detailed information was purposely withheld, not only from the masses, but from most scholars as well.[18] This science was preserved by the elders of the Sanhedrin, who were charged with proclaiming the New Moon and establishing the calculations upon which such proclamations were based and was transmitted by them to selected scholars from generation to generation.

This information was preserved as an esoteric science in order to prevent dissension or controversy which could easily have created a schism among Jews. The *Mishnah, Rosh HaShanah* 25a, tells of a dispute which did in fact break out between R. Joshua and Rabban Gamliel. The latter was head of the Sanhedrin and, in that capacity, proclaimed the New Moon to have occurred on a certain day. R. Joshua, on the basis of his own astronomical calculations, challenged Rabban Gamliel's determination. The dispute would have resulted in Rabban Gamliel and R. Joshua, and their respective disciples, observing *Yom Kippur* on different days. Rabban Gamliel demanded of R. Joshua that he appear before him with his staff and money on the day that, according to the latter's

---

Chazon Ish, Orach Chaim 138:4, explains that the method promulgated by Shmuel was the product of an oral tradition received at Sinai. Its lack of precision, explains *Chazon Ish,* is simply an example of the approximation reflected in other calculations accepted by the halachic tradition, e.g., the value of *pi* and the fractional excess of the length of a diagonal over the side of a square. Those discrepancies, asserts *Chazon Ish,* constitute margins of error accepted by Halachah on the basis of oral tradition in order to facilitate fulfillment of divine obligations by human beings of "imperfect intellect." In contradistinction, the calculations of Rav Adda, opines *Chazon Ish,* were not the product of an oral tradition and hence are subject to refinement at some future time for the purpose of determining the veracity of witnesses testifying to appearances of the New Moon.

For an attempt to harmonize the methods of Shmuel and Rav Adda, see R. Betzalel haKohen of Vilna, *Teshuvos Reishis Bikkurim,* introduction, pp. 3-4 and no. 10, as well as R. Shlomo haKohen of Vilna, *Atzei Beroshim,* no. 60.

18. Cf. *Kesubos* 111a and the commentaries of Rashi and *Tosafos ad loc.;* see also R. Meir Shapiro, *Teshuvos Or haMeir,* no. 13, sec. 3, s.v. *ulefi.*

reckoning, would have been *Yom Kippur.* R. Joshua was understandably reluctant to do so until his colleagues, R. Akiva and R. Dosa ben Hurkinos, convinced him that, by virtue of his office as head of the Sanhedrin, Rabban Gamliel's actions were efficacious even if based upon erroneous astronomical assumptions. Even if he was wrong with regard to the empirical facts, Rabban Gamliel's determination was correct nonetheless because, with regard to the proclamation of the New Moon, the Torah conveys ultimate authority and halachic infallibility upon the head of the Sanhedrin. Thus, writes *Yesod Olam,* in order to forestall similar disputes, which might have resulted in less happy endings, the Sages jealously preserved the astronomical "secret" upon which the calendar is based.

The destruction of the Temple and the dispersion of Israel gave rise to a state of affairs which led to a *volte face* with regard to this policy: 1) The Sanhedrin, shorn of its power and authority, was no longer able to proclaim the New Moon every month. The principles governing the calculations of the calendar and intercalations were in danger of being forgotten. Therefore, these principles had to be taught and publicized as widely as possible. 2) The promulgation of a permanent calendar minimized the likelihood of a schism. Once the calendrical system of Hillel II was adopted, there no longer existed a monthly occasion for possible dissension upon proclamation of the New Moon.[19] Accordingly, we find recorded in the Gemara narratives concerning various Sages telling of how they imparted to their colleagues and students fundamental astronomical data with regard to the length of the lunation and the halachic grounds that would justify periodic intercalations. This knowledge was transmitted as a tradition that, quite obviously, had earlier been withheld from the multitude of scholars.

Nevertheless, even in the earliest of times, the basic principles of the calendar had to be conveyed to the entire people. Otherwise, not only would they have been ignorant of the detailed calculations of the Sanhedrin, but the very purpose of such calculations

---

19. This did not, however, prevent the promulgation of sectarian calendars, most notably by the Karaites in Geonic times, whose efforts in this area met with forceful resistance on the part of R. Saadia Gaon.

would have been incomprehensible to them. They would have been at a loss to understand why the length of the various months and years did not follow a regular and fixed pattern or sequence. They had to be assured that the seemingly erratic nature of the calendar did have rhyme and reason. Accordingly, it was widely taught that the *mitzvah* "Preserve the month of Aviv" required reconciliation of the lunar months with the solar year. This required imparting at least approximate information with regard to the length of the solar year.

This, explains *Yesod Olam,* was the motive underlying dissemination of Shmuel's *tekufah.* This reckoning was known to be imprecise, and kept so, purposely for the reasons indicated. But it served to explain to the uninitiated the nature of the concerns underlying the more precise calculations of the Sanhedrin that, in turn, were accepted with implicit faith by the populace.[20]

These explanations clarify not only a seeming inaccuracy on the part of Shmuel, but also what otherwise seems to be an anomaly of halachah. The calendar, as we possess it, employs both Shmuel's reckoning of the *tekufah* as well as the *tekufah* of Rav Adda. The *tekufah* of Rav Adda is followed for purposes of intercalation, i.e., for reconciliation of the lunar calendar with the solar year in order to assure that *Pesach* does not occur in *Tekufas Teves.* In other words, *Pesach* must always occur in the spring, in *Tekufas Nisan* as determined by Rav Adda's more accurate calculation, but without taking account of Shmuel's *tekufah.*

Determination of the date of *Tekufas Nisan,* is, in actuality, the calculation of the date of the vernal equinox that marks the beginning of spring. Since the year reckoned in the Jewish calendar is somewhat longer than the true solar year, the date established as the day of the *tekufah* is later in the solar year than the true equinox. Since the length of the solar year according to Shmuel is even longer than according to Rav Adda, *Tekufas Nisan,* according to Shmuel, occurs even later in the solar year than it does according to Rav Adda. Thus, the calendar of Hillel II, because it is based upon Rav Adda's *tekufah,* allows *Pesach* — which cannot

---

20. Cf. the commentary of R. Ovadiah ben David, *Hilchos Kiddush haChodesh* 10:1, who expresses the differing view that the true *tekufah* was not publicized in order to withhold that information from sorcerers; see also *Teshuvos Or haMeir,* no. 13, sec. 3.

occur before *Tekufas Nisan* — to occur earlier than according to Shmuel's calculation.[21]

However, for purposes of recitation of the *tal umatar* prayer, as well as for purposes of *Bircas haChammah*, as shall be shown, the *tekufah* of Shmuel is followed. Hence, recitation of *tal umatar* is commenced on the 60th day of *Tekufas Tishrei*, as calculated by Shmuel's reckoning. The reason for this is that recitation of *tal umatar* and *Bircas haChammah* are essentially individual, private rituals to be performed by vast numbers of people. Rav Adda's calculations are simply too difficult for everyone to grasp.[22] Determination of the proper date

---

21. This can result in the rather odd situation in which *Bircas haChammah* — which marks the date of *Tekufas Nisan* — is recited on *Pesach*, as occurred in the year 5601 when *Bircas haChammah* was recited on the second day of *Yom Tov*, even though *Pesach* must not occur before the *tekufah*. The explanation is that *Pesach* must indeed occur after the *tekufah*, but only after the *tekufah* of Rav Adda, not the *tekufah* of Shmuel. Shmuel's *tekufah* is always later than that of Rav Adda and can indeed occur on, or, as is frequently the case, even after *Pesach*. (See *Teshuvos Masais Binyamin*, no. 101.) It is the later date of Shmuel's *tekufah* that governs the date for recitation of *Bircas haChammah*.

The progressive discrepancy between the *tekufah* of Shmuel and the *tekufah* of Rav Adda can, in theory, lead to an even greater paradox. *Tal umatar* is recited on the 60th day of *Tekufas Tishrei* as determined by Shmuel's calculations. That date moves ahead in the solar year approximately 7⅘ days every 1000 years. Rav Adda's *tekufah* also advances and occurs later in the true solar year, but at the slower rate of approximately 4½ days each 1000 years. Thus, the date of *tal umatar* will move closer to *Pesach* by about three days each 1000 years. In approximately 42,000 years the date for *tal umatar*, which is reckoned according to Shmuel's *tekufah*, and the date of *Pesach*, which is entirely independent of Shmuel's *tekufah*, will coincide! This oddity is amplified by the fact that *tal umatar*, associated with the rains of the late fall and winter, is not recited after the first day of *Pesach* when prayers for spring dew are recited. This simply underscores our faith that the present calendar will be abrogated long before that time and the original method of proclaiming the New Moon will be reinstituted. Cf. Elkin, p. 104.

22. Cf. R. Chaim Yosef David Azulai, *Birkei Yosef*, *Shiyurei Berachah*, *Orach Chaim* 229:1, who remarks that Shmuel adopted a simple and readily understandable system of calculating the *tekufah* for purposes of commencement of the *tal umatar* prayers anticipating that later *Batei Din* would correct the calculations from time to time. Since the lapse of a central authority with the power to modify this mode of calculation prevented adoption of any change, Shmuel's promulgation remains in effect. See also *Alfasi Zuta*, *Berachos* 59b.

For a discussion of the acceptance of Shmuel's calculations with regard to the practice of not drinking water at the time of the *tekufah*, see the explanation of R. Yom Tov Lipman Heller, the author of *Tosefos Yom Tov*, in a responsum addressed to R. Menachem Mendel Krochmal and published in the latter's *Teshuvos Tzemach Tzedek*, no. 14.

Cf., also R. Isaac Lampronti, *Pachad Yitzchak*, "Chammah beTekufosah," who further suggests that the discrepancy between the actual *tekufah* and the *tekufah* as determined

for *Pesach* is not a private matter. The community, through the *Beth Din*, is commanded to *preserve the month of Aviv.*[23] Accordingly, the more complicated, but more accurate, *tekufah* of Rav Adda was employed by Hillel II in establishing the date of *Pesach*.[24]

Since calculations based upon Shmuel's *tekufah* follow the pattern of a 365-day year with allowance for an intercalated day every four years, the dates of Shmuel's *tekufos* occur each year on the same date in the civil calendar, which is also 365 days in length. (An exception occurs in the *tekufah* preceding a leap year when there is a one-day difference.) Since the date of *tal umatar* follows the date of *Tekufas Tishrei* by sixty days, counting the day of the *tekufah* as the first day, recitation of *tal umatar* always begins on the same day of the month in the civil calendar. Thus, as is shown in the chart that appears in the appendix, pp. 210-214, in common years, *Tekufas Tishrei* always occurs on October 7th and recitation of *tal umatar* begins on the eve of December 5th. In the autumn preceding a leap year, the *tekufah* occurs on October 8th and recitation of *tal umatar* begins on the eve of December 6th.[25]

Over the centuries the civil date for commencement of *tal umatar* does, however, move forward because of the nature of the Gregorian calendar. Since the Gregorian calendar does not provide for a leap year in centurial years (except those which after dropping the last two zeros are evenly divisible by four), while Shmuel's calculation of the *tekufah* assumes the addition of an extra day *every* four years, including centurial years, the date of *tal umatar* moves forward in the civil calendar by one day each century. Thus, while throughout the 19th century the date for

---

for purposes of *Bircas haChammah* is not a matter of consequence since, in his opinion, a "blessing of praise" (*bircas hashevach*) is never a blessing in vain and, with regard to this blessing, God does indeed constantly renew "the work of creation."

23. Cf. *Beitzah* 5b.

24. Cf. R. Yechiel Michel Tucatzinsky, *Tekufas haChammah uBirchosah* (Jerusalem, 1953), pp. 13 and 16.

25. Cf. R. Shimon ben Zemach Duran, *Teshuvos Tashbatz*, III, no. 123. The instruction found in most *siddurim* indicating that *tal umatar* prayers commence on December 6 in a leap year is inaccurate. The intended meaning is that *tal umatar* prayers begin on December 6 in the winter seasons that span a leap year.

commencement of *tal umatar* prayers was on December 4th, in the 20th century the date advanced one day to December 5th. Since the year 2000 was a leap year, *tal umatar* will continue to commence on December 5th throughout the 21st century. As is shown in the chart that appears in the appendix, pp. 210-214, the date for commencement of *tal umatar* will move foward by one day in the 22nd century.

Similarly, since Shmuel's *tekufos* occur each year on the same date of the civil calendar, *Tekufas Nisan,* which occurs 182½ days following *Tekufas Tishrei,* always occurs on April 8th during the course of the 20th and 21st centuries. Accordingly, the date of *Bircas haChammah* which, as will be discussed, is recited every twenty-eight years on the occurrence of *Tekufas Nisan,* is always April 8th during these centuries.[26]

The establishment of a calendrical system that allows for a patterned sequence of years that can be repeated, at least theoretically, *ad infinitum* necessitates a certain degree of imprecision. However, when each year, and indeed each month, can be established independently, without regard to what has preceded and what must follow, such constraints do not exist. Sanctification of the New Moon each month allows for highly accurate calendrical determinations, subject only to conditions imposed by the requirements of religious observances.

Chasam Sofer, in his work on astronomical calculation, *Et Sofer, klal 110,* chap. 1,[27] stresses that when the Sages speak of the *sod ha'ibbur,* or the "mystery" of calendrical intercalation, they do not refer to the calculations upon which the calendar of Hillel II was predicated, but to the full complement of astronomical and mathematical knowledge that is necessary in order to determine the astronomical year with absolute precision. It was that data which

---

26. Although according to Shmuel's calculations *Tekufas Nisan* occurs on April 8th, the astronomical phenomenon marking the vernal equinox occurs on March 21, some 18 days earlier. Hence, there is a significant discrepancy between the solar phenomenon celebrated by *Bircas haChammah* and the date on which the blessing is recited. A number of proposals have been advanced suggesting alternative dates for *Bircas haChammah* that would be in closer conformity with astronomical phenomena. For a review and critique of those proposals see this writer's *Contemporary Halakhic Problems,* II (New York, 1983), 37-43.

27. Reprinted in *Po'al haShem,* I (Bnei Brak, 5728).

was used by the *Beth Din* in determining whether or not testimony of witnesses was to be accepted for purposes of sanctifying the New Moon upon the expiration of twenty-nine days or whether the month should be allowed to have a full complement of thirty days and in determining whether or not it was necessary to intercalate an additional month by proclaiming a leap year in order to reconcile the lunar year with the solar year.

This science was known to Jews with precision from time immemorial. The Midrash tells us, "Our father Abraham possessed great astronomical wisdom and the nations of the world clamored at his door" seeking to share in that wisdom. The Gemara, *Shabbos 75a*, describes the astronomical calculations upon which the Jewish calendar is based as an example of the wisdom of the Jewish nation. Scripture declares: *Behold, I have taught you statutes and ordinances... Keep them and do them for that is your wisdom and understanding in the eyes of the nations who... will say, "Surely, this great nation is a wise and understanding people"* (*Deuteronomy* 4:5-6). In explaining the meaning of this verse, the Gemara comments: "What is the 'wisdom and understanding' which is in the 'eyes of the nations'? That is the calculation of *tekufos* and *mazalos*." The Gemara interprets the "wisdom and understanding" that this verse ascribes to the Jewish people as a specific reference to the insight necessary for reconciling the lunar months with the solar year and the fashioning of the lunisolar calendar. The remarkable accuracy of this calendar is eloquent testimony to the highly developed knowledge of astronomy and mathematics that our ancestors possessed in antiquity. This knowledge is far too complex and difficult for most people to master. Not everyone has the intellectual acumen to become proficient in the scientific and mathematical studies required for this undertaking.

So long as it was incumbent upon the *Beth Din* to proclaim the New Moon and to establish whether each month was to be twenty-nine or thirty days in length, this corpus of knowledge was preserved by at least a select number of Jewish scholars. With the exile and dispersion of Israel, a relatively simple calendar had to be promulgated. Moreover, it had to be one whose principles and calculations might readily be grasped even by persons possessing only a modicum of scholarship. Accordingly, accuracy was sacrificed for simplicity. *Chasam Sofer* declares that, in promulgating a calendar subject in some small measure to error, the Sages exercised the power vested in them willfully to establish the New Moon, and hence the festivals, in an inaccurate manner, if they found it necessary to do so. Commenting on the verse אֵלֶּה מוֹעֲדֵי ה' מִקְרָאֵי קֹדֶשׁ אֲשֶׁר תִּקְרְאוּ אֹתָם בְּמוֹעֲדָם — *These are the festivals of* HASHEM . . . *those* [אֹתָם] *that you shall proclaim in their appointed time* (*Leviticus* 23:4), the Gemara, *Rosh HaShanah* 25a, takes note of the spelling of the word אֹתָם, *those,* with the deletion of the letter *vav,* and indicates that for purposes of exegesis the letters *alef, tav,* and *mem* should not be vocalized as "*osam,*" meaning "them," but as "*atem,*" meaning "you." The verse is accordingly understood as meaning, "These are the festivals that you [אַתֶּם] shall proclaim, i.e., 'you,' even if you are in error; 'you,' even if you are willfully inaccurate; 'you,' even if you are misled." By virtue of biblical law, the actions of the *Beth Din* in proclaiming the New Moon and in establishing the calendar are endowed with legitimacy regardless of the accuracy of the *Beth Din* or even of its motivation. The power to promulgate a calendar, to ordain *Rosh Chodesh* and to establish the dates of the festivals is delegated to the Sages to be used at their discretion in order to assure and perpetuate the service of God.

The introduction of a permanent calendar by Hillel II notwithstanding, the Gemara, *Shabbos* 75a, declares that it is a *mitzvah* incumbent upon us to calculate the *tekufos* and the progressive movement of the signs of the zodiac (*mazalos*). Citing the verse, "Observe and do them, for this is your wisdom and understanding in the eyes of the nations" (*Deuteronomy* 4:6), the Gemara queries, "What is the wisdom and understanding that is [recognized] by the eyes of the nations? It is calculation of the *tekufos* and *mazalos.*" One of the *Amora'im* declared even more forcefully, "Whosoever knows how to calculate the *tekufos* and *mazalos* but does not make the calculations, of him the verse says, 'But they do not look upon the work of the Lord nor have they seen the product of His hands' (*Isaiah* 5:12)."[28]

---

28. That dictum is cited by Rambam in the introduction to his *Sefer haMitzvos, shoresh* 2.

Since the calendar is now predetermined, no practical purpose is served in our era by actually engaging in such calculations. Rambam was asked, if so, why was such importance attached to engaging in so difficult and esoteric a pursuit? In his *Teshuvos Pe'er haDor,* no. 53, Rambam responds by paraphrasing the admonition of the Sages, "Scrutinize His works for from that you will recognize He Who declared and the world came into being."[29] In his *Hilchos Yesodei haTorah* 2:2, Rambam also defines the commandment "And you shall love the Lord your God" (*Deuteronomy* 6:5) in light of that concept. Rambam explains that love of God is acquired by examining and comprehending the wondrous nature of the created universe. In his *Sefer haMitzvos, mitzvos aseh,* no. 3, Rambam develops that concept at greater length and describes intellectual appreciation of God's "commandments, utterances and works" as constituting the love of God that is incumbent upon us.[30]

Thus, the occasion of *Bircas haChammah* serves not only as the opportunity for recitation of a blessing acknowledging the awesome power of the Deity but also as an opportunity to investigate the wondrous nature of creation reflected in the complexities of the calendar and, in doing so, to enhance fulfillment of the commandment "And you shall love the Lord your God."

---

29. Cf. *Sifri, Deuteronomy* 6:6.

30. Cf. Rambam, *Hilchos Yesodei haTorah* 2:2, where he states that both this commandment and the commandment "And the Lord your God shall you fear" (*Deuteronomy* 6:13) are fulfilled by reflecting "upon His wondrous and great works and creations."

Chapter Three
❧ The Sources

Bircas haChammah, in its essence, consists of the blessing "who makes the work of creation." This blessing is pronounced on the occasion of the sun's return to the position in the heavens that it occupied at the time of the sun's original creation, but not on every such occasion. The sun returns to its original position once each year at the time of *Tekufas Nisan*. *Bircas haChammah*, however, is pronounced only when the sun's return to its original position takes place on the same day of the week and at the same hour of the day as the original creation. Creation of the sun took place at the beginning of the fourth day of the week. The sun was created in the position that it occupies at the time of the vernal equinox. Accordingly, *Bircas haChammah* is recited when the vernal equinox, as calculated by the Jewish calendar, occurs at the beginning of the fourth day, i.e., at 6:00 P.M. on Tuesday evening. As will be shown, the vernal equinox takes place on Tuesday evening at 6:00 P.M. only once every twenty-eight years. Since the sun is not visible in all places at that hour, the Sages ordained that the blessing be recited the next morning.

◌৻ The Beraisa: Bircas haChammah

The primary source for *Bircas haChammah* is the following *Beraisa* accompanied by the Amora Abaye's elucidation, which is found in the Gemara, *Berachos* 59b:

תָּנוּ רַבָּנָן הָרוֹאֶה חַמָּה בִּתְקוּפָתָהּ לְבָנָה בִּגְבוּרָתָהּ וְכוֹכָבִים בִּמְסִילוֹתָם וּמַזָּלוֹת כְּסִדְרָן אוֹמֵר בָּרוּךְ עוֹשֶׂה בְרֵאשִׁית וְאֵימַת הָוֵי אָמַר אַבַּיֵי כָּל כ"ח שְׁנִין וַהֲדַר מַחֲזוֹר וְנָפְלָה תְּקוּפַת נִיסָן בְּשַׁבְּתַאי בְּאוֹרְתָּא דִּתְלַת נַגְהֵי אַרְבַּע.

Our Rabbis taught: He who sees the sun at its turning point, the moon in its power, the planets in their orbits or the signs of the zodiac in their order should say: Blessed are You who makes the work of creation.[1]

---

1. For an analysis of the blessing "Who makes the work of creation" and of why it was ordained in conjunction with such disparate phenomena as the sighting of tall mountains or deep canyons, lightning, and the renewal of the solar cycle, see this author's *BeNesivos haHalachah*, II (New York, 5759), 83-86 (reprinted below, pp. 223-227).

And when [does this happen]? Abaye said: Every twen-ty-eight years when the cycle begins again and the Nisan [Spring] equinox falls in Saturn on the evening of Tuesday, going into Wednesday.

Abaye's explanation of the *Beraisa* is based upon the dictum of Shmuel, *Eruvin 56a:*

אָמַר שְׁמוּאֵל אֵין תְּקוּפַת נִיסָן נוֹפֶלֶת אֶלָּא בְּאַרְבָּעָה רְבְעֵי הַיּוֹם אוֹ בִּתְחִלַּת הַיּוֹם אוֹ בִּתְחִלַּת הַלַּיְלָה אוֹ בַּחֲצִי הַיּוֹם אוֹ בַּחֲצִי הַלַּיְלָה וְאֵין תְּקוּפַת תַּמּוּז נוֹפֶלֶת אֶלָּא אוֹ בְּאַחַת וּמֶחֱצָה אוֹ בְּשֶׁבַע וּמֶחֱצָה בֵּין בַּיּוֹם וּבֵין בַּלַּיְלָה וְאֵין תְּקוּפַת תִּשְׁרֵי נוֹפֶלֶת אֶלָּא אוֹ בְּשָׁלֹשׁ שָׁעוֹת אוֹ בְּתֵשַׁע שָׁעוֹת בֵּין בַּיּוֹם וּבֵין בַּלַּיְלָה וְאֵין תְּקוּפַת טֵבֵת נוֹפֶלֶת אֶלָּא אוֹ בְּאַרְבַּע וּמֶחֱצָה אוֹ בְּעֶשֶׂר וּמֶחֱצָה בֵּין בַּיּוֹם וּבֵין בַּלַּיְלָה וְאֵין בֵּין תְּקוּפָה לִתְקוּפָה אֶלָּא תִּשְׁעִים וְאֶחָד יוֹם וְשֶׁבַע שָׁעוֹת וּמֶחֱצָה.

Shmuel stated: The vernal equinox occurs only at the beginning of one of the four quarters of the day, either at the beginning of the day or at the beginning of the night or at midday or at midnight. The summer solstice occurs only either at the end of one and a half, or at the end of seven and a half hours of the day or the night. The autumnal equinox occurs only at the end of three, or nine hours of the day or the night, and the winter solstice occurs only at the end of four and a half, or ten and a half hours of the day or the night. The duration of a season of the year is no other than ninety-one days and seven and a half hours.

Shmuel reckons the solar year as having 365¼ days divided into four seasons of equal length. Taking *Tekufas Nisan,* i.e., the vernal equinox, as the starting point, and assuming (as Abaye states explicitly) that the first *tekufah* of Nisan occurred at the beginning of the night, i.e., at 6:00 P.M., the next *tekufah* must occur 91 days and 7½ hours later. 6:00 P.M. marks the beginning of the night at *Tekufas Nisan* since at the time of the equinox day and night are of equal duration. Ninety-one days equal 13 weeks exactly. Thus, if *Tekufas Nisan* occurs at 6:00 P.M., the next *tekufah, Tekufas Tammuz,* which marks the summer solstice, must occur on the same day of the week as the first *tekufah,* but will occur another

7½ hours later in the day at 1:30 A.M. The following *tekufah,* which marks the autumnal equinox, *Tekufas Tishrei,* will occur another 7½ hours later in the day at 9:00 A.M. The final *tekufah, Tekufas Teves,* which marks the winter solstice, will occur yet another 7½ hours later in the day at 4:30 P.M.

The next occurrence of *Tekufas Nisan,* which begins the second year of the cycle, will of necessity occur 7½ hours later than the previous *Tekufas Teves,* i.e., at 12:00 midnight of the next day of the week. *Tekufas Tammuz* will follow at 7:30 A.M.; *Tekufas Tishrei* at 3:00 P.M.; and *Tekufas Teves* at 10:30 P.M.

In the third year, *Tekufas Nisan* occurs at 6:00 A.M.; *Tekufas Tammuz* at 1:30 P.M.; *Tekufas Tishrei* at 9:00 P.M.; and *Tekufas Teves* at 4:30 A.M.

In the fourth year, *Tekufas Nisan* occurs at 12:00 noon; *Tekufas Tammuz* at 7:30 P.M.; *Tekufas Tishrei* at 3:00 A.M.; and *Tekufas Teves* at 10:30 A.M.

In the fifth year, *Tekufas Nisan* again occurs at 6:00 P.M., as it did in the first year, and thus the entire cycle is repeated every four years.

Examining these times, it is readily apparent that *Tekufas Nisan* occurs only at 6:00 P.M., 12:00 midnight, 6:00 A.M., and 12:00 noon or, as Shmuel put it, "only at the beginning of one of the four quarters of the day, either at the beginning of the day (6:00 A.M.), or at the beginning of the night (6:00 P.M.), or at midday or at midnight." *Tekufas Tammuz* occurs only at 7:30 A.M. (at the end of 1½ hours of the day), 1:30 P.M. (at the end of 7½ hours of the day), 7:30 P.M. (at the end of 1½ hours of the night), or at 1:30 A.M. (at the end of 7½ hours of the night). *Tekufas Tishrei* occurs only at 9:00 A.M. (at the end of 3 hours of the day), 3:00 P.M. (at the end of 9 hours of the day), 9:00 P.M. (at the end of 3 hours of the night), or at 3:00 A.M. (at the end of 9 hours of the night). *Tekufas Teves* occurs only at 10:30 A.M. (at the end of 4½ hours of the day), 4:30 P.M. (at the end of 10½ hours of the day), 10:30 P.M. (at the end of 4½ hours of the night), or at 4:30 A.M. (at the end of 10½ hours of the night).

It is therefore evident that each of the *tekufos* can occur at one of four hours of the day. But the advent of any one of the four *tekufos* will be at the same hour as its original occurrence only after completing a four-year cycle. However, the *tekufah,* when it recurs at its original time in the fifth year, will not recur on the day of the week on which it occurred in the first year. Since each *tekufah* advances 7½ hours, each successive *tekufah* occurs 13 weeks and 7½ hours later than the previous *tekufah.* Each successive *tekufah* then occurs 7½ hours later in the day. In the course of the four *tekufos* of the year, the *tekufah* advances 30 hours. Thus, any given *tekufah* will recur the following year precisely one day and 6 hours later in the week.

It is evident that each of the four *tekufos* advances 30 hours each successive year if it is remembered that the solar year normally has 365¼ days, which equal 52 weeks plus 1¼ days. Accordingly, for example, the first day of the solar year moves ahead one day in the week each year. Since one day is added to the solar year every four years, the first day of the second four-year cycle will occur five days later in the week. Therefore, if, for example, *Tekufas Nisan* occurs on a Wednesday in the first year of the first cycle, it will, of necessity, occur on a Monday in the first year of the second cycle. Following this pattern, *Tekufas Nisan* will occur on Saturday in the first year of the third cycle, on Thursday in the first year of the fourth cycle, on Tuesday in the fifth cycle, on Sunday in the sixth cycle and on Friday in the seventh. Although *Tekufas Nisan* recurs at the same hour, viz., 6:00 P.M., at the beginning of each of these four-year cycles, it does not occur on the same day of the week. Only after completion of seven four-year cycles, that is, after twenty-eight years, at the beginning of the eighth cycle, will *Tekufas Nisan* again occur at 6:00 P.M. on the same day of the week as its very first occurrence.

This, then, is precisely the meaning of Abaye's statement defining the meaning of "the sun in its *tekufah.*" Abaye explains that the *Beraisa* refers to the occurrence of the *tekufah* at the hour of the day and on the day of the week that are identical with the hour and the day at which the sun was created. *Genesis* 1:14-19 states explicitly that the sun was created on the fourth day. Abaye's statement is based upon the premise that the sun was created at the beginning of the fourth day, i.e., "on the evening of Tuesday going into Wednesday," and fixed in the heavens at the position of the vernal equinox, which is *Tekufas Nisan.*

Yet another astrological phenomenon occurs "on the evening of Tuesday going into Wednesday." Abaye describes the *tekufah* as occurring in the hour of *Shabbetai* or Saturn, on the evening of Tuesday going into Wednesday. Each of the seven planets, Saturn (שַׁבְּתַאי), Jupiter (צֶדֶק), Mars (מַאְדִּים), the sun, Venus (נוֹגַה), Mercury (כּוֹכָב), and the moon, is described as ruling over the various hours of the day in recurring sequences.[2]

Since the planets are seven in number and the week contains 168 hours, a number which is exactly divisible by seven, the cycle of the ascendancy of the planets corresponds precisely to the seven days of the week. Each planet is in the ascendancy every seventh hour and each planet "rules" 24 times (168 divided by 7) during the course of a week. The planets begin a new cycle each week on the same day and at the same time as the previous week. Therefore, any specific hour of the week is governed by the same planet each week. Saturn, which ruled at the time of the creation of the sun on the first hour of Wednesday, is always in ascendancy at the beginning of the fourth day. Abaye identifies the hour of *Tekufas Nisan* to which the *Beraisa* refers as occurring on Tuesday evening in the hour during which Saturn is in the ascendancy, i.e., 6:00 P.M. Saturn, which "ruled" at the hour of the first *tekufah*, is also in ascendancy at the same hour of the same day at the time of the *tekufah* twenty-eight years later. Thus, it is the configuration of *Tekufas Nisan* with the ascendancy of Saturn that occasions *Bircas haChammah*.[3]

These, then, are the astronomical premises which underlie the establishment of *Bircas haChammah*. There are, however, other

_____

2. The planets are viewed as instruments of divine providence in the ordering of human affairs. The term מַזָּל associated with the signs of the zodiac is derived from the verb לְהַזִּיל "to cause to flow." Divine guardianship "flows" or is channeled through the celestial bodies. In particular, it is channeled through the various planets in an ordered sequence. The planets Uranus and Neptune (and Pluto as well, if it is to be classified as a planet) were, of course, unknown to astronomers of antiquity. It has been suggested that they are not included in the tradition concerning planetary influence because, in light of their great distance from the earth, they do not serve as channels of influence and hence their existence is of no astrological significance. Cf. R. Yechiel Michel Tucatzinsky, *Tekufas haChammah uBirchosah* (Jerusalem, 5713), p. 19.

3. The reference is not, however, to the return of Saturn to its original place in the firmament, since the orbit of Saturn around the sun is reckoned at 29 years and 167 days, but rather to the astrological influence of Saturn.

factual assumptions accepted by Halachah which appear to contradict those upon which *Bircas haChammah* is based. The first and most obvious discrepancy involves the date of the creation of the universe.

There is a well-known dispute among the *Tanna'im, Rosh HaShanah,* 10b-11a, regarding the date of the creation of the world. R. Joshua maintains that the world was created on the first day of Nisan. R. Eliezer disagrees and declares that the world was created on the first day of Tishrei.[4] It is quite obvious that Abaye's explanation of the *Beraisa* is predicated upon the premise that the world was created in Nisan, which is in accordance with the opinion of R. Joshua.[5] However, as all know, Jewish law accepts the calendar as beginning with the month of Tishrei and reckons the beginning and the end of sabbatical and jubilee years accordingly. The year is also deemed to begin with the month of Tishrei for purposes of assigning a number to each year. Ostensibly, this practice is in accordance with the opinion of R. Eliezer.[6]

There is thus an apparent inconsistency between Abaye's acceptance of R. Joshua's view that the world was created in Nisan and the acceptance of R. Eliezer's opposing view in other areas of Halachah.[7] A solution to this difficulty may be found in a statement of the Gemara, *Rosh HaShanah* 12a. The Gemara declares that the opinion of R. Eliezer is accepted for purposes of numeration of

---

4. See *Tosafos, Rosh HaShanah* 8a, s.v. *letekufos,* who explain that the controversy is actually with regard to the creation of Adam and that the first day of creation occurred on 25 Adar according to R. Joshua or on 25 Elul according to R. Eliezer.

5. Shmuel's dictum, *Eruvin* 56a, is also obviously based upon the same premise. See *Tosafos, Rosh HaShanah* 8a, s.v. *letekufos.* According to R. Eliezer it follows that the sun was created on Tuesday evening at 6:00 and placed in the firmament at the position it occupies on *Tekufas Tishrei.* Accordingly, the time pattern for the occurrence of the *tekufos* is quite different for R. Eliezer from that described by Shmuel. Thus *Bircas ha-Chammah* for R. Eliezer should occur every twenty-eight years in the month of Tishrei, not in Nisan.

6. The *piyyut* in the *Rosh HaShanah* liturgy that begins: "This day is the beginning of Your creation" (זֶה הַיּוֹם תְּחִלַּת מַעֲשֶׂיךָ) also appears to reflect the position of R. Eliezer. See, however, *Tosafos, Rosh HaShanah* 27a and *Ran, Rosh HaShanah* 16a.

7. *Tosafos, Rosh HaShanah* 8a, certainly recognize a factual dispute between R. Eliezer and R. Joshua. Cf., however, *Bi'ur haGra, Orach Chaim* 581:1, who maintains that there is no factual controversy and attributes that view to *Ran, Rosh HaShanah* 16a. Nevertheless, it should be noted that *Ran,* in the comment cited by *Bi'ur HaGra,* maintains that creation took place in Tishrei.

years,[8] but that the opinion of R. Joshua is accepted for purposes of calculating the *tekufos*. *Tosafos, ad loc.*,[9] explains that the factual decision is in accordance with the opinion of R. Joshua.[10] The *tekufos*, which represent an empirical fact, are reckoned according to R. Joshua. The calendar year, which is only a halachic convention, is reckoned in accordance with the opinion of R. Eliezer.[11]

But why should there be such ambivalence? Why do the months of the calendar year not correspond to the months of creation?

One explanation that has been advanced[12] is based upon the Midrash, *Bereishis Rabbah* 10:4, which states that prior to the sin of Adam the planets and spheres travelled at an extremely rapid speed. Only as a result of the sin of Adam, declares the Midrash, were the planetary orbits enlarged and was their speed diminished. Thus it may be postulated that R. Joshua and R. Eliezer do not disagree regarding facts of cosmogony. Both may be in agreement that the universe was created in Nisan, that is, that when the heavenly bodies were placed in the firmament on the fourth day of creation they were placed in the positions which they occupy on *Tekufas Nisan*. However, due to the rapid rate of speed of the planetary bodies, by the time that Adam was created on the sixth day, the planets had already completed the equivalent of a six-

---

8. It should be noted that R. Joshua agrees that the sabbatical and jubilee years commence with the month of Tishrei. This practice is based upon an Oral Law tradition which is not the subject of dispute, but for which, according to R. Joshua, there is no apparent rationale. See *Aruch laNer, Rosh HaShanah* 12a.

9. See also *Tosafos, Rosh HaShanah* 8a.

10. Elsewhere, *Rosh HaShanah* 27a, *Tosafos* state that R. Eliezer merely means to say that the intention to create the universe arose in Tishrei but all agree that, in actuality, creation took place in Nisan.

11. Other authorities assert that the halachah is, in reality, in accordance with R. Eliezer who maintains that the world was created in Tishrei. Their position reflects the literal meaning of the Gemara, *Rosh HaShanah* 27a, which declares that our recitation of the *piyyut* זֶה הַיּוֹם תְּחִלַּת מַעֲשֶׂיךָ is in accordance with the opinion of R. Eliezer. See *Ritva, ad loc.*; Rambam, *Hilchos Shmittah veYovel* 10:2; R. Ovadiah ben David, *Hilchos Kiddush haChodesh* 9:3; Ramban, *Genesis* 8:5; *Targum Yonasan ben Uziel, Genesis* 8:4; and *Birkei Yosef, Orach Chaim* 229:1. *VaYikra Rabbah* 29:1; *Yalkut Shimoni, Parashas Pinchas* 29; and *Zohar, Parashas Emor*, p. 100b, are also in accordance with the position of R. Eliezer. According to these sources the difficulty with regard to why the *tekufos* — and *Bircas haChammah* — are reckoned in accordance with the opinion of R. Joshua is even greater. For another explanation see R. Meir David Hertzberg, *Or haChammah, Me'orei Or*, p. 13a.

12. See *Or haChammah*, pp. 6b-7b.

month journey and had progressed in their orbits to the positions they now assume at the autumnal equinox, on *Tekufas Tishrei.* According to this explanation, insofar as calculation of the *tekufos* is concerned, R. Eliezer also concedes that reckoning must begin with *Tekufas Nisan;* he disagrees only with regard to the numbering of years which, in his view, begins with the creation of man. Although the creation of man occurred but two days later, it took place in what both R. Eliezer and R. Joshua agree was astronomically the month of Tishrei. According to the Midrash, Tishrei, in the year of creation, came two days after Nisan!

There is a second discrepancy regarding the date of *Bircas ha-Chammah.* Abaye's definition of the "sun at its *tekufah*" implicitly accepts the reckoning of the *tekufos* in accordance with the calculations of Shmuel. However, according to the more precise reckoning of the *tekufos* as calculated by Rav Adda, the *tekufah* occurs on an entirely different date. Moreover, according to Rav Adda, the *tekufah* of Nisan virtually never occurs at the beginning of the fourth day. Indeed, following Rav Adda's calculations, *Tekufas Nisan* has, in fact, in the 5768 years that have elapsed since creation, never recurred at its original hour.[13] Hence, Rav Adda's *tekufah* could not possibly serve as a basis for instituting *Bircas haChammah.*[14]

---

13. See *Tekufas haChammah uBirchosah,* p. 17. *Teshuvos Masais Binyamin,* no. 101, states that according to the *tekufah* of Rav Adda there never will be an occasion for this blessing. See also R. Shlomo haKohen of Vilna, *Teshuvos Atzei Beroshim,* no. 60. Rabbi Tucatzinsky also states that the Sages could not have ordained a blessing based upon the *tekufah* of Rav Adda, but for a somewhat different reason. Rabbi Tucatzinsky notes that the *tekufah* of Rav Adda was not popularly known. The vast majority of people knew only the *tekufah* of Shmuel. A blessing based upon calculations of the *tekufah* that are not consistent with those of Shmuel would have been baffling and incomprehensible to them. Cf. the discussion in *Yesod Olam,* cited above, p. 59. See also *Chazon Ish, Orach Chaim* 138:4. For other explanations see R. Moshe Schick, *Teshuvos Maharam Shik, Orach Chaim,* no. 90 and R. Meshullam Roth, *Teshuvos Kol Mevaser,* no. 51.

14. See above, p. 62 Curiously, *Sheyarei Kenesses haGedolah, Orach Chaim* 229:2, states that "earlier" it was not the custom to recite *Bircas haChammah. Teshuvos Chasam Sofer, Orach Chaim,* no. 56, explains that perhaps this was because those who did not recite *Bircas haChammah* believed Abaye's halachah to be only in accordance with the position of Shmuel, but contrary to the accepted opinion of Rav Adda. See, however, above, pp. 57-67, for sources indicating that Shmuel was well aware of the greater accuracy of Rav Adda's calculations. *Chasam Sofer* himself concludes by pointing out that *Rif, Rambam, Rosh, Tur* and *Shulchan Aruch,* all of whom were well aware of the normative validity of Rav Adda's *tekufos,* cite Abaye's halachah with regard to *Bircas haChammah,* and accordingly *Chasam Sofer* declares that one should not deviate from

It should be pointed out that the beginning of each *machzor katan*, or nineteen-year cycle, is not an appropriate occasion for instituting a blessing in praise of God "who makes the work of creation." The completion of a nineteen-year cycle marks no particular astronomical event, much less a replication of a cosmological event associated with the original creation. As perceived by Rav Adda, the nineteen-year cycle is simply the period of time at the close of which the lunar and solar years are reconciled in Hillel's calendar.[15]

◄§ The Beraisa: Other Phenomena

Recurrence of *Tekufas Nisan* on the eve of Wednesday at 6:00 P.M. is not the only phenomenon reminiscent of creation for which a blessing was ordained. The *Beraisa* in *Berachos* 59b speaks of "the הַחַמָּה בִּתְקוּפָתָהּ לְבָנָה בִּגְבוּרָתָהּ וְכוֹכָבִים בִּמְסִילוֹתָם וּמַזָּלוֹת כְּסִדְרָן, sun at its turning point, the moon in its power, the planets in their orbits and the signs of the zodiac in their order." *Rif* and *Rosh* apparently had a variant reading: לְבָנָה בְּטָהֳרָהּ כּוֹכָבִים בִּמְשִׁמְרוֹתָם מַזָּלוֹת

---

the accepted halachah. See also R. Yitzchak of Posen, *Teshuvos Be'er Yitzchak,* no. 4; and *Machazik Berachah, Orach Chaim* 229:9-10.

See also R. Akiva Eger, *Orach Chaim* 229:2, who reports that the Maharal of Prague recited the blessing without *shem umalchus.* R. Abraham David of Buczacz, *Eshel Avraham, Orach Chaim* 229, comments that the obligation may have been regarded as a matter of doubt because according to Rav Adda there is no basis for *Bircas haChammah.* R. Moshe Kunitz, a great-grandson of Maharal, *Ben Yocha'i,* no. 281, comments that Maharal omitted *shem umalchus* because he did not regard the blessing to be talmudic in origin because he had a variant manuscript reading of *Berachos* 59b.

R. Joseph Shneituch, *Teshuvos Rivam Shneituch,* reports that an earlier authority directed the *shliach tzibbur* to recite the blessing on behalf of the entire congregation in order to minimize the possible infraction. See also *Yizrach Or* 12:4 and R. Yitzchak Yaakov Weisz, *Teshuvos Minchas Yitzchak,* VIII, no. 15.

15. See *Tekufas haChammah uBirchosah,* pp. 17-18. Cf., however, *Teshuvos Masais Binyamin,* no. 101, who assumes that at the beginning of each nineteen-year cycle the sun and moon return to the respective positions that they occupied at the time of creation. *Masais Binyamin* explains that, nevertheless, neither the sun nor the moon returns to its position on the same day or hour as that of the original creation. Rabbi Tucatzinsky points out that the question is based upon an erroneous assumption, since at the beginning of each of Rav Adda's cycles the *molad,* or "birth" of the moon, is 9 hours and 642 *chalakim* after the sun's *tekufah,* presumably because Rav Adda's cycle of the reconciliation of the solar and lunar years is entirely artificial. This reconciliation began with the promulgation of a permanent calendar but was not followed in that precise manner when intercalation was determined on an *ad hoc* basis by the Sanhedrin. Thus, although the length of nineteen solar and lunar years is equal, the sun and the moon are not precisely synchronized at the beginning of the cycle.

בְּעִתָּם, "the moon in its purity, the planets in their watch, the signs of the zodiac in their season." Rambam, *Hilchos Berachos* 10:18, followed by *Tur* and *Shulchan Aruch,* explains that the terms לְבָנָה בְּטָהֳרָהּ כּוֹכָבִים בְּמִשְׁמְרוֹתָם or בִּגְבוּרָתָהּ וְכוֹכָבִים בִּמְסִילוֹתָם refer to when "the moon returns to *mazal teleh* at the beginning of the month and does not incline either to the north or to the south; and similarly, when one of the other five planets returns to the beginning of *mazal teleh* and does not incline either to the north or to the south; and also at every time that one sees *mazal teleh* ascend from the furthermost point in the east."[16]

The *mazalos,* or signs of the zodiac, refer to the stars that sweep across the heaven. In its journey across the sky the sun travels under the path of these stars. This band of stars that circle the earth is divided into twelve sectors of thirty degrees each. Each sector is given a name according to the perceived shape of the configuration of stars in that section of the sky. This zone of the heaven is known in the vernacular as the zodiac (from the Greek word ζψδίων meaning "little animal," presumably because many of the twelve sectors represent animals). The names assigned to each of these twelve sectors of the heaven are טָלֶה (Aries), שׁוֹר (Taurus), תְּאוֹמִים (Gemini), סַרְטָן (Cancer), אַרְיֵה (Leo), בְּתוּלָה (Virgo), מֹאזְנַיִם (Libra), עַקְרָב (Scorpio), קֶשֶׁת (Sagittarius), גְּדִי (Capricorn), דְּלִי (Aquarius), and דָּגִים (Pisces).[17] Six of these are north of the equator and six are south of the equator.

The sun does not rise in the same portion of the eastern sky each day. From Nisan until Tammuz the sun moves in a northerly direction, rising each day a bit further to the north. From Tammuz until Tishrei, the sun returns to the celestial equator which is the

---

16. Cf. R. Jacob Emden, *Mor uKetzi'ah* 229, who expresses ignorance of the phenomenon depicted by Rambam as well as of why it should be a rare, rather than daily, occurrence.

17. For the symbolic representations of these signs and the events with which they are associated, see *Pesikta Rabbasi* 20, 27 and 28. The zodiac and the succession of the planets are significant in Judaism primarily as a reflection of the complexity, majesty and grandeur of creation. As is evident from *Deuteronomy* 18:11, it is forbidden for Jews to consult astrologers for purposes of acting upon their advice. The Gemara, *Shabbos* 156a, declares, "Israel is immune to the influence of the *mazal*" and in this connection, cites the prophetic verse, *Thus says HASHEM, learn not the way of the nations and be not dismayed at the signs of the heaven, for the gentile nations are dismayed by them* (*Jeremiah* 10:2).

midline between the sun's northerly and southerly declination in the sky. From Tishrei on it begins to rise a bit more to the south each day. In the period of a year, the sun travels through the course of the *mazalos*, rising in a slightly different position each day. Each day the sun rises in a position approximately one degree distant from the point at which it rose the day before. The twelve full moons also occur in successive parts of the sky in the course of one full year.

Each of the twelve *mazalos*, or signs of the zodiac, coincides with the position in the sky of the rising sun for a period of one month. Thus, at the time of *Tekufas Nisan*, the sun rises and continues along its orbit at the beginning of *mazal teleh* (which is the first of the *mazalos*), etc. Similarly, the moon and the planets, when they rise in the sky, rise at different points under the various *mazalos*, each in accordance with its own orbit, and continue their journey, each at its own fixed rate of speed. The blessing of which the *Beraisa* speaks is to be recited when each of the planets returns to its original position under *mazal teleh*, the first of the *mazalos*, and is aligned precisely with *mazal teleh*, "neither inclining to the north nor to the south."

The concluding phrase: מַזָּלוֹת כְּסִדְרָן or מַזָּלוֹת בְּעֵתָּם, is defined by Rambam as the occasion on which "one sees *mazal teleh* rising in the east," as it did at the time of creation. This is referred to as the occasion on which the signs of the zodiac are "in their order," because when *mazal teleh* rises in the east, the other *mazalos* are in the respective positions that they occupied at the time of their creation.[18]

It is curious that although the *Beraisa* prescribes that the blessing pronounced upon the return of the sun to its *tekufah* also be recited upon the appearance of the moon and the planets in *mazal teleh*, and upon the appearance of *mazal teleh* in the east, it is nevertheless not our custom to do so.[19] A number of reasons

---

18. It is thus quite clear that the *Beraisa* speaks of three distinct phenomena, each of which occasions the recitation of a blessing: 1) the sun at its *tekufah;* 2) the moon and planets when they appear in *mazal teleh;* and 3) *mazal teleh* when it appears in the east. Cf. R. Yaakov Emden, *Mor uKetzi'ah, Orach Chaim* 229, who expresses difficulty in understanding Rambam's definition of מַזָּלוֹת בְּעֵתָּם but offers no alternative explanation. See also *Ateres Tiferes,* I, 60a-62a, who seeks to clarify Rambam's position.

19. See *Mishnah Berurah* 229:9.

have been advanced in explanation of our failure to pronounce the blessing on the latter occasions. *Teshuvos Beis Efrayim, Orach Chaim,* no. 7, quotes the view of R. Jacob Landau (the son of the *Noda biYehudah*) as well as of *Chida, Machazik Berachah, Orach Chaim* 229:9, who maintain that we do not pronounce this blessing on such occasions for the simple reason that only a skilled astronomer is able to make the appropriate calculations.[20] Indeed, so early an authority as the thirteenth-century commentator, Rabbeinu Yonah, in his remarks on *Rif, Berachos* 59b, states that the times of the occurrence of these celestial events are "known to the astronomers," implying that the information is not widely known. It may be inferred from the very words of the Gemara, *Berachos* 59b, that we are ignorant of the precise times at which these events occur. The *Beraisa* records the general halachah regarding the blessing both as it applies to the sun and the other planets without stating with precision the time at which any of these events occurs. Abaye amplifies the halachah recorded in the *Beraisa* only as it applies to the sun in its *tekufah*. Abaye offers no information with regard to when the blessing as associated with the other celestial bodies is to be pronounced. Apparently, then, "the sun in its *tekufah*" is an occasion which readily lends itself to calculation, whereas the others can be determined only with great difficulty.

In his *Teshuvos Yehudah Ya'aleh, Orach Chaim,* no. 7, R. Judah Asad, known as *Maharya,* advances a different reason in explanation of why this blessing is not recited upon the other occasions enumerated in the *Beraisa.* He points to the fact that the Gemara requires that a blessing be pronounced only when one "sees" these astronomical events. Thus, even *Bircas haChammah,* according to *Maharya,* is not recited on a cloudy day when the sun cannot be seen.[21] Therefore, declares *Maharya,* with regard to the other phenomena, since it is virtually impossible to observe them other than by means of a telescope, and since they are brief in nature, it is not very often that the blessing can be pronounced.[22]

---

20. See also R. Joseph Stern, *Teshuvos Zecher Yehosaf,* no. 119.

21. For a discussion of conflicting opinions with regard to this point, see below, pp. 106-109

22. R. Pinchas Schwartz, *Yizrach Or,* chap. 7, suggests, somewhat tenuously, on the

Chida, Birkei Yosef, Shiyurei Berachah, Orach Chaim 229:2, of-fers a differing interpretation of the phrase כּוֹכָבִים בִּמְסִילוֹתָם מַזָּלוֹת בְּעִתָּם. *Chida* quotes a certain Rabbeinu Yonason who explains that this phenomenon is an occurrence which parallels the event described as "the sun at its *tekufah*." The latter event signifies the return of the sun to the position that it occupied at the time of cre-ation. The term מַזָּלוֹת בְּעִתָּם, declares this authority, similarly refers to the time that each of the heavenly bodies returns to the point it occupied at the time of creation. Although we do know when the sun returns to its original position, the time at which each of the heavenly bodies returns to its original position is described as hav-ing been known only to *chachmei hakochavim*, those proficient in the way of the stars. Since we, however, are ignorant of when these phenomena occur, we cannot recite the blessing on such occasions.

✑§ The Yerushalmi

The Talmud *Yerushalmi, Berachos* 9:2, presents a somewhat dif-ferent formulation of the occasions on which the blessing is to be recited:

> הָרוֹאֶה אֶת הַחַמָּה בִּתְקוּפָתָהּ וְאֶת הַלְּבָנָה בִּתְקוּפָתָהּ וְאֶת הָרָקִיעַ בְּטִיהֲרוֹ אוֹמֵר בָּרוּךְ עוֹשֶׂה בְרֵאשִׁית אָמַר רַב הוּנָא הֲדָא דְתֵימַר בִּימוֹת הַגְּשָׁמִים בִּלְבָד לְאַחַר ג' יָמִים הֲדָא דִכְתִיב וְעַתָּה לֹא רָאוּ אוֹר [בָּהִיר הוּא בַּשְּׁחָקִים וְרוּחַ עָבְרָה וַתְּטַהֲרֵם]

> *He who sees the sun at its turning point, the moon in its strength and the firmament in its clarity should say: Blessed is He who makes [the work of] creation. Rav Huna said: This is said with regard to the rainy season and only after three days [of rain], as it is said, "And now they do not see light when it is bright in the skies but a wind passes and clears them" (Job 37:21).*

The *P'nei Moshe* commentary on the *Yerushalmi* understands the comment of Rav Huna as explaining the very last clause, i.e.,

---

basis of the comments of *Zohar Chadash, Seder Bereishis,* that the blessing *"ma'ariv aravim,"* which speaks of the ordering of the stars, encompasses praise for these events as well. Cf. *Pesach haDvir, Orach Chaim* 229:6.

"the firmament in its purity."[23] Rav Huna qualifies the halachah by stating that the blessing is to be recited only in "the rainy season" and even then only after a three-day period of rain during which the sun cannot be seen.[24] Afterwards, when the sun disperses the rain clouds, the firmament, entirely free of clouds, is perceived in its clarity. It is this phenomenon that is referred to in *Job* 37:21: *And now they do not see light when it is bright in the skies but a wind passes and clears them.* When that phenomenon is perceived, one is required to pronounce the blessing "who makes the work of creation" because it is then that the firmament is perceived in its splendor. According to *P'nei Moshe,* there is no conflict between *Berachos* 59b and the Talmud *Yerushalmi* with regard to *Bircas haChammah.* On the contrary, these two sources complement one another. Abaye explains only the first clause, i.e., "the sun at its *tekufah,*" while Rav Huna explains the last clause of the dictum as cited in the *Yerushalmi,* i.e., "the firmament in its purity."[25] This latter phrase does not occur in the *Beraisa* cited in *Berachos* 59b.[26]

---

23. See also R. Elijah, Gaon of Vilna, commentary on the *Yerushalmi, ad loc.*

24. *Teshuvos Chasam Sofer, Orach Chaim,* no. 56, suggests that the blessing is recited after a three-day absence of sunlight because the reappearance of the sun after a three-day interval is reminiscent of the original creation of the sun, the sun having been created only on the fourth day. He also suggests that "perhaps" the correct textual reading of Rav Huna's statement is "thirty days" rather than three days. This would have the effect of rendering this blessing comparable to the blessing recited, for example, upon sighting the "Great Sea." That blessing is recited only if the sea has not been seen for a full thirty-day period. Similarly, the blessing upon sighting the sun is recited, according to this interpretation of the *Yerushalmi,* only if it has not been seen for a full thirty days.

25. See also R. Betzalel Ze'ev Shafran, *Teshuvos Ravaz,* no. 32, sec. 2; R. Chaim Moshe Amarillo, *Teshuvos Dvar Moshe,* no. 18, s.v. *veattah;* R. Abraham Meshullam Zalman Ashkenazi, *Teshuvos Divrei Rav Meshullam,* no. 7; and *Sefer Kovetz, Hilchos Berachos* 10:18.

26. The phrase הָרָקִיעַ בְּטִיהֲרוֹ is absent in the *Beraisa* as cited in *Berachos* 59b. However, the Gemara, *Berachos* 59a, states:

> R. Joshua ben Levi said: If one sees the sky in all its purity, one says, "Blessed is He who makes the work of creation." When does he say so? Abaye said: When there has been rain all the night and in the morning the north wind comes and clears the heavens. And they differ from Rafram bar Papa, quoting R. Chisda. For Rafram bar Papa said, in the name of R. Chisda: Since the day when the Temple was destroyed there has never been a perfectly clear day, as it says: *I clothe the heavens with blackness and I make a sackcloth their covering (Isaiah 50:3).*

The *Yerushalmi* and R. Joshua ben Levi both posit an obligation with regard to a blessing after a period of rain. The sole difference is that for Rav Huna, as recorded in the

This interpretation of the *Yerushalmi* is, however, apparently contradicted by a parallel text that appears in the Midrash, *VaYikra Rabbah* 23:8, which reads:

תָּנָא הָרוֹאֶה חַמָּה בִתְקוּפָתָהּ לְבָנָה בְּכַדּוּרָהּ כּוֹכָבִים בִּמְסִילוֹתָם
מַזָּלוֹת כְּסִדְרָן אוֹמֵר בָּרוּךְ עוֹשֶׂה מַעֲשֵׂה בְרֵאשִׁית. אָמַר רַב הוּנָא
הֲדָא דְאַתְּ אָמַר בִּימוֹת הַגְּשָׁמִים וּבִלְבַד לְאַחַר שָׁלֹשׁ יָמִים.

It was taught: He who sees the sun at its turning point, the moon in its circle, the planets in their orbits, or the signs of the zodiac in their order, should say: Blessed is He who makes the work of creation. Rav Huna said: That which you said applies to the rainy season, and then only after three days.

The same Midrash is found in *Yalkut Shimoni, Job* 922, in the identical language except that in the *Yalkut* the name R. Jeremiah appears instead of Rav Huna. The crucial difference between the *Yerushalmi* and the Midrash is that the latter makes no reference to "the firmament in its purity" and hence, as presented in the Midrash, Rav Huna's explication can have no reference other than to "the sun in its *tekufah*."

Radal, one of the commentators on the Midrash, endeavors to reconcile the textual reading of the Midrash with that of the *Yerushalmi* by adding the words רָקִיעַ בְּטָהֳרָתָהּ "the firmament in its purity" to the text of the Midrash. This would have the effect of eliminating any need to posit a conflict between the Midrash

---

Yerushalmi, it is recited only after three days of rain, whereas for Abaye it is recited after but a single night's rain. It is, however, entirely possible that there is a fundamental difference between these two sources with regard to the specific factor that occasions the obligation to pronounce the blessing. Abaye requires that the blessing be pronounced even after a single night's rain. Certainly, there is nothing extraordinary about the sun's reappearance after a single night since this is a regular occurrence. For Abaye it would appear that it is the clarity of the sky that occasions the blessing. The brilliance and clarity of the sky after the clouds have been dispersed by the north wind following a night's rain that has flushed and "cleansed" the sky is reminiscent of the purity of the sky at the time of creation, and this phenomenon occasions the blessing "who makes the work of creation." For Rav Huna it is the reappearance of the light of the sun following a period of darkness, rather than the actual purity of the sky *per se,* that occasions the blessing. Appearance of the sun after a three-day hiatus is a reenactment, in a minuscule sense, of the original creation of the sun on the fourth day following a three-day period of darkness. Cf. *Teshuvos Chasam Sofer, Orach Chaim,* no. 56. We do not recite the blessing on such occasions because the halachah is in accordance with the opinion of Rafram bar Papa. See *Teshuvos Beis Efrayim, Orach Chaim,* no. 7.

or the *Yerushalmi* and the *Bavli*, as indeed is the position of *P'nei Moshe.*

Of further interest with regard to a possible controversy between the *Bavli* and the *Yerushalmi* with regard to *Bircas ha-Chammah* is one definition of *chammah betekufosah* found in the *Aruch*, s.v. *chammah*. The *Aruch* quotes the reference *chammah betekufosah* in *Berachos* 59b and proceeds to offer two different interpretations of that term. The first is identical with the explanation of Abaye; the second is identical with the statement of Rav Huna[27] as found in the *Yerushalmi.*[28] It is clear that the *Aruch* cites both statements as explanations of the term *chammah*

---

27. The latter interpretation is also cited by *Meiri, Berachos* 59b, in the name of anonymous "yesh meforshim." See also R. Yitzchak Palaggi, *Yafeh LeLev,* II, *Orach Chaim* 229:40. It seems evident that the two explanations of *chammah betekufosah* cited by the *Aruch* are intended by him as references to those of *Berachos* 59b and the *Yerushalmi* respectively. The halachah, then, is clearly in accordance with the *Bavli, Berachos* 59b. R. Akiva Eger, *Gilyon haShas, Berachos* 59b, states that the second explanation cited by the *Aruch* is based upon a variant text of *Berachos* 59b in which Abaye's explanation of the *Beraisa* is absent. See also *Teshuvos Be'er Yitzchak,* no. 4, and *Teshuvos Koach Shor,* no. 27. Cf., however, *Teshuvos Chasam Sofer, Orach Chaim,* no. 56. This would then call into question the very basis of the halachah with regard to recitation of *Bircas ha-Chammah.* Indeed, for this reason, *Sheyarei Kenesses haGedolah* and *Teshuvos Masais Binyamin,* no. 101, consider the blessing to be a *safek berachah.* See also the view of Maharal of Prague, as cited in *Ben Yocha'i,* no. 281, as well as *Teshuvos Dvar Moshe,* no. 18, cited in *Hagahos R. Akiva Eger, Orach Chaim* 229:2. This position is rejected by virtually all other authorities, precisely, it would appear, because there is no reason to assume that the *Aruch* had a different textual reading of *Berachos* 59b. See, for example, *Adnei Paz, Orach Chaim* 229:2. Cf. R. Ben Zion Lichtman, *No'am,* VIII (5724), pp. 362-363.

28. R. Joshua Horowitz of Dzikov, in his letter of approbation to *Boker Yizrach,* suggests that the *Yerushalmi* does not completely ignore Abaye's interpretation of the *Beraisa.* The *Yerushalmi,* he argues, means to add a further stipulation. The blessing is to be recited on the day of the *tekufah,* but only if the sun has not appeared for a period of three days previously. [This interpretation of the *Yerushalmi* was actually advanced earlier by R. Jacob Landau; see *Teshuvos Beis Efrayim,* no. 7.] Cf. *Or haChammah, Me'orei Or,* p. 10, who professes failure to comprehend the rationale of the *Yerushalmi* according to this analysis. It would appear, however, that according to Rabbi Horowitz' understanding of the *Yerushalmi,* the blessing is to be recited only if the occasion is fully comparable to the state which existed at the time of the original creation, i.e., not only must the sun appear at the position that it occupied when it was created and return to that position on the same day and hour as that of creation, but the sun must also not have appeared (because of rain) for a full three days previously, as was the case at the time of the original creation of the sun on the fourth day. For a fuller discussion see this writer's *BeNesivos haHalachah,* II, 86 (reprinted below, p. 226).

Auguring in favor of this latter analysis of the *Yerushalmi* is the fact that the words חַמָּה בִּתְקוּפָתָהּ do not seem to be at all related to Rav Huna's explanation; see, however, below, note 29, Cf. also R. Shlomo Segner, *Or haChammah* (Munkacs, 5657), pp. 6a-6b.

betekufosah[29] since in the *Aruch* there is no mention whatsoever of "the firmament in its purity."[30]

Teshuvos Chasam Sofer, Orach Chaim, no. 56, adheres to the view that there *is* a controversy between the *Bavli* and the *Yerushalmi. Chasam Sofer* suggests that Rav Huna disagreed with Abaye's understanding of the phrase *chammah betekufosah* and hence sought to explain the *Beraisa* in a different vein because Abaye's interpretation — as we have seen earlier — is predicated upon Shmuel's calculation of the *tekufos.* Rav Huna, suggests *Chasam Sofer,* accepted the reckoning of Rav Adda and hence felt constrained to advance an alternative explanation of the *Beraisa. Chasam Sofer* concedes, however, that Rambam and subsequent authorities had no difficulty in ruling in accordance with Abaye even though they accept the fact that our calendar is based upon the *tekufah* of Rav Adda.[31]

It is therefore more likely that a basis for the controversy between *Berachos* 59b and the *Yerushalmi* (if such a controversy does in fact exist) is to be found in another dispute. As noted earlier, R. Joshua and R. Eliezer disagree with regard to whether the world was created in Tishrei or in Nisan. Abaye's halachah, as has been explained earlier, is obviously in accordance with the view that the world was, in fact, created in Nisan. However, the Midrash, *VaYikra Rabbah* 29:1, declares that Adam was created in Tishrei on *Rosh HaShanah.* Rav Huna, assuming that he maintains

---

29. See *Teshuvos Beis Efrayim,* no. 7, who suggests that the correct textual reading of the *Yerushalmi* should then be חַמָּה בְּתוֹקְפָּתָהּ in the sense of בְּתוֹקְפָּהּ, i.e., the "sun at its strength," meaning that, after having been obscured by the rain, the sunlight is then perceived in its full strength. [Cf. *Siddur R. Saadiah Gaon,* p. 90 and commentary of *Rabbeinu Bachya, Genesis* 1:14.] He further suggests that חַמָּה בִּתְקוּפָתָהּ may indeed mean "the sun at its *tekufah,*" meaning on the day of any one of its *tekufos.* This would mean that, according to Rav Huna, the blessing is recited only if the sun appears on the day of the *tekufah,* when it shines most strongly (see *Chullin* 60b), after three days of rain.

30. *Mor uKetzi'ah, Orach Chaim* 229, endeavors to explain the *Aruch's* second definition as an explication of רָקִיעַ בְּטִיהֲרוֹ; this, however, is simply not borne out by the text of the *Aruch.* See R. Meir David Hertzberg, *Or haChammah, Me'orei Or* (Przemysl, 5684), p. 11.

31. Indeed, as noted earlier, both Ibn Ezra and *Yesod Olam* maintain that in actuality there is no contradiction between Shmuel's dictum and the *tekufah* of Rav Adda. See, however, *Machazik Berachah* 229:9, who advances a thesis identical to that of *Chasam Sofer* in explanation of *Sheyarei Kenesses haGedolah* cited above, note 27.

that the world was created in Tishrei,[32] would have had strong reason to reject Abaye's halachah and to advance his own explanation of the Beraisa.[33]

32. See Rashi, Genesis 47:2, who states that Midrash Rabbah has as its source the aggados of the Yerushalmi. If Rav Huna, whose view is recorded in the Yerushalmi, rejected Abaye's explanation of the Beraisa because the Yerushalmi accepted the tradition that the world was created in Tishrei, it is understandable that it is this view that is reflected in Midrash Rabbah.
33. See Boker Yizrach, Sha'arei Mizrach, chap. 1.

Chapter Four

✍ The Laws

[1] One who sees the sun on the morning following the vernal equinox when the equinox, as reckoned by the Jewish calendar, occurs at 6:00 P.M. (Jerusalem solar time) on Tuesday evening — an event which occurs at intervals of twenty-eight years — should pronounce the following blessing:

The proper term is *Bircas haChammah* (Blessing of the Sun) rather than *Kiddush haChammah* (Sanctification of the Sun). The latter term is, however, found in *Teshuvos Chasam Sofer, Orach Chaim*, no. 56, and is used by R. Meir David Hertzberg who includes a chapter entitled *"Hilchos Kiddush haChammah"* in his *Or haChammah* (Przemysl, 5684) as well as by several other scholars. The appellation *"Kiddush haChammah"* is a colloquialism borrowed from the term *"Kiddush Levanah"* (Sanctification of the Moon), which is used to denote the blessing and accompanying liturgy recited each month upon the reappearance of the new moon. The term *"kiddush"* or *"sanctification"* used in conjunction with the lunar blessing is also somewhat of a misnomer since no act of "sanctification" is involved. Use of the term stems from the fact that in the time of the Sanhedrin the month was proclaimed by the *Beth Din* upon the testimony of witnesses who had sighted the nascent moon. Subsequent to interrogation by the *Beth Din*, the head of the court proclaimed that day as the first day of the new month by declaring, *"Mekudash* — it is sanctified."* The term was borrowed and applied to the blessing upon the new moon even though the blessing is in no way connected with the actual sanctification of the new moon. See R. Pinchas Schwartz, *Yizrach Or* (Nagyvarad, 5685), p. 23b.

[1] For a discussion of whether recitation of the blessing is obligatory or discretionary, see R. Moshe Sofer, *Teshuvos Chasam Sofer*, no. 56, as well as R. Zevi Pesach Frank, *Teshuvos Har Zevi, Orach Chaim*, I, no. 119.

Bircas haChammah is recited on the Wednesday morning following *Tekufas Nisan*, when *Tekufas Nisan* occurs the previous evening according to the reckoning of Shmuel's *tekufos*. This occurs every 28 years. *Tekufas Nisan*, and hence *Bircas haChammah*, generally occur some time during the month of Nisan. The latest day of the occurrence of *Bircas haChammah* in the Jewish calendar, at least in recent centuries, was on 26 Nisan 5629 (April 7, 1869). However, on rare occasions, *Bircas haChammah* occurs late in the month of Adar. Thus, in 5461 it occurred on 27 Adar II (April 6, 1701) and will occur on 29 Adar II 5993 (April 10, 2233).

The last two occasions of *Bircas haChammah* were 23 Nisan 5713 (April 8, 1953) and 4 Nisan 5741 (April 8, 1981).[1] *Bircas haChammah* will be recited this year on 14 Nisan,

---

[1] 1. The dates given by J.D. Eisenstein, *Jewish Encyclopedia*, XI, 591, and in his *Otzar Yisrael*, X, 189, as well as those given by *Encyclopedia Judaica*, XV, 518, are in error. Eisenstein's dates are apparently based upon his own calculations of

בָּרוּךְ אַתָּה יהוה אֱלֹהֵינוּ מֶלֶךְ הָעוֹלָם עוֹשֶׂה מַעֲשֵׂה בְרֵאשִׁית

Blessed are You, HASHEM, our God, King of the universe, who makes the work of creation.

Recitation of additional psalms and prayers is discretionary and not a matter of fixed custom.

---

erev Pesach 5769, which corresponds to April 8, 2009.[2] This occasion will mark the commencement of the 207th 28-year solar cycle since the beginning of creation. Subsequent occasions for recitation of *Bircas haChammah* in the 21st century are April 8th in the years 2037, 2065 and 2093. In the 22nd century, the date for *Bircas haChammah* is April 9th in the years 2121, 2149 and 2177. A chart showing the appropriate dates for *Bircas haChammah* from creation until the end of the sixth millennium (*elef hashishi*) and of the twenty-third century is included in the Appendix.

The time of the equinox, i.e., the time at which the sun crosses the equator, is given as the precise solar time in Jerusalem at the moment at which this event occurs. Similarly, in announcing the *molad*[3] on the

---

the *tekufah*, not upon the *tekufah* of Shmuel. Such calculations are presented by Eisenstein in an article in *HaDo'ar*, August 8, 1952, but are not consistent either with the principles of the Jewish calendar or with the astronomical facts. Moreover, the dates given in *HaDo'ar* contradict those presented in *Otzar Yisrael* and the *Jewish Encyclopedia*. Most significantly, for purposes of *Bircas haChammah*, any innovative calculation of the *tekufah* is of absolutely no halachic validity. See A.A. Akabiyah, *HaDo'ar*, November 7, 1952; Arthur Spier, *HaDo'ar*, September 5, 1952; and Arthur Spier, *Jewish Life*, January-February, 1953, p. 53. It appears that the author of the article in *Encyclopedia Judaica* sought to copy the dates of *Bircas haChammah* from the *Jewish Encyclopedia* and compounded the error by copying inaccurately.

2. The 22 Nisan 5713 issue of *Hamodia* published a report recounting that on the occasion of *Bircas haChammah* in 5685, which occurred on *erev Pesach*, the *Ostrovtzer Rebbe* declared that since the creation of the world, *Bircas haChammah* had occurred on *erev Pesach* on only two prior occasions, namely in the year of the Exodus from Egypt, and in the year in which Mordecai and Esther, seeking to avert the evil decree of Ahasuerus, proclaimed a three-day fast beginning on *erev Pesach*. The *Ostrovtzer* sought to draw a parallel between the coincidence of *erev Pesach* and *Bircas haChammah* and the salvation of the Jewish people. He prayerfully anticipated the coming of Messiah subsequent to the third such occurrence. A report of his remarks was subsequently published in the *Ostrovtzer's Meir Einei Chachamim, Mahadura Tinyana* (New York, 5712), p. 52.

The *Ostrovtzer Rebbe's* observation is intriguing. However, as reflected in the accompanying chart, prepared by Mr. Moishe Miller and confirmed by Professor Irvin Bromberg of the University of Toronto, the *Ostrovtzer's* information is at variance with the facts. Neither the year of the Exodus (2448) nor the year preceding Purim (3404) marked the beginning of a new twenty-eight year solar cycle. Hence, *Bircas haChammah* could not have been recited in either of those two years and obviously not on *erev Pesach*. This writer has been unable to find a source or explanation that would account for the *Ostrovtzer's* remark.

Shabbos preceding *Rosh Chodesh*, the *molad* is always given as the time in Jerusalem at which this phenomenon occurs.[4]

The conventional system of measuring time, based upon Greenwich mean time, provides for the division of the world into 24 time zones of 15 degrees each. Since the sun completes its revolution around the earth (or, more accurately, since the earth completes its rotation upon its axis) completing a full circuit of approximately 360 degrees once every twenty-four hours, it traverses a distance of 15 degrees from east to west each hour. Thus, for example, if the sun is directly overhead (i.e., at noon) at a given point, it is one hour before noon 15 degrees to the west because the sun will be directly overhead at the latter point one hour later. Division of time zones into one-hour segments of sun travel is a mere convention. Precision and accuracy would require establishing many more time zones

As shown in the accompanying chart, *Bircas haChammah* has occurred on *erev Pesach* four times since our present calendar was introduced by Hillel II in the fourth century of the common era. From the time of the Exodus until the age of Hillel II, determination of *Rosh Chodesh* and hence of the day of the week on which *erev Pesach* occurred depended upon sanctification by the *Beth Din*. We have no record of which months any particular year were thirty rather than twenty-nine days in length. Prior to the commandment "This month shall be unto you the beginning of months" (Exodus 12:2), there was no formal Jewish calendar. See *Chazon Ish, Orach Chaim* 140:3, s.v. *vehineh hada-*

Bircas haChammah on Erev Pesach			
Jewish Calendar		Civil Calendar	
1821	יד ניסן	March 26	1940 B.C.E.
1905	יד ניסן	March 26	1856 B.C.E.
2437	יד ניסן	March 26	1324 B.C.E.
2521	יד ניסן	March 26	1240 B.C.E.
3137	יד ניסן	March 26	624 B.C.E.
3753	יד ניסן	March 26	8 B.C.E.
3837	יד ניסן	March 26	77 C.E.
4369	יד ניסן	March 26	609 C.E
4453	יד ניסן	March 26	693 C.E.
5069	יד ניסן	March 26	1309 C.E.
5685	יד ניסן	April 8	1925 C.E.
5769	יד ניסן	April 8	2009 C.E.

var. Nevertheless, hypothetically extending Hillel's calendar retrospectively, the beginning of the twenty-eight year solar cycle coincided with *erev Pesach* on a total of eleven occasions. *Bircas haChammah* in the year 5769 will be the twelfth such occasion.

With the coming of the Messiah our present calendar will be superseded by sanctification of each month by the *Beth Din*. However, if our calendar is projected into the future there will not be an occurrence of *Bircas haChammah* on *erev Pesach* until the year 6301 which will coincide with April 12, 2541, a gap of about five hundred years. The two will again coincide after a much briefer period in 6385 on April 13, 2625.

3. As the moon revolves around the earth in its monthly cycle it becomes progressively more obscured and ultimately invisible as it passes between the earth and the sun. As the moon emerges from between the earth and the sun it becomes progressively more visible. *Rosh Chodesh*, or the "New Moon," marks the reappearance of the moon after it has become obscured. The *molad* is the moment that the moon is precisely between the earth and the sun and marks the end of the previous cycle and the "birth" (*molad*) of a new cycle.

4. See *Ba'al haMa'or, Rosh HaShanah* 20b; *Chazon Ish, Kuntres Yud-Ches Sha'os*, sec. 15; *Chazon Ish, Orach Chaim* 138:7; R. Yechiel Michel Tucatzinsky, *Luach leEretz Yisrael*; and R. Yosef Eliyahu Henkin, *Edus leYisrael*, p. 258 and *Ezras Torah Luach Minhagei Beis haKenesses*, pocket ed., p. 7.

[2] **I**n many places it was customary to announce at the close of *Ma'ariv* services on Tuesday evening that *Bircas haChammah* would be recited the next morning and to call upon the members of the community to assemble at the proper time so that they might recite *Bircas haChammah* collectively since בְּרָב עָם הַדְרַת מֶלֶךְ, *the glory of the King is in the multitude of the populace* (*Proverbs* 14:28).

In *Eretz Yisrael*, in the years 5657 [1897] and 5685 [1925], the rabbinical authorities directed that the sextons wake each householder before sunrise as was the custom on the first day of *Selichos*.

---

separated from one another by mere moments — a situation that would lead to confusion and inconvenience. Hence, when, for example, the time is given as 12:00 noon the sun is directly overhead only at a point in the direct center of the time zone. Seven and a half degrees to the east it is really a half hour after noon since the sun has already traveled one half hour beyond that point, while seven and a half degrees to the west the true sun time[5] is still one half hour before noon since the sun will pass directly overhead only one half hour later. True sun time[5] varies four minutes with each degree.

True solar time in Jerusalem is 21 minutes later than the conventional clock time. Thus, the actual time of the *tekufah* in Jerusalem is 5:39 P.M. Jerusalem standard time which corresponds to 6:00 P.M. true solar time.[6]

[2] In Eretz Yisrael the following text was used in announcing *Bircas haChammah* in the year 5713:

בהתאם למנהג ישראל ועל דעת רבותינו גאוני עיר־קדשנו ירושלים תו״ב אנו מכריזים על קיום מצות ברכת החמה, מחר בבוקר יום רביעי כ״ג בניסן, עם שעת הנץ החמה. הקהל יתאסף לברכה במקומות המיועדים.

ויהי רצון שנזכה לברך ברכת החמה הבאה עלינו ועל כל ישראל לטובה ולברכה בבנין בית הבחירה במהרה בימינו אמן.

In accordance with the custom of Israel and with the sanction of our teachers, the sages of our holy city, Jerusalem, may it speedily be rebuilt and reestablished, we issue a proclamation with regard to the fulfillment of the *mitzvah of Bircas haChammah* tomorrow morning, Wednesday, the 23rd of Nisan, at the moment of sunrise.

---

5. More precisely, it is the average sun time that is here described. The "true" sun time at any point varies throughout the year and may be as much as 15 minutes earlier or later than the average sun time.

6. See R. Yechiel Michel Tucatzinsky, *Bein haShemoshos*, p. 105 and *Luach leEretz Yisrael*. Cf. R. Shmuel David Siegel, *Achuzas Sadeh* (Baltimore, 5740), pp. 73-74.

[3] A quorum of ten is not required. It is, however, preferable to recite the blessing in the company of a large assemblage because בְּרָב עָם הַדְרַת מֶלֶךְ, *the glory of the King is in the multitude of the populace.*

[4] Some authorities maintain that it is preferable to pronounce the blessing immediately upon seeing the sun in the morning (even before reciting the morning prayers) even if this entails pronouncing the blessing in private. Others

---

The public shall assemble for the blessing at the designated places.

May it be His will that we be privileged to pronounce the forthcoming *Bircas haChammah,* which comes upon us and all Israel for good and for blessing, with the rebuilding of the Temple speedily in our days. Amen. [*Seder Bircas haChammah* (Jerusalem, 5713), pp. 14-15.]

R. David Meldola, *Boker Yizrach* (London, 5601), and *Magen Avraham* 229:5, citing *Likkutei Maharil,* state that in the year 5181 [1421] Maharil directed the sexton of the community to announce that every person "should be vigilant to pronounce the blessing 'who makes the work of creation' upon seeing the rise of the sun." It is evident that the announcement was necessary because, in Maharil's opinion, it is preferable that each person recite the blessing individually immediately at sunrise. If, as is our practice, the blessing is recited after morning prayers in the synagogue, there is less need for an

announcement the previous evening since it is to be assumed that everyone will be present in the synagogue. Cf. *Or haChammah, Me'orei Or,* p. 10b.

[3] See R. Chaim Yosef David Azulai, *Machazik Berachah* 229:7. The blessing *oseh ma'aseh bereishis* is identical with the blessing recited upon observing various wondrous phenomena. A *bircas hoda'ah* of this nature is an individual, personal obligation and, hence, may be recited in private.[1]

[4] The Gemara states that "he who sees the sun at its turning point" must recite the blessing. Abaye adds that this occurs every 28 years "on the evening of the third [day of the week] going on the fourth [day of the week]." Rambam, followed by all other halachic codifiers, rules that the blessing is to be recited on the Wednesday morning following the *tekufah* that occurred the previous evening.

Rambam clearly recognized that

---

[3] 1. *Sedei Chemed, asifas dinim, ma'areches berachos,* sec. 33, suggests that an onlooker observing the ceremony might suspect that it is a form of sun worship, but that any such suspicion is dispelled if the blessing is recited publicly, since a "multitude" is not subject to suspicion (see *Avodah Zarah* 43b).

maintain that it is preferable to pronounce the blessing in the company of a large assemblage and that, for this reason, the blessing should be delayed and pronounced outside the synagogue after morning services. If clouds threaten to obscure the sun, all agree that the blessing should be recited without delay.

---

the *tekufah* occurs on Tuesday evening at an hour at which the sun is no longer visible. Accordingly, the Sages, in ordaining a blessing upon "seeing" the sun, could not have intended that the blessing be recited at night. Their edict, then, must require that the blessing be recited at the earliest opportunity following the *tekufah*, viz., the very next morning after sunrise.[1]

Rabbi Eliyahu David Rabinowitz

(known as the "*Aderes*"), renowned rabbi of Mir in Russia and later of Jerusalem, observed that, although the sun could not be seen in *Eretz Yisrael* and Babylonia at the beginning of the seventh hour because sunset occurs earlier in those countries,[2] nevertheless, in places located at a more northerly latitude sunset occurs at a much later hour. Rabbi Rabinowitz contends that such is the case in Russia.[3] In such a locale the

---

[4] 1. See *Teshuvos Koach Shor*, no. 27 and *Teshuvos Or Pnei Meir*, no. 14. Cf., however, Rabbi David Meldola, *Boker Yizrach*, and *Or haChammah, Me'orei Or*, p. 11b.

2. Actually, as noted earlier, the *tekufah* occurs on April 7 at 5:39 P.M., Jerusalem standard time, which is well before sunset in Jerusalem, (which will occur at 7:03 P.M.). However, as has been shown elsewhere (see p. 55), with the passage of time, the *tekufah* of Shmuel occurs progressively later in the solar year. See *Achuzas Sadeh*, pp. 74-75, who remarks that in the days of Shmuel the *tekufah* fell "early in March," at which time the *tekufah* occurred after sunset. In point of fact, in Shmuel's day the *tekufah* occurred on March 20 or 21. At present, sunset in Jerusalem on those dates occurs at approximately 5:50 P.M., approximately 11 minutes after the *tekufah*, which theoretically would allow for a brief period for *Bircas haChammah* on Tuesday afternoon. It should, however, be remembered that the Gemara, *Niddah* 65b, states that at the time of the *tekufah* day and night are of equal duration. Thus, for halachic purposes, the *tekufah* is assumed to coincide with the beginning of the fourth day. See R. Ze'ev Biednovitz, *Toras Eretz Yisrael*, vol. I, no. 69 (reprinted in *KeTzes haShemesh* [Jerusalem, 5741], p. 44).

Indeed, in Jerusalem pronouncement of *Bircas haChammah* before sunset would be paradoxical. The *tekufah* is calculated as occurring "on the evening of Tuesday, going into Wednesday," i.e., at the beginning of Wednesday. As explained earlier, Shmuel ignored the true astronomical *tekufah*. However, at the time of the creation of the sun, the actual *tekufah* did indeed coincide with the beginning of the fourth day. Since *Bircas haChammah* commemorates the creation of the sun, which occurred at the beginning of the fourth day, it would be inconsistent to recite the blessing prior to sunset the previous day.

3. See *Over Orach, Orach Chaim* 229, published as an appendix to the second volume of R. Nachman Kahana of Spinka's *Orchos Chaim*. This statement is quoted by *Yizrach Or*, chap. 12. See also *Teshuvos Ravaz*, no. 32, sec. 6. Cf., however, Rabbi

sun is perfectly visible at the time of the *tekufah*. Rabbi Rabinowitz therefore ruled that the blessing be recited on Tuesday evening at the actual time of the *tekufah* rather than be delayed until the next morning. However, no other authority suggests that the blessing may actually be pronounced on Tuesday evening. This may be because, in the opinion of those authorities, the Sages, living as they did in places where the sun was not visible on Tuesday evening, ordained that *Bircas haChammah* be pronounced only on the morning following the *tekufah* and ordained that Jews throughout the world follow the same practice.[4] This would explain why Rambam adds the phrase "in the morning," which is not found in the Gemara, in stating that one should pronounce the blessing "when one sees [the sun] on Wednesday *in the morning*."[5]

The generally accepted practice is not to recite the blessing earlier than sunrise. Sunrise this year on Wednesday morning, April 8, occurs at 6:28 A.M. Daylight Saving Time in New York City.[6] The time of sunrise is reckoned as the time at which the crest of the sun appears over the horizon. Rabbi Yechiel Michel Tucatzinsky, *Tekufas haChammah*

Cohen, *Bircas haChammah* 1:8, note 15, who asserts that the discrepancy in the time of sunset between northerly countries and Jerusalem in the early part of April is no greater than approximately 15 minutes. Of course, this issue would be germane in isolated locales lying more than 180 degrees west of Jerusalem.

However, in point of fact, according to information provided by the U.S. Naval Observatory, sunset on April 7, 1925 occurred at 4:52 P.M. in Mir, Belarus. The time of sunset for a specific date in the civil calendar varies little from year to year. Thus, sunset in Mir on April 7 takes place *after* the time of the *tekufah*, which occurs at 5:39 P.M. Jerusalem time, which is 4:39 P.M. in Mir.

4. *Me'orei Or, Or haChammah*, p. 13b, argues that although the luminaries were created or suspended in the firmament on Tuesday evening, they did not give light until the end of the third hour on Wednesday. This is also the opinion of *Tiferes Yisrael* in the introduction to his commentary on the Mishnah, *Seder Mo'ed, Shevilei deRaki'a*, sec. 34. Cf. *Teshuvos Koach Shor*, no. 17, and *Chazon Ish, Orach Chaim* 138:1. Indeed, *Tiferes Yisrael, Shevilei deRaki'a*, sec. 32, maintains that the blessing should be pronounced only upon the expiration of three hours of the day on Wednesday. This also appears to be the view of another authority cited by *Divrei Chamudos, Berachos*, chap. 9, sec. 42. If, at the time of creation, the sun did not shine until Wednesday, the rabbinic edict may require that the blessing be recited only in the morning since it is only in the morning that the sun actually became visible at the time of its original creation. See also Rabbi Cohen, *Bircas haChammah* 1:2, note 5.

5. Rambam, in incorporating this phrase, may, however, have meant to limit the recitation of the blessing to the morning hours only, or perhaps even to the first three hours in the day. See below, p. 102.

6. For halachic purposes sunrise is defined as the earliest time at which the crest of the sun is visible over the horizon. See Rabbi Tucatzinsky, *Bein haShemoshos*, p. 47, and R. Meir Posen, *Kuntres haNeshef* (London, 5728), p. 14. This is the time customarily given in tables listing the times of sunrise and sunset that are published in the U.S. Thus, *Tables of Sunrise, Sunset and Twilight*, published by the U.S. Naval Observatory (Washington, 1962), p. 9 states: "Sunrise and sunset are considered to occur when the *upper edge* of the disk of the Sun *appears* to be exactly on the horizon. The times ... given ... are for an unobstructed horizon, with normal atmospheric conditions, at zero elevation above the Earth's surface in a level region." Cf. *Kuntres haNeshef*, introduction.

uBirchosah (Jerusalem, 5713), pp. 43 and 74, is of the opinion that *Bircas haChammah*, which is occasioned by the actual sighting of the sun, should not be recited until the entire circumference of the sun is visible. This occurs approximately 2½ minutes later than the time of the sun's first appearance.[7]

There is disagreement among halachic authorities with regard to whether it is preferable to recite *Bircas haChammah* as early as possible or whether it is preferable to delay recitation of the blessing until after morning services so that the blessing may be recited collectively by a large assemblage of people.[8]

Machazik Berachah 229:7 notes that *Bircas haChammah* does not require a *minyan*, a quorum of ten, for its recitation. Accordingly, he rules that it is preferable to be alacritous in pronouncing the blessing immediately upon seeing the sun at sunrise, even before recitation of the morning prayers,[9] rather than to delay recitation until after the morning service in order to recite the blessing with a larger assemblage.[10] *Machazik Berachah* categorizes the practice of reciting *Bircas haChammah* with a *minyan* as "a custom that later rabbis sought to promulgate because of בְּרָב־עָם הַדְרַת מֶלֶךְ, *the glory of the King is in the multitude of the populace.*" This principle, he asserts, is overridden by the more compelling principle of זְרִיזִין מַקְדִּימִין לְמִצְוֹת, *the alacritous perform mitzvos as early as possible.* Moreover, he observes, reason augurs

---

7. See R. Chaim Joseph David Azulai, known as *Chida, Machazik Berachah* 229:4, who states that "it is proper" to recite the blessing in a place where the "globe (*galgal*) of the sun" is visible. *Kaf haChaim, Orach Chaim* 229:11, seems to equate the appearance of the *galgal hachammah* with sunrise. Cf., however, Rabbi Cohen, *Bircas haChammah* 1:2, note 6.

Rabbi Cohen, *loc. cit.*, questions whether it is absolutely necessary to see the entire globe of the sun or whether it is merely preferable to wait until the sun is visible in its entirety. That issue is significant in the event that the sun is only partially visible and it is evident that the sun will not become completely visible during the period in which the blessing may be recited.

8. A person who delays the blessing in order to recite it together with a large assemblage may partake of food before pronouncing the blessing. See Rabbi Gerlitz, *Bircas haChammah keHilchosah*, sec. 41.

9. See *Or haChammah, Me'orei Or*, p. 11b, and *Tekufas haChammah uBirchosah*, pp. 44-52. Cf. also *Teshuvos Har Zevi, Orach Chaim*, I, no. 119, who is of the opinion that the blessing should be recited immediately upon seeing the sun, even before recitation of the morning prayers, despite the consideration that prayer is a more frequently performed *mitzvah. Har Zevi* asserts that the principle that one does not "pass by" or ignore a *mitzvah* (*ein ma'avirin al hamitzvos*) supersedes the principle that priority is accorded to the more frequently performed *mitzvah* (*tadir veshe'eino tadir, tadir kodem*).

However, if one sights blossoms of a fruit tree for the first time in the season at the same time as one is about to recite *Bircas haChammah*, the principle *tadir kodem* applies. Hence, the blessing *oseh ma'aseh bereishis* should be recited before pronouncing the blessing for the blossoms. See *Peninei Rabbeinu haKehillos Yaakov* (Bnei Brak, 5746), I, 66.

10. Cf. *Rosh HaShanah* 32b. For possible alternative explanations of the source in *Rosh HaShanah* see *Boker Yizrach, Sha'arei Mizrach*, pp. 35ff. and *Tekufas haChammah uBirchosah*, p. 54.

that the blessing be recited at the time of sunrise because it should, properly speaking, be recited as close to the moment of the equinox as possible.[11] In pronouncing *Bircas haChammah* immediately upon sunrise, the blessing is recited as close as possible to the moment at which the sun has returned to the spot it occupied at the time of its original creation. Arguments in support of this position are presented by R. Yekusiel Aryeh Kamelhar, *Boker Yizrach, Sha'arei Mizrach* (Cracow, 5656), chap. 3. This ruling was accepted by *Chayyei Adam* 63:5 and 68:6; *Kaf haChaim* 229:14; R. Chaim Palaggi, *Ruach Chaim, Orach Chaim* 229:3; R. Isaac Singer, *Zoharei Chammah* (Cracow, 5656), p. 14; and *Or haChammah, Me'orei Or,* p. 11a. This appears to be the position of *Likkutei Maharil* as well, as noted earlier.[12]

However, a number of authorities, including *Yosef Ometz*, no. 378, and *Teshuvos Mayim Chaim*, no. 22, maintain that it is preferable to recite *Bircas haChammah* in the company of a larger number of people and hence, if necessary, its recitation may be delayed until after the morning prayers. This practice is also sanctioned by *Teshuvos Masais Binyamin*, no. 101; *Teshuvos Chasam Sofer*, no. 56; and *Tekufas haChammah uBirchosah*, pp. 44-60 and 74.[13]

It may also be added that, for reason of בְּרָב עָם הַדְרַת מֶלֶךְ, *the glory of the King is in the multitude of the populace*, it is preferable for the *chazzan* to pronounce the blessing on behalf of the assembled congregation and for each person to respond "Amen" rather than for every person to pronounce the blessing individually.[14] Rabbi Tucatzinsky reports that in many houses of worship in *Eretz Yisrael* it was the practice to begin the morning prayers at an early hour and to recite *Shemoneh Esreh* at the precise moment of sunrise (as was the practice of the *vasikin*, as reported in the Gemara, and which indeed is the optimal hour for prayer) and then to

---

11. It appears to this writer that if the blessing is to be pronounced at the earliest possible opportunity the prefatory verses should be recited prior to sunrise or omitted. Cf., however, Rabbi Cohen, *Bircas haChammah* 1:12. *Birchos haTorah* must, of course, be pronounced before reciting biblical verses.

12. See also additional sources cited by Rabbi Cohen, *Bircas haChammah* 1:1, note 19 and Rabbi Gerlitz, *Bircas haChammah keHilchosah*, p. 69, note 20.

R. Shlomo haKohen of Vilna, *Atzei Beroshim*, no. 60, reports that in the year 5657 he instructed the townspeople of Vilna to assemble at an elevated location outside the city and to recite *Bircas haChammah* immediately upon sunrise and then to return to their synagogues for morning prayers.

13. See additional sources cited by Rabbi Cohen, *Bircas haChammah* 1:11, note 20.

R. Chaim Kanievsky reports that on the occasion of *Bircas haChammah* in the year 5713, *Chazon Ish* recited the blessing after morning prayers before the recitation of *Aleinu*. See Rabbi Cohen, ibid., p. 54.

For an analysis of whether priority is to be assigned to *rov am* or to *zerizin makdimin*, see this writer's *BeNesivos haHalachah*, II, 86-93 (reprinted below, pp. 227-232). See also *Torah Temimah, Bereishis* 17:26, sec. 53 and *Aruch haShulchan, Yoreh De'ah* 262:8.

14. See *Berachos* 53a; *Ma'adanei Yom Tov, Berachos* 6:33; *Kesef Mishneh, Hilchos Berachos* 1:12; *Shulchan Aruch, Orach Chaim* 298:14; *Magen Avraham* 298:18; *Magen Avraham* 213:7; and *Shulchan Aruch, Orach Chaim* 167:1. Cf. *Magen Avraham* 698:10. Cf. also *Yizrach Or*, p. 16b and R. Shlomo Kluger, *Chochmas Shlomo, Orach Chaim* 426:3.

[5] When the blessing is recited after morning services, some have the custom of reciting the blessing while yet attired in *tallis* and *tefillin*.

[6] It is proper to wear dignified clothing while reciting the blessing.

[7] The blessing should be recited while standing.

---

assemble in the courtyard of the synagogue and immediately recite *Bircas haChammah*[15] even before the reader's repetition of *Shemoneh Esreh*. Rabbi Tucatzinsky cautions, however, that if, as a result of this procedure, some of the assembled will not return to the synagogue and there attentively listen to the repetition of the *Shemoneh Esreh*, it is preferable to complete the morning prayers in their entirety and then to pronounce *Bircas haChammah*.[16]

R. Yehoshua Leib Diskin, cited by R. Chaim Dov Spitzer, *Nivreshes leNetz haChammah beTzion*, I, 43a, rules that the assembled should not leave the synagogue in order to recite the blessing until after the reader's repetition of *Shemoneh Esreh* because of the principle that one does not "pass by" a *mitzvah*.

[5] This custom is described by Rabbi Tucatzinsky in his *Tekufas haChammah uBirchosah*, p. 75, as having been the common practice in *Eretz Yisrael*. For reasons underlying

this practice, see Rabbi Gerlitz, *Bircas haChammah keHilchosah*, p. 75, note 35.

[6] In consideration of the fact that *Bircas haChammah* is usually recited in a large gathering, dignified clothing is worn in honor of the assemblage and also in honor of the singularity of the rare occurrence of *Bircas haChammah*. See *Yizrach Or* 13:8 and p. 23a.

[7] This practice is noted by Rabbi Tucatzinsky, *TekufashaChammah uBirchosah*, p. 73. See also *Magen Avraham* 25:20. *Yizrach Or* 13:8 states that the blessing should be recited while standing as is the practice with regard to *Kiddush Levanah*. *Tekufas haChammah uBirchosah*, p. 88, also states that this is the accepted custom. Cf., however, *Yizrach Or*, chap. 17, who cites an earlier authority who correctly points out that the Gemara, *Sanhedrin* 42a, states that *Kiddush Levanah* should be recited while standing in honor of the Divine Presence. As will

---

15. According to Rabbi Tucatzinsky, for purposes of *Bircas haChammah*, sunrise is the actual appearance of the entire circumference of the sun; while, for purposes of *Shemoneh Esreh*, sunrise is defined as the emergence of the sun's crest over the horizon. This allows both *Shemoneh Esreh* and *Bircas haChammah* to be recited successively at the optimal time for each.

16. Cf. also *Kaf haChaim* 229:13.

[8] The blessing may be recited while standing under a roof or even when observing the sun through a window from inside a building.

[9] The blessing should be pronounced as early in the day as possible but should not be delayed

---

be discussed in the next section, that consideration may not be applicable to *Bircas haChammah*. Nevertheless, *Yizrach Or* states that in a large assemblage the blessing should be recited while standing in honor of the assembled. It should also be noted that *Birkei Yosef, Orach Chaim* 8:2, states that although the Gemara mandates recitation of *Kiddush Levanah* while standing because of the honor of the Divine Presence, nevertheless, even in the absence of that consideration, it would be preferable, albeit not mandatory, to recite *Kiddush Levanah* while standing. Rabbi Cohen, *Bircas haChammah* 4:9, note 18, applies that comment to *Bircas haChammah* as well.

More significantly, *Tekufas haChammah uBirchosah* 5:2, sec. 6, cites *Bet Yosef, Orach Chaim* 8, who maintains that most blessings, with some exceptions such as blessings pronounced as acknowledgment of benefit, should be recited while standing. The statement of Abaye, *Sanhedrin* 42a, to the effect that *Kiddush Levanah* is recited while standing in honor of the Divine Presence, he explains, is because *Kiddush Levanah* might otherwise be construed as a *bircas hanehenin* expressing gratitude for the illumination provided by the moon. See also R. Reuven Margulies, *Margalios haYam, Sanhedrin* 42a.

[8] *Kiddush Levanah* should preferably be recited while standing under the open sky because *Kiddush*

Levanah is compared by the Gemara, *Sanhedrin* 42a, to receiving the Divine Presence. Accordingly, one should exit from one's abode in order to recite the blessing just as one would emerge from one's house to welcome a king. See *Mishnah Berurah* 426:21. This consideration does not apply to *Bircas haChammah*. See *Yizrach Or* 16:1 and *Tekufas haChammah uBirchosah*, p. 63 and 73. Cf., however, *Or haChammah, Me'orei Or*, chap. 16, as well as Rabbi Gerlitz, *Bircas haChammah keHilchosah*, p. 80, note 27, who vigorously argues that *Bircas haChammah* is also an occasion of greeting the Divine Presence (see also *ibid.*, notes 35, 36, 38, 43, 54, 64 and 67.) See also Rabbi Mordecai Kahane, *Bircas haChammah* (Jerusalem, 5781), sec. 9.

According to the authorities who maintain that *Bircas haChammah* may be recited indoors, the blessing may be pronounced even if the window is closed. See *Yizrach Or*, p. 10a; *Or haChammah*, p. 18b; *Tekufas haChammah uBirchosah* 4:4, sec. 5; and R. Joshua Horowitz, *Teshuvos Ateres Yeshu'ah*, I, no. 29.

Both *Kiddush Levanah* and *Bircas haChammah* may be recited even if the sun or the moon is seen only through eyeglasses and even if the person would be unable to see the sun or the moon without glasses. See *Sha'arei Teshuvah, Orach Chaim* 426:1; *Yizrach Or*, p. 10b; and *Tekufas haChammah uBirchosah*, p. 63.

later than the end of the third hour. According to the most permissive view, the end of the third hour on April 8th, 2009 occurs in New York City at 9:43 A.M. Daylight Saving Time. In case of delay, or if the sun is overcast by clouds earlier in the day, the blessing, according to some authorities, may be recited until midday, which, on April 8th, 2009 occurs in New York City at 12:58 P.M. Daylight Saving Time. The corresponding times for other major centers of Jewish population are listed on pp. 196-198 of this volume.

---

[9] There is considerable difference of opinion with regard to how late in the day the blessing may be recited. Rambam records that the blessing should be recited "in the morning." *Magen Avraham* 229:5 states that it may not be pronounced later than the expiration of three hours of the day.[1]

Adnei Paz, Orach Chaim 229:2, explains that *Magen Avraham's* position is based on the fact that Saturn is in ascendancy during the third hour of Wednesday morning, as it is at the beginning of the fourth day of the *tekufah*. Although the blessing must be postponed until morning,

Magen Avraham, according to this explanation, asserts that it should not be delayed beyond the hour of the day that is under the influence of Saturn. For this reason, *Adnei Paz*, in disagreement with other authorities, states that it is preferable to wait until the beginning of the third hour before reciting *Bircas haChammah*.[2]

Rabbi Joseph Saul Nathanson, author of *Sho'el uMeshiv*, offers a very beautiful, albeit homiletical, explanation of why *Magen Avraham* asserts that *Bircas haChammah* must be recited before the completion of the third hour. *Koheles* 3:1 declares,

---

[9] 1. This is also the opinion of *Levush, Orach Chaim* 229:2; *Teshuvos Panim Me'iros*, II, no. 38; *Teshuvos Chasam Sofer, Orach Chaim*, no. 56; R. Shlomo Kluger, *Chochmas Shlomo, Orach Chaim* 229:2; *Teshuvos Zera Emes*, II, no. 24; *Pri Megadim, Eshel Avraham* 229:5; R. Jacob of Lissa, *Siddur Derech haChaim, Dinei Berachos Pratiyos*, sec. 6; *Kaf haChaim* 229:16 and R. Abraham David Wahrman of Buczacz, *Eshel Avraham* 229:2. Cf., however, *Or haChammah, Me'orei Or*, p. 14a.

R. Yitzchak Lampronti, *Pachad Yitzchak, Chammah beTekufosah*, reports that in Ferrara, "on 7 Nisan 5489, April 6, 1729, according to the calendar of the Christians, we recited *Bircas haChammah* in the general yeshivah after the study within the first three hours."

2. Others explain that the blessing is not recited after the third hour because although the sun was created on Tuesday evening, it was not suspended in the firmament until the end of the third hour on Wednesday morning. See above, section 4, note 4. *Teshuvos Koach Shor*, no. 27, understands this as meaning that the sun did not achieve its full power of illumination until the end of the third hour on Wednesday. For a different explanation based on *Tosafos, Rosh HaShanah* 8a, see R. Betzalel haKohen of Vilna, *Reishis Bikkurim* (Jerusalem, 5729), pp. 4 and 148.

For everything there is a season, and a time for every matter under the heaven, and then proceeds to list a series of twenty-eight examples, e.g., a time to be born and a time to die, a time to plant and a time to pluck, etc. *Sho'el uMeshiv* explains that *Koheles* seeks to demonstrate that everything which has a beginning also has an end; everything which is generated is also destroyed. Hence, wherever there is degeneration and destruction there must also previously have been generation and creation. Therefore, everything which is subject to time is created. The purpose of *Bircas haChammah*, declares *Sho'el uMeshiv*, is to negate pagan belief in the sun as a deity. This negation of the sun's divinity follows demonstrably from the fact that the sun returns to its original point in the heavens. If the sun were not subject to God's will, it would continue in its travels without being curbed in any way. The Almighty, however, establishes the sun's orbit, commanding it to travel so far and no further, and then to return to its original course. The twenty-eight examples of *Koheles* correspond to the twenty-eight years of the sun's apparent travels before it returns to its original position at the day and at the hour of its original creation. The twenty-eight years symbolize that the sun is subject to time and hence is created by God.

The Gemara, *Berachos* 7a, states that each day God is angered when the kings of the East and of the West arise, place their crowns upon their heads and prostrate themselves before the sun. Elsewhere, *Berachos* 9b, the Mishnah states that even monarchs who enjoy the luxury of morning sleep arise by the end of the third hour of the day. Therefore, concludes *Sho'el uMeshiv*, *Bircas haChammah*, which is designed to negate sun worship, is to be recited at the time that is identical to that at which the pagans were wont to prostrate themselves before the sun, that is, during the first three hours of the day. See *Yizrach Or*, chap. 15 (pp. 22b-23a) and cf. *ibid.*, p. 17a.

Rabbi Ezekiel Landau, in his commentary on the *Shulchan Aruch*, *Dagul meRevavah*, states that, in his opinion, the blessing may be recited any time during the course of the entire day.[3] He suggests that Rambam's use of the phrase "in the morning" is intended only to establish the optimal time for reciting *Bircas haChammah* in the sense of "zerizin makdimin lemitzvos — the alacritous perform *mitzvos* at the earliest opportunity."[4]

Dagul meRevavah further states that, even if Rambam's phraseology is to be understood in a restrictive sense, it must be understood as serving to limit recitation of *Bircas haChammah* to the forenoon, and to exclude only the afternoon hours "when the sun inclines to the west."[5] *Dagul meRevavah* reports that in the year 5545 "when the sun did not shine until an hour before noon" he himself recited the blessing in the prescribed manner in the late morning.

---

3. R. Judah Asad, *Teshuvos Yehudah Ya'aleh, Orach Chaim,* no. 7, similarly maintains that the blessing may be recited during the course of the entire day.

4. See, however, above, p.96, note 5.

5. *Mor uKetzi'ah* argues that in this regard *Bircas haChammah* should be comparable to *Kiddush Levanah*. *Kiddush Levanah* may be recited during the entire period of time in which the illumination of the moon increases, i.e., until half the month has elapsed. Similarly, he argues, *Bircas haChammah* may be recited until the sun's illumination has reached full strength, i.e., until midday. Cf. also *Teshuvos Koach Shor,* no. 27.

Indeed, a significant number of authorities rule that the blessing may be recited until midday. Among these authorities are *Teshuvos Beis Efrayim*, no. 7[6]; *Divrei Chamudos, Berachos* 9:42; *Malbushei Yom Tov* 229:3 cited by *Eliyahu Rabbah, Orach Chaim* 229:2;[7] R. Jacob Emden, in his commentaries on *Seder Olam* and on *Megillas Taanis*, chap. 10, and in his *Mor uKetziah* 229; *Yeshuos Yaakov, Orach Chaim* 229:2; *Tzedah laDerech*, p. 61; *Birkei Yosef, Orach Chaim* 229:2; *Machazik Berachah* 229:8; *Chayyei Adam* 63:5; *Sha'arei Teshuvah, Orach Chaim* 229:3; *Aruch haShulchan* 229:3; and *Sedei Chemed, asifas dinim, ma'areches berachos*, sec. 33.[8] See also *Teshuvos Koach Shor*, no. 27 as well as additional

---

6. *Beis Efrayim* rules that the blessing may not be delayed beyond one hour prior to midday and attributes that position to *Dagul MeRevavah*. Cf., however, *Sha'arei Teshuvah* 229:3 and Rabbi Cohen, *Bircas haChammah* 1:5, note 12.

7. *Malbushei Yom Tov* and *Eliyahu Rabbah* suggest that the blessing may be recited even during the course of the entire day. See also the newly published manuscript of R. Yedidyah Theo Weil of Karlsruhe included in *Siach Tefillah: Otzar Genuzos veKisvei Yad miGeonei uPoskei haDoros* (Jerusalem, 5759), pp. 197-8.

8. See also *Mishnah Berurah* 229:8. If a person has delayed, or has been unable to recite, *Bircas haChammah* until an hour at which there is dispute with regard to whether or not it may be recited, some authorities rule that one may avail oneself of the following expedient: One may orally study the *Beraisa* in *Berachos* 59b or the halachah as recorded in the *Shulchan Aruch*, including the full text of the blessing, with the conditional intention of fulfilling the *mitzvah* thereby if obligated to do so but, if no longer obligated to fulfill the *mitzvah*, the vocalization be deemed an act of Torah study only. In this manner, the full text of the blessing may be pronounced, since, in terms of normative halachah, even the Divine Name may be pronounced in the course of study. See *Derech Pekudecha*, no. 4, sec. 10, note 5, regarding *Kiddush Levanah* under analogous circumstances, and *Yizrach Or*, p. 16b. Cf., however, *Magen Avraham, Orach Chaim* 215:5; *Machatzis haShekel, ad loc.*, and *Mishnah Berurah* 216:14.

It should be noted that even those authorities who maintain that one should not pronounce the Divine Name in the course of studying a text containing a blessing agree that the Divine Name may be pronounced in the course of providing instruction to children. Hence, it seems to this writer that, according to all authorities, the above outlined expedient may be utilized while teaching a child the *Beraisa* or the halachah as recorded in *Shulchan Aruch*.

Another expedient suggested by *Derech Pekudecha* is recitation of the blessing in the Aramaic form: "*Brich Rachamana Mara Malka dealma ...*" See *Eshel Avraham* (*Rav* of Buczacz) 229:2 who records that he recited *Bircas haChammah* in this manner when the sun was obscured by clouds. *Shulchan Aruch, Orach Chaim* 167:10, 187:1, and 219:4 rules that the obligation with regard to various blessings may be fulfilled in this manner while many authorities maintain that a blessing recited in this manner does not constitute a *berachah levatalah*, a blessing pronounced in vain. Hence, according to these authorities, this expedient may be utilized in cases of doubtful obligation. See also *Aruch haShulchan, Orach Chaim* 202:3.

Actually, the suggestion of pronouncing the blessing in Aramaic in cases of doubt was advanced by *Teshuvos Zecher Simchah, Orach Chaim*, no. 232, and ascribed to the author of *Teshuvos Chamudei Daniel* who recommended that this procedure be followed with regard to the blessing over the *arba minim* when there is reason to suspect that the *esrog* may be a hybrid. See also *Da'as Kedoshim, Gidulei HaKodesh* 19:15; *Teshuvos Bikkurei Shlomo, Orach Chaim*, no. 39; and *Sedei Chemed, ma'areches lamed, klal* 141, sec. 32. *Chasam Sofer* is reported to have used a similar Aramaic formula for *Kiddush Levanah* on one occasion when it was doubtful whether the blessing might

sources cited by Rabbi Cohen, *Bircas haChammah* 1:5, note 12 and Rabbi Gerlitz, *Bircas haChammah ke-Hilchosah*, p. 65, note 14.

Most authorities maintain that the 3-hour period established by *Magen Avraham* is not reckoned on the basis of clock hours but as *sha'os zemaniyos*.

In calculating *sha'os zemaniyos* the period between sunrise and sunset[9] is divided into twelve equal parts, each one being a single hour of *sha'os ze-maniyos*, or what is known to astron-omers as temporary hours. Among those who state that the hours are to be reckoned as *sha'os zemaniyos* are

---

be pronounced; see *Ha'amek She'elah, she'ilta* 53, sec. 2, and *Tzitz Eliezer*, X, no. 11.

Nevertheless, numerous authorities maintain that a blessing in the form of *Brich Rachamana* does constitute a *berachah levatalah*. See *Teshuvos R. Akiva Eger*, no. 25; *Chasam Sofer* in his commentary on *Nedarim* 2a (which contradicts the earlier cited position attributed to *Chasam Sofer*); *Pri Megadim, Mishbetzos Zahav* 219:3; *Chavas Da'as, Yoreh De'ah* 110, *Beis haSafek*, sec. 20; *Maharam Shik al Taryag Mitzvos*, no. 69, and *Ha'amek She'elah, She'ilta* 53, sec. 2. See also *Mishnah Berurah* 115:19. Hence, according to these authorities, the expedient of *Brich Rachamana* cannot be utilized in cases of doubtful obligation. See also R. Moshe Feinstein, *Iggeros Moshe, Orach Chaim*, IV, no. 40, sec. 27. *Teshuvos Rivash*, no. 408, advises that one recite "Baruch attah Hashem" etc., in all cases of doubtful obligation. That procedure is advised with regard to *Bircas haGomel* of doubtful obligation by R. Yaakov Breisch, *Chelkas Yaakov*, II, no. 9. See also R. Pinchas Zelig Schwartz, *Likkutei Pinchas al Hilchos Pidyon haBen* 305:106. For further sources see this author's *Contemporary Halakhic Problems*, III (New York, 1989), p. 35, note 5.

9. Although R. Elijah, the Gaon of Vilna, maintains that, for halachic purposes such as *zman Krias Shema* and *zman tefillah*, the day is always reckoned as beginning with sunrise and ending with sunset, *Magen Avraham* disagrees and maintains that, for example, for purposes of *zman Krias Shema* and *zman tefillah*, the day is reckoned from dawn (*alos hashachar*) until dark (*tzes hakochavim*). Nevertheless, for purposes of *Bircas haChammah*, the day must certainly be considered as beginning with the ap-pearance of the sun. Accordingly, it is logical that the three-hour period be reckoned on the basis of the length of the day from sunrise to sunset. See *Zoharei Chammah*, p. 15, and *Tekufas haChammah uBirchosah*, p. 43. *Eshel Avraham* (Rav of Buczacz), however, maintains that, according to *Magen Avraham*, the 3-hour period is calculated in the usual manner. See also *Or haChammah, Me'orei Or*, p. 15b and Rabbi Gerlitz, *Bircas haChammah keHilchosah*, p. 64, note 13. [According to the above cited com-ments of *Sho'el uMeshiv*, it is entirely logical that *Bircas haChammah* should not be recited after the conclusion of *zman Krias Shema*. *Zman Krias Shema* extends to the hour at which royalty are accustomed to arise.]

According to this method of calculation, the period between dawn and dark is di-vided into 12 hours and the latest time for *Bircas haChammah* is determined by add-ing three hours to the time of *alos hashachar*. Reckoned in this manner, the latest time for *Bircas haChammah* in N.Y.C. is 9:07 A.M. This calculation is based upon reckoning *alos hashachar* as occurring uniformly 72 minutes before sunrise. If both *alos hashachar* and *tzes hakochavim* are deemed to occur when the sun is 16.1 degrees below the horizon, the time is 9:01 A.M. Varying calculations of *tzes hakochavim* will yield differing times. If *alos hashachar* is deemed to occur when the sun is 16.1 degrees below the horizon and *tzes hakochavim* is reckoned as *gimul riva'ei mil* after sunset, the end of the 3-hour period is 8:43 A.M.

If the 3-hour period beginning at dawn is calculated on the basis of clock hours, the latest time for *Bircas haChammah* in New York City is 8:16 A.M., assuming that *alos hashachar* always occurs 72 minutes before sunrise. If *alos hashachar* is assumed to occur when the sun is 16.1 degrees below the horizon, the latest time for *Bircas ha-Chammah* in New York City is 8:03 A.M.

Pri Megadim, Eshel Avraham 229:5; Teshuvos Chasam Sofer, Orach Chaim no. 56; the Rav of Buczacz in his Eshel Avraham 229:2; Teshuvos Pnei Moshe, no. 14; R. Chaim Knoller, Bircas haChammah (Przemysl, 5684), p. 4; Seder Bircas haChammah, published by Eliyahu Volk (Warsaw, 5657), p. 8; Zoharei Chammah, p. 15; and Tekufas haChammah uBirchosah, p. 15.

However, one authority, R. Meir David Hertzberg, Or haChammah, Me'orei Or, p. 14a, maintains that the 3 hours are the usual clock hours. His argument is based on the fact that the reckoning of the tekufos must be in accordance with the usual, fixed 60-minute hour rather than according to sha'os zemaniyos. The reasoning upon which this view is based is entirely obvious. The sun travels in its orbit at a fixed rate of speed which does not vary in accordance with the length of the day or night. Magen Avraham states that the blessing may not be pronounced after 3 hours in the day have elapsed, for at that time "kvar ovrah mimekomah," i.e., the sun has passed too far beyond the point of the tekufah. Since Magen Avraham indicates that the 3-hour period is a measure of distance of the sun's travel, it is logical, argues Rabbi Hertzberg, that the time be reckoned in terms of clock hours.[10] Since sunrise in New York City on April 8th occurs at 6:28 A.M. (Daylight Saving Time), Bircas haChammah, according to this opinion, should be recited before 9:28 A.M.

Since Bircas haChammah marks the return of the sun to the place it occupied in the heavens at the time

of creation, it might be anticipated that the proper time for its recitation would be simultaneous throughout the world. This is, after all, an astronomical event totally unrelated to time zones.[11] Thus, if, for example, Bircas haChammah may be recited only until noon in Jerusalem it should logically not be recited later in any other locale. Given a seven-hour time difference it would be impossible to recite Bircas haChammah in the United States since at the hour of sunrise in New York City it is already after noon in Jerusalem.

It is nevertheless clear that the sun (or for some authorities, its illumination) must actually be perceived in order that one may pronounce the blessing. As explained in section 4 of this chapter, even in the Land of Israel the blessing is delayed until Wednesday morning, even though the tekufah occurs the previous evening, because at the time of the tekufah the sun is not yet visible. Thus, the blessing is ordained only upon the appearance of the sun. Accordingly, the blessing is not pronounced within a time period that is simultaneous all over the world, but is associated with a specific period of solar time as measured in any given locale. This regulation is particularly cogent if the blessing is understood as evocative in nature, designed to cause us to reflect upon the continual creation of the universe, as explained in chapter one. Thus, the blessing is pronounced when the sun is perceived as having returned to its original position rather than at the precise moment of the occurrence of this astronomical phenomenon.

10. Similarly, if the three-hour period is established because Saturn is in ascendancy during the third hour, it should be presumed that the hours are calculated as clock hours. See Or haChammah, Me'orei Or, pp. 14b-15a.

11. See R. Yosef Eliyahu Henkin, Edus leYisrael, p. 258, who declares that this is indeed the case with regard to calculation of the time-period during which Kiddush Levanah may be recited even though the nascent moon is not perceived simultaneously in all places.

[10] The blessing should not be recited if the sun is obscured by clouds. However, the blessing may be recited on a cloudy day if the

---

[10] There is considerable controversy with regard to the proper procedure to follow when the sun is not visible because of clouds. *Teshuvos Panim Me'iros*, II, no. 38, rules that the blessing may be recited even if the sun is entirely obscured.[1] Unlike the blessing of *Kiddush Levanah* that is recited each month upon the appearance of the new moon, *Bircas haChammah*, argues *Panim Me'iros*, is not a blessing occasioned by the sighting of the sun, but by the return of the sun to its original place in the heavens. *Panim Me'iros* adds the phrase "and benefit is derived from it," indicating that the blessing is, in part, occasioned by the benefit derived from the sun's illumination. Hence, he states, benefit is derived from the light of the sun even though the sun itself is completely obscured. Therefore, concludes *Panim Me'iros*, the blessing may be recited even though the sun is not directly visible.

R. Abraham Benjamin Sofer, *Teshuvos Kesav Sofer, Orach Chaim*, no. 34, agrees that the blessing may be recited even if the sun is obscured by clouds. He explains the terminology employed by both the Gemara and Rambam by stating that one who "sees" the sun may pronounce the blessing immediately upon sunrise, but when the sun is obscure the blessing may be pronounced only later in the day when benefit can be derived from the sun's light even though the sun is beclouded.[2] This was also the view of R. Wolf Hamburger, *Nachalas Binyamin*, pp. 132-133.

However, many authorities disagree. *Chasam Sofer* argues that the phraseology of the Gemara, "He who *sees* the sun at its *tekufah*," indicates that an individual must actually see the sun in order to recite the blessing. Thus, in codifying the halachah, Rambam states that the blessing is to be recited "when one sees [the sun] on Wednesday in the morning."[3] This is quite evidently also the opinion of *Dagul meRevavah*, who reports that he waited to recite the blessing until

---

[10] 1. See *Yizrach Or*, p. 9b, who cites the phraseology of *Ra'avan* no. 200. In omitting any mention of "seeing" the sun, *Ra'avan* appears to agree with *Panim Me'iros*. See also Rabbi Gerlitz, *Bircas haChammah keHilchosah*, p. 100, no. 8.

R. Saul Brach, *Beis Va'ad laChachamim* (Satmar, 5685), cites *Teshuvos Nachlas Binyamin* and reports that in the years 5545 and 5573 the sun was completely obscured in his locale but that the blessing was nevertheless recited. That is also the position of R. Isaac of Komarne as recorded in his *Shulchan haTahor* 229:3.

That view is also reflected in a calendar published by the community of Frankfurt am Main in 5601. However, when meteorologists predicted a cloudy day for the occasion of *Bircas haChammah*, in the year 5713, R. Joel Teitelbaum, the Satmar Rebbe, in accordance with the ruling of *Chasam Sofer*, advised that, if the sun would indeed be obscured, the blessing should not be recited. See Rabbi Gerlitz, *Bircas haChammah keHilchosah*, p. 103, note 79.

2. That thesis is developed by *Kesav Sofer* only after his initial comment that *Dagul meRevavah* and *Chasam Sofer* constitute a majority versus *Panim Me'iros*. *Kesav Sofer* then prefaces his own agreement with *Panim Me'iros* with the phrase, "Were it not that I am unfit." Cf. Rabbi Cohen, *Bircas haChammah* 3:3, note 6, s.v. *gam da'as*.

outline of the sun can be perceived beneath the clouds or if any portion of the sun is visible between the clouds.

the clouds dispersed. This is also the position of *Ruach Chaim* 229:6; R. Chaim haKohen Rapoport, *Teshuvos Mayim Chaim*, no. 22; and R. Shlomo Kluger, in his commentary on the *Shulchan Aruch, Chochmas Shlomo, Orach Chaim* 229:2; *Teshuvos Yehudah Ya'aleh, Orach Chaim*, no. 7; *Koach Shor*, no. 27; *Yeshuos Yaakov, Orach Chaim* 229:2; *Kaf haChaim* 229:16; *Eshel Avraham* (Rav of Buczacz) 229:2; *Reishis Bikkurim*, pp. 4 and 148; *Atzei Beroshim*, no. 60; *Aruch haShulchan* 229:3; *Mishnah Berurah* 228:8; and *Tekufas haChammah uBirchosah*, p. 62.

However, even those authorities who maintain that *Bircas haChammah* may not be recited when the sun is beclouded, assert that this is the case only if the sun is completely obscured. According to most authorities, even if

---

3. *Panim Me'iros*, however, argues that the term "sees the sun" should not be understood literally. The Gemara states that one who hears a cock crow must recite the blessing "who gives the rooster wisdom to distinguish between day and night." Yet, *Tosafos, Berachos* 60b, rules that one need not actually hear the rooster crow in order to pronounce this blessing. The blessing, for *Tosafos*, is primarily an expression of thanksgiving for the benefit of daylight. Similarly, argues *Panim Me'iros, Bircas haChammah* is occasioned primarily by the awareness of the return of the sun to its original position in the heavens.

Teshuvos Yehudah Ya'aleh counters by pointing out that Rambam, *Hilchos Tefillah* 7:4 and *Shulchan Aruch* 46:8 disagree with the position of *Tosafos* and rule that the blessing should not be recited unless one actually hears the rooster crow. Later authorities who affirm the view that the blessing may be recited even though the rooster is not heard, do so, argues *Yehudah Ya'aleh*, on the basis of the comments of *Rosh, Berachos* 9:23. *Rosh* states that, although the word "sechvi" means "rooster" in Aramaic, in the blessing the word means "heart," which is the Hebrew meaning of the word, as in the verse *Who gave understanding to the heart* (Job 38:36). The blessing is thus one of thanksgiving to God for having endowed the human heart with the understanding necessary to distinguish between day and night.

Ostensibly, the essence of the controversy is whether *Bircas haChammah* was ordained as a form of *bircas hanehenin*, i.e., as a blessing of thanksgiving for a received benefit, or whether it is a form of *bircas hoda'ah*, a blessing of thanksgiving in recognition of the wondrous nature of creation. Rabbi Kahana, *Bircas haChammah*, quotes R. Shlomo Kluger as being of the opinion that the blessing is "akin" (ke'eilu) to a *bircas hanehenin*. However, it appears to this writer that all authorities agree that the blessing is essentially a *bircas hoda'ah* and that the controversy is limited to whether the blessing is occasioned simply by the cognitive awareness of the astronomical event or whether recitation of the blessing is also conditioned upon perception of an empirical manifestation of the phenomenon.

A practical halachic difference arises in a situation in which the sun becomes visible briefly and again becomes obscured before there is an opportunity to recite the blessing. A *bircas hanehenin* can be recited only before, or while, the benefit is experienced; the blessing may not be recited even immediately after the benefit has been experienced. A *bircas hoda'ah*, however, may be recited even immediately (*toch kedei dibbur*) after the event. See *Bi'ur Halachah* 426:3 for an analysis of *Kiddush Levanah* in that context. If *Bircas haChammah* is a *bircas hoda'ah* which, for some authorities,

only a portion of the sun is visible the blessing may be recited.[4] See *Yizrach Or*, p. 9a and the practice of *Chazon Ish* as cited by Rabbi Cohen, *Bircas haChammah*, p. 54. Moreover, *Sedei Chemed, asifas dinim, pe'as hasadeh, ma'areches berachos*, no. 33, citing R. David Meldola, *Boker Yizrach*, states that "there is no doubt" that if the clouds are not too dense and the outline of the sun may be perceived in its position,[5] "the blessing may be recited, even according to those who would maintain that, under similar circumstances, *Kiddush Levanah* should not be recited."[6] This is also the opinion of *Chasam Sofer*, who reports that his teacher, the renowned Rabbi Nathan Adler, recited *Bircas haChammah* in the year 5545 when only "the outline of the sun was perceivable between the clouds."[7]

R. Shalom Mordecai Schwardron, author of *Teshuvos Maharsham, Daas Torah Orach Chaim* 229:2 and 426:1, in his glosses to *Orchos Chaim* 426:6 as well as in a note appended to

his letter of approbation to R. Isaac Singer's *Zoharei Chammah*, adduces evidence in support of this position from *Menachos* 98a. The Gemara states that in the Temple, not only the Ark itself, but also the poles with which the Ark was carried were completely hidden behind a *paroches* or curtain. Nevertheless, their shape was discernible through the displaced fabric of the curtain. In demonstrating that the poles could not be seen, the Gemara cites the verse: *And the poles were so long that the ends of the poles were seen from the holy place* (I Kings 8:8). The poles are described as having been "seen" because they could be perceived as protrusions even though the material of the *paroches* intervened. Similarly, argues *Maharsham*, even when the sun is not clearly visible, nevertheless, it may be deemed to be "seen" when it is perceived behind the clouds.[8]

R. Chaim Knoller, *Bircas haChammah*, pp. 6-7, refuting this argument, draws attention to the concluding

---

is occasioned by an empirical observation rather than by an actual benefit, the blessing may be recited immediately after the sun becomes obscured. Cf. Rabbi Gerlitz, *Bircas haChammah keHilchosah*, p. 106, note 36.

4. A similar but subtly different position was advanced by R. Yedidyah Theo Weil of Karlsruhe who asserts that the blessing should be recited if the rays of the sun can be seen at the margin of the clouds. That phenomenon, he suggests, can readily be observed in the east at the time of sunrise. See *Siach Tefillah*, p. 198.

5. For this reason the blessing may be recited from behind a translucent curtain that does not completely obscure the sun. See *Mishnah Berurah* 426:2 and *Tekufas haChammah uBirchosah* 4:4, sec. 4. Similarly, the blessing may be recited while one is wearing sunglasses. See Rabbi Cohen, *Bircas haChammah* 3:9.

6. The normative ruling, however, is that even *Kiddush Levanah* is recited under such circumstances. See *Mishnah Berurah* 426:3.

7. This is also the opinion of *Reishis Bikkurim*, p. 148, and *Atzei Beroshim*, no. 60. However, *Sedei Chemed* cites *Ruach Chaim* 229:6 who rules that if the sun "is covered by a cloud one should recite the blessing without *shem umalchus*" and concludes that since *Ruach Chaim* fails to distinguish between a situation in which the sun's "outline is perceivable" and one in which it is not perceivable, it should be inferred that *Ruach Chaim* disagrees with *Chasam Sofer* and maintains that the blessing should not be pronounced with *shem umalchus* on a cloudy day, even if the sun's outline is perceivable. However, this inference is not compelling.

8. Cf. *Teshuvos Ravaz*, no. 32, who cites *Yoma* 54a in support of the view that only that which is visible can be deemed to be seen. See also *Sedei Chemed, Asifas Dinim*,

[11] If one commences recitation of the blessing but the sun becomes hidden by a cloud before the blessing is completed, the blessing should nevertheless be recited in its entirety. However, if before commencing the blessing it is apparent that there will not be sufficient time to complete the blessing before the sun is obscured, the blessing should not be recited.

[12] On an overcast day, if the sun becomes visible while one is in the midst of reciting *Pesukei deZimrah*, one should interrupt to recite *Bircas haChammah*.

---

phrase of the very same verse. The final words of the verse read, "but they could not be seen outside." The latter portion of the verse describes the poles concealed behind the curtain as not being "seen" despite the protrusion of their form through the intervening material. The entire verse, argues R. Chaim Knoller, must accordingly be understood as stating that, while it could be "seen" that there was an object located behind the curtain, the object itself could not be seen.[9]

[11] This rule is formulated by *Magen Avraham* 426:1 with regard to *Kiddush Levanah* on the basis of the ruling of R. David ibn Zimra, *Teshuvos Radvaz*, I, no. 156.

Commencement of the blessing is defined as utterance of the Divine Name.

[12] The rule regarding interruption of *Krias Shema* and its blessings is formulated by R. Ezekiel Landau, *Teshuvos Noda biYehudah, Mahadura Kamma, Orach Chaim*, no. 41, with regard to *Kiddush Levanah* in circumstances in which the period during which the blessing may be recited will lapse if the blessing is delayed. See also *Sha'arei Teshuvah, Orach Chaim* 426:9. *Magen Avraham* 66:5 similarly rules that upon hearing thunder one should interrupt *Krias Shema* in order to pronounce the appropriate blessing. *Mishnah Berurah*

---

ma'areches berachos, no. 2, sec. 18; Rabbi Moskowitz, *Bircas haChammah,* sec. 32 and Rabbi Gerlitz, *Bircas haChammah keHilchosah,* p. 99, note 79.

9. Cf., however, *Teshuvos Tashbatz,* I, no. 30, who comments upon the practice of covering the phylactery placed on the head with the *tallis*. The verse *And all the peoples of the earth shall see that the name of* HASHEM *is called upon you and they shall be afraid of you* (Deut. 28:10) is understood as describing the reaction of non-Jewish nations who behold the *tefillin shel rosh* upon the heads of Jews. *Tashbatz* states that this function of the *tefillin* is not defeated by covering them because, although the *tefillin* are covered by the *tallis*, their shape may yet be discerned and the phrase "and all the peoples of the earth shall see" remains applicable.

If the sun becomes visible while one is in the midst of reciting *Krias Shema* or the blessings preceding or following *Krias Shema* and the sun is likely again to become obscured, most authorities maintain that one should interrupt in order to recite the blessing. However, unless there is concern that the sun will immediately be obscured, recitation of the blessing of *Bircas haChammah* should be delayed until the paragraph of *Krias Shema* or of the blessing preceding *Krias Shema* being recited is completed. Nevertheless, if the sun becomes visible during recitation of the blessing following *Krias Shema*, *Bircas haChammah* should be pronounced immediately and not be delayed until conclusion of the blessing *Go'al Yisrael*.

When prayer is interrupted for recitation of *Bircas haChammah* only the blessing *oseh ma'aseh bereishis* should be pronounced. Other portions of the *Bircas haChammah* prayers should be omitted or recited subsequently upon completion of the morning prayers.

66:19 records conflicting views with regard to recitation of the blessing upon hearing thunder but is silent with regard to *Kiddush Levanah*.

Mishnah Berurah rules that interruption is permissible only between blessings and paragraphs. That is also the view of *Chayyei Adam* 20:4. There is some controversy with regard to whether the first paragraph of *Krias Shema* is deemed a "paragraph" separate from the preceding blessing.

Disagreeing with those authorities, *Yizrach Or*, p. 23, rules that one should not interrupt *Krias Shema* or its blessings either for *Kiddush Levanah* or *Bircas haChammah*. *Yizrach Or*

reasons that a person engaged in performing a *mitzvah* is exempt from other *mitzvos*. Although interruption is certainly appropriate in order to respond to *Kaddish*, *Kedushah*, and *Borachu*, *Yizrach Or* contends that such interruption is permitted only because failure to respond together with the congregation is tantamount to an expression of disdain for the congregation and "perhaps" results in the perception that the person who fails to respond is a non-believer.

However, *Sefer Chasidim*, no. 807, asserts that the rule that a person engaged in a *mitzvah* should not interrupt for purposes of performing another *mitzvah* does not apply

The blessing of *Bircas haChammah* may not be recited:

(i) while donning *tefillin*

(ii) during recitation of the *Shema Yisrael* verses and *Baruch shem kevod malchuso*

(iii) between pronouncing the word *Elokeichem* at the conclusion of *Krias Shema* and the word *emes* that constitutes the first word of the ensuing blessing

(iv) between the concluding phrase of the blessing *Go'al Yisrael* and *Shemoneh Esreh*.

(v) during *Shemoneh Esreh* itself; the supplication *Elokai Netzor* appended to *Shemoneh Esreh* may be interrupted in order to recite *Bircas haChammah*.

[13] If the sun is obscured but becomes visible during the course of a meal and is likely again to become obscured, the meal should be interrupted for recitation of *Bircas haChammah*. If bread had previously been eaten, upon resuming the meal after *Bircas haChammah*, hands should again be washed but without pronouncing the attendant blessing.

---

to a *mitzvah overes*, i.e., a *mitzvah* whose fulfillment, if delayed, will be foregone entirely. Thus, according to *Sefer Chasidim*, interruption for *Bircas haChammah* would be appropriate. See also Rabbi Gerlitz, *Bircas haChammah*, sec. 48 and p. 111, note 100.

[13] The general rule with regarding to washing of hands is recorded by *Rema, Orach Chaim* 178:2 and *Mishnah Berurah* 178:47. If a quantity of bread equal in weight to that of an olive was not consumed before the interruption, the blessing for bread must be repeated. See *Mishnah*

Berurah 178:28.

If the sun becomes visible after the blessing upon handwashing has been recited it is permissible to pronounce *Bircas haChammah* before reciting the blessing for bread. See *Shulchan Aruch, Orach Chaim* 167:1, who does not categorically forbid interruption before reciting the blessing for bread. See also Rabbi Gerlitz, *Bircas haChammah keHilchosah*, sec. 42. In such an instance only the blessing *oseh ma'aseh bereishis* should be pronounced without the accompanying liturgy. Upon completion of the blessing of *Bircas haChammah* hands should again be washed without the

[14] The four blessings comprising the Grace after Meals should not be interrupted in order to recite *Bircas haChammah*. There are no restrictions with regard to interruption of the supplementary supplications and verses recited upon completion of those blessings.

[15] In any situation in which *Bircas haChammah* cannot be recited because of doubt, e.g., the sun is obscured, but lightning is observed, the blessing *oseh ma'aseh bereishis* should be recited with the intention of satisfying the requirement of *Bircas haChammah* as well. Moreover, if thunder is heard, the blessing *oseh ma'aseh bereishis* (rather than the usual blessing *shekocho ugevuroso mole olam*) should be recited with the same intention.

[16] If the sun is completely obscured throughout the morning, the blessing should be delayed until shortly before midday. At that time the blessing should be recited with the omission

---

attendant *al netilas yadayim* blessing and then the blessing over bread should be recited.

[14] The general rule prohibiting any interruption of the Grace after Meals is recorded in *Shulchan Aruch, Orach Chaim* 183:8 and *Mishnah Berurah* 183:30. See also Rabbi Gerlitz, *Bircas haChammah keHilchosah*, p. 98, note 77.

[15] The blessing *oseh ma'aseh bereishis* is entirely appropriate for the hearing of thunder. See *Shulchan Aruch, Orach Chaim* 227:1. Cf., also, the comments of Rabbi Gerlitz, *Bircas haChammah keHilchosah*, p. 106,

note 82.

[16] *Teshuvos Panim Me'iros* reports that although he believed his opinion to be correct and that the blessing should be recited even when the sun is not visible, nevertheless, he hesitated to rule in accordance with his opinion. Accordingly, when on the occasion of *Bircas haChammah* in the year 5489 it transpired that the sun was not visible, he directed that the blessing be recited with the omission of *shem umalchus*. He thus directed that the formula "Blessed are You who makes the work of creation" be used, eliminating the phrase "HASHEM, our God, King of

of *shem umalchus* (the words הָעוֹלָם מֶלֶךְ אֱלֹהֵינוּ ה',
HASHEM, our God, King of the universe). The
blessing should then be pronounced as follows:
בְּרֵאשִׁית מַעֲשֵׂה עוֹשֶׂה אַתָּה בָּרוּךְ, *Blessed are You who
makes the work of creation.*

[17] Once the blessing has been recited in this
manner, regardless of the hour at which

---

the universe." In ruling in this manner, *Panim Me'iros* relied upon the
opinion of *Ra'avad* who maintains
that all the various blessings of praise
recorded in *Perek haRo'eh*, e.g., the
blessings recited upon seeing lightning, hearing thunder, etc., may val-
idly be pronounced without mention
of *shem umalchus*.

R. David Meldola, *Boker Yizrach*,
similarly rules in accordance with the
position of *Panim Me'iros* that the
blessing may be pronounced even if
the sun is hidden by clouds, but advises that it is preferable to omit *shem
umalchus* in pronouncing the blessing.[1]

Sha'arei Teshuvah 229:3 states that
one who conducts himself in accordance with the opinion of those who
maintain that *Bircas haChammah*

may be recited only until noon should
not, on a cloudy day, recite *Bircas
haChammah* without *shem umalchus* before the end of the third hour
in an attempt to fulfill the obligation
in at least this manner according to
the opinion of the opposing authorities. This should not be done because,
according to *Ra'avad*, the obligation
is fulfilled even without *shem umalchus* and hence the blessing may not
be repeated afterwards with *shem
umalchus* when the clouds disperse.[2]
One who does, however, conduct himself in accordance with the ruling of
Magen Avraham, who maintains that
Bircas haChammah may not be pronounced after the third hour, should,
on a cloudy day, recite the blessing
without *shem umalchus* before the
third hour.[3]

---

[16] 1. *Eshel Avraham* (*Rav* of Buczacz) 229:2 appears to agree with the position of
Panim Me'iros. See *Or haChammah, Me'orei Or*, p. 17b.

2. *Eshel Avraham* reports that, on one occasion when the sun was yet obscured at
the close of the third hour, he recited the blessing omitting the Divine Name. Upon
dispersal of the clouds after the third hour, he repeated the text of the blessing again
omitting *shem umalchus*. However, in accordance with *Taz, Orach Chaim* 62:1, he did
invoke the Divine Name mentally (*hirhur*); cf. *Sha'agas Aryeh*, no. 3.

3. *Eshel Avraham* further suggests that the blessing be recited in this manner condi-
tionally, i.e., with the stipulation that if the sun will emerge from behind the clouds
the blessing be reckoned as naught so that it may later be recited in the proper manner
with *shem umalchus*. Although he does not cite *Ra'avad*, it would appear that this
conditional pronouncement of the blessing would be efficacious even taking into account *Ra'avad's* position that a blessing without *shem umalchus* satisfies the requirement for blessings of this nature. However, for a general discussion of the validity of
conditional fulfillment of a *mitzvah*, see *Teshuvos Oneg Yom Tov*, no. 3, and R. Zevi
Pesach Frank, *Mikro'ei Kodesh, haYomim haNora'im*, p. 88.

it was recited, the full text of the blessing should not be repeated, even if the sun becomes visible before midday.

[18] However, if the sun becomes visible, even if only late in the day, the blessing should be repeated, but only with the omission of *shem umalchus.*

---

[17] The full text of the blessing should not be repeated even though it has previously been pronounced with the omission of *shem umalchus* because numerous authorities maintain that the obligation is fulfilled even though the sun is obscured by clouds and because *Ra'avad* maintains that the obligation with regard to this blessing may be fulfilled even with omission of *shem umalchus.*[1] See *Sha'arei Teshuvah* 229:3. That position is, however, disputed by *Atzei Beroshim*, no. 60.

However, when the sun becomes visible the blessing should be repeated, but again with the omission of *shem umalchus.* See *Sha'arei Teshuvah, Orach Chaim* 229:3 and *Kaf haChaim* 229:16. Other portions of the prayer service need not be repeated. See *Atzei Beroshim*, no. 60.

[18] The blessing should be repeated in order to fulfill the obligation according to those authorities who maintain that the obligation was not discharged by the earlier recitation of the blessing during the period in which the sun was obscured. The blessing cannot be repeated with *shem umalchus* because, according to the opinion of other authorities, the obligation was discharged through the first recitation of the blessing even though the sun was obscured. Both the first stipulation, providing for recitation of the blessing with the omission of *shem umalchus* when the sun is obscured, and the second stipulation, requiring a repetition of the blessing, but again without *shem umalchus*, when the sun reappears, are based upon consideration of *Ra'avad's* opinion that the obligation is satisfied even with the omission of *shem umalchus.* Once the obligation with regard to a blessing is satisfied,

---

[17] 1. See *Ra'avad's* commentary on *Ba'al haMa'or, Berachos* 54a, and as cited by Meiri, *Berachos* 54a and *Tur Shulchan Aruch, Orach Chaim* 218. *Ra'avad* concludes his comments with the statement, "... if one pronounces [the blessing] with mention of *shem umalchus* one suffers no loss." See also *Sha'arei Teshuvah, Orach Chaim* 218:1, who declares that, even according to *Ra'avad*, inclusion of *shem umalchus* does not entail a blessing pronounced in vain. It is logical to assume that such is the case only if *shem umalchus* is included in the original pronouncement of the blessing. However, once the obligation has been discharged without *shem umalchus* any subsequent pronouncement of the blessing incorporating *shem umalchus* would constitute a blessing pronounced in vain. Accordingly, when the blessing is repeated after the sun becomes visible, *shem umalchus* should be omitted.

[19] The *shehecheyanu* blessing is not recited in conjunction with *Bircas haChammah*.

any repetition with *shem umalchus* constitutes a *berachah levatalah* — a blessing pronounced in vain — and is forbidden.

[19] The blessing, "who has sustained us in life, preserved us and brought us to this season," recited upon performance of most *mitzvos* that are incumbent only on specific occasions, is not recited in conjunction with *Bircas haChammah*. Nor is this blessing recited on the occasion of the monthly *Kiddush Levanah*. *Teshuvos Kesav Sofer, Orach Chaim*, no. 34, explains that the blessing is omitted in both cases for the identical reason. At the time of creation the moon was as bright as the sun and the sun was many times brighter than at present. At the time of *Kiddush Levanah* we pray:

וִיהִי רָצוֹן מִלְּפָנֶיךָ יהוה אֱלֹהַי וֵאלֹהֵי אֲבוֹתַי לְמַלֹּאות פְּגִימַת הַלְּבָנָה וְלֹא יִהְיֶה בָּהּ שׁוּם מִעוּט, וִיהִי אוֹר הַלְּבָנָה כְּאוֹר הַחַמָּה וּכְאוֹר שִׁבְעַת יְמֵי בְרֵאשִׁית כְּמוֹ שֶׁהָיְתָה קֹדֶם מִעוּטָהּ.

May it be Your will ... to restore the deficiency of the moon so that it no longer be reduced in size; may

the light of the moon again be like the light of the sun as its light was during the seven days of creation, as it was before its diminution."

The diminution of the sun and the moon was caused by the sin of Adam. Ultimately, when mankind is fully repentant and totally dedicated to the service of God, these luminaries will be restored to their original brilliance. In the interim, the rituals associated with the sun and the moon, while joyous in nature, are also mingled with an element of sadness because they remind us of our present imperfect spiritual state. Accordingly, the blessing of *shehecheyanu* is not pronounced.

Rabbi Tucatzinsky, *Tekufas haChammah uBirchosah*, p. 73, dismisses the question of the absence of the *shehecheyanu* blessing by pointing out that this blessing is associated only with a pleasurable experience or the joyous performance of a *mitzvah*.[1] The blessing of *Kiddush Levanah*, he states, is ordained as an expression of gratitude for the pleasurable benefit derived from the illumination of the moon. Each month

---

[19] 1. A similar explanation is advanced by R. Moshe Schick, *Teshuvos Maharam Shik, Orach Chaim*, no. 90. For a discussion of the basic principle see *Teshuvos haRashba*, I, no. 126; *Avudraham, sha'ar* 3; R. Shimon ben Tzemach Duran, *Yavin Shemuah, maamar chametz*; and *Machazik Berachah, Orach Chaim* 432: 1. Cf., however, the novel view of *Teshuvos Chavos Ya'ir*, no. 70, who maintains that a person should pronounce *shehecheyanu* upon reaching his seventieth birthday. Cf. also *Pesach haDvir*, III, *Hashmottos leOrach Chaim* 219:7 (pp. 315a-316a), who cites (but hesitates to give credence to) a report that in the year 5601 [1841] R. Chaim Palaggi donned a new garment in order to recite *shehecheyanu* in conjunction with *Bircas haChammah*. If this report is true, R. Chaim Palaggi followed this procedure because of a possible obligation to recite *shehecheyanu* on the occasion of *Bircas haChammah*. *Teshuvos Minchas Yitzchak*, VIII, no. 15, reports that a similar view is recorded in a manuscript written by R. Akiva Yosef Schlesinger, author of *Lev Ivri*, and that the late R. Pinchas Epstein, who served as head of the *Beis Din* of the *Eidah haChareidis*, donned a new garment and recited the *shehecheyanu* on behalf of the entire assemblage. See also R. Zevi Moskowitz, *Bircas haChammah*, p. 31. See below, pp. 184-185,

we experience a renewed benefit that constitutes a pleasurable experience. Hence, the halachic commentaries seek to explain why the *shehecheyanu* blessing is omitted on the occasion of *Kiddush Levanah*.[2] However, *Bircas haChammah*, he argues, is not an acknowledgment of the pleasure derived from the illumination of the sun,[3] nor, technically speaking, does

---

for the formula of thanksgiving appended to the יְהִי רָצוֹן by *Pesach haDvir* in lieu of the *shehecheyanu* blessing.

Eliyahu Rabbah is quoted as suggesting two reasons why *shehecheyanu* is not recited in conjunction with *Kiddush Levanah*. The first reason is that the recitation may occur within a thirty-day period of a prior recitation of *Kiddush Levanah* (cf. *Magen Avraham* 422:5 and *Eliyahu Rabbah* 422:10). *Eliyahu Rabbah* further cites an early authority, *Tanya*, who declared that pronouncement of *shehecheyanu* would be superfluous since a blessing has already been recited upon "renewal" of the moon. R. Joseph Zecharya Stern, *Teshuvos Zecher Yehosef*, *Orach Chaim*, no. 119, points out that, according to *Eliyahu Rabbah*, recitation of *shehecheyanu* in conjunction with *Bircas haChammah* should be contingent upon which of those explanations is accepted. For a discussion of other possible considerations precluding recitation of *shehecheyanu* see Rabbi Kahane, *Bircas haChammah*, sec. 5, and *Bircas haChammah keHilchosah*, p. 61, note 8.

Somewhat surprisingly, one writer, R. Mordechai Fogelman, *Teshuvos Beis Mordechai*, no. 31, is of the opinion that the *shehecheyanu* blessing should be recited in thanksgiving for having been privileged to pronounce *Bircas haChammah*.

2. Actually, if the *shehecheyanu* blessing is occasioned by pleasure or benefit received rather than by virtue of performance of a *mitzvah* associated with joy, the appropriate blessing would be *hatov vehametiv*, "who is good and who bestows beneficence," rather than *shehecheyanu*. *Shehecheyanu* is pronounced only when the benefit or pleasure befalls a single person; *hatov vehametiv* is pronounced when two or more individuals share the same benefit or pleasure. Thus the Mishnah, *Berachos* 54a, prescribes that following a period of drought the blessing *hatov vehametiv* be pronounced when rain falls. The Gemara, *Sanhedrin* 42a, does indeed question why *hatov vehametiv* is not pronounced each month for the renewed illumination of the moon. In response the Gemara declares: כֵּיוָן דִּהֲדַיִינוּ אוֹרְחֵיהּ לֹא מְבָרְכִינָן, "Since this is its nature we do not pronounce the blessing." The principle enunciated by the Gemara is that no blessing is occasioned by the reappearance of the moon each month since this is a regular phenomenon and not a novel occurrence. *Pesach haDvir* (p. 315a) aptly notes that *hatov vehametiv* is not recited on the occasion of *Bircas haChammah* for the identical reason.

3. Cf., however, *Panim Me'iros*, II, no. 38, who describes the blessing as being occasioned, at least in part, by the benefits derived from the sun. Similarly, *Zera Emes*, III, no. 24, rules that a blind person must recite the blessing because even the blind receive benefit from the light of the sun. However, even according to these authorities, there is no cause for this blessing as explained above, note 2.

4. This point was made earlier by *Pesach haDvir* (p. 315b). Cf. *Zoharei Chammah*, *Bircas Kiddush haChammah* (J. Thayer: Frankfurt a.M., 5685), p. 11.

5. See also *Teshuvos Maharam Shik*, *Orach Chaim*, no 90. *Shevilei David*, *Orach Chaim* 229, states that the *shehecheyanu* blessing is not recited in conjunction with *Bircas haChammah* because the blessing "*oseh ma'aseh bereishis*" is identical with the blessing occasioned by thunder and the like and hence is not novel. Cf. *Or haChammah*, *Me'orei Or*, p. 19a and R. Raphael Rubinstein, *Birkas Refael: Pesach*, no. 92. See also the analysis of the *Rogatchover*, R. Joseph Rosen, *Teshuvos Tzofnas Pa'ane'ach* (Jerusalem, 5728), II, no. 2.

Tekufas haChammah uBirchosah, 5:2, sec. 6, *inter alia*, declares that recitation of a blessing does not occasion an additional *shehecheyanu*. See also *Taharas haShulchan*

[20] Women may recite the blessing, although in some places it was the custom for women not to do so.

it constitute a *mitzvah* or commandment.[4] Rather, it is an acknowledgment of divine omnipotence. Such an acknowledgment does not necessitate the *shehecheyanu* blessing.[5]

[20] In many places it was the practice for women not to recite *Bircas haChammah*. The reason for this custom is rather obscure. Indeed, *Teshuvos Chasam Sofer, Orach Chaim*, no. 56, states that he knows of no reason why they should not do so. Nevertheless, he was reluctant to tamper with the practice, particularly because some few authorities question the entire basis of *Bircas haChammah*.[1]

The question is a twofold one: (1) whether or not women are obligated to recite *Bircas haChammah*; (2) whether, if they are not obligated to do so, they are permitted voluntarily to pronounce the blessing just as they customarily fulfill certain *mitzvos* that are not incumbent upon them such as *shofar* and *arba minim*.

It may be argued that the obligation with regard to *Bircas haChammah* is one "that is contingent upon time" [מִצְוַת עֲשֵׂה שֶׁהַזְמַן גְּרָמָא] and hence women are not obligated to discharge this obligation, just as they are not bound by other positive commandments that must be performed at a stipulated time. This argument

is consistent with the position of *Tosafos, Berachos* 20b, who maintain that the exemption of women from *mitzvos aseh shehazman gerama* extends not only to biblical obligations but to rabbinic obligations as well. Rashi, however, maintains that the exemption is limited to biblical precepts, but the women are not excluded for this reason from similar rabbinic obligations.[2] They may, however, be exempt from specific rabbinic obligations on other grounds.

Rabbi Kamelhar, *Boker Yizrach, Sha'arei Mizrach*, chap. 7, argues quite cogently that *Bircas haChammah* cannot be characterized as a *mitzvas aseh shehazman gerama*. That concept encompasses *mitzvos* that are bound to a set time-period or to a specific date in the calendar. The *mitzvos* of *Succos* must be performed on a specific day; *Krias Shema* must be recited during the prescribed time periods. *Bircas haChammah* is intrinsically no different from the blessing recited upon hearing thunder or seeing lightning. Similarly, *Bircas haChammah* is recited on the occasion of the unfolding of an astronomical phenomenon reminiscent of creation. As such, it is an empirical event that occasions the blessing. The fact that it occurs only at a specific time is an "accident" or a matter extraneous to the nature of the obligation; the time at which the blessing is pronounced

---

229. Rabbi Cohen, *Bircas haChammah* 4:2, note 3, cites R. Yaakov Zev haLevi, *Nitzutzei Chammah* (Jerusalem, 5685), who suggests that the *shehecheyanu* is delayed and recited on the festivals as determined by reconciliation of the lunar and solar cycles in the same manner that *shehecheyanu* upon constructing a *succah* is delayed and recited on the festival.

[20] 1. See above, p. 78, note 14.

is not intrinsic to the obligation itself. Hence, argues Rabbi Kamelhar, it should not be regarded as a *mitzvas aseh shehazman gerama*. The same considerations are formulated by R. Joshua Leib Diskin, *Teshuvos Maharil Diskin*, II, *kuntres acharon*, no. 5, sec. 26. Cf. R. Binyamin Silber, *Birur Halachah* 229:7.

There may, however, be other considerations that prompted the Sages to exclude women from this obligation. *Magen Avraham*, in his introductory remarks to *Orach Chaim* 426, states that women are excluded from *Kiddush Levanah* because it was Eve who was responsible for the sin that caused the moon to be diminished.[3] *Chasam Sofer*, however, points out that this consideration does not apply to *Bircas haChammah*.[4] *Maharam Shik, Orach Chaim*, no. 90, argues that women are exempt from *Bircas haChammah* for another reason. The Gemara, *Shabbos* 75a, categorizes the astronomical calculations upon which the calendar is based as "wisdom," a branch of knowledge that can be acquired only by means of arduous

study. Since women are exempt from the obligation of Torah study, argues *Maharam Shik*, they are exempt from the aspect of study associated with *Bircas haChammah* as well. Since, unlike men, they are under no obligation to make the astronomical calculations that would enable them to reckon the time of the sun's return to its original place in the heavens, they are also exempt from the blessing attendant upon that event.[5]

These arguments exempting women from *Bircas haChammah* are not accepted by all authorities. Furthermore, there remains the second question, namely, may women voluntarily fulfill the obligation of *Bircas haChammah* even if they are not formally bound to do so? Some authorities maintain that women who voluntarily perform *mitzvos* from which they are exempt should not pronounce the prescribed blessing prior to performance of the *mitzvah*. Their reasoning is that women ought not to pronounce the liturgical formula וְצִוָּנוּ "and has commanded us," since, in point of fact, they

---

2. See also *Teshuvos Har Zevi, Orach Chaim*, I, no. 119.

3. See, however, R. Eliezer Deutsch, cited in *Yizrach Or*, p. 12b, who argues that, contrary to the position of *Magen Avraham*, women no longer bear responsibility for the sin of Adam and Eve. This is so, he argues, because the Sages indicate that the sin of Adam would have been rectified at the time of the acceptance of the Torah at Mount Sinai if not for the sin of the Golden Calf. Women, who did not participate in that sin, did indeed remedy the sin of Eve and, therefore, deserve to enjoy the original brilliance of the moon. The moon remains diminished, he argues, not because of women, but on the contrary, because of men. For this reason, explains Rabbi Deutsch, women were given *Rosh Chodesh* as a holiday; women, for their part, have rectified the blemish of the moon and granting them the day of the new moon as a holiday is *middah keneged middah*.

[The generally accepted explanation of why *Rosh Chodesh* is a holiday for women is that women refused to contribute their gold adornments for purposes of fashioning the Golden Calf. However, when the Tabernacle was constructed, they joyously presented their gold and silver jewelry. The Tabernacle was erected for the first time on the first day of the month of Nisan. In recognition of the exemplary piety of the women they were given *Rosh Chodesh* as a special holiday. See *Pirkei deRabbi Eliezer* 45 and the commentary of *Radal*, chap. 45, sec. 20.]

4. See, however, *Teshuvos Minchas Yitzchak*, VIII, no. 15. See also the reason advanced by that authority, *ibid.*, no. 34.

have not been commanded. In many Sephardic communities this is the established practice and women do not pronounce such blessings. However, women cannot be excluded from *Bircas haChammah* on these grounds because, in this instance, the blessing is one of thanksgiving, and does not include the words "who has commanded us."[6]

Rabbi Joshua Horowitz and Rabbi Eliezer Deutsch, *Yizrach Or*, p. 13a,[7] state that women were not accustomed to recite the blessing since *Bircas haChammah* was customarily recited in a public assemblage in the synagogue courtyard and it was deemed unseemly for women to mingle with men.[8] Rabbi Horowitz, however, adds that the concern is solely with regard to decorum and that it is entirely proper for women to recite the blessing.[9]

Teshuvos Kesav Sofer, Orach Chaim, no. 34, advances a somewhat complex reason in explaining why it is that in some places women did not recite *Bircas haChammah*. Women customarily perform many *mitzvos* from which they are exempt and, when doing so, pronounce the appropriate blessing. In such cases the blessing is secondary to the performance of the *mitzvah* and is properly pronounced by anyone performing the *mitzvah*. *Magen Avraham* 296:11 states that women are exempt from all rabbinic *mitzvos* that consist solely of the recitation of a blessing (as distinct from *birchos hanehenin*) and that women should not voluntarily recite such blessings. In such cases, women cannot appropriately recite the blessing, according to *Magen Avraham*, because they are specifically exempted from its recitation. *Magen Avraham* explains that it is for this reason that *Rema* declares that women should

---

5. A similar explanation regarding the exemption of women from the obligation of *Kiddush Levanah* was advanced earlier by *Yeshu'os Ya'akov, Orach Chaim* 426:1.

6. See *Magen Avraham* 226:11 and *Yizrach Or*, p. 10a as well as sources cited by Rabbi Cohen, *Bircas haChammah* 2:4, note 5. Cf., also, R. Aaron Vermez, *Me'orei Or*, p. 117b, cited in *Yizrach Or*, pp. 10a and 17a.

7. See also R. Eliezer Deutsch, *Teshuvos Pri haSadeh*, I, no. 103, and R. Judah Leib Graubart, *Teshuvos Chavalim BeNe'imim*, III, no. 8.

8. *Chasam Sofer, Shabbos* 21a, states that since Chanukah lights were kindled outside the entrance to the home, women do not kindle lights individually. See also Rabbi Gerlitz, *Bircas haChammah keHilchosah*, p. 126, note 120.

9. R. Joseph Saul Nathanson, *Teshuvos Sho'el uMeshiv, mahadura tinyana*, IV, no. 168, explains the practice of women not to recite *Bircas haChammah* on the basis of a tenuous argument with which other scholars disagree sharply. *Sho'el uMeshiv* cites *Jeremiah* 7:18 which states that, at that time, women were wont to offer sacrifices to the מְלֶכֶת הַשָּׁמַיִם, "queen of the heaven." *Radak* interprets "queen of the heaven" as a reference to the sun. On the basis of this reference, *Sho'el uMeshiv* opines that it is the custom for women not to recite *Bircas haChammah* lest they erroneously consider the ceremony to be a form of sun worship. See *Da'as Torah, Orach Chaim* 229:2. R. Joshua Horowitz (in his letter of approbation to *Boker Yizrach*, p. 14) forcefully argues that normative halachah cannot be predicated upon such a far-fetched allusion, particularly one that is not contained in a halachic source. Indeed, *Sho'el uMeshiv* himself, as cited earlier, asserts that the very purpose of *Bircas haChammah* is to eradicate any false belief in the divinity of the sun. Moreover, *Pesikta Rabbasi* (Vienna, 1880), chap. 31, p. 143a, identifies *"meleches hashamayim"* as the stars. See also R. Isaiah Joseph Margolin, *Tiferes Maharshim*, II, no. 13 and Rabbi Kahane, *Bircas haChammah*, sec. 9.

[21] An *onen* (a bereaved person during the period between death and burial of a relative for whom the laws of mourning must be observed) should not pronounce the blessing prior to burial of the deceased.

[22] A mourner should pronounce the blessing but should not attend synagogue

---

not recite *havdalah* at the conclusion of *Shabbos*. *Kesav Sofer* advances this consideration as a reason why women should not recite the blessing of *Bircas haChammah*.[10]

There are, however, numerous other authorities who maintain that women should recite *Bircas haChammah*. Among these are *Noheg keTzon Yosef*, p. 36b; *Be'er Sheva*, p. 117a; *Ateres haChaim*, no. 28, sec. 8; *Pesach haDvir* 229:4; R. Aaron Vermez, *Me'orei Or*, p. 117b; R. Joel Ungar, *Teshuvos Riva*, no. 16; *Orchos Chaim* 229; *Chacham Zevi*, quoted by *Yalkut haGershuni*, no. 426; R. Pinchas Schwartz, *Yizrach Or*, p. 10a; R. Joseph Schwartz, cited in *Yizrach Or*, p. 11a; and R. Joshua Horowitz and R. Shlomo Segner, *Or haChammah*, p. 6b. This is also the ruling of *Teshuvos Maharil Diskin*, *kuntres acharon*, no. 26; and *Teshuvos Har Zevi*, *Orach Chaim*, no. 226. See also *Teshuvos Hillel Omer*, no. 147. It is the established custom in Jerusalem that women pronounce the blessing.

It has been stated earlier that it is preferable for the *chazzan* to recite the blessing aloud on behalf of the assembled and for the assembled then to answer "Amen" with intention thereby to fulfill their obligation. There is no question that, in this manner, women may participate in *Bircas haChammah* even in a locale in which it is the custom for women not to recite the blessing. The Sephardic authority, *Ben Ish Chai*, *Shanah Rishonah*, *Parshas Ekev*, no. 19, reports that, in the year 5657, he personally recited the blessing on behalf of the assembled women of his community.[11] Women may, without doubt, recite the other prayers which form part of the liturgy of *Bircas haChammah*.

[21] See *Ruach Chaim* 229:8; *Or haChammah*, p. 18a; *Orchos Chaim* 229:2; and *Kaf haChaim* 229:8. An *onen* is exempt from the performance of positive *mitzvos* and does not pronounce blessings prior to the burial of his deceased relative; see *Shulchan Aruch, Yoreh De'ah* 341:1.

---

10. This explanation is rather problematic since women certainly recite the identical blessing "who makes the work of creation" upon seeing lightning, etc., and pronounce other *birchos hoda'ah* as well, including, according to many authorities, *bircas hagomel*. A distinction must be drawn between these blessings and *havdalah*. The former are analogous to *birchos hanehenin*, recited upon experiencing sensory pleasure. Women, no less than men, are clearly obligated to recite such blessings. Blessings offered in response to specific phenomena are occasioned by emotions of gratitude and thanksgiving and hence women are obligated to recite these blessings as well. *Havdalah* is not ordained as a response to a perceivable phenomenon but as a *mitzvah sui generis*

for this purpose during the period of *shivah*. A mourner during the period of *shivah* should omit the psalms and the talmudic selections recited in conjunction with the blessing.

[23] A blind person should request another person reciting the blessing to recite it on his behalf as well, and the blind person should

---

[22] See *Pesach haDvir* 229:5; *Yizrach Or*, p. 13a; *Or haChammah*, p. 18a; *Orchos Chaim* 229:2; *Kaf haChaim, Orach Chaim* 229:8; and *Teshuvos Hillel Omer*, no. 146. Following the burial of his relative a mourner is obligated to perform all *mitzvos*, even during the period of *shivah*. Since the blessing can be pronounced in private there is no reason for *shivah* restrictions to be suspended in order for the mourner to attend synagogue for this purpose.[1]

If the sun is visible through a window or door the mourner should not leave his home. Otherwise, the mourner may recite the blessing in his courtyard or in a place in close proximity to his home.[2]

During *shivah* the mourner, who is forbidden to engage in Torah study because study of Torah "gladdens the heart," should not recite the psalms and talmudic selections associated with *Bircas haChammah* since this constitutes a form of Torah study. See *Yizrach Or*, p. 18a.[3]

[23] The Mishnah, *Megillah* 24a, states that a blind person recites the blessing "who creates the luminaries" preceding the *Shema* in the morning service. The Gemara explains that a blind person derives benefit from illumination even though he does not see. In explaining this concept, the Gemara relates that, one night, R. Yose saw a blind man walking with a torch in his hand. R. Yose asked the blind man to what purpose he carried a torch. The blind man replied that by means of the light of the torch people were able to see him and preserve him from danger. *Maharshal* rules that, similarly, a blind person should recite *Kiddush Levanah* since, even though he is blind, he may, in like manner, derive benefit from the light of the moon. *Radvaz*, however, disagrees and rules that a blind person should not recite *Kiddush Levanah*.[1]

---

and therefore, women, according to *Magen Avraham*, are exempt. *Bircas haChammah* would appear to belong to the general category of blessings of thanksgiving.

11. See also *Kaf haChaim* 229:8. Cf. *Hillel Omer*, no. 146.

[22] 1. Cf., however, *Tekufas haChammah uBirchosah*, pp. 65-66.

2. Cf. the rulings of *Eliyahu Rabbah, Orach Chaim* 426:15, and *Mishnah Berurah* 426:11 regarding *Kiddush Levanah*. See *Tekufas haChammah uBirchosah*, chap. 7.

3. Cf. also *Mishnah Berurah* 559:20; 554:7 and 46:28.

[23] 1. See *Sha'arei Teshuvah* 426:1.

himself respond "Amen." A blind person who pronounces the blessing himself should omit *shem
umalchus.*

R. David Meldola cites a certain R. Jacob ibn Na'im who main-
tained that the selfsame controversy
would extend to recitation of *Bircas
haChammah* by a blind person.[2]
However, this parallelism is not compelling. *Magen Gibborim, Elef haMa-
gen,* no. 103, notes that, according to
those who maintain that the blessing may be recited even if the sun
is completely obscured by clouds, a
blind person may certainly recite this
blessing. For those authorities the
blessing is not occasioned by "seeing" the sun, but by the awareness
that it has returned to the position
in which it was placed at the time of
creation.

On the other hand, *Maharshal,*
who maintains that a blind person
should recite *Kiddush Levanah,* might
well agree that he should not recite
Bircas haChammah.[3] The blessing

of *Kiddush Levanah* is, according to
Maharshal, comparable to the blessing *yotzer hame'oros.* Both were ordained in acknowledgment of the
benefit derived from the luminaries,
a benefit in which, as noted earlier,
the blind share as well. The blessing
of *Bircas haChammah* is not a blessing pronounced because of benefit
derived from the sun, but a blessing
pronounced upon perceiving an empirical event. Hence, even according
to *Maharshal,* the blind, who cannot
perceive the event, may perhaps not
be included among those who recite
the blessing.[4]

Most authorities, including
Shemesh Tzedakah, R. Chaim Yosef
David Azulai, *Machazik Berachah*
229:6, and R. Chaim Palaggi, *Ruach
Chaim* 229:7, maintain that the obligation on the part of the blind is
doubtful and, therefore, as is the case

---

2. This authority adds the words "for both are stated in the same clause: one who
sees the moon *bechiddushah* and the sun *betkufasah.*" See also R. Shlomo Kluger,
Chochmas Shlomo 229:2, who makes a similar statement with regard to recitation of
the blessing when the sun is obscured by clouds. These statements appear to be in
error. The halachah of *levanah bechiddushah,* referring to the appearance of the new
moon each month, is recorded in *Sanhedrin* 42a. The *Beraisa, Berachos* 59b, which
speaks of both the sun and the moon, speaks of *levanah begevurasah* and does not at
all refer to the appearance of the new moon but to the return of the moon and its entry
into *mazal teleh,* as is clearly stated by Rambam, *Hilchos Berachos* 10:18. Cf. *Tekufas
haChammah uBirchosah,* p. 35, note 1. Cf., however, *Yizrach Or,* p. 9a.

3. Thus, basing himself upon *Maharshal, Teshuvos Zera Emes,* III, no. 24, rules that a
blind person should recite the blessing.

4. See *Pesach haDvir,* III, *Hashmottos leOrach Chaim* 219:6 (p. 315a) and *Tekufas
haChammah uBirchosah,* pp. 64-65. However, one authority, *Zera Emes,* III, no. 24,
maintains that *Bircas haChammah* is occasioned by the benefit derived from the sun.
Accordingly, he rules that a blind person must recite the blessing even according to
the opinion of those who maintain that the blessing is not recited when the sun is
hidden by clouds. Since the sun may be perceived by others, he argues, the blind
receive benefit as well. See also *Panim Me'iros,* II, no. 38, who similarly describes
the blessing as being occasioned, at least in part, by the benefits derived from the
sun.

[24] Minors who have reached the age of training in *mitzvos* and who understand the nature of a blessing should be taught to recite the blessing.

[25] *Bircas haChammah* is recited on *Yom Tov* even when the occasion for its recitation coincides with the festival of *Pesach*.

[26] If a circumcision is to be performed on the day of *Bircas haChammah,* the circumcision

---

in every situation in which the obligation with regard to recitation of a blessing is in doubt, it should not be recited or be recited without *shem umalchus*. *Kaf haChaim* 229:8 advises that a blind person should fulfill his obligation by hearing the blessing as it is recited by another person who recites it on behalf of both.[5]

[24] See *Zoharei Chammah*, p. 19 and *Yizrach Or*, p. 18a. With reference to blessings, *Shulchan Aruch, Orach Chaim* 215:3, distinguishes between a child who has reached the age of *chinnuch* (training in *mitzvos*) and a child of a younger age. See also *Mishnah Berurah* 215:16.

[25] R. Chaim haKohen Rapoport, *Teshuvos Mayim Chaim*, no.

22, reports that the blessing "was recited in a great assembly" on the second day of *Pesach* in the year 5601 [1841].[1] See also *Ruach Chaim* 229:4. *Bircas haChammah* also occurred on the second day of *Pesach* in the year 5517 (1757). See Rabbi Kahane, *Bircas haChammah*, sec. 10.[2] Most of the reasons for not reciting *Kiddush Levanah* on *Shabbos* or *Yom Tov*[3] are not applicable to *Bircas haChammah*. Moreover, even *Kiddush Levanah* may be recited on *Yom Tov* when it is otherwise impossible to recite the blessing. See *Be'er Hetev, Orach Chaim* 426:5, and *Or haChammah, Me'orei Or*, p. 18b.

The next occurrence of *Bircas haChammah* on *Yom Tov*, according to the present calendrical system,

---

5. See also *Pesach haDvir*, loc. cit.

[25] 1. The text of *Teshuvos Mayim Chaim* reads "on the second day of *Yom Tov* of *Chol haMo'ed Pesach*." The words "*Chol haMo'ed*" are obviously a misprint. Wednesday, April 7, 1841, which was the date for *Bircas haChammah*, coincided with the second day of *Yom Tov*.

2. *Bircas haChammah*, which is on a Wednesday, can never occur on either the first or last day of *Pesach*, since those days never fall on a Wednesday.

3. See *Teshuvos haRashba*, IV, no. 48; *Teshuvos Shevus Yaakov*, III, no. 31 and *Mahadura Basra*, no. 12; *Margaliyos haYam*, Sanhedrin 42a, sec. 4; and *Mishnah Berurah, sha'ar hatziyyun* 426:12. For an informative survey of those reasons see Rabbi Cohen, *Bircas haChammah* 1:14, note 26.

should be performed before *Bircas HaChammah* is pronounced. On a cloudy day, if there is a concern that the sun may become obscured, the blessing should be recited before the circumcision, but recitation of the other portions of the liturgy should be delayed until after the circumcision.

---

will be in the year 5881 [2121], when it will occur on the seventh day of *Pesach.*

[26] Both circumcision and *Bircas haChammah* become incumbent simultaneously at sunrise. Circumcision takes precedence because it is a biblical obligation whereas the obligation of *Bircas haChammah* is rabbinic in nature. In addition, circumcision is a more frequently performed *mitzvah* (*tadir*) and therefore is accorded priority. It is reported in the 5 Nisan 5657 edition of *HaTzefirah* that the community of Metz conducted themselves in this manner on the occasion of *Bircas haChammah* in the year 5461. See R. Zevi Cohen, *Bircas haChammah: Halachos uMinhagim haShalem* (Jerusalem, 5741), 1:10, note 18*. (This work is also appended to Rabbi Cohen's *Erev Pesach shechal beShabbos* published the same year.)

On a cloudy day *Bircas haChammah* takes precedence because, under such circumstances, it is a *mitzvah overes*, i.e., a *mitzvah* that, if delayed, will be entirely foregone. See Rabbi Gerlitz, *Bircas haChammah keHilchosah,* sec. 65.

Chapter Five

≈§ The Prayers

The Prayers

Bircas haChammah consists of the blessing עוֹשֶׂה מַעֲשֶׂה בְרֵאשִׁית, *who makes the work of creation*. The identical blessing is pronounced upon witnessing unusual natural phenomena, such as shooting stars or lightning. When recited upon witnessing other phenomena the blessing is accompanied by no liturgical embellishment. However, over the course of centuries, an entire order of prayer came to surround this blessing when recited every twenty-eight years upon the return of the sun to the position in the heavens which it occupied at the time of creation. Similarly, much earlier in time, an extended order of prayer became associated with the blessing מְחַדֵּשׁ חֳדָשִׁים, *who renews the months*, which constitutes the essence of *Kiddush Levanah*.

The parallel between these two orders of prayer is underscored by R. Chaim haKohen Rapoport, *Teshuvos Mayim Chaim*, no. 22. This authority introduced a more elaborate prayer service for *Bircas haChammah*, stating that he did so, "For I said, 'Why should it be worse than the blessing of the moon which we pronounce each and every month while *Bircas haChammah* comes only at intervals of twenty-eight years?' certainly, it is seemly for us to glorify and praise the Master of all things who has caused us to reach this occasion. May He similarly cause us to see and be seen in our holy Temple speedily in our days."

There is no single accepted text for the service associated with *Bircas haChammah*. The most commonly used liturgy for the order of *Bircas haChammah* is found in a small pamphlet entitled *Boker Yizrach*. This, in turn, combines the *Seder Bircas haChammah* according to the practice of Sephardic Jews with the *Seder Bircas haChammah* instituted by *Chasam Sofer*. Over the years, other liturgies for *Bircas haChammah* have been prepared and published. The latter are based primarily upon the text of *Boker Yizrach*, but contain various additions.

In the present volume a variety of type-faces have been utilized in order to indicate sources and relative degrees of emphasis. The order of *Bircas haChammah* as presented by *Boker Yizrach* and *Chasam Sofer* appears in large-size type. In the past, some expanded services gained wide currency in certain locales. Additional psalms and prayers included in the *Seder Bircas haChammah* prepared by *Pesach haDvir* and in the text published in *Sedei Chemed* have been

typeset in this volume in intermediate-size type. Supplementary
material incorporated in the liturgy by yet other authorities did not
receive widespread acceptance. Accordingly, this latter material is
here presented in small-size type.

◆§ A Bibliographic Note
Sources and Development of *Seder Bircas haChammah*

Since *Bircas haChammah* is recited so infrequently, relatively little has been written on the sources
and content of the accompanying liturgy. The few monographs
and halachic compendia which do
discuss these prayers are, by and
large, unavailable and virtually
unknown. Accordingly, additional
bibliographic details concerning the
sources of *Seder Bircas haChammah* are here presented for the benefit of the interested reader.

The *Seder Bircas haChammah*
presented in *Boker Yizrach* is itself
based upon an older order of service
whose source is somewhat obscure.
The earliest extant[1] published additions to the blessing עוֹשֶׂה מַעֲשֵׂה
בְרֵאשִׁית in the liturgy of *Bircas
haChammah* are found in a prayer-
book entitled *Tefillah Zakkah*, compiled by R. Abraham Isaac Castillo
and published in Leghorn, Italy, in

5549 [1789], pp. 217b-218b. This
work contains the order of *Bircas
haChammah* as it was recited in
Leghorn on the 25th of Nisan 5545[2]
[1785], some four years prior to the
publication of *Tefillah Zakkah*.

The order of *Bircas haChammah*
as it appears in *Tefillah Zakkah*
was subsequently published in
London in the year 5601 [1841] as
a separate pamphlet bearing the
title *Boker Yizrach*.[3] That edition,
which includes a number of ex-
pository notes dealing with various
aspects of the laws pertaining to
Bircas haChammah, was published
by R. David Meldola at the behest
of his father, R. Raphael Meldola,
who served as *Chacham* of the
Sephardic community in London.[4]
Boker Yizrach was subsequently republished in Czernowitz in 5627
[1867] and in 5652 [1892].

The *Seder Bircas haChammah*

---

1. See below, note 4.

2. *Tefillah Zakkah* gives the date as 29 Nisan 5544, but this is obviously a typographical error.

3. That pamphlet is actually a reprint of an earlier edition published in London in 5573
[1813]. That edition, edited by R. Raphael Meldola, was published by L. Alexander
and sold exclusively by B. Abrahams, a Hebrew bookseller. Only one page of this
pamphlet is extant. A photo offset of that page is appended to a limited edition reprint
of the 5601 [1841] version published by Abraham Schischa (London, 1981).

4. In a parenthetical note in the preface of *Boker Yizrach*, R. David Meldola states that
the order of *Bircas haChammah* had already been published, presumably in pamphlet
form, in 5545 [1785], prior to the appearance of *Tefillah Zakkah*. A similar reference
on the title page also speaks of the original publication as having been in Leghorn
in 5545. Actually, there were two earlier editions of *Boker Yizrach*. The first edition,
as noted earlier, was published in 5545 [1785] by R. Jacob Meldola (presumably in
Leghorn) and bore the title *Seder veTikkun Bircas haChammah beTekufosah*. A
second edition, bearing the title *Boker Yizrach*, was published in London, 5573 [1813].
See *supra*, note 3.

as presented in *Boker Yizrach*, and which earlier appeared in *Tefillah Zakkah*, is ascribed to R. Jacob Meldola. R. Jacob Meldola, scion of an illustrious Sephardic family, lived in Leghorn and was a distant cousin of R. David Meldola. This version of *Seder Bircas haChammah* is described in *Tefillah Zakkah* as having been followed in Leghorn in 5545 [1785] and is depicted by R. David Meldola as being in accordance with the usage of "the cities of Italy" and as having received "the approbation of all the rabbis." It is therefore evident that this order of *Bircas haChammah* reflects a firmly rooted *minhag*. Thus it appears that Sephardic Jews had a long tradition of liturgical additions to the *Seder Bircas haChammah*. An order of *Bircas haChammah* quite similar to that of R. Jacob Meldola seems to have constituted a well-established and accepted liturgy in *Eretz Yisrael*. (See Eliyahu Volk, *Seder Bircas haChammah*, p. 5.)

The identical order of *Bircas haChammah* was followed by the Sephardic authority, R. Eliezer Papo in the year 5573 [1813] and is incorporated in his halachic compendium, *Chesed laAlafim* (Salonica, 5610) 221-230:28. The very same liturgy is also found in a compendium of prayers entitled *Ateres haChaim* (Salonica, 5601) compiled by the Sephardic scholar, R. Chaim Palaggi.

The service as found in *Tefillah Zakkah* and *Boker Yizrach* begins with the verse כִּי שֶׁמֶשׁ וּמָגֵן ה' (*Psalms* 84:12), followed by four verses

whose initial letters form an acrostic spelling the Divine Name, and Psalm 148:1-6. All of these passages are recited prior to pronouncing the blessing. Following the blessing, R. Jacob Meldola incorporates Psalms 19 and 121 as well as the text of the *Beraisa* found in *Berachos* 59b together with a selection from the final Mishnah of *Makkos*, רִ' חֲנַנְיָא בֶּן עֲקַשְׁיָא אוֹמֵר. This is followed by the *Kaddish deRabbanan*. The liturgical order concludes with a יְהִי רָצוֹן, a supplicatory prayer for longevity and redemption accompanied by restoration of the original lumination of the moon, as well as the enhanced brilliance of the sun as vouchsafed in the end of days.

Similar liturgies associated with *Bircas haChammah* apparently did not arise among Ashkenazic Jews until somewhat later. R. Moshe Sofer, *Teshuvos Chasam Sofer, Orach Chaim*, no. 56 — who quite evidently was unaware of the additions recorded in *Tefillah Zakkah* — reports that on the occasion of *Bircas haChammah* in 5573 [1813] he recited Psalm 148 prior to the blessing. After the blessing he recited the prayer אֵל אָדוֹן (from the *Shabbos* morning service) as well as Psalm 19. This was followed by *Aleinu* and *Kaddish*. It is obvious from the phraseology employed by *Chasam Sofer* that in introducing these embellishments he was not following an already established custom.[5]

Chasam Sofer's order of *Bircas haChammah* parallels that of R. Jacob Meldola in the incorporation of Psalms 148:1-6[6] and 19, but

---

5. Cf. comments in *Seder Bircas haChammah* published by Eliyahu Volk (Warsaw, 5657), p. 16; the author is identified only as י.פ.פ.

6. However, *Chasam Sofer* may have recited Psalm 148 in its entirety. See *Teshuvos Chasam Sofer, Orach Chaim*, no. 56.

excludes other interpolations found in *Tefillah Zakkah*. It is clear that recitation of אֵל אָדוֹן and *Aleinu* originates in the practice of *Chasam Sofer*. It is of interest to note that when R. David Meldola reprinted the *Bircas haChammah* service of *Tefillah Zakkah* in his *Boker Yizrach* he added אֵל אָדוֹן, attributing its recitation to *Chasam Sofer*. Apparently without exception, subsequent Sephardic authorities incorporated אֵל אָדוֹן in the *Seder Bircas haChammah* and ascribed its inclusion to *Chasam Sofer*. *Aleinu* is also included in the order of *Bircas haChammah* presented in *Boker Yizrach*.

Both אֵל אָדוֹן and עָלֵינוּ were also independently introduced into the order of *Bircas haChammah* by R. Chaim haKohen Rapoport in 5701 [1841]. In his *Teshuvos Mayim Chaim*, no. 22, R. Chaim Rapoport notes that when he inaugurated recitation of these prayers he was not aware that *Chasam Sofer* had preceded him in this practice. In addition, the prayer אָנָּא בְּכֹחַ and Psalm 67 were included by R. Chaim Rapoport following the blessing.

Other additions stem from diverse sources. R. Joseph Saul Nathanson, author of *Teshuvos Sho'el uMeshiv*, introduced the chanting of Psalm 150 following אֵל אָדוֹן on the occasion of *Bircas haChammah* in the year 5629 [1869].

More extensive additions were made by another Sephardic scholar, R. Chaim Binyamin Pontremoli. These additions which are found in his *Pesach haDvir*, III (Smyrna, 5633), *Hashmottos leOrach Chaim* 229:9[7] (pp. 316a-b), include a prefatory selection of verses from the Pentateuch (*Genesis* 1:14-19), the

Prophets (*Jeremiah* 31:34-39) and the Hagiographa (*Psalms* 136:1-9) and a *LeShem Yichud* meditation composed in a manner appropriate to *Bircas haChammah*. *Pesach haDvir* also incorporated the brief selection from *Perek Shirah* which describes the praises sung to God by the sun and inserted this selection immediately following the *Beraisa*, *Berachos* 59b.

Two brief emendations occur in the prayers following the blessing עוֹשֶׂה מַעֲשֵׂה בְרֵאשִׁית. In including אֵל אָדוֹן, which is taken from the *Shabbos* service, *Chasam Sofer* understandably concluded the selection immediately prior to the words "לָאֵל אֲשֶׁר שָׁבַת ... בַּיּוֹם הַשְּׁבִיעִי — To God who rested ... on the seventh day" since that section of the liturgy is clearly not germane to *Bircas haChammah*. *Pesach haDvir* similarly omits that section but does, however, include the final passage which is certainly appropriate to the occasion:

שִׁמְךָ ה' אֱלֹהֵינוּ יִתְקַדֵּשׁ וְזִכְרְךָ מַלְכֵּנוּ יִתְפָּאַר בַּשָּׁמַיִם מִמַּעַל וְעַל הָאָרֶץ מִתַּחַת תִּתְבָּרַךְ מוֹשִׁיעֵנוּ עַל שֶׁבַח מַעֲשֵׂה יָדֶיךָ וְעַל מְאוֹרֵי אוֹר שֶׁעָשִׂיתָ יְפָאֲרוּךָ סֶּלָה.

Your Name, O HASHEM, our God, shall be hallowed and Your mention, O our King, shall be glorified in the heavens above and on the earth beneath. You shall be blessed, O our Deliverer, for the excellence of Your handiwork and for the luminaries of light which You have made; they shall glorify You. Selah.

Finally, since *Seder Bircas haChammah* does not include a formal *shehechiyanu* blessing, *Pesach haDvir* prefaces the concluding prayer with words expressing similar sentiments:

---

7. The caption appears as 219:9; this is obviously a typographical error.

מוֹדִים אֲנַחְנוּ לָךְ וּמְהַלְלִים לְשֵׁם תִּפְאַרְתֶּךָ בְּרָכוֹת וְהוֹדָאוֹת לְשִׁמְךָ הַגָּדוֹל וְהַקָּדוֹשׁ עַל שֶׁהֶחֱיִיתָנוּ וְקִיַּמְתָּנוּ וְהִגַּעְתָּנוּ עַד הַיּוֹם הַזֶּה לְבָרֵךְ בִּרְכַּת הוֹדָאָה זוֹ לְפָנֶיךָ.

We give thanks unto You and praise Your glorious Name. Blessings and thanksgiving to Your great and holy Name for having sustained us in life, for having preserved us and for having caused us to reach this day to pronounce the blessing of thanksgiving before You.

One very widely used *Seder Bircas haChammah* is that of R. Chaim Chizkiyahu Medini, author of the encyclopedic halachic work, *Sedei Chemed*. This order of prayer is included immediately following *ma'areches chanukah*, VII, 74-77 (New York, 5722).[8] This volume of *Sedei Chemed* was first published in 5657 [1897], a year in which *Bircas haChammah* was recited, and apparently was originally published as a separate pamphlet. In a prefatory note, the author of *Sedei Chemed* states that the *Seder Bircas haCham- mah* which he presents is taken from *Pesach haDvir* and also incorporates the additions of R. Chaim haKohen Rapoport. In point of fact, *Sedei Chemed* also includes one other se- lection not found in any of the pre- viously noted works, a prefatory se- lection taken from the introduction to the *Tikkunei Zohar*. The identical selection from the *Tikkunei Zohar* is found in many prayerbooks as an introductory meditation prior to the morning service.

The אֲדוֹן עוֹלָם hymn is men- tioned in the report delivered by the Sephardic authority *Ben Ish Chai* regarding the order of *Bircas haChammah* which he recited in 5657 [1897],[9] the same year as that of the publication of *Sedei Chemed's* service.

R. Pinchas Zelig Schwartz pres- ents an enhanced liturgy for *Bircas haChammah* in his *Yizrach Or* pub- lished in 5685 [1925]. This version includes Psalm 8 among the psalms recited after the blessing, Psalm 33 before *Aleinu*, Psalm 74 follow- ing *Aleinu*, as well as אֵין כֵּאלֹהֵינוּ immediately preceding the יְהִי רָצוֹן prayer. Also included in *Yizrach Or* is a much longer and more elaborate concluding prayer in lieu of the יְהִי רָצוֹן. This prayer was composed in 5657 [1897] by R. Eliezer Chaim Deutsch, author of *Teshuvos Pri haSadeh*.

The *Seder Bircas haChammah* is customarily recited in a festive man- ner. R. Yechiel Michel Tucatzinsky writes that it was the practice in Jerusalem to repeat the verses of the various psalms after the *chazzan* and that Psalm 67 and אֵל אֲדוֹן were sung rather than recited. Similarly, in the report of the *Bircas haChammah* service conducted in the presence of R. Joseph Saul Nathanson, we are told that Psalm 150 was sung by the cantor and choir of Lemberg. In a similar vein, *Ben Ish Chai* remarks that the verses of Psalm 136:1-9 are to be sung with a melodious tune.

From time to time, these services

---

8. *Seder Bircas haChammah* is found in vol. IX, pp. 3850-53, in the *Kehot* edition of *Sedei Chemed* (New York, 5736).

9. The order of prayers presented by *Ben Ish Chai* is somewhat different. In his version *Seder Bircas haChammah* consists of Psalm 19; Psalm 48; the various biblical verses which precede the blessing in *Boker Yizrach*; Genesis 1:14-19; *LeShem Yichud*; the blessing; Psalm 136:1-9; *Kel Adon; Aleinu; Adon Olam; Yehi Ratzon;* R. Chananya ben Akashya Omer; and *Kaddish deRabbanan.*

were embellished in various ways. In conjunction with the service conducted in Lemberg in 5629 [1869] the chief rabbi of the city, R. Joseph Saul Nathanson, delivered an inspirational address. The text of this *derashah* was published in the periodical *HaMaggid* and is reprinted in *Yizrach Or*, chap. 15. Earlier, on the occasion of *Bircas haChammah* which coincided with the second day of Pesach 5601 [1841], R. Jacob Ettlinger, author of *Aruch laNer*, himself composed a prayer in honor of the event. It is of historical interest to note that this *tefillah* invokes divine blessings upon Sir Moses Montefiore for his intervention on behalf of those Jews who were imprisoned at the time of the Damascus libel in 1840. This prayer with accompanying translation as well as the text of a sermon delivered in German were published in pamphlet form by the Altona community. An English translation of that sermon was published in *Jewish Studies*, a publication of Yeshivas Dvar Yerushalayim, no. 30 (Spring, 5741) as well as in the monograph *The Blessing on the Sun* published by that yeshivah in 5741.

⋙ Publications Occasioned by Bircas haChammah 5741

Bircas haChammah in 5741, which marked the beginning of the 206th twenty-eight year solar cycle, was a singular event in Jewish religious life. Unprecedented numbers of Jews both in Israel and in the United States gathered for impressive public observances of this ritual. The zeal with which the ritual was performed was reflected in the extraordinary number of scholarly publications dealing with this observance to which but a brief paragraph is devoted in the *Shulchan Aruch*. Many more monographs and articles devoted to this subject were published in conjunction with this most recent observance of *Bircas haChammah* than had been published in conjunction with all such previous events combined. The most comprehensive work to be published on this topic is *Sefer Bircas haChammah keHilchosah* by a Jerusalem scholar, R. Menachem Gerlitz, which includes an appendix containing relatively inaccessible halachic discussions, responsa and homilies of earlier scholars. Another comprehensive and erudite work is *Bircas haChammah* by Rabbi Zevi Cohen, author of *Tevilas Kelim* and *Hag'alas Kelim*. As in his other volumes, Rabbi Cohen's work on *Bircas haChammah* is exemplary both in its organization and analysis.

A brief compendium, *Bircas haChammah*, was also published by R. Moshe Sternbuch. Another pamphlet dealing with this observance, *Barah kaChammah*, was published by R. Shlomoh Schweitzer of Spring Valley, N.Y. R. Yehoshua Heschel Deutsch of Los Angeles compiled a booklet entitled *Kuntres Berachah veYeshu'ah*. A major portion of a hitherto unpublished work, *Davar beItto*, authored by R. Akiva Schlesinger (known as the *Lev Ivri*), deals with the Blessing of the Sun. Edited by R. Moshe Nachum Shapiro, this work contains additional responsa authored by the editor as well as by R. Shmuel Wosner and R. Yitzchak Yaakov Weisz.

Many works published in conjunction with earlier observances of *Bircas haChammah* were also republished. A valuable new edition of R. Yechiel Michel Tucatzinsky's informative and authoritative *Tekufas haChammah uBirchosah* was widely disseminated. This work first appeared eighty-four years ago, was republished with additions twenty-eight years later, and was republished by the author's son in 5741 with the addition of a number of important notes. Also republished was R. Pinchas Zelig Schwartz' *Yizrach Or* which may be familiar to many readers as a result of its wide circulation in the United States in 1953. Two classic works, *Boker Yizrach* by R. Yekutiel Aryeh Kamelhar and *Or haChammah* by R. Meir Dan Hertzberg, were reprinted in a single paperback edition together with *Kuntres keTzes haShemesh* by R. Gavriel Zinner. This volume was published by Yeshiva Machazikei Hadas of Belz. Rabbi Zinner's *Kuntres keTzes haShemesh* was also published separately by the student organization of Yeshiva Kehilath Yakov of Pupa. Supplementary discussions by Rabbi Zinner, entitled *Kuntres keTzes haShemesh, Mahadura Tinyana*, appear as an appendix to his *Milei dePischa*.

Particularly noteworthy is a booklet entitled *keTzes haShemesh* published by Mesifta Maharam Schick in Jerusalem containing important responsa and source material. Also of interest is a collection of articles and responsa, *Tovim Me'oros sheBara*, compiled by R. Samuel Isaac Roth. Another pamphlet, *Tizrach haShemesh*, contains material gleaned from the writings of R. Nachman of Braslav.

A number of items also appeared in English, including the first edition of this book and an interesting article by a mathematician, Charles Elkin, which appears in the *Proceedings of the Association of Orthodox Jewish Scientists*, vol. VI (1980). Elkin presents much intriguing information regarding the Jewish calendar in general and the astronomical premises which form the basis of *Bircas haChammah*. Also of interest is *A Blessing for the Sun: A Study of Birkat ha-Hammah from Early Time until the Present* by R. Nehemia Polen and *Yiroucho Im Shemesh* by R. Avraham Blumenkrantz as well as *The Blessing on the Sun* published by Yeshivat Dvar Yerushalayim.

Articles in the periodical literature discussing various aspects of *Bircas haChammah* include R. Zevi Sloucz, *Shevilin*, Kislev 5741; R. Moshe Nachum Shapiro, *Moriah*, Shevat 5741; R. Eliyahu Baruch Kepetsh, *HaMa'ayan*, Nisan 5741; R. Nehemia Polen, *Tradition*, Spring 1981; R. J. David Bleich, *HaPardes*, Adar 5741 and *Beis Yitzchok* 5742 (reprinted in the author's *BeNesivos haHalachah*, vol. II). A document describing recitation of *Bircas haChammah* despite difficult weather conditions in Cologne, Germany, in the year 5545, was published by Manfred R. Lehmann in the Tishrei-Cheshvan 5741 issue of *Sinai*.

סדר התפילות

וִיהִי נֹעַם אֲדֹנָי אֱלֹהֵינוּ עָלֵינוּ, וּמַעֲשֵׂה יָדֵינוּ כּוֹנְנָה עָלֵינוּ, וּמַעֲשֵׂה יָדֵינוּ כּוֹנְנֵהוּ.

פָּתַח אֵלִיָּהוּ

פָּתַח אֵלִיָּהוּ הַנָּבִיא זָכוּר לַטוֹב וְאָמַר. רִבּוֹן עָלְמִין דְּאַנְתְּ הוּא חַד וְלָא בְחֻשְׁבָּן. אַנְתְּ הוּא עִלָּאָה עַל־כָּל עִלָּאִין, סְתִימָא עַל־כָּל סְתִימִין. לֵית מַחֲשָׁבָה תְּפִיסָא בָךְ כְּלָל. אַנְתְּ הוּא דְאַפִּיקַת עֲשַׂר תִּקּוּנִין, וְקָרֵינָן לוֹן עֲשַׂר סְפִירָן. לְאַנְהָגָא בְהוֹן עָלְמִין סְתִימִין דְּלָא אִתְגַּלְיָין, וְעָלְמִין דְּאִתְגַּלְיָין. וּבְהוֹן אִתְכַּסִּיאַת מִבְּנֵי נָשָׁא, וְאַנְתְּ הוּא דְקָשִׁיר לוֹן וּמְיַחֵד לוֹן. וּבְגִין דְּאַנְתְּ מִלְּגָאו, כָּל מַאן דְּאַפְרִישׁ חַד מִן חַבְרֵה, מֵאִלֵּין עֲשַׂר סְפִירָן, אִתְחֲשִׁיב לֵיה כְּאִלּוּ אַפְרִישׁ בָּךְ. וְאִלֵּין עֲשַׂר סְפִירָן אִינוּן אָזְלִין כְּסִדְרָן, חַד אֲרִיךְ וְחַד קְצַר וְחַד בֵּינוּנִי. וְאַנְתְּ הוּא דְּאַנְהִיג לוֹן. וְלֵית מַאן דְּאַנְהִיג לָךְ לָא לְעֵילָא וְלָא לְתַתָּא וְלָא מִכָּל סִטְרָא. לְבוּשִׁין תְּקִינַת לוֹן דְּמִנַּיְיהוּ פָּרְחִין נִשְׁמָתִין לִבְנֵי נָשָׁא. וְכַמָּה גוּפִין תְּקִינַת לוֹן דְּאִתְקְרֵיאוּ גוּפִין לְגַבֵּי לְבוּשִׁין דִּמְכַסְּיָין עֲלֵיהוֹן. וְאִתְקְרֵיאוּ בְּתִקּוּנָא דָא. חֶסֶד דְּרוֹעָא יְמִינָא, גְּבוּרָה דְּרוֹעָא שְׂמָאלָא, תִּפְאֶרֶת גּוּפָא, נֶצַח וְהוֹד תְּרֵין שׁוֹקִין, יְסוֹד סִיּוּמָא דְגוּפָא אוֹת בְּרִית קוֹדֶשׁ, מַלְכוּת פֶּה תּוֹרָה שֶׁבְּעַל פֶּה קָרֵינָן לָה. חָכְמָה מוֹחָא אִיהִי מַחֲשָׁבָה מִלְּגָו, בִּינָה לִבָּא וּבָהּ הַלֵּב מֵבִין, וְעַל אִלֵּין תְּרֵין כְּתִיב: הַנִּסְתָּרוֹת לַיהוֹה אֱלֹהֵינוּ, כֶּתֶר עֶלְיוֹן אִיהוּ כֶּתֶר מַלְכוּת, וַעֲלֵיה אִתְּמַר: מַגִּיד מֵרֵאשִׁית אַחֲרִית, וְאִיהוּ קַרְקַפְתָּא דִּתְפִלִּין, מִלְּגָו אִיהוּ יוֹ"ד ה"א וָי"ו ה"א דְּאִיהוּ אֹרַח אֲצִילוּת, אִיהוּ שַׁקְיוּ דְאִילָנָא בִּדְרוֹעוֹי וְעַנְפוֹי, כְּמַיָּא דְּאַשְׁקֵי לְאִילָנָא וְאִתְרַבֵּי בְּהַהוּא שַׁקְיוּ.

רִבּוֹן הָעוֹלָמִים, אַנְתְּ הוּא עִלַּת הָעִלּוֹת, וְסִבַּת הַסִּבּוֹת, דְּאַשְׁקֵי לְאִילָנָא בְּהַהוּא נְבִיעוּ. וְהַהוּא נְבִיעוּ אִיהוּ כְּנִשְׁמָתָא לְגוּפָא דְּאִיהִי חַיִּים לְגוּפָא. וּבָךְ לֵית דִּמְיוֹן וְלֵית דִּיוּקְנָא מִכָּל מַה דִּלְגָו וּלְבַר. וּבָרָאתָ שְׁמַיָּא וְאַרְעָא. וְאַפִּיקַת מִנְּהוֹן שִׁמְשָׁא וְסִיהֲרָא וְכֹכְבַיָּא וּמַזָּלַיָּא. וּבְאַרְעָא, אִלָּנִין וּדְשָׁאִין וְגִנְּתָא דְעֵדֶן וְעִשְׂבִּין וְחֵיוָן וְעוֹפִין וְנוּנִין, וּבְנֵי נָשָׁא. לְאִשְׁתְּמוֹדַע בְּהוֹן עִלָּאִין, וְאֵיךְ יִתְנַהֲגוּן בְּהוֹן עִלָּאִין וְתַתָּאִין, וְאֵיךְ אִשְׁתְּמוֹדְעָאן מֵעִלָּאֵי וְתַתָּאֵי, וְלֵית דְּיָדַע בָּךְ כְּלָל. וּבַר מִנָּךְ לֵית יְחוּדָא בְּעִלָּאֵי וְתַתָּאֵי, וְאַנְתְּ אִשְׁתְּמוֹדַע עִלַּת עַל כֹּלָּא, אֲדוֹן עַל־כֹּלָּא, וְכָל־סְפִירָן, כָּל־

⊱ The Order of the Prayers

Psalms 90:17

May the pleasantness of the Lord, our God, be upon us; our handiwork, establish for us; our handiwork, establish it.

⊱ Pasach Eliyahu

[The kabbalistic terminology found in this selection from *Tikkunei Zohar* does not lend itself to a readily comprehensible translation. Accordingly, the following synopsis is offered in lieu of a translation.]

This selection, taken from the introduction to the *Tikkunei Zohar*, presents in capsule form a number of fundamental kabbalistic doctrines. God is described as One, as an absolute unity. God is completely removed from human experience and cannot be perceived by the mortal mind. God is omnipotent and omnipresent. The existence of all created beings depends directly upon the existence of God. Save for the continued existence of God, Who is the preserving force of all creation, created beings would be "as bodies without souls."

God's grace and blessing are channeled through the *Sephiros* which emanate from God. They are ten in number. The term *"Sephirah"* is derived from the Hebrew word *sappir*, meaning "sapphire." This term is used because the *Sephiros* reflect the radiance of God whose brightness is likened to that of the sapphire.

The emanation described in the *Tikkunei Zohar* is

⊱ וִיהִי נֹעַם — **Vihi Noam**

נֹעַם — *Pleasantness.*

The *Shechinah* (*Rashi*). As in לַחֲזוֹת בְּנֹעַם ה׳ — *to behold the pleasantness of HASHEM* (*Psalms* 27:4).

כּוֹנְנָה עָלֵינוּ — *Establish for us.*

May our endeavor be without flaw or defect (*Metzudas David*). Recited immediately prior to the blessing of *Bircas haChammah*, this verse is a supplication that the blessing be

uttered with proper *kavannah* and sincerity and be free of defect.

כּוֹנְנֵהוּ — *Establish it.*

The reference is to the Tabernacle. These words were uttered by Moses upon completion of the Tabernacle. *Rashi* notes that the verse contains a twofold prayer: 1) that the *Shechinah* rest upon the Tabernacle and 2) that all the endeavors of Israel be blessed by God.

חַד אִית לֵיהּ שֵׁם יָדִיעַ וּבְהוֹן אִתְקְרִיאוּ מַלְאָכַיָּא. וְאַנְתְּ לֵית
לָךְ שֵׁם יָדִיעַ, דְּאַנְתְּ הוּא מְמַלֵּא כָל־שְׁמָהָן. וְאַנְתְּ הוּא שְׁלִימוּ
דְּכֻלְּהוּ. וְכַד אַנְתְּ תִּסְתַּלֵּק מִנְּהוֹן אִשְׁתָּאֲרוּ כֻּלְּהוּ שְׁמָהָן, כְּגוּפָא
בְּלָא נִשְׁמָתָא. אַנְתְּ חַכִּים וְלָא בְּחָכְמָה יְדִיעָא. אַנְתְּ הוּא מֵבִין
וְלָא מִבִּינָה יְדִיעָא. לֵית לָךְ אֲתַר יְדִיעָא, אֶלָּא לְאִשְׁתְּמוֹדְעָא
תּוּקְפָךְ וְחֵילָךְ לִבְנֵי נָשָׁא, וּלְאַחֲזָאָה לוֹן אֵיךְ אִתְנַהֵיג עָלְמָא
בְּדִינָא וּבְרַחֲמֵי, דְּאִינוּן צֶדֶק וּמִשְׁפָּט, כְּפוּם עוֹבְדֵיהוֹן דִּבְנֵי נָשָׁא.
דִּין אִיהוּ גְּבוּרָה, מִשְׁפָּט עַמּוּדָא דְאֶמְצָעִיתָא, צֶדֶק מַלְכוּתָא
קַדִּישָׁא, מֹאזְנֵי צֶדֶק תְּרֵין סַמְכֵי קְשׁוֹט. הִין צֶדֶק אוֹת בְּרִית
קֹדֶשׁ. כֹּלָּא לְאַחֲזָאָה אֵיךְ אִתְנַהֵיג עָלְמָא, אֲבָל לָא דְּאִית לָךְ
צֶדֶק יְדִיעָא דְּאִיהוּ דִין, וְלָאו מִשְׁפָּט יְדִיעָא דְּאִיהוּ רַחֲמֵי. וְלָא
מִכָּל אִלֵּין מִדּוֹת כְּלָל. קוּם רַבִּי שִׁמְעוֹן וְיִתְחַדְּשׁוּן מִלִּין עַל־יְדָךְ,
דְּהָא רְשׁוּתָא אִית לָךְ לְגַלָּאָה רָזִין טְמִירִין עַל־יְדָךְ, מַה דְּלָא
אִתְיְהִיב רְשׁוּ לְגַלָּאָה לְשׁוּם בַּר נָשׁ עַד־כְּעַן.

קָם רַבִּי שִׁמְעוֹן, פָּתַח וְאָמַר לְךָ יְהוָה הַגְּדוּלָה וְהַגְּבוּרָה
וְהַתִּפְאֶרֶת וְהַנֵּצַח וְהַהוֹד, כִּי כֹל בַּשָּׁמַיִם וּבָאָרֶץ, לְךָ יְהוָה
הַמַּמְלָכָה וְהַמִּתְנַשֵּׂא לְכֹל לְרֹאשׁ: עִלָּאִין שְׁמָעוּ, אִינוּן דִּמְכִין
דְּחֶבְרוֹן וְרַעְיָא מְהֵימְנָא אִתְעָרוּ מִשְּׁנַתְכוֹן. הָקִיצוּ וְרַנְּנוּ שׁוֹכְנֵי
עָפָר, אִלֵּין אִינוּן צַדִּיקַיָּא, דְּאִינוּן מִסִּטְרָא דְּהַהוּא דְּאִתְּמַר בָּהּ
אֲנִי יְשֵׁנָה וְלִבִּי עֵר, וְלָאו אִינוּן מֵתִים, וּבְגִין דָּא אִתְּמַר בְּהוֹן
הָקִיצוּ וְרַנְּנוּ שׁוֹכְנֵי עָפָר. רַעְיָא מְהֵימְנָא, אַנְתְּ וְאַבְהָן הָקִיצוּ
וְרַנְּנוּ לְאִתְעָרוּתָא דִשְׁכִינְתָּא, דְּאִיהִי יְשֵׁנָה בְּגָלוּתָא, דְּעַד כְּעַן
צַדִּיקַיָּא כֻּלְּהוּ דְּמִכִין וְשֵׁנָתָא בְּחוֹרֵיהוֹן. מִיָּד יְהִיבַת שְׁכִינְתָּא
תְּלַת קָלִין לְגַבֵּי רַעְיָא מְהֵימְנָא, וְיֵימָא לֵיהּ, קוּם רַעְיָא מְהֵימְנָא,
דְּהָא עֲלָךְ אִתְּמַר קוֹל דּוֹדִי דוֹפֵק לְגַבָּאי בְּאַרְבַּע אַתְוָון דִּילֵיהּ.
וְיֵימָא בְּהוֹן, פִּתְחִי לִי אֲחוֹתִי רַעְיָתִי יוֹנָתִי תַמָּתִי, דְּהָא תַם עֲוֹנֵךְ
בַּת צִיּוֹן לֹא יוֹסִיף לְהַגְלוֹתֵךְ. שֶׁרָאשִׁי נִמְלָא טָל, מַאי נִמְלָא טָל,
אֶלָּא אָמַר קוּדְשָׁא בְּרִיךְ הוּא, אַנְתְּ חֲשִׁיבַת דְּמִיּוֹמָא דְּאִתְחָרַב
בֵּיהּ מַקְדְּשָׁא דְּעָאלְנָא בְּבֵיתָא דִילִי וְעָאלְנָא בִּישׁוּבָא, לָאו
הָכִי, דְּלָא עָאלְנָא כָּל זִמְנָא דְּאַנְתְּ בְּגָלוּתָא, הֲרֵי לָן סִימָנָא,
שֶׁרֹאשִׁי נִמְלָא טָל, ה״א שְׁכִינְתָּא בְּגָלוּתָא. שְׁלִימוּ דִּילָהּ וְחַיִּים
דִּילָהּ אִיהוּ טָל. וְדָא אִיהוּ יוֹ״ד ה״א וא״ו. וה״א אִיהִי שְׁכִינְתָּא
דְּלָא מֵחוּשְׁבַּן ט״ל, אֶלָּא יוֹ״ד ה״א וא״ו דְּסַלְּיקוּ אַתְוָון לְחֻשְׁבַּן
ט״ל, דְּאִיהוּ מַלְיָא לִשְׁכִינְתָּא מִנְּבִיעוּ דְּכָל מְקוֹרִין עִלָּאִין. מִיָּד
קָם רַעְיָא מְהֵימְנָא וַאֲבָהָן קַדִּישִׁין עִמֵּיהּ. עַד כָּאן רָזָא דְּיִחוּדָא.
בָּרוּךְ יְהוָה לְעוֹלָם אָמֵן וְאָמֵן.

in the form of *Adam Kadmon* or "primordial man."
The ten *Sephiros* are portrayed as aligning themselves
in the form of a human being and his limbs. The right
arm is associated with *Chesed* (Lovingkindness); the
left arm with *Gevurah* (Power); *Tiferes* (Beauty) with
the torso; *Netzach* (Victory) and *Hod* (Splendor) with
the two feet; and *Yesod* (Foundation) with circumcision which is the sign of the covenant. *Malchus* (Sovereignty) is here associated with the mouth and the
Oral Law. In addition there are three other *Sephiros*,
known as the "higher" *Sephiros*, associated with divine thought: *Chochmah* (Wisdom) is associated with
the brain or mind and *Binah* (Understanding) with
the heart which is the seat of reason. The highest of
the *Sephiros* is *Keser* (Crown) which the *Tikkunei
Zohar* describes as being associated with the spot on
the head upon which the phylactery is placed. It is
from the head of *Adam Kadmon* that "lights" shine
forth. These lights combine to form the names of God.
This depiction is, of course, symbolic in nature. The
souls of mankind are also described as rooted in the
Sephiros.

The concluding section of this selection describes
the exile of Israel and the exile of the *Shechinah* and
calls upon Moses and the Patriarchs to arise and to
arouse the *Shechinah*. The return of the *Shechinah*
will be accompanied by the redemption of Israel.

בראשית
א:יד-יט

וַיֹּאמֶר אֱלֹהִים יְהִי מְאֹרֹת בִּרְקִיעַ הַשָּׁמַיִם לְהַבְדִּיל בֵּין הַיּוֹם וּבֵין הַלָּיְלָה, וְהָיוּ לְאֹתֹת וּלְמוֹעֲדִים וּלְיָמִים וְשָׁנִים. וְהָיוּ לִמְאוֹרֹת בִּרְקִיעַ הַשָּׁמַיִם לְהָאִיר עַל־הָאָרֶץ, וַיְהִי־כֵן. וַיַּעַשׂ אֱלֹהִים אֶת־שְׁנֵי הַמְּאֹרֹת הַגְּדֹלִים, אֶת־הַמָּאוֹר הַגָּדֹל לְמֶמְשֶׁלֶת הַיּוֹם וְאֶת־הַמָּאוֹר הַקָּטֹן לְמֶמְשֶׁלֶת הַלַּיְלָה וְאֵת הַכּוֹכָבִים. וַיִּתֵּן אֹתָם אֱלֹהִים בִּרְקִיעַ הַשָּׁמָיִם, לְהָאִיר עַל־הָאָרֶץ. וְלִמְשֹׁל בַּיּוֹם וּבַלַּיְלָה וּלֲהַבְדִּיל בֵּין הָאוֹר וּבֵין הַחֹשֶׁךְ, וַיַּרְא אֱלֹהִים כִּי־טוֹב. וַיְהִי־עֶרֶב וַיְהִי־בֹקֶר יוֹם רְבִיעִי.

ירמיהו
לא:לד-לט

כֹּה אָמַר יהוה, נֹתֵן שֶׁמֶשׁ לְאוֹר יוֹמָם, חֻקֹּת יָרֵחַ וְכוֹכָבִים לְאוֹר לָיְלָה, רֹגַע הַיָּם וַיֶּהֱמוּ גַלָּיו, יהוה צְבָאוֹת שְׁמוֹ:

⋖§ Selections from Torah, Nevi'im and Kesuvim.

These selections speak of the creation of the celestial bodies as well as of the regularity and reliability of the sun and the moon in performing their assigned tasks.

⋖§ Torah (*Genesis 1:14-19*)

14. יְהִי מְאֹרֹת — *Let there be luminaries.*

The singular form יְהִי is employed rather than the plural יִהְיוּ. Although *Rashbam, Ibn Ezra* and *Radak* point out that such usage is not unusual, *Rabbeinu Bachya* ascribes use of the singular to the fact that only the sun actually gives forth its own light. The light of the moon is reflected light.

בִּרְקִיעַ הַשָּׁמַיִם — *In the firmament of the heavens.*

רָקִיעַ is the appellation of the level of the stratosphere in which the luminaries are placed. Other strata of the heavens are located above the firmament. Thus the phrase *in the firmament of the heavens* means the

firmament which is spread out beneath the heavens (*Rashbam*).

וְהָיוּ לְאֹתֹת — *And they shall serve as signs.*

The eclipse of the luminaries is an ill omen for the world. However, when man obeys the commandments of God he need have no fear thereof as stated in *Jeremiah 10:2*, *Be not dismayed at the signs of heaven* (*Rashi*). Other commentators understand "signs" as meaning navigational aids.

וּלְמוֹעֲדִים — *And for seasons.*

Rashi translates this word as "and for festivals," i.e., as constituting the basis of the calendrical system which determines the occurrence of the festivals.

Genesis
1:14-19

¹⁴ God said, "Let there be luminaries in the firmament of the heavens to separate between the day and the night; and they shall serve as signs, and for seasons, and for days and years; ¹⁵ and they shall serve as luminaries in the firmament of the heavens to shine upon the earth." And it was so. ¹⁶ And God made the two great luminaries, the greater luminary to dominate the day and the lesser luminary to dominate the night; and the stars. ¹⁷ And God set them in the firmament of the heaven to give light upon the earth, ¹⁸ to dominate by day and by night, and to separate between the light and the darkness. And God saw that it was good. ¹⁹ And there was evening and there was morning, a fourth day.

Jeremiah
31:34-39

³⁴ Thus said HASHEM, Who gives the sun as a light by day and the laws of the moon and the stars as a light by night; Who agitates the sea so that its waves roar; HASHEM, Master of Legions, is His Name:

---

16. שְׁנֵי הַמְּאֹרֹת הַגְּדֹלִים — *The two great luminaries.*

The moon was originally equal in size to the sun, but the moon complained to God, "Can two rulers reign together as equals?" The moon sought to be made superior to the sun, but was punished by being made inferior (*Chullin* 60b; *Rashi*).

18. וְלִמְשֹׁל — *To dominate.*

The dominion to which reference is made is not identical with the previously described illumination of the sun and the moon. The sun "rules" by day causing growth of vegetation; the "rule" of the moon by night causes tides to occur (*Ramban*).

וַיַּרְא אֱלֹהִים כִּי־טוֹב — *And God saw that it was good.*

Had the sun been made larger or been placed closer to earth, the intensity of its heat would have scorched the earth, making life impossible. Had the sun been made smaller or been placed at a greater distance from

earth, the earth would have been too cold to support life. Similarly, each of the stars and constellations is placed in a precise orbit; any deviation would have resulted in chaos and destruction (*Abarbanel*).

◈§ Nevi'im (Jeremiah 31:34-39).

34. רֹגַע הַיָּם — *Who agitates the sea.*

On behalf of the children of Israel when they departed from Egypt (*Radak*). According to *Rashi* this phrase means "who stirs up the sea."

וַיֶּהֱמוּ גַלָּיו — *So that its waves roar.*

Even though the waves roared, nevertheless they split and did not flow in their accustomed manner (*Radak*).

The immediately preceding verses speak of Israel's repentance and return to God. Just as God suspended the laws of nature in splitting the Sea of Reeds so will He transform the nature of man of whom it is said (*Genesis* 8:21): *"for the inclination of the heart of man is evil from his youth"* (*Radak*).

אִם־יָמֻשׁוּ הַחֻקִּים הָאֵלֶּה מִלְּפָנַי נְאֻם־יהוה גַּם, זֶרַע
יִשְׂרָאֵל יִשְׁבְּתוּ מִהְיוֹת גּוֹי לְפָנַי כָּל־הַיָּמִים. כֹּה אָמַר
יהוה, אִם־יִמַּדּוּ שָׁמַיִם מִלְמַעְלָה, וְיֵחָקְרוּ מוֹסְדֵי־אֶרֶץ
לְמַטָּה, גַּם־אֲנִי אֶמְאַס בְּכָל־זֶרַע יִשְׂרָאֵל, עַל־כָּל־אֲשֶׁר
עָשׂוּ נְאֻם־יהוה. הִנֵּה יָמִים בָּאִים נְאֻם־יהוה, וְנִבְנְתָה
הָעִיר לַיהוה, מִמִּגְדַּל חֲנַנְאֵל עַד־שַׁעַר הַפִּנָּה. וְיָצָא
עוֹד קָו הַמִּדָּה נֶגְדּוֹ, עַל גִּבְעַת גָּרֵב, וְנָסַב גֹּעָתָה. וְכָל־
הָעֵמֶק הַפְּגָרִים וְהַדֶּשֶׁן, וְכָל־הַשְּׁדֵמוֹת עַד־נַחַל קִדְרוֹן
עַד־פִּנַּת שַׁעַר הַסּוּסִים מִזְרָחָה, קֹדֶשׁ לַיהוה, לֹא־
יִנָּתֵשׁ וְלֹא־יֵהָרֵס עוֹד לְעוֹלָם.

---

35. אִם־יָמֻשׁוּ הַחֻקִּים הָאֵלֶּה ... גַּם זֶרַע
יִשְׂרָאֵל יִשְׁבְּתוּ מִהְיוֹת גּוֹי — *If these laws
could be removed ... so could the seed
of Israel cease from being a people.*

Israel will endure as a nation so
long as the fixed order of the sun, the
moon and the stars endures, i.e., forever (*Metzudas David*).

מִהְיוֹת גּוֹי לְפָנַי — *From being a people
before Me.*

I.e., from being a nation which
serves God (*Radak*). Just as the ordinances of heaven and earth are im-
mutable, so also shall Israel always
remain servants of God.

Maharal explains that these verses
underscore the immutability of the
election of Israel. The sun, the moon
and the stars are necessary for the
continued existence of the universe;
it is inconceivable that God will forsake Israel, His chosen nation. The
unique spiritual quality of the people
of Israel is no more subject to change
than is the nature of the heavenly
bodies. The world, as we know it,
could not exist without the sun and
the moon; similarly, the world, as we
conceive of it, could not exist without
Israel.

This is true when Israel is exiled,
downtrodden and oppressed no less
so than when Israel is an independent
people in its own land. Exile and oppression should not be mistaken as a
sign of rejection of Israel as a chosen
people. Just as God gives the moon
and the stars ability to illuminate the
night, so does God give Israel the
power to preserve its unique spiritual
quality even in the darkness of exile.
Maharal states that, while Israel is
compared to the sands surrounding
the sea, the sea itself represents the
nations of the world. The nations of
the world plot against Israel but God
thwarts their plans. It is God who
split the sea and its waves roared; it
is He who diffuses the power of the
"sea," i.e., of the nations of the world
(*Netzach Yisrael*, chap. 10).

36. אִם־יִמַּדּוּ שָׁמַיִם מִלְמַעְלָה — *If the
heavens above could be measured.*

If the height of the heavens could
be measured (*Rashi*).

מוֹסְדֵי אֶרֶץ לְמַטָּה — *The foundations of
the earth ... below.*

I.e., the depth of the foundations
(*Metzudas David*).

³⁵ *If these laws could be removed from before Me — the word of HASHEM — so could the seed of Israel cease from being a people before Me forever.* ³⁶ *Thus said HASHEM: If the heavens above could be measured or the foundations of the earth plumbed below, so too would I reject the entire seed of Israel because of everything they did — the word of HASHEM.* ³⁷ *Behold, days are coming — the word of HASHEM — when the City will be built up unto HASHEM, from the Tower of Hananel until the Corner Gate.* ³⁸ *The measuring line will once again be stretched out over Gareb Hill and around to Goah.* ³⁹ *And all the valley of the corpses and the place of the ashes and all the fields up to the brook Kidron until the corner of the Horses' Gate to the east will be holy unto HASHEM; it will not be abandoned nor destroyed again forever.*

---

37. וְנִבְנְתָה הָעִיר לַה' — *When the City will be built up unto HASHEM.*

This is a prophecy regarding the rebuilding of Jerusalem (*Radak*).

מִמִּגְדַּל חֲנַנְאֵל — *From the Tower of Chananel.*

This tower was located at the north of the wall of Jerusalem (*Radak;* cf. *Nehemiah* 3:1; *Nehemiah* 12:39; *Zechariah* 14:10).

שַׁעַר הַפִּנָה — *The Corner Gate.*

This gate was located at the southern wall of Jerusalem (*Radak;* cf. II *Kings* 14:13; II *Chronicles* 29:9).

38. גִּבְעַת גָּרֵב ... גֹּעָתָה — *Gareb Hill ... to Goah.*

The rebuilt city will be enlarged beyond its original boundaries and will encompass these areas which earlier were outside the city (*Metzudas David*).

39. וְכָל־הָעֵמֶק הַפְּגָרִים — *And all the valley of the corpses.*

The valley in which there lay the bodies of the camp of Sennacherib (*Rashi*). The Assyrian army under the leadership of Sennacherib besieged Jerusalem. Miraculously, 185,000 soldiers were killed in one night by an angel of God. (See II *Kings* 19:35 and *Isaiah* 37:36.)

וְהַדֶּשֶׁן — *And the place of the ashes.*

This is a reference to the place to which the ashes of the sacrifices were removed for disposal. This spot was outside the city limits of Jerusalem during the time of the Temple but will one day be encompassed within the expanded boundaries of the city (*Rashi*).

וְכָל הַשְּׁרֵמוֹת — *And all the fields.*

This translation is in accordance with *Metzudas David.* According to *Targum Yonason* and *Radak* the term refers to canals which irrigate the fields.

נַחַל קִדְרוֹן — *The brook Kidron.*

This brook is located in the east of Jerusalem near the Temple precincts, separating the city from the Mount of Olives. See II *Samuel* 15:23 and 15:30.

קֹדֶשׁ לַה' — *Holy unto HASHEM.*

This entire area will be endowed with the sanctity of Jerusalem (*Metzudas David*).

הוֹדוּ לַיהוה כִּי־טוֹב,
כִּי לְעוֹלָם חַסְדּוֹ.
הוֹדוּ לֵאלֹהֵי הָאֱלֹהִים,
כִּי לְעוֹלָם חַסְדּוֹ.
הוֹדוּ לַאֲדֹנֵי הָאֲדֹנִים,
כִּי לְעוֹלָם חַסְדּוֹ.
לְעֹשֵׂה נִפְלָאוֹת גְּדֹלוֹת לְבַדּוֹ,
כִּי לְעוֹלָם חַסְדּוֹ.
לְעֹשֵׂה הַשָּׁמַיִם בִּתְבוּנָה,
כִּי לְעוֹלָם חַסְדּוֹ.
לְרֹקַע הָאָרֶץ עַל־הַמָּיִם,
כִּי לְעוֹלָם חַסְדּוֹ.
לְעֹשֵׂה אוֹרִים גְּדֹלִים,
כִּי לְעוֹלָם חַסְדּוֹ.
אֶת־הַשֶּׁמֶשׁ לְמֶמְשֶׁלֶת בַּיּוֹם,
כִּי לְעוֹלָם חַסְדּוֹ.
אֶת־הַיָּרֵחַ וְכוֹכָבִים לְמֶמְשְׁלוֹת בַּלָּיְלָה, כִּי לְעוֹלָם חַסְדּוֹ.

⋹§ **Kesuvim** (*Psalms 136:1-9*).

1. כִּי לְעוֹלָם חַסְדּוֹ — *For His kindness endures forever.*

The ensuing verses refer to God's providence exercised both through natural processes and miraculous intervention. We thank God for His constant lovingkindness in all its guises (*Malbim*).

Metzudas David points out that, in contradistinction to human beneficence which is but transitory, God's lovingkindness is permanent, unchanging and endures for all of eternity.

This phrase serves as the refrain in each of the twenty-six verses of Psalm 136. Only the first nine verses which include references to the heavenly bodies are recited in the *Seder Bircas haChammah*. *Rashi* notes that the twenty-six refrains parallel the twenty-six generations of man which existed between creation and the giving of the Torah. In the absence of Torah and its merit the world (עוֹלָם) existed only by virtue of the lovingkindness of the Almighty (חַסְדּוֹ).

2. לֵאלֹהֵי הָאֱלֹהִים — *To the God of the heavenly powers.*

Literally, the God of gods, but since there is no other but He (*Deut.* 4:35),

such a translation is patently erroneous. Accordingly, *Ibn Ezra* translates the phrase as *the God of angels*.

The term אֱלֹהִים as an appellation of God connotes God as Ruler of the universe whose power is manifest in nature. The root meaning of the term אֱלֹהַּ is "force" or "power." See *Kuzari*, Fourth Treatise, section 1. Angels are divine messengers for implementation of God's will as manifest in the forces of nature. God, however, is Author of all forces of nature and source of all angelic powers. He is therefore described as the God of angels.

3. לַאֲדֹנֵי הָאֲדֹנִים — *To the Lord of the lords.*

I.e., the angels who are the "lords" of earth (*Ibn Ezra*).

4. לְעֹשֵׂה — *To Him Who ... performs.*

In the ensuing verses the present tense of the verb is used, rather than the past. This usage reflects the teaching that the universe is constantly being recreated by God (*Malbim*).

נִפְלָאוֹת גְּדֹלוֹת — *Great wonders.*

These include heaven, earth, sun and moon of which the following verses speak (*Rashi*).

לְבַדּוֹ — *Alone.*

The heaven, earth, sun and moon were created by God alone; they were

Give thanks to HASHEM for He is good,
for His kindness endures forever.

Give thanks to the God of the heavenly powers,
for His kindness endures forever.

Give thanks to the Lord of the lords,
for His kindness endures forever.

To Him Who alone performs great wonders,
for His kindness endures forever.

To Him Who makes the heavens with understanding,
for His kindness endures forever.

To Him Who spreads out the earth upon the waters,
for His kindness endures forever.

To Him Who makes great lights,
for His kindness endures forever;

the sun to rule by day,
for His kindness endures forever;

the moon and the stars to rule by night,
for His kindness endures forever.

---

created before the creation of angels (*Rashi*). All of these are the direct creation of God who created them without intermediary.

5. לַעֹשֵׂה הַשָּׁמַיִם בִּתְבוּנָה — *To Him Who makes the heavens with understanding.*

The term תְבוּנָה literally means "understanding" or "discernment" (see *Jeremiah* 10:12). Ostensibly, the reference here is to divine anticipation of the needs of man which led God to create the sun and the moon in order to sustain life. Perhaps the reference to תְבוּנָה in conjunction with the general term "heavens," rather than with the sun and the moon specifically, serves to teach that the celestial bodies set in the heavens had to be created with utmost precision and accuracy, else they would not long remain in their particular orbits but would collide and destroy one another. The term has the same root as the word בִּינָה

which connotes understanding in the sense of deductive inference (מֵבִין דָּבָר מִתּוֹךְ דָּבָר). The heavens and their hosts were created with full understanding of the effect each heavenly body would have upon all others. Only by virtue of that understanding could the heavens be created in a manner which would enable them to endure (cf. *Hirsch*).

5-9. These verses constitute a brief outline of the Creation and portray God to us as אֱלֹהֵי הָאֱלֹהִים (*Hirsch*).

8. אֶת־הַשֶּׁמֶשׁ לְמֶמְשֶׁלֶת בַּיּוֹם — *The sun to rule by day.*

Maharal comments that the sun is the guardian of the order of nature. The sun is described as "ruling" because the role of the sun is analogous to that of a king. The king watches over and preserves the social order; the sun preserves the natural order (*Tiferes Yisrael*, chap. 4).

[143] BIRCAS HACHAMMAH / *The Prayers*

לְשֵׁם יִחוּד קוּדְשָׁא בְּרִיךְ הוּא וּשְׁכִינְתֵּיהּ בִּדְחִילוּ
וּרְחִימוּ, וּרְחִימוּ וּדְחִילוּ, לְיַחֲדָא שֵׁם
י״ה בו״ה בְּיִחוּדָא שְׁלִים, בְּשֵׁם כָּל יִשְׂרָאֵל. הִנֵּה אֲנַחְנוּ
בָּאִים לְבָרֵךְ עַל־רְאִיַּת הַחַמָּה בִּתְקוּפָתָהּ כְּמוֹ שֶׁתִּקְּנוּ
לָנוּ חֲכָמֵינוּ זִכְרוֹנָם לִבְרָכָה, וּלְתַקֵּן אֶת־שָׁרְשָׁהּ
בִּמְקוֹם עֶלְיוֹן. וַאֲנַחְנוּ מְכַוְּנִים לְפָאֵר שִׁמְךָ מַלְכֵּנוּ,
שָׁאַתָּה הוּא רִבּוֹן כָּל־הַמַּעֲשִׂים אֲדוֹן כָּל־הָעוֹלָמִים,
עֶלְיוֹנִים וְתַחְתּוֹנִים וּצְבָא הַשָּׁמַיִם לְךָ מִשְׁתַּחֲוִים, נוֹטֶה
שָׁמַיִם וְיוֹסֵד אָרֶץ, אֲשֶׁר הֲכִינוֹתָ וּפָעַלְתָּ זָהֲרֵי חַמָּה.

🌼 לְשֵׁם יִחוּד — LeShem Yichud

The *LeShem Yichud*, which is kabbalistic in origin, is recited prior to the performance of a *mitzvah* and is designed to consecrate the act about to be performed to the service of God. According to R. Elijah de Vidas, *Reishis Chochmah, Sha'ar haAhavah,* chap. 9, the recitation of *LeShem Yichud* is predicated upon the following passage in the *Zohar:*

R. Eliezer said: All man's deeds should be carried out for the sake of the Holy Name. What does "for the sake of the Holy Name" mean? Man should mention the Holy Name with his mouth whenever he performs any act so that it is performed for His service and [then] the *sitra achara* (lit., "other side," meaning "demonic forces") will not rest upon it, because [the *sitra achara*] is always in attendance upon man and may rest upon that deed (*Zohar, Tazri'a* 51b).

Other authorities cite Psalms 45:2: רָחַשׁ לִבִּי דָּבָר טוֹב אֹמֵר אָנִי מַעֲשַׂי לְמֶלֶךְ which they understand as "My heart has acquired a good thing, I declare

'My works are on behalf of a King'" and interpret as an allusion to the need for verbal dedication of a virtuous act to the service of God. (See R. Baruch haLevi Epstein, *Baruch sheAmar* [Tel Aviv, 5730], p. 38.)

According to the Kabbalists, there is a direct causal relationship between man's physical acts and particular metaphysical effects. The actions of man, no matter how trivial and insignificant they may appear, can, at times, have profound cosmic significance. Performance of *mitzvos,* in particular, is of utmost importance in perfecting the world-order and in bringing about the ultimate redemption.

The Kabbalah teaches that beneficence and blessing emanate to man through the *Sephiros.* Channels for the flow of divine grace and mercy are opened when harmony exists among the *Sephiros.* Man, through good deeds and virtuous actions, contributes to the promotion of this harmony. Conversely, if man sins, he causes disharmony to occur among the *Sephiros* and thus impedes the flow of divine blessing through the

◆§ LeShem Yichud

[This *LeShem Yichud* meditation was composed and added by a latter-day Sephardic scholar, R. Chaim Binyamin Pontremoli. As noted in the commentary below, many authorities do not favor the recitation of the *LeShem Yichud*.]

For the sake of the unification of the Holy One, blessed is He, and His Presence, in fear and love, love and fear, to unify the Divine Name in perfect unity, in the name of all Israel.

Behold we come to pronounce the blessing when seeing the sun at its equinox as the Sages, of blessed memory, ordained for us; and to perfect its root on High. It is our intention to glorify Your Name, our King, for You are the Lord of all created things. Master of all the worlds, [both] higher and lower; and the hosts of the heavens bow before You, Who has spread out the heavens and founded the earth, Who has prepared and made the radiance of the sun.

---

channels of grace.

The harmony of the realm of the *Sephiros* depends ultimately upon the union of two *Sephiros*, viz., *Tiferes* (Beauty) and *Malchus* (Kingship or Sovereignty). *Tiferes* is depicted as the active principle and *Malchus* as the passive principle. In the *Zohar*, the term "the Holy One, blessed is He," is a cognomen for *Tiferes* and the term "*Shechinah*" is identified with *Malchus*. As a result of man's sins the *Shechinah* is in exile. This is understood as meaning that the *Shechinah* and the Holy One, blessed is He, i.e., the *Sephiros* of *Malchus* and *Tiferes*, are separated from one another. Restoration of the harmony of the *Sephiros* depends upon the mystical union of the active and passive principles, viz., of the Holy One blessed is He and the *Shechinah*.

Man aids in this ultimate unification by performing good deeds. Each such act causes the release of "sparks of holiness" which are embodied in *kelipos*, "shells" or "husks" of material substance into which they have fallen. It is the *Shechinah* which is in exile. The sparks of holiness arouse the love of the Holy One, blessed is He, causing an emanation towards the *Shechinah*. This leads to a mystical union between the *Shechinah* and the Holy One, blessed is He.

The Kabbalists taught that in order to achieve this effect each deed must be specifically dedicated to achieving this goal. Accordingly, they advised that this intention be expressed verbally before performing any *mitzvah*. The deed, to achieve the desired end, must be carried out "for the sake of the unification of the Holy One, blessed is He, and His *Shechinah*." This liturgical formula constitutes the essence of the *LeShem Yichud*. The *LeShem Yichud* often includes further references to the nature and function of the particular *mitzvah* about to be performed.

This *LeShem Yichud* makes specific reference to our intention to praise God as the Creator of the heavenly

וַאֲנַחְנוּ מְקַבְּלִים עָלֵינוּ וְעַל־זַרְעֵנוּ וְעַל־זֶרַע זַרְעֵנוּ עַד־
סוֹף כָּל־הַדּוֹרוֹת, אֲדנוּתָךְ וֶאֱלָהוּתָךְ יִתְבָּרַךְ שְׁמָךְ,
וְאַהֲבָתָךְ וְיִרְאָתָךְ וְיִחוּדָךְ, לַעֲשׂוֹת רְצוֹנָךְ כִּרְצוֹנֶךְ,
וּלְעָבְדָךְ בֶּאֱמֶת בְּלֵבָב שָׁלֵם. וְתַעֲלֶה לְפָנֶיךָ בְּרָכָה
זוּ כְּאִלּוּ כֻּוְּנוּ בְּכָל־הַכַּוָּנוֹת הָרְאוּיוֹת לְכַוֵּן. וְיַחֵד
לְבָבֵנוּ לְאַהֲבָה וּלְיִרְאָה אֶת־שְׁמֶךָ, לֵב טָהוֹר בְּרָא
לָנוּ אֱלֹהֵינוּ וְרוּחַ נָכוֹן חַדֵּשׁ בְּקִרְבֵּנוּ. וְשָׁמְרֵנוּ
וְתַצִּילֵנוּ מִכָּל־פְּגָעִים וּמִקְרִים רָעִים הַמִּתְחַדְּשִׁים
לָבוֹא בַּמַּחֲזוֹר זֶה בְּכָל־יוֹם וָיוֹם, וּבְכָל־שָׁעָה וְשָׁעָה,
וּבְכָל רֶגַע וָרֶגַע. וּבְצֵל כְּנָפֶיךָ תַּסְתִּירֵנוּ, כְּנֶשֶׁר
יָעִיר קִנּוֹ עַל־גּוֹזָלָיו יְרַחֵף. וּשְׁמוֹר צֵאתֵנוּ וּבוֹאֵנוּ
מֵעַתָּה וְעַד־עוֹלָם. וְגַם עַד־זִקְנָה וְשֵׂיבָה אֱלֹהִים אַל
תַּעַזְבֵנִי, עַד־אַגִּיד זְרוֹעֲךָ לְדוֹר לְכָל־יָבוֹא גְּבוּרָתֶךָ.

---

hosts and contains a prayer for the eradication of idolatry.

The author of *Pesach haDvir*, who composed this *LeShem Yichud*, writes that he incorporated those references in order to negate any possibility that *Bircas haChammah* might be construed as an act of sun worship. According to some interpretations, the possibility of such an erroneous assumption is ascribed to R. Judah, *Tosefta, Berachos* 6:11. See below, p. 174.

◆§ The Controversy

The need for, and indeed the propriety of, recitation of the *LeShem Yichud* is the subject of considerable controversy. The earliest recorded references to the need for specific kabbalistic *kavannah*, or intention, in the performance of a *mitzvah* are found in sixteenth-century writings. R. Chaim Vital, *Sha'ar haMitzvos*, p. 2, speaks of the need to have the specific intention of uniting the name of

the Holy One, blessed is He, and the *Shechinah* when performing a *mitzvah*, but provides no specific formula to be recited. The identical concept is presented, with additional elaboration, by R. Elijah de Vidas in his *Reishis Chochmah, Sha'ar haAhavah*, chap. 9. A specific text of the *LeShem Yichud* appears for the first time in a collection of kabbalistic prayers entitled *Sha'arei Zion*, which was compiled by R. Nathan of Hanover and published in Prague in the year 5422 [1662].

R. Ezekiel Landau vehemently opposed recitation of the *LeShem Yichud*. His views are recorded in a responsum included in his *Teshuvos Noda biYehudah, Mahadura Kamma, Yoreh De'ah*. no. 93. In this responsum, dated 5536 [1776], *Noda biYehudah* describes the recitation of the *LeShem Yichud* as an innovation popularized by its recent inclusion in various prayerbooks.

It is noteworthy that *Noda*

We accept Your sovereignty and Your divinity, may Your Name be blessed, upon ourselves and upon our children and children's children until the end of all generations, to love, fear, and unify You in order to perform Your will in accordance with Your will and to serve You in truth and with a perfect heart.

May this blessing ascend before You as if we had meditated upon all the intentions upon which it is proper to meditate. Unite our hearts to love and fear Your Name. Create for us a pure heart, O our God, and renew within us a steadfast spirit. Safeguard us and preserve us each day, every hour and every moment, from all afflictions and evil occurrences which may come upon us in the coming cycle. Shelter us in the shadow of Your wings "as an eagle that stirs up its nest hovering over its young" (Deut. 32:11). Watch over our going out and coming in from this time forth and for evermore. "And even unto old age and advanced years, O God, do not forsake me, until I have declared Your strength unto the next generation, Your might to everyone that is to come" (Psalms 71:18).

biYehudah does not at all challenge any of the kabbalistic premises upon which the *LeShem Yichud* is based. He does indeed chastise those of his generation who "have forsaken the spring of living waters, namely the two Talmuds, Babylonian and Palestinian, to hew for themselves broken cisterns" in concentration upon kabbalistic studies to the exclusion of Talmud study. But his objection to recitation of *LeShem Yichud* is, in a fundamental sense, predicated upon considerations which are themselves kabbalistic in nature.

In terms of strictly halachic considerations, *Noda biYehudah* views pronouncement of the *LeShem Yichud* to be entirely superfluous. A sacrifice must be offered upon the altar with a particular intention (*lishmah*). For example, a sin-offering must be offered with the intention that it constitute a sin-offering, not a burnt-offering

or a peace-offering. However, although the intention to sacrifice a sin-offering as a burnt-offering does indeed disqualify the sacrifice, there is no need for a verbal declaration, or even for an express mental intention, to sacrifice the sin-offering for its proper purpose, i.e., as a sin-offering. The halachic principle reflected in these regulations is that a contradictory intention serves to invalidate the sacrifice but, nevertheless, an act may be carried out without any specific intention (*setama*) because the sacrifice automatically serves the purpose for which it has been set aside.

Similarly, argues *Noda biYehudah*, a *mitzvah* automatically serves to achieve the purpose for which it has been ordained by God. In his talmudic commentary, *Tziun leNefesh Chayah (Tzlach)*, *Berachos* 28b, *Noda biYehudah* gives assurances that one will not be punished for failing to

וְעוֹרְרָה אֶת־גְּבוּרוֹתֶיךָ לְהַעֲבִיר גִּלּוּלִים מִן־הָאָרֶץ,
וְהָאֱלִילִים כָּרוֹת יִכָּרֵתוּן, לְתַקֵּן עוֹלָם בְּמַלְכוּת שַׁדַּי.
יֵבְשׁוּ כָּל־עוֹבְדֵי פֶסֶל הַמִּתְהַלְלִים בָּאֱלִילִים, וְהֵמָּה
מִשְׁתַּחֲוִים קֵדְמָה לַשֶּׁמֶשׁ. יֹאבְדוּ כָל־אוֹיְבֶיךָ יהוה,
וְאֹהֲבָיו כְּצֵאת הַשֶּׁמֶשׁ בִּגְבֻרָתוֹ. וְקַיֵּם לָנוּ יהוה אֱלֹהֵינוּ
מִקְרָא שֶׁכָּתוּב, כִּי־אָז אֶהְפֹּךְ אֶל־עַמִּים שָׂפָה בְרוּרָה,
לִקְרֹא כֻלָּם בְּשֵׁם יהוה, לְעָבְדוֹ שְׁכֶם אֶחָד וְהָיָה יהוה
לְמֶלֶךְ עַל־כָּל־הָאָרֶץ, בַּיּוֹם הַהוּא יִהְיֶה יהוה אֶחָד
וּשְׁמוֹ אֶחָד. יִהְיוּ לְרָצוֹן אִמְרֵי פִינוּ וְהֶגְיוֹן לִבֵּנוּ לְפָנֶיךָ,
יהוה צוּרֵנוּ וְגֹאֲלֵנוּ. לְךָ יוֹם אַף לְךָ לָיְלָה, אַתָּה הֲכִינוֹתָ
מָאוֹר וָשָׁמֶשׁ. כִּי שֶׁמֶשׁ וּמָגֵן יהוה אֱלֹהִים, חֵן וְכָבוֹד
יִתֵּן יהוה, לֹא יִמְנַע טוֹב לַהֹלְכִים בְּתָמִים.

תהלים
פד:יב
כִּי שֶׁמֶשׁ וּמָגֵן יהוה אֱלֹהִים, חֵן וְכָבוֹד יִתֵּן יהוה
לֹא יִמְנַע־טוֹב לַהֹלְכִים בְּתָמִים.

---

pray in accordance with kabbalistic mysteries: "On the contrary, you will be rewarded for separating yourself from these matters and as a result you will inherit eternal life."

According to *Noda biYehudah*, recitation of *LeShem Yichud* is not only superfluous, but fraught with spiritual danger as well. He notes that the Sages advised that it is preferable that no declaration of intention be made prior to the offering of a sacrifice. This practice serves to prevent any confusion which might lead to an error invalidating the sacrifice. *A fortiori*, argues *Noda biYehudah*, it is preferable not to concentrate upon kabbalistic intentions while performing a *mitzvah* since there is the ever-present danger that a person conducting himself in this manner may entertain incorrect intentions. This would have the effect of "cutting the plantings" (*kitzutz banetiyos*).

In kabbalistic writings, "cutting the plantings" is the archetype of all great transgressions; it entails disruption of harmony among the *Sephiros* and introduction of division into divine unity.

A defense of retention of the *LeShem Yichud* meditation was advanced by R. Chaim ben Solomon in his *Sha'ar haTefillah* (Sudilkov, 5573), pp. 3-10. Earlier, R. Chaim Yosef David Azulai (*Chida*) in his *Simchas haRegel*, a commentary on *Megillas Ruth* (Leghorn, 5542) p. 5a, advised that the comments of *Noda biYehudah* should be ignored. *Chida* emphasizes the need for specific intention on the part of those who study the mysteries of the Kabbalah "in holiness and humility" and argues that *Noda biYehudah*'s remarks are not directed against such persons.

In practice, *chassidim* customarily recite the *LeShem Yichud* while

Arouse Your might to remove idols from the earth and may false gods be totally eradicated and the world be perfected through the reign of the Almighty. May idol-worshippers who glory in false gods and who bow toward the east to the sun be put to shame. "May all Your enemies perish, O HASHEM; but they that love Him be as the sun when it goes forth in its might" (Judges 5:31).

Fulfill for us, HASHEM, our God, the verse that is written: For then will I turn to the peoples a clear language that they may all call upon the Name of HASHEM to serve Him with one mind (Zephaniah 3:9). HASHEM shall be King over all the earth; on that day HASHEM shall be One and His Name One (Zechariah 14:9).

May the words of our mouth and the meditations of our heart be acceptable before You, HASHEM, our Rock and our Redeemer. "Yours is the day, Yours also is the night; You have established luminary and sun" (Psalms 74:16). "For HASHEM God is a sun and shield; HASHEM bestows favor and honor, He does not withhold good from those who walk in perfection" (Psalms 84:12).

Psalms 84:12 **F**or *HASHEM God is a sun and shield; HASHEM bestows favor and honor, He does not withhold good from those who walk in perfection.*

---

misnagdim generally follow the advice of the *Noda biYehudah.*

◄§ כִּי שֶׁמֶשׁ — Ki Shemesh

כִּי שֶׁמֶשׁ וּמָגֵן ה' אֱלֹהִים — *For a sun and a shield is HASHEM God.*

God has always been as a sun and as a shield to us, therefore we are confident that He will yet bestow favor and honor upon us (*Metzudas David*).

Ibn Ezra understands the verse as referring to those who journey to the Temple in Jerusalem. They require sunlight for their travels but must also be shielded from excessive heat. God will also grant them favor and honor in every place through which they pass, since they undertake the arduous journey with sincerity of purpose.

Ibn Ezra, in his introduction to *Koheles*, describes the paradoxical powers of the sun which "blackens the laundryman even while it bleaches the laundry." In the days of the Messiah the sun will burn brightly and destroy the wicked, while for the righteous it will remain a source of warmth. God is described as both a sun and a shield; he causes the sun to shine brightly, but He shields the righteous from its full force (*Malbim*).

[For an intriguing explanation of this verse as a simile describing God's immanence in nature, see *Tanya, Sha'ar haYichud vehaEmunah*, chap. 4.]

עב:ה **יִירָאֽוּךָ** עִם־שָֽׁמֶשׁ, וְלִפְנֵי יָרֵֽחַ, דּוֹר דּוֹרִים.

עה:ב **הוֹדִֽינוּ** לְּךָ אֱלֹהִים, הוֹדִֽינוּ וְקָרוֹב שְׁמֶֽךָ, סִפְּרוּ נִפְלְאוֹתֶֽיךָ.

מלאכי ג:כ **וְזָרְחָה** לָכֶם יִרְאֵי שְׁמִי שֶֽׁמֶשׁ צְדָקָה, וּמַרְפֵּא בִּכְנָפֶֽיהָ, וִיצָאתֶם וּפִשְׁתֶּם כְּעֶגְלֵי מַרְבֵּק.

תהלים צז:ו **הִגִּֽידוּ** הַשָּׁמַֽיִם צִדְקוֹ, וְרָאוּ כָל־הָעַמִּים כְּבוֹדוֹ.

תהלים קמח א־ז **הַלְלוּיָהּ**, הַלְלוּ אֶת־יהוה מִן־הַשָּׁמַֽיִם, הַלְלֽוּהוּ בַּמְּרוֹמִים. הַלְלֽוּהוּ כָל־מַלְאָכָיו, הַלְלֽוּהוּ כָּל־צְבָאָו. הַלְלֽוּהוּ שֶֽׁמֶשׁ וְיָרֵֽחַ, הַלְלֽוּהוּ כָּל־כּֽוֹכְבֵי אוֹר. הַלְלֽוּהוּ שְׁמֵי הַשָּׁמָֽיִם, וְהַמַּֽיִם

◆§ יִירָאֽוּךָ — Yiraucha

The initial letters of each of the following four verses combine to form an acrostic spelling the Divine Name.

יִירָאֽוּךָ — *They will fear You.*

King Solomon, the author of this psalm, prays that Israel learn to be God-fearing (*Rashi*).

עִם שֶֽׁמֶשׁ וְלִפְנֵי יָרֵֽחַ — *As long as the sun and moon endure.*

At the time of the shining of the sun and in the presence of the moon's illumination, i.e., at all times (*Metzudas David*); or, so long as the sun and the moon continue to exist, i.e., forever (*Rashi*).

דּוֹר דּוֹרִים — *Generation after generation.*

May each generation teach the next to be God-fearing (*Metzudas David*).

The verse admonishes man to serve God constantly and without deviation just as the sun and the moon continuously and unfailingly fulfill the Divine will (*Malbim*).

הוֹדִֽינוּ ... הוֹדִֽינוּ — *We have aknowledged ... we have aknowledged.*

The double expression is employed to indicate that man must give thanks for misfortune as well as for good (*Rashi*).

וְקָרוֹב שְׁמֶֽךָ — *And Your Name is near.*

Your Name is constantly in our mouths, i.e., we praise God unceasingly, regardless of the vicissitudes of fortune (*Rashi*). Your Name is constantly in our mouths as we pray for deliverance and salvation (*Metzudas David*).

סִפְּרוּ נִפְלְאוֹתֶֽיךָ — *They recounted Your wondrous deeds.*

The verse does not state explicitly who recounts God's praises. *Rashi* understands the words וְקָרוֹב שְׁמֶֽךָ and סִפְּרוּ נִפְלְאוֹתֶֽיךָ as forming one clause which expresses a single concept: Your Name is close to us. We, in our day, constantly praise You just as previous generations always recounted Your wonders. *Ibn Ezra* maintains that it is the prophets who

Pslams
72:5
They will fear You as long as the sun and moon endure, generation after generation.

Psalms
75:2
We have acknowledged You, O God, we have acknowledged, and Your Name is near; they recounted Your wondrous deeds.

Malachi
3:20
But a sun of righteousness will shine for you who fear My Name, with healing in its wings, and you will go out and flourish like calves [fattened] in the stall.

Psalms
97:6
The heavens declare His righteousness, and all the peoples saw His glory.

Psalms
148:1-6
Halleluyah! Praise HASHEM from the heavens; praise Him in the heights. ²Praise Him, all His angels; praise Him, all His legions. ³Praise Him, sun and moon; praise Him, all bright stars. ⁴Praise Him, the most exalted of the heavens and the waters

have recounted God's wondrous acts (סִפְּרוּ נִפְלְאוֹתֶיךָ), thereby teaching us that God is always near to us, ready to respond to our needs (וְקָרוֹב שְׁמֶךָ).

שֶׁמֶשׁ צְדָקָה — *But a sun of righteousness.*

The word צְדָקָה may be understood as meaning "charity." The verse then means that the deeds of charity performed by those who fear God's name afford them great merit, "shining" on their behalf as does the sun (*Metzudas David*).

וּמַרְפֵּא בִּכְנָפֶיהָ — *With healing in its wings.*

The sun casts its rays over the earth in a manner similar to the way a bird spreads its wings. Those who fear God will not be harmed by the sun (*Ibn Ezra*).

The sun's rays will be protective rather than destructive. This verse is no doubt included in the order of *Bircas haChammah* as a reminder that in the days of the Messiah the sun will destroy the wicked, but serve as a source of healing for the righteous.

וִיצָאתֶם וּפִשְׁתֶּם כְּעֶגְלֵי מַרְבֵּק — *And you will go out and flourish like calves [flattened] in the stall.*

Wherever you go you shall experience pleasure and plenty just as calves delight in being fattened in their stables (*Metzudas David*).

הַשָּׁמַיִם — *The heavens.*

Those who dwell in the heavens (*Ibn Ezra*). God's omnipotence is readily apparent to all, but only the angels, whose knowledge of the divine purpose is far superior to ours, can properly proclaim God's righteousness. Thus, those who dwell in *the heavens* recount God's righteousness, while *all the nations* can perceive only His honor.

◆§ הַלְלוּיָהּ — **Psalms 148:1-6**

2. כָּל-צְבָאָיו — *All His legions.*

The spheres and the constellations of the zodiac all praise God (*Metzudas David*).

3. כּוֹכְבֵי אוֹר — *All bright stars.*

Rashi interprets this as meaning the stars of the night; *Metzudas*

אֲשֶׁר מֵעַל הַשָּׁמָיִם. יְהַלְלוּ אֶת־שֵׁם יהוה, כִּי הוּא
צִוָּה וְנִבְרָאוּ. וַיַּעֲמִידֵם לָעַד לְעוֹלָם, חָק־נָתַן וְלֹא
יַעֲבוֹר.

⚜ נוסח הברכה

בָּרוּךְ אַתָּה יהוה אֱלֹהֵינוּ מֶלֶךְ הָעוֹלָם,
עוֹשֶׂה מַעֲשֵׂה בְרֵאשִׁית.

David understands the phrase as a reference to the planets.

5. כִּי הוּא צִוָּה וְנִבְרָאוּ — *For He commanded and they were created.*

These verses are recited in conjunction with both *Bircas haChammah* and *Kiddush Levanah* to emphasize our negation of pagan belief in, and worship of, the sun and the moon. The passage serves as a clear proclamation acknowledging that it is God alone who created the sun and the moon and established them as luminaries in the heavens. The heavenly bodies are the products of divine creation, subject to God's will, and not independent powers.

6. חָק נָתַן וְלֹא יַעֲבוֹר — *He issued a decree that will not change.*

Literally, חָק נָתַן means "He gave a law." Each of the celestial bodies is bound to serve at a certain time; they cannot violate these laws which are inherent in their nature (*Rashi* and *Radak*).

⚜ נוֹסַח הַבְּרָכָה — The Blessing

בָּרוּךְ ... עוֹשֶׂה מַעֲשֵׂה בְרֵאשִׁית — *Blessed are ... who makes the work of creation.*

The proper formula of the blessing to be pronounced on the occasion of *Bircas haChammah* is the subject of some dispute. The accepted version, as recorded by all latter-day

authorities, is "who makes the work of creation." Nevertheless, some confusion has arisen because the blessing pronounced upon witnessing extraordinary phenomena, as recorded in the Mishnah, *Berachos* 54a, in the *Yerushalmi, Berachos* 9:2, and in the *Tosefta, Berachos* 6:1 as well as in the *Beraisa* cited in *Berachos* 59b, which speaks of *Bircas haChammah* specifically, is עוֹשֶׂה בְרֵאשִׁית "who makes creation." However, in our texts of the Gemara, *Berachos* 59a, the reading עוֹשֶׂה מַעֲשֵׂה בְרֵאשִׁית "who makes the work of creation" occurs in the discussion of the blessing as it is cited in the context of the blessing pronounced upon sighting wondrous natural phenomena.

Many early authorities, including *Rif, Rambam* and *Shulchan Aruch*, record the blessing as בָּרוּךְ עוֹשֶׂה בְרֵאשִׁית. Other authorities, including *Rosh, Tur, Levush, Eliyahu Rabbah, Pri Megadim, Panim Me'iros* and *Chasam Sofer* as well as numerous later authorities record the blessing as עוֹשֶׂה מַעֲשֵׂה בְרֵאשִׁית. It may be assumed that the definitive version of the blessing is עוֹשֶׂה מַעֲשֵׂה בְרֵאשִׁית, as indicated by the Gemara, *Berachos* 59a. If so, the *Beraisa* contains an elliptical version omitting the word "מַעֲשֵׂה" and relies upon the reader's or student's general familiarity with the blessing. This abridged version

that are above the heavens. ⁵Let them praise the Name of HASHEM, for He commanded and they were created. ⁶And He established them forever and ever, He issued a decree that will not change.

◄§ The Blessing

Blessed are You, HASHEM our God, King of the universe, who makes the work of creation.

---

was copied by the early authorities cited above, who, in so copying, did not intend to delete the word "מַעֲשֵׂה" but cited the shortened version on the assumption that the student would be familiar with the full text. Indeed, R. Joseph Karo, who omits the word "מַעֲשֵׂה" in the *Shulchan Aruch*, incorporates the phrase "מַעֲשֵׂה בְרֵאשִׁית" in his commentary on the *Rambam*, *Kesef Mishneh*, *Hilchos Berachos* 10:18, without even noting that *Rambam* omits the word "מַעֲשֵׂה". It may be assumed that he found nothing remarkable in *Rambam's* omission, and assumed that *Rambam* was in agreement that the complete text is "עוֹשֶׂה מַעֲשֵׂה בְרֵאשִׁית". In a like manner, R. Joseph Karo himself utilized the shortened version in the *Shulchan Aruch*, relying upon the reader's familiarity with the text. Elsewhere in *Shulchan Aruch, Orach Chaim* 227 and 228, the full text is recorded.

One commentary on the Mishnah, *Meleches Shlomo, Berachos* 9:2, does, however, declare that the proper text is the shorter version, עוֹשֶׂה בְרֵאשִׁית. He regards the accepted version, עוֹשֶׂה מַעֲשֵׂה בְרֵאשִׁית as erroneous. This opinion is followed by the anonymous author of the introductory note to the *Seder Bircas haChammah* published by Eliyahu Volk (Warsaw 5657), but is rejected by all subsequent scholars. Another authority, Rabbi Meir

David Hertzberg, *Or haChammah, Me'orei Or*, p. 19a, suggests that none of the earlier authorities makes a point of establishing either of the two versions as the correct one because the two versions were used interchangeably and accepted by all authorities as being of equal validity. However, following *Eshel Avraham* (*Rav of Buczacz*) 229:2, he prefers the lengthier version עוֹשֶׂה מַעֲשֵׂה בְרֵאשִׁית. R. Shlomo haKohen of Vilna, *Atzei Beroshim*, no. 60, suggests that, in order to satisfy all opinions, it is proper to recite בָּרוּךְ אַתָּה ה' ... עוֹשֶׂה בְרֵאשִׁית, and then immediately to add the "corrected" formula עֹשֶׂה מַעֲשֵׂה בְרֵאשִׁית.

The formula בָּרוּךְ עוֹשֶׂה בְרֵאשִׁית does appear in the *Baruch sheAmar* prayer contained in the morning service. It is explained that the *Baruch sheAmar* prayer omits the word מַעֲשֵׂה because, for kabbalistic reasons, as stated by *Tur* in the name of *Sefer Hecholos*, it is designed to contain precisely 87 words. It may, however, be noted that some texts, e.g., *Machzor Vitri*, have the reading בָּרוּךְ עוֹשֶׂה מַעֲשֵׂה בְרֵאשִׁית in the *Baruch sheAmar* prayer as well.

There is indeed little substantive difference between these variant formulae. The term "who makes creation" is identical in meaning with "who makes the work of creation."

אָנָּא בְּכֹחַ גְּדֻלַּת יְמִינְךָ תַּתִּיר צְרוּרָה. קַבֵּל רִנַּת
עַמְּךָ שַׂגְּבֵנוּ טַהֲרֵנוּ נוֹרָא. נָא גִבּוֹר דּוֹרְשֵׁי
יִחוּדְךָ כְּבָבַת שָׁמְרֵם. בָּרְכֵם טַהֲרֵם רַחֲמֵם צִדְקָתְךָ
תָּמִיד גָּמְלֵם. חֲסִין קָדוֹשׁ בְּרוֹב טוּבְךָ נַהֵל עֲדָתֶךָ.
יָחִיד גֵּאֶה לְעַמְּךָ פְּנֵה זוֹכְרֵי קְדֻשָּׁתֶךָ. שַׁוְעָתֵנוּ קַבֵּל
וּשְׁמַע צַעֲקָתֵנוּ יוֹדֵעַ תַּעֲלוּמוֹת. בָּרוּךְ שֵׁם כְּבוֹד
מַלְכוּתוֹ לְעוֹלָם וָעֶד.

The *Baruch sheAmar* prayer could contain either without its meaning being altered. However, when recited upon witnessing wondrous phenomena such as lofty mountains, or upon seeing lightning, etc., the blessing is more specific in nature. On such occasions, the blessing acknowledges God's creation of the universe, but, more specifically, praises Him for particular phenomena of creation. Accordingly, the phrase the "work of creation," of which each phenomenon occasioning the blessing is an example, is more appropriate. On the other hand, בָּרוּךְ עוֹשֶׂה בְרֵאשִׁית appears more appropriate in the context of the *Baruch sheAmar* prayer. *Baruch sheAmar* is an entirely different form of blessing in the nature of a more general praise of God as Creator of the universe.

The blessing upon the occasion of *Bircas haChammah* could have been ordained as עוֹשֶׂה מַעֲשֵׂה בְרֵאשִׁית in praise of God upon the specific phenomenon of the sun's return to its original position or, since that is hardly an event of which man would spontaneously be aware, the blessing which was ordained might well be the more general form of praise for all creation עוֹשֶׂה בְרֵאשִׁית. However, it should be remembered that *Bircas haChammah* is one of a series of phenomena which occasion a blessing of this nature. Accordingly, it is probable

that a single blessing was ordained for all such events. Cf. R. Shlomo Segner, *Or haChammah*, p. 11a.

s§ אָנָּא בְּכֹחַ — **Ana beKoach.**

This prayer, which is kabbalistic in origin, contains 42 words symbolizing the Divine Name of 42 letters to which reference is made in *Kiddushin* 71a. The prayer is found in the *Tikkunei Zohar*, *tikkun* 21, and attributed by some to the *Tanna*, R. Nechuniah ben Hakanah.

The initial letters of the words of this prayer, it is asserted, form an acrostic containing the 42-letter Divine Name. אָנָּא בְּכֹחַ is included in the *Seder Bircas haChammah* by virtue of the fact that the *Zohar* states that this Name appears in the firmament preceding the sun as it shines in the morning. (See R. Chaim Knoller, *Bircas haChammah*, p. 15.)

בְּכֹחַ גְּדֻלַּת יְמִינְךָ — *With the strenght of Your right hand's greatness.*

This phrase is based upon *Exodus* 15:6: יְמִינְךָ ה' נֶאְדָּרִי בַּכֹּחַ — *Your right hand, O HASHEM, glorious in power.*

צְרוּרָה — *The bound.*

This is the accepted reading and is a prayer for release from the bondage of exile. However, *Iyun Tefillah* suggests that the proper reading should be צְרוֹרָה. If so, the term means "bundle" and refers to a bundle of iniquities as in חָתוּם בִּצְרוֹר פִּשְׁעִי, *My transgression is sealed up in a bundle (Job*

*W*e beg You! With the strength of Your right hand's greatness, untie the bound. Accept the prayer of Your people; strengthen us, purify us, O Awesome One. Please, O Strong One — those who foster Your Oneness, guard them like the pupil of an eye. Bless them, purify them, show them pity, may Your righteousness always recompense them. Powerful Holy One, with Your abundant goodness guide Your congregation. One and only Exalted One, turn to Your people, which proclaims Your holiness. Accept our entreaty and hear our cry, O Knower of mysteries. Blessed is the Name of His glorious Kingdom for all eternity.

14:17). The prayer is then a supplication for forgiveness of sins so that the sins not intervene and prevent acceptance of prayer.

נָא — *Please.*

A shortened form of אָנָּא.

דּוֹרְשֵׁי יִחוּדְךָ — *Those who foster Your Oneness.*

The term דּוֹרְשֵׁי also has the connotation "those who seek" or "those who search" and may be an allusion to the kabbalistic concern for unification of the Holy One, blessed is He, and the *Shechinah* (*Etz Yosef*).

כְּבָבַת שָׁמְרֵם — *Guard them like the pupil of an eye.*

Similar to בְּבָבַת עֵינוֹ, *in the apple of his eye* (*Zechariah* 2:12). The *Targum* renders the word בָּבַת as "eyeball." *Iyun Tefillah* suggests that the word means the "iris" of the eye and is related to the word בּוֹאָה meaning "shadow." The iris is called a "shadow" because a person can see his reflection in the iris of another person's eye. A similar phrase שָׁמְרֵנִי כְּאִישׁוֹן בַּת עָיִן, *Guard me as the apple of the eye,* occurs in *Psalms* 17:8.

רַחֲמֵם — *Show them pity.*

Etz Yosef records an alternative reading: רַחֲמֵי צִדְקָתְךָ תָּמִיד גָּמְלֵם, *the mercy of Your righteousness always bestow upon them.* This reading is found in the text of the *Siddur*

Amudei Shamayim compiled by R. Yaakov Emden.

תָּמִיד — *Always.*

Iyun Tefillah suggests that the proper reading is תָּמִים — *O perfect One.* This would conform to the form of the other lines of the prayer, each of which includes an attribute of praise to the Almighty.

חָסִין — *Powerful One.*

As in מִי כָמוֹךָ חֲסִין יָהּ — *Who is mighty like unto You, O God?* (*Psalms* 89:9).

לְעַמְּךָ פְּנֵה — *Turn to Your people.*

As promised in *Leviticus* 26:9, וּפָנִיתִי אֲלֵיכֶם — *And I will turn toward you.* God assures Israel that He will turn to them in blessing.

יוֹדֵעַ תַּעֲלֻמוֹת — *O Knower of mysteries.*

In *Psalms* 44:22 the Almighty is depicted as knowing man's innermost intentions, כִּי הוּא יֹדֵעַ תַּעֲלֻמוֹת לֵב, *For He knows the secrets of the heart.*

בָּרוּךְ שֵׁם — *Blessed is the Name.*

The Mishnah, *Yoma* 66a, records that when the High Priest pronounced the *shem hameforash,* the ineffable Name, on *Yom Kippur,* those assembled in the Temple precincts prostrated themselves and responded בָּרוּךְ שֵׁם כְּבוֹד מַלְכוּתוֹ לְעוֹלָם וָעֶד, *Blessed is the Name of His glorious kingdom for ever and ever.* This

לַמְנַצֵּחַ בִּנְגִינֹת מִזְמוֹר שִׁיר. אֱלֹהִים יְחָנֵּנוּ וִיבָרְכֵנוּ, יָאֵר פָּנָיו אִתָּנוּ סֶלָה. לָדַעַת בָּאָרֶץ דַּרְכֶּךָ, בְּכָל-גּוֹיִם יְשׁוּעָתֶךָ. יוֹדוּךָ עַמִּים, אֱלֹהִים, יוֹדוּךָ עַמִּים כֻּלָּם. יִשְׂמְחוּ וִירַנְּנוּ לְאֻמִּים, כִּי-תִשְׁפֹּט עַמִּים מִישׁוֹר, וּלְאֻמִּים בָּאָרֶץ תַּנְחֵם סֶלָה. יוֹדוּךָ עַמִּים, אֱלֹהִים, יוֹדוּךָ עַמִּים כֻּלָּם. אֶרֶץ נָתְנָה יְבוּלָהּ, יְבָרְכֵנוּ אֱלֹהִים אֱלֹהֵינוּ. יְבָרְכֵנוּ אֱלֹהִים, וְיִירְאוּ אֹתוֹ כָּל-אַפְסֵי-אָרֶץ.

---

declaration is uttered at the conclusion of אָנָּא בְּכֹחַ because the prayer, containing 42 words, symbolizes the Divine Name of 42 letters. Hence the recitation of אָנָּא בְּכֹחַ is, as it were, tantamount to pronouncing the Divine Name, which occasions the response בָּרוּךְ שֵׁם כְּבוֹד מַלְכוּתוֹ לְעוֹלָם וָעֶד.

⧼ לַמְנַצֵּחַ בִּנְגִינֹת — Psalm 67 ⧽

This psalm is universal in its message, summoning all peoples to acknowledge God. *Radak* considers the psalm to be a prophecy regarding the Redemption. At the time of the Redemption God's graciousness toward Israel will lead the nations of the world to worship Him.

1. לַמְנַצֵּחַ — *For the conductor.*
According to *Ibn Ezra* and *Radak* the psalms prefaced by this superscription were sung by the Levites in the Temple under the direction of the conductor. King David composed these psalms *for the conductor*, i.e., to be transmitted to the Levite who served as conductor, for use in conjunction with the Temple service.
Rashi also explains that these psalms were sung by the Levites in the Temple but understands the term as being derived from נִצָּחוֹן meaning triumph. Each Levite is a מְנַצֵּחַ, "a triumphant one" because each Levite triumphs over himself in striving to perform the divine service in the most exemplary manner possible.

בִּנְגִינֹת — *With instrumental music.*
The precise nature of the נְגִינֹת is obscure. The commentators agree that the reference is to musical instruments. *Radak* understands the word as describing a specific, but to us unknown, instrument used in the Temple. *Malbim*, in his introduction to the Book of Psalms, declares that it is impossible for us to know with precision the nature of the musical instruments described in various psalms and decries any effort to identify them as a futile attempt to build מִגְדָּלִים הַפּוֹרְחִים בָּאֲוִיר עַל כַּנְפֵי רוּחַ — "castles in the sky."

2. אֱלֹהִים יְחָנֵּנוּ — *May God favor us.*
Redeem us on account of Your חֵן, i.e., as an act of grace, even though we are undeserving (*Sforno*).

אֱלֹהִים יְחָנֵּנוּ וִיבָרְכֵנוּ יָאֵר פָּנָיו אִתָּנוּ — *May God favor us and bless us, may He illuminate His countenance with us.*
These phrases parallel the wording of the priestly blessing (*Numbers* 6:24-25), יְבָרֶכְךָ ה' — *May* HASHEM *bless you,* ... יָאֵר ה' פָּנָיו אֵלֶיךָ — *May* HASHEM *shine His face toward you,* וִיחֻנֶּךָ — *and show you favor* (*Rashbam*).

סֶלָה — *Selah.*
The word סֶלָה occurs repeatedly in the Book of Psalms but, with the exception of three instances in *Habakkuk*, is not found elsewhere

Psalms 67

¹ For the conductor with instrumental music, a psalm, a song. ² May God favor us and bless us, may He illuminate His countenance with us, Selah. ³ To make known Your way on earth, among all nations Your salvation. ⁴ The peoples will acknowledge You, O God; the peoples will acknowledge You — all of them. ⁵ Let the nations be glad and sing for joy, because You will judge the peoples fairly and guide the nations upon the earth, Selah. ⁶ The peoples will acknowledge You, O God; the peoples will acknowledge You — all of them. ⁷ The earth will then have yielded its produce; may God, our God, bless us. ⁸ May God bless us, and may all the ends of the earth fear Him.

---

in Scripture. *Targum* translates the word as meaning "forever." This translation is supported by *Eruvin* 54a which states, "Wherever the words נֶצַח, סֶלָה, וָעֶד are used, they mean 'forever, without an end' סֶלָה ... as it says עַד עוֹלָם סֶלָה — 'forever, Selah' (Psalms 48:9)." *Ibn Ezra* understands סֶלָה as a reaffirmation of the preceding statement, i.e., all of the preceding is true and certain. *Radak* explains סֶלָה as a form of choral instruction, indicating that the voice is to be raised. According to *Radak* the term סֶלָה is derived from סוּל, "to raise," as in the verse סֹלּוּ סֹלּוּ הַמְסִלָה, *Build up, build up the road* (Isaiah 62:10). The members of the choir are instructed to raise their voices.

3. לָדַעַת בָּאָרֶץ דַּרְכֶּךָ — *To make known Your way on earth.*

So that the entire world may know that You reward those who believe in You. God's graciousness toward Israel will lead the nations of the world to serve Him (*Ibn Ezra*).

5. יִשְׂמְחוּ וִירַנְּנוּ לְאֻמִים כִּי תִשְׁפֹּט עַמִּים מִישֹׁר — *Let the nations be glad and sing for joy, because You will judge the peoples fairly.*

You will judge Gog and Magog with equity; this will cause the other nations to rejoice (*Radak*).

וּלְאֻמִים בָּאָרֶץ תַּנְחֵם — *And guide the*

nations upon the earth.

You will guide those nations who rejoice in Your justice (*Metzudas David*).

6. יוֹדוּךָ עַמִּים — *The peoples will acknowledge You.*

The repetition of this phrase which occurs in verse 4 signifies, "Let the peoples thank You for this *as well*," i.e., because You judge and compensate each nation in accordance with its deeds (*Ibn Ezra*).

7. אֶרֶץ נָתְנָה יְבוּלָהּ — *The earth will then have yielded its produce.*

That the earth has yielded its produce is also a cause to praise God (*Rashi* and *Ibn Ezra*). According to *Metzudas David* verses 6 and 7 must be understood as meaning that when "the nations will give thanks to God, *then* shall the earth give its produce."

8. יְבָרְכֵנוּ אֱלֹהִים וְיִירְאוּ אוֹתוֹ כָּל אַפְסֵי אָרֶץ — *May God bless us, and may all the ends of the earth fear Him.*

In the blessing which God bestows upon us even those nations who dwell in the ends of the earth and who have not heard of the greatness of God will recognize His Providence and they will fear Him (*Ibn Ezra*).

אַפְסֵי אָרֶץ — *The ends of the earth.*

Ibn Ezra, in his commentary on

[בְּרוֹב קְהִלּוֹת אֵין אוֹמְרִים]

הַלְלוּיָהּ, הַלְלוּ־אֵל בְּקָדְשׁוֹ, הַלְלוּהוּ בִּרְקִיעַ עֻזּוֹ. הַלְלוּהוּ תהלים קנ
בִּגְבוּרֹתָיו הַלְלוּהוּ כְּרֹב גֻּדְלוֹ. הַלְלוּהוּ בְּתֵקַע שׁוֹפָר,
הַלְלוּהוּ בְּנֵבֶל וְכִנּוֹר. הַלְלוּהוּ בְּתֹף וּמָחוֹל, הַלְלוּהוּ בְּמִנִּים וְעֻגָב.
הַלְלוּהוּ בְצִלְצְלֵי שָׁמַע, הַלְלוּהוּ בְּצִלְצְלֵי תְרוּעָה. כֹּל הַנְּשָׁמָה
תְּהַלֵּל יָהּ, הַלְלוּיָהּ.

[בְּרוֹב קְהִלּוֹת אֵין אוֹמְרִים]

לַמְנַצֵּחַ עַל־הַגִּתִּית, מִזְמוֹר לְדָוִד. יהוה אֲדֹנֵינוּ, מָה־אַדִּיר תהלים ח
שִׁמְךָ בְּכָל־הָאָרֶץ, אֲשֶׁר תְּנָה הוֹדְךָ עַל־הַשָּׁמָיִם. מִפִּי
עוֹלְלִים וְיֹנְקִים יִסַּדְתָּ עֹז, לְמַעַן צוֹרְרֶיךָ, לְהַשְׁבִּית אוֹיֵב וּמִתְנַקֵּם.
כִּי־אֶרְאֶה שָׁמֶיךָ מַעֲשֵׂה אֶצְבְּעֹתֶיךָ, יָרֵחַ וְכוֹכָבִים אֲשֶׁר כּוֹנָנְתָּה.
מָה־אֱנוֹשׁ כִּי־תִזְכְּרֶנּוּ, וּבֶן־אָדָם כִּי תִפְקְדֶנּוּ. וַתְּחַסְּרֵהוּ מְּעַט
מֵאֱלֹהִים, וְכָבוֹד וְהָדָר תְּעַטְּרֵהוּ. תַּמְשִׁילֵהוּ בְּמַעֲשֵׂי יָדֶיךָ, כֹּל
שַׁתָּה תַחַת־רַגְלָיו. צֹנֶה וַאֲלָפִים כֻּלָּם, וְגַם בַּהֲמוֹת שָׂדָי. צִפּוֹר
שָׁמַיִם וּדְגֵי הַיָּם, עֹבֵר אָרְחוֹת יַמִּים. יהוה אֲדֹנֵינוּ, מָה־אַדִּיר
שִׁמְךָ בְּכָל־הָאָרֶץ.

Psalms 2:8, explains the word אַפְסֵי in the term אַפְסֵי אָרֶץ as identical with the genitive plural of the word אֶפֶס in the phrase (כִּי אָפֵס כָּסֶף) *for our money is totally depleted* (*Genesis* 47:15). In this context the term refers to areas devoid of population.

◄§ הַלְלוּיָהּ — Psalm 150

This psalm, which is the concluding chapter of the Book of Psalms, calls for God to be praised both in the *firmament of His power*, i.e., by the cosmos itself, and by every animate creature. The resounding song of the instruments echoes the music of the spheres, orchestrating a grand finale to the songs of praise of the Book of Psalms. This psalm was added to the *Seder Bircas haChammah* by the author of *Teshuvos Sho'el uMeshiv* who directed that it be sung in his city

with choral accompaniment.

Bereishis Rabbah 14:11 renders the final verse כֹּל הַנְּשָׁמָה תְּהַלֵּל יָהּ as הַנְּשִׁימָה תְּהַלֵּל יָהּ, *Let every "breath" praise God*. R. Levi in the name of R. Chanina adds the statement: "Man ought to praise his Creator for each and every breath." According to this midrashic interpretation, the psalmist here affirms God's continuous providential guardianship. As has been explained in chapter 1, it is an awareness of this fundamental principle which *Bircas haChammah* is designed to evoke.

◄§ לַמְנַצֵּחַ עַל הַגִּתִּית — Psalm 8

Although not recited in most communities, the reason for the inclusion of this psalm by some is self-evident. The psalm eloquently depicts the wonder and awe which man experiences

[In most communities the following psalm is not recited.]

Psalms 150

¹ **H**alleluyah! *Praise God in His Sanctuary; praise Him in the firmament of His power;* ²*praise Him for His mighty acts; praise Him as befits His abundant greatness;* ³*praise Him with the blast of the shofar; praise Him with lyre and harp;* ⁴*praise Him with drum and dance; praise Him with organ and flute;* ⁵*praise Him with clanging cymbals; praise Him with resonant trumpets.* ⁶*Let all souls praise God, Halleluyah!*

[In most communities the following psalm is not recited.]

Psalms 8

¹ **F**or the conductor, on the gittis, a psalm by David. ²*HASHEM, our Master, how mighty is Your Name throughout the earth, [You] Who places Your majesty on the heavens.* ³*Out of the mouths of babes and sucklings You have established strength, because of Your enemies, to silence foe and avenger.* ⁴*When I behold Your heavens, the work of Your fingers, the moon and the stars that You have set in place, [I think,]* ⁵*"What is frail man that You should remember him, and the son of mortal man that You should be mindful of him?"* ⁶*Yet, You have made him but slightly less than the angels, and crowned him with soul and splendor.* ⁷*You give him dominion over Your handiwork, You placed everything under his feet:* ⁸*sheep and cattle, all of them, even the beasts of the field;* ⁹*the birds of the sky and the fish of the sea; for [man] even traverses the lanes of the sea.* ¹⁰*HASHEM, our Master, how mighty is Your Name throughout the earth!*

---

when contemplating the grandeur of the heavens and the celestial bodies.

The grandeur and majesty of the heavens and their hosts testify to the existence of a Creator. *Hirsch*, commenting on the verse, *Out of the mouths of babes and sucklings You have established strength, because of Your enemies,* remarks that acknowledgment of God's existence is so compelling that it can never be totally eradicated. Even when the teachings of religion are forcibly suppressed, a new generation arises to rediscover their verity. The intuitive quest for God among the youth of each generation is a phenomenon which, in and of itself, refutes atheistic contentions. It is *from the mouths of babes* that *enemies* are vanquished. One need but reflect upon the contemporary revival of religious commitment among youth in totalitarian regimes which, for decades, have suppressed all religious teaching to recognize the validity of *Hirsch's* interpretation.

לַמְנַצֵּחַ מִזְמוֹר לְדָוִד. הַשָּׁמַיִם מְסַפְּרִים כְּבוֹד־
אֵל, וּמַעֲשֵׂה יָדָיו מַגִּיד הָרָקִיעַ. יוֹם לְיוֹם
יַבִּיעַ אֹמֶר, וְלַיְלָה לְּלַיְלָה יְחַוֶּה־דָּעַת. אֵין־אֹמֶר
וְאֵין דְּבָרִים, בְּלִי נִשְׁמָע קוֹלָם. בְּכָל־הָאָרֶץ יָצָא
קַוָּם וּבִקְצֵה תֵבֵל מִלֵּיהֶם, לַשֶּׁמֶשׁ שָׂם־אֹהֶל בָּהֶם.
וְהוּא כְּחָתָן יֹצֵא מֵחֻפָּתוֹ, יָשִׂישׂ כְּגִבּוֹר לָרוּץ אֹרַח.

◆§ לַמְנַצֵּחַ מִזְמוֹר לְדָוִד — Psalm 19 ◆§

2. הַשָּׁמַיִם מְסַפְּרִים כְּבוֹד־אֵל — *The heavens declare the glory of God.*

The stars and constellations testify to God as Creator. The regularity and orderliness of their movements reflect the guidance of divine wisdom (cf. *Radak*). The wonders of the heavens prompt man to recount God's praises (*Targum* and *Rashi*).

Rambam interprets this verse in light of his view that the spheres are animate and rational (*Hilchos Yesodei haTorah* 3:9). Accordingly, he understands these words quite literally. Although *there is no speech and there are no words* (verse 4), the heavens praise God without speech. They are capable of thought and seek to express and communicate praise of God (*Guide of the Perplexed*, Book II, chap. 5).

3. יוֹם לְיוֹם יַבִּיעַ אֹמֶר — *Day following day utters speech.*

Each day the wonders of God are perceived (*Metzudas David*).

Rashi understands the phrase as meaning "from day to day," i.e., creation is reenacted each day in the setting of the sun at night and its reappearance in the morning.

Ibn Ezra explains the phrase as meaning "each day," i.e., each day there is new testimony to the miracles of God because each day the stars and constellations are arranged in a different configuration. The identical

configuration is never precisely repeated. Each day the continued preservation of the universe is a fresh miracle.

Man should reflect upon nature and the wondrous manner in which the world is ordered. The care and precision with which every created entity is fashioned in order to achieve its purpose is testimony to the existence of God. If man will continuously ponder the marvels of nature he will discover new evidence of divine wisdom each day. This is the meaning of *Day following day utters speech* (*Chovos haLevavos, Sha'ar haBechinah*, chap. 6). Moreover, each day man should be prompted to renewed repentance because each day recognition of God's greatness is increased and man realizes how much he has been remiss in serving God (*Chovos haLevavos, Sha'ar Avodas haElokim*, chap. 3).

יַבִּיעַ — *Utters.*

This translation is in accordance with *Metzudas Zion* and an alternative explanation advanced by *Ibn Ezra*. *Rashi*, citing the grammarian Menachem ben Saruk, as well as *Ibn Ezra* in his initial comments, understands the word as meaning "to pour forth," as an underground stream unceasingly pours forth its waters. The verse would then mean that each day God's praise flows forth continuously.

וְלַיְלָה לְּלַיְלָה יְחַוֶּה דָּעַת — *And night*

Psalms 19 ¹ **F**or the conductor, a psalm by David. ²*The heavens declare the glory of God, and the firmament tells of His handiwork.* ³*Day following day utters speech, and night following night declares knowledge.* ⁴*There is no speech and there are no words; their sound is not heard.* ⁵*[But] their line goes forth throughout the earth, and their words reach the end of the inhabited world. In their midst He has set up a tent for the sun,* ⁶*which is like a groom emerging from his bridal chamber, it rejoices like a powerful warrior*

---

following night declares knowledge.

Day and night follow one another with unfailing regularity. This phenomenon bespeaks divine wisdom in establishing the world order (*Rashi*). The regularity and sequence of day and night in the past foretells the regular recurrence of a sequence of day and night in the future (*Radak*).

4. אֵין אֹמֶר וְאֵין דְּבָרִים בְּלִי נִשְׁמָע קוֹלָם — *There is no speech and there are no words; their sound is not heard.*

Ibn Ezra explains that the terms דְּבָרִים, אֹמֶר and קוֹל are not synonymous, but convey different meanings. אֹמֶר connotes a proposition conveying an entire thought. דְּבָרִים are single words which do not convey a message individually. קוֹל is a sound which, in and of itself, is not cognitive. Thus, the verse declares that the heavens communicate neither complete sentences, nor individual words, nor even isolated verbal sounds. Yet, although there is no verbal communication, man's intellect can discern the message which the heavens do indeed convey.

5. קַוָּם — *[But] their line.*

The skyline is spread out over all the earth (*Rashi*).

תֵּבֵל — *The world.*

The word תֵּבֵל refers to the inhabited areas of the earth (*Ibn Ezra* and *Malbim*).

לַשֶּׁמֶשׁ שָׂם אֹהֶל — *He has set up a tent*

for the sun.

The sun is encased in a "tent" (אֹהֶל) or "case" (תִּיק) which serves as a protective shield preventing the full force of the sun's rays from generating oppressive heat and even destroying life on earth (*Rashi*). Cf. *Berachos* 27a (cited by *Rashi, Genesis* 18:1), הַקָּדוֹשׁ בָּרוּךְ הוּא הוֹצִיא חַמָּה מִנַּרְתִּיקָהּ — "The Holy One, blessed is He, removed the sun from its sheath" and *Avodah Zarah* 3b, הַקָּדוֹשׁ בָּרוּךְ הוּא הוֹצִיא חַמָּה מִנַּרְתִּיקָהּ, רְשָׁעִים נִידוֹנִין בָּהּ צַדִּיקִים מִתְרַפְּאִין בָּהּ ... — "God will bring forth the sun from its sheath ... the wicked will be punished by it and the righteous will be healed by it."

6. וְהוּא כְּחָתָן יֹצֵא מֵחֻפָּתוֹ — *Which is like a groom emerging from his bridal chamber.*

The sun comes forth with joy to shine upon the earth just as the bridegroom emerges from his chamber with joy (*Metzudas David*).

The bridegroom is eager to return to his bride; so does the sun return each day to its original place (*Radak*, in the name of his father).

כְּגִבּוֹר לָרוּץ אֹרַח — *Like a powerful warrior to run the course.*

The strong man is happy to run because he does not tire (*Ibn Ezra*). Similarly, the sun is certain that it will run its course without impediment (*Metzudas David*).

מִקְצֵה הַשָּׁמַיִם מוֹצָאוֹ, וּתְקוּפָתוֹ עַל־קְצוֹתָם; וְאֵין
נִסְתָּר מֵחַמָּתוֹ. תּוֹרַת יהוה תְּמִימָה, מְשִׁיבַת נָפֶשׁ;
עֵדוּת יהוה נֶאֱמָנָה, מַחְכִּימַת פֶּתִי. פִּקּוּדֵי יהוה
יְשָׁרִים, מְשַׂמְּחֵי־לֵב; מִצְוַת יהוה בָּרָה, מְאִירַת
עֵינָיִם. יִרְאַת יהוה טְהוֹרָה, עוֹמֶדֶת לָעַד; מִשְׁפְּטֵי־

---

7. וּתְקוּפָתוֹ עַל־קְצוֹתָם — *And its circuit is to their end.*

Daily the sun begins its circuit at one end of the heavens and completes its circuit by setting at the other end of the sky (*Metzudas David*).

וְאֵין נִסְתָּר מֵחַמָּתוֹ — *Nothing is hidden from its heat.*

The heat of the sun extends to every place on earth. This is true of the sun's heat but not of the sun's light. A person can shut out the light of the sun, but he cannot insulate himself entirely from its heat (*Radak*).

On the day of judgment no one will be hidden from the punishing heat of the sun (*Rashi*).

8. תּוֹרַת ה׳ תְּמִימָה מְשִׁיבַת נָפֶשׁ — *The Torah of HASHEM is perfect, restoring the soul.*

Both nature and Torah testify to God's existence. Man can perceive God by means of rational proof and logical inference based upon contemplation of the wonders of creation. God can also be known on the basis of Revelation as recorded in the Torah. The psalmist teaches that the testimony of Revelation is *more reliable* than proofs based upon observation of nature (*Ibn Ezra* and *Malbim*).

The immediate awareness of God as He is apprehended by means of Revelation leaves no doubt. Thus Torah is מְשִׁיבַת נָפֶשׁ, it *restores the soul* in the sense that it dispels any lingering doubts which may remain if God's existence is demonstrated on the basis of a teleological proof alone. The Torah is תְּמִימָה — *perfect*

because it is independently capable of establishing the existence of God and requires no corroboration (*Ibn Ezra*). The Torah is *perfect* because the Torah in its totality provides for all man's needs, both in this world and in the world-to-come (*Radak*).

R. Bachya ibn Pakuda explains that sensual desires, which are constantly reinforced, interfere with the exercise of the intellectual faculty. Man was given the Torah in order to overcome this hindrance. Study of Torah strengthens the intellect, making it more perceptive. Thus, *The Torah of HASHEM is perfect, restoring the soul*, i.e., the Torah enables man to overcome his corporeal nature, restores the balance, and allows the intellectual faculty to perceive the existence and glory of God (*Chovos haLevavos, Sha'ar Avodas haElokim*, chap. 2).

Rambam understands the verse as stating that the Torah eschews the extremes both of asceticism and sensual excess. Thus, unlike other religions of antiquity, the Torah and its *mitzvos* do not entail either withdrawal from the world or orgiastic rites. *The Torah of HASHEM is perfect, restoring the soul*, i.e., its *mitzvos* preserve our balance, fostering moral and intellectual perfection (*Guide of the Perplexed*, Book II, chap. 39).

R. Joseph Albo comments that the Torah is תְּמִימָה — *perfect* because every single narrative contained in it comes to teach an eternal lesson. There is nothing in the Torah which is not designed to instruct mankind

to run the course. [7] Its source is the end of the heavens and its circuit is to their end; nothing is hidden from its heat. [8] The Torah of HASHEM is perfect, restoring the soul; the testimony of HASHEM is trustworthy, making the simple one wise; [9] the precepts of HASHEM are upright, gladdening the heart; the commandment of HASHEM is clear, enlightening the eyes; [10] the fear of HASHEM is pure, enduring

---

(*Sefer haIkkarim*, Book III, chap. 25). He translates מְשִׁיבַת נָפֶשׁ as *causes the soul to return*, i.e., the teachings of the Torah cause the soul of man to return to its Creator (Book I, chap. 8).

עֵדוּת ה' נֶאֱמָנָה מַחְכִּימַת פֶּתִי — *The testimony of HASHEM is trustworthy, making the simple one wise.*

There are specific commandments which testify to Israel's acceptance of God and to God's acceptance of Israel as His chosen people. Those *mitzvos* are known as עֵדוּת — "testimony," indicating that they constitute reliable and trustworthy indications of this relationship (*Radak*).

Mitzvos are termed עֵדוּת — testimony — because they testify that those who fulfill them believe in God (*Metzudas David*).

R. Joseph Albo understands עֵדוּת ה' as referring to the intellectual verities taught by Torah. For example, the Torah teaches that the universe is created and not eternal. The *testimony of HASHEM* עֵדוּת ה', as found in the Torah, is *reliable and true* נֶאֱמָנָה (*Sefer haIkkarim*, Book I, chap. 8).

Malbim understands עֵדוּת as referring to the narrative sections of the Torah. These narratives are not mere parables, but are true and reliable. Moreover, they are described as מַחְכִּימַת פֶּתִי, *making the simple one wise*, since their messages are readily perceived and understood even by the simple and untutored.

9. פִּקּוּדֵי ה' יְשָׁרִים מְשַׂמְּחֵי לֵב — *The precepts of HASHEM are upright, gladdening the heart.*

פִּקּוּדִים constitute those *mitzvos* whose rationale is readily perceived. They are called פִּקּוּדִים because God placed them (הִפְקִידָם) in the intellect of man, i.e., God made it possible for man to fathom the meaning of these *mitzvos*. Since these commandments are readily comprehensible they gladden the "heart." The heart is viewed as the seat of the intellect. Man derives satisfaction from his intellectual understanding of these *mitzvos* (*Radak*).

Some commentators contrast this verse with the preceding description of the sun. Thus, *Ibn Ezra* remarks that the sun shines only by day, whereas the *mitzvos* gladden the heart at all times. Similarly, *Metzudas David* observes that, in contradistinction to the sun which causes worry and concern lest its heat cause harm, *mitzvos* always gladden the heart.

מִצְוַת ה' בָּרָה — *The commandment of HASHEM is clear.*

Every *mitzvah* is flawless and free of imperfection (*Radak*).

The commandment of God shines clearly and brightly. The sun, in contradistinction, is, at times, obscured by clouds (*Ibn Ezra*).

מְאִירַת עֵינָיִם — *Enlightening the eyes.*

Mitzvos are superior to the sun since one who gazes into the light of the sun is blinded (*Metzudas David*).

10. יִרְאַת ה' טְהוֹרָה — *The fear of HASHEM is pure.*

Ibn Ezra understands this phrase as a reference to the negative

יהוה אֱמֶת, צָדְקוּ יַחְדָּו. הַנֶּחֱמָדִים מִזָּהָב וּמִפַּז רָב,
וּמְתוּקִים מִדְּבַשׁ וְנֹפֶת צוּפִים. גַּם־עַבְדְּךָ נִזְהָר בָּהֶם,
בְּשָׁמְרָם עֵקֶב רָב. שְׁגִיאוֹת מִי־יָבִין מִנִּסְתָּרוֹת נַקֵּנִי.
גַּם מִזֵּדִים חֲשֹׂךְ עַבְדֶּךָ, אַל־יִמְשְׁלוּ־בִי, אָז אֵיתָם,
וְנִקֵּיתִי מִפֶּשַׁע רָב. יִהְיוּ לְרָצוֹן אִמְרֵי־פִי, וְהֶגְיוֹן
לִבִּי לְפָנֶיךָ, יהוה צוּרִי וְגֹאֲלִי.

---

commandments. An individual who does not defile himself by transgressing the negative commandments attains purity.

Meiri, Malbim and *Hirsch* understand this phrase as a reference to *chukkim,* i.e., those *mitzvos* which must be accepted on the basis of fear of God rather than on the basis of reason.

צָדְקוּ יַחְדָּו — *Altogether righteous.*

The Divine commandments are not contradictory to one another (*lbn Ezra* and *Radak*).

מִשְׁפְּטֵי ה' אֱמֶת צָדְקוּ יַחְדָּו — *The judgments of HASHEM are true, altogether righteous.*

R. Joseph Albo renders this verse: *The judgments of HASHEM are true and together they are righteous.* He explains that although, at times, the righteous are oppressed and the wicked prosper, this is so only when viewed from the perspective of this world. However, when account is taken of reward and punishment in the world-to-come as well, it will then become clear that both the wicked and the righteous have received their just deserts. The *judgments of* God are perceived as *righteous* when reward and punishment in this world and in the world-to-come are examined *together* (*Sefer halkkarim,* Book I, chap. 8).

11. הַנֶּחֱמָדִים מִזָּהָב וּמִפַּז רָב — *They are*

more desirable than gold, than even much fine gold.

Ibn Ezra and *Radak* explain that it is the benefits of Torah study which are contrasted with the value of gold and precious stones. Torah is inalienable; it cannot be stolen or lost. Knowledge of Torah is preserved in death as well as in life. Moreover, money or gold which is spent is no longer available. Torah, however, can be taught to others and, in the process, the teacher does not diminish his own knowledge but rather increases it.

וּמְתוּקִים מִדְּבַשׁ — *And sweeter than honey.*

lbn Ezra explains that the pleasures of taste are transitory while the intellectual pleasure derived from study of Torah is constant and enduring. *Radak* comments that wisdom is superior to honey because, although honey is the sweetest of foods, overindulgence leads to sickness, yet a person cannot have a surfeit of wisdom.

וְנֹפֶת צוּפִים — *And dripping of the honeycombs.*

Rashi translates נֹפֶת as "sweetness" or, alternatively, citing *Menachem,* as "drop" or "dripping." *Metzudas Zion* renders נֹפֶת as "flow" and defines צוּפִים as "honeycombs."

12. בְּשָׁמְרָם עֵקֶב רָב — *In observing them there is great reward.*

The literal translation of עֵקֶב is "heel." The "heel" is located at the

forever; the judgments of HASHEM are true, altogether righteous. [11]*They are more desirable than gold, than even much fine gold; and sweeter than honey, and dripping of the honeycombs.* [12] *Also, when Your servant is scrupulous in them, in observing them there is great reward.* [13]*Who can discern mistakes? Cleanse me from unperceived faults.* [14] *Also from intentional sins restrain Your servant; let them not rule me, then I shall be perfect; and I will be cleansed of great transgression.* [15] *May the expressions of my mouth and the thoughts of my heart find favor before You, HASHEM, my Rock and my Redeemer.*

"end" of the body and, hence, the word is here used in the sense of "end," i.e., the reward which is the end-result of the observance of *mitzvos* (*Radak*).

Hirsch remarks that appreciation of *mitzvos* is attained by man, not in the abstract, but only in the process of observance. Thus, only בְּשָׁמְרָם *in observing them* does man gain an appreciation of עֵקֶב רָב, their *great reward.*

13. שְׁגִיאוֹת מִי יָבִין — *Who can discern mistakes?*

שְׁגִיאוֹת are inadvertent sins. No person is totally free of unintentional error (*Rashi* and *Radak*).

14. מְזֵדִים — *From intentional sins.*

According to *Rashi* and *Radak* זֵדִים means "willful transgressions" and the reference is to the sins. However, *Ibn Ezra* understands the word as a reference to the sinners, individuals who transgress knowingly and willfully.

חֲשׂךְ עַבְדֶּךָ — *Restrain Your servant.*

Strengthen my heart so that I will not commit transgressions (*Metzudas David*).

אַל יִמְשְׁלוּ בִי — *Let them not rule me.*

Let the desire for sinful pleasure not overcome me (*Metzudas David*). According to *Ibn Ezra* the meaning

would be: Do not allow transgressors to have dominion over me and compel me to sin.

אָז אֵיתָם — *Then I shall be perfect.*

A contraction of the words אֶהְיֶה תָמִים, *I shall be perfect* (*Rashi*).

If You will cleanse me from inadvertent sin and prevent me from committing willful transgressions, I will then be perfect since I will certainly not sin rebelliously (*Radak*).

Midrash Shocher Tov (cited by *Rashi*) explains verses 13 and 14 by means of a parable. A crafty beggar asks first merely for a glass of water. Upon receiving the water, he asks for an insignificant item, a small onion. When he obtains the onion, he complains that the onion cannot be eaten without salt. When he is given the salt he asks for some bread so that he may be able to eat the sharp onion. Similarly, David asks for forgiveness first for שְׁגִיאוֹת, *inadvertent sins,* afterwards for זֵדִים, *willful transgressions,* and finally for פֶּשַׁע רָב, *rebellious misdeeds.*

15. וְהֶגְיוֹן לִבִּי — *And the thoughts of my heart.*

The thoughts which I cannot express verbally. There are many things which a person may feel but not be able to express in words (*Radak*).

שִׁיר לַמַּעֲלוֹת; אֶשָּׂא עֵינַי אֶל־הֶהָרִים, מֵאַיִן
יָבֹא עֶזְרִי. עֶזְרִי מֵעִם יהוה,
עֹשֵׂה שָׁמַיִם וָאָרֶץ. אַל־יִתֵּן לַמּוֹט רַגְלֶךָ, אַל־יָנוּם
שֹׁמְרֶךָ. הִנֵּה לֹא־יָנוּם וְלֹא יִישָׁן, שׁוֹמֵר יִשְׂרָאֵל.
יהוה שֹׁמְרֶךָ, יהוה צִלְּךָ עַל־יַד יְמִינֶךָ. יוֹמָם
הַשֶּׁמֶשׁ לֹא־יַכֶּכָּה וְיָרֵחַ בַּלָּיְלָה. יהוה יִשְׁמָרְךָ
מִכָּל־רָע, יִשְׁמֹר אֶת־נַפְשֶׁךָ. יהוה יִשְׁמָר־צֵאתְךָ
וּבוֹאֶךָ, מֵעַתָּה וְעַד־עוֹלָם.

⧓ שִׁיר לַמַּעֲלוֹת — Psalm 121 ⧓

1. שִׁיר לַמַּעֲלוֹת — *A song to the ascents.*
Each of psalms 120-134 begins with a reference to "ascents." The "ascents" refer to the fifteen steps separating the courtyard of the Temple (עֶזְרַת יִשְׂרָאֵל) from the women's courtyard. On the occasion of שִׂמְחַת בֵּית הַשּׁוֹאֵבָה (Rejoicing at the place of Water-drawing), the festive celebration of the eve of the intermediate days of *Succos*, Levites were positioned on each of these steps. Each group sang, in turn, a different one of these fifteen psalms with the accompaniment of instrumental music (Mishnah, *Succah* 51b).

In an aggadic narrative the Gemara relates that the fifteen "ascents" were sung by King David at the time of the construction of the Temple. In the course of building the Temple, David dug pits which uncovered waters deep within the recesses of the earth. The waters thus released threatened to inundate the earth. David wrote the Divine Name upon a shard and cast it into the waters, thereby causing them to recede. This, in turn, caused the water table to recede precipitously, threatening to make all water inaccessible. Thereupon David chanted these psalms, each one causing the water to rise to some extent until the waters returned to their original level (*Succah* 53a).

Radak suggests that these psalms are called psalms of "ascent" because they were composed in anticipation of Israel's "ascent" from exile. The content of these psalms focuses upon the hardships of exile and the promise of deliverance.

לַמַּעֲלוֹת — *To the ascents.*
In each of the other fourteen psalms the term הַמַּעֲלוֹת is employed. *Rashi* comments that this psalm employs the term לַמַּעֲלוֹת, literally "to the ascents," because, although recorded as the second of the fifteen psalms, in the Temple it was the first to be sung by the Levites at the *Succos* celebration. This psalm, then, is "to the ascent," i.e., to mark the beginning of the ascent.

אֶשָּׂא עֵינַי — *I raise my eyes.*
It is the wont of those waiting for rescue to ascend to the top of the hills and to gaze into the distance with longing and anticipation (*Ibn Ezra* and *Radak*).

Psalms 121

¹ A song to the ascents. I raise my eyes upon the mountains; whence will come my help? ² My help is from HASHEM, who makes heaven and earth. ³ He will not allow your foot to falter; your Guardian will not slumber. ⁴ Behold, He neither slumbers nor sleeps, the Guardian of Israel. ⁵ HASHEM is your Guardian; HASHEM is your protective Shade at your right hand. ⁶ By day the sun will not harm you, nor the moon by night. ⁷ HASHEM will protect you from every evil; He will guard your soul. ⁸ HASHEM will guard your departure and your arrival, from this time and forever.

---

2. עֹשֵׂה שָׁמַיִם וָאָרֶץ — *Who makes heaven and earth.*

"Who makes" is in the present tense. God continually recreates heaven and earth. Hence, heaven and earth are subject to His rule at every moment in time. Therefore, it is to God alone that man must constantly look for help and assistance (*Hirsch*).

4. לֹא יָנוּם וְלֹא יִישָׁן — *He neither slumber nors sleeps.*

God will not withhold or withdraw His providence from Israel (*Metzudas David*).

שׁוֹמֵר יִשְׂרָאֵל — *The Guardian of Israel.*

God promised Jacob, "I will watch over you wherever you will go" (*Genesis* 28:15). Although Jacob was asleep at the time, God never "sleeps," but constantly watches over Israel (*Ibn Ezra*).

5. ה' צִלְּךָ — *HASHEM is your protective Shade.*

God will shield Israel, just as the shade shields from the heat of the sun (*Metzudas David*).

יַד יְמִינֶךָ — *Your right hand.*

The right hand is the more powerful of the two hands. God will shield

Israel in a manner which will protect and preserve Israel's full power and strength.

יוֹמָם הַשֶּׁמֶשׁ לֹא יַכֶּכָּה — *By day the sun will not harm you.*

This psalm is apparently included in the order of *Bircas haChammah* because of the presence of this verse. Life cannot exist on earth without the sun, but its heat may not always be an unmitigated blessing. This verse is a prayer that the sun's rays always be a blessing rather than an affliction.

וְיָרֵחַ בַּלָּיְלָה — *Nor the moon by night.*

May the darkness of the moon, i.e., of the night, not bring sickness (*Ibn Ezra*).

7. מִכָּל רָע — *From every evil.*

There are two types of evil or misfortune, internal and external, i.e., physical and spiritual. The psalmist prays that Israel be preserved from both (*Ibn Ezra* and *Malbim*).

8. צֵאתְךָ וּבוֹאֶךָ מֵעַתָּה וְעַד עוֹלָם — *Your departure and your arrival from this time and forever.*

Divine guardianship extends to all places and to all times (*Malbim*).

תָּנוּ רַבָּנָן: הָרוֹאֶה חַמָּה בִּתְקוּפָתָהּ אוֹמֵר: בָּרוּךְ
עוֹשֶׂה בְרֵאשִׁית. וְאֵימַת הָוֵי, אָמַר אַבַּיֵי,
כָּל כ"ח שְׁנִין וַהֲדַר מַחֲזוֹר, וְנָפְלָה תְּקוּפַת נִיסָן
בְּשַׁבְּתַאי בְּאוּרְתָּא דִתְלָת נַגְהֵי אַרְבַּע.

שֶׁמֶשׁ אוֹמֵר: שֶׁמֶשׁ יָרֵחַ, עָמַד זְבֻלָה, לְאוֹר חִצֶּיךָ
יְהַלֵּכוּ, לְנֹגַהּ בְּרַק חֲנִיתֶךָ. וְאוֹמֵר: קוּמִי אוֹרִי
כִּי בָא אוֹרֵךְ, וּכְבוֹד יהוה עָלַיִךְ זָרָח.

◂§ **תָּנוּ רַבָּנָן** The Beraisa.

It is this *Beraisa, Berachos* 59b,
which is the source of the obligation
to recite *Bircas haChammah.* Abaye
explains that the blessing upon seeing the sun "at its turning point" is
recited on the occasion of the return
of the sun to the position which it occupied at the time of creation when
this occurs on the same day and at
the precise time of its original creation. At the time of creation the sun
was placed in the position it occupies
at the time of the vernal equinox. The
Sages teach that creation of the sun
took place on the eve of the fourth day,
i.e., on Tuesday evening, at the hour
subject to the influence of Saturn, i.e.,
the first hour of the evening. Thus
the blessing is recited only when the
vernal equinox occurs on a Tuesday
evening at 6:00 P.M. This occurs
only once every twenty-eight years.
For a fuller discussion of this *Beraisa*
and of parallel sources see chapter
three.

◂§ **פֶּרֶק שִׁירָה** — Perek Shirah

Perek Shirah, the "Chapter of
Song," or, as it is often known, "The
Beraisa of *Perek Shirah*" consists of
biblical verses depicted as being sung
in praise of God by heavenly and
earthly bodies as well as by plants
and animals. R. Joseph Albo, *Sefer*

halkkarim, Book III, chap. 1, cites
a rabbinic dictum which declares,
"Whoever recites *Perek Shirah* each
day is assured a share in the world-
to-come." Although, as indicated in
Seder Avodas Yisrael (Roedelheim,
5628), p. 547, we have no talmudic
record of this saying, or of the specific contents of *Perek Shirah,* there
are, however, ample talmudic and
midrashic references to the fact that
animals do sing *shirah* in praise of
God. (See *Chullin* 64b; *Sanhedrin* 95b;
Avodah Zarah 24b; *Rosh HaShanah*
8a; *Yerushalmi, Avodah Zarah* 2:8;
Yalkut Shimoni, Tehillim 889.) In particular, the Gemara, *Avodah Zarah*
25a, speaks specifically of *shirah*
sung by the sun. Thus, although the
earliest specific references to *Perek
Shirah* are found in the literature of
the Geonic period, there is every reason to assume that at least portions
of the text of *Perek Shirah* date at least
to the time of the *Tana'im.* R. Moshe
ben Joseph Trani (*Mabit*), in his
work *Bet Elokim,* ascribes ultimate
authorship of *Perek Shirah* to King
David.

The notion of animals and inanimate objects singing praises to God is
not necessarily to be understood in a
literal manner. In explaining a similar reference, *Tosafos, Avodah Zarah*
17a, indicate that the words ascribed

Beraisa Berachos 59b

Our Rabbis taught: *He who sees the sun at its turning point should say: Blessed are You who makes the work of creation. And when [does this happen]? Abaye said: Every twenty-eight years when the cycle begins again and the Nisan [Spring] equinox falls in Saturn on the evening of Tuesday, going into Wednesday.*

Perek Shirah

The sun says: *The sun and moon stood still in their habitation; by the light of Your arrows did they go, by the illumination of Your shining spear (Habakkuk 3:11). And [the sun] says: Arise, shine, for your light has come and the glory of HASHEM will shine over you (Isaiah 60:1).*

---

to inanimate objects constitute a reflection of the very nature of created things and represent what those beings or entities would say if they were capable of speech. Alternatively, declare *Tosafos*, the words may be understood as being those of the guardian angels of these entities. (See also *Tosafos, Chullin* 7a.)

Sefer haIkkarim explains that the reward vouchsafed for recitation of *Perek Shirah* is not gained by mere rote repetition of the words, but rather by virtue of fully comprehending their import. The message of *Perek Shirah*, declares *Sefer haIkkarim*, is that one must recognize that every creature has something to teach man, a good quality, a moral lesson or some wise inference. Thus, the introductory query which prefaces the statements of *Perek Shirah*, such as, for example, "What do the heavens say?" does not refer to vocal speech on the part of the heavens but means, "What do the heavens signify?" The response, "The heavens declare the glory of God, etc." conveys the lesson that from the motion of the heavens we may infer that there is a Being who moves them and that He is omnipotent.

עָמַד וְזֵבָלֹה — *Stood still in their*

habitation.

I.e., in their orbits. *Radak* understands the verse as referring to the stopping of the sun in the midst of its course at the time of Joshua and the subsequent military victory of Israel as a result of divine intervention.

לְאוֹר חִצֶּיךָ יְהַלֵּכוּ — *By the light of Your arrows did they go.*

I.e., Israel did go (*Rashi*). The reference according to *Metzudas David* is, here too, to the time of Joshua. *Radak* interprets this phrase as a reference to the journey of Israel at the time of the Exodus from Egypt.

The Gemara, *Nedarim* 39b, understands this verse as meaning *they* (i.e., the sun and the moon) *go by the light of Your arrows* and explains that the sun and the moon are reluctant to rise at their appointed times because when they appear they become objects of pagan worship. They emerge and proceed in their orbits only because, figuratively speaking, they are prodded by God's arrows.

כִּי בָא אוֹרֵךְ — *For your light has come.*

The verse alludes to the redemption of Israel and the ensuing manifestation of the *Shechinah* (*Radak*).

אֵל אָדוֹן עַל כָּל הַמַּעֲשִׂים, בָּרוּךְ וּמְבֹרָךְ בְּפִי כָל־נְשָׁמָה, גָּדְלוֹ וְטוּבוֹ מָלֵא עוֹלָם, דַּעַת וּתְבוּנָה סוֹבְבִים אוֹתוֹ. הַמִּתְגָּאֶה עַל־חַיּוֹת הַקֹּדֶשׁ, וְנֶהְדָּר בְּכָבוֹד עַל־הַמֶּרְכָּבָה, זְכוּת וּמִישׁוֹר לִפְנֵי כִסְאוֹ, חֶסֶד וְרַחֲמִים לִפְנֵי כְבוֹדוֹ. טוֹבִים מְאוֹרוֹת שֶׁבָּרָא אֱלֹהֵינוּ, יְצָרָם בְּדַעַת בְּבִינָה וּבְהַשְׂכֵּל. כֹּחַ וּגְבוּרָה נָתַן בָּהֶם, לִהְיוֹת מוֹשְׁלִים בְּקֶרֶב תֵּבֵל. מְלֵאִים זִיו וּמְפִיקִים נֹגַהּ, נָאֶה זִיוָם בְּכָל־הָעוֹלָם, שְׂמֵחִים בְּצֵאתָם וְשָׂשִׂים בְּבוֹאָם, עֹשִׂים בְּאֵימָה רְצוֹן קוֹנָם. פְּאֵר וְכָבוֹד נוֹתְנִים לִשְׁמוֹ, צָהֳלָה וְרִנָּה לְזֵכֶר מַלְכוּתוֹ, קָרָא לַשֶּׁמֶשׁ וַיִּזְרַח אוֹר, רָאָה וְהִתְקִין צוּרַת הַלְּבָנָה.

⧉ אֵל אָדוֹן — Kel Adon

אֵל אָדוֹן — *God, Master …*

The initial letters of each phrase of אֵל אָדוֹן are arranged in accordance with the sequence of the Hebrew alphabet. The hymn praises God as the Creator of the celestial bodies, including the sun, moon, and five planets. The initial letters of five words of the penultimate phrase שֶׁבַח נוֹתְנִים לוֹ כָּל־צְבָא מָרוֹם are the initials of the Hebrew names of the five planets: שַׁבְּתַאי (Saturn), נֹגַהּ (Venus), כּוֹכָב (Mercury), צֶדֶק (Jupiter), and מַאְדִּים (Mars). The two final phrases contain six words each, corresponding to the 12 constellations of the zodiac.

בְּפִי כָּל־נְשָׁמָה — *In the mouth of every soul.*

This phrase is based upon the final verse of Psalm 150, כֹּל הַנְּשָׁמָה תְּהַלֵּל יָהּ, *Let every soul praise God.*

הַמִּתְגָּאֶה עַל־חַיּוֹת הַקֹּדֶשׁ — *He Who is exalted above the holy beings.*

The reference is to the vision described in the first chapter of Ezekiel.

זְכוּת וּמִישׁוֹר — *Purity and uprightness.*

The translation *purity* (rather than the more obvious "merit") is in accordance with the commentary of R. Yitzchak Seligmann Baer in his *siddur, Avodas Yisrael.* He comments that the phrase זְכוּת וּמִישׁוֹר, *purity and uprightness*, parallels Proverbs 21:8: וְזַךְ יָשָׁר פָּעֳלוֹ, *But as for the pure, his work is right.*

טוֹבִים מְאוֹרוֹת — *Good are the luminaries.*

As stated in *Genesis* 1:18, וַיַּרְא אֱלֹהִים כִּי טוֹב, *And God saw that it was good.*

לִהְיוֹת מוֹשְׁלִים — *That they may have dominion.*

As stated in *Genesis* 1:16 the great luminary was created לְמֶמְשֶׁלֶת הַיּוֹם, *to rule the day,* and the small luminary was created לְמֶמְשֶׁלֶת הַלַּיְלָה, *to rule the night.*

שְׂמֵחִים בְּצֵאתָם — *Joyous in their rising.*

$\mathbf{G}$od, Master over all created things, blessed and praised in the mouth of every soul. His greatness and goodness fill the universe; knowledge and understanding surround Him.

He Who is exalted above the holy beings, and is adorned with glory above the chariot. Purity and uprightness are before His throne; lovingkindness and mercy are before His glory.

Good are the luminaries which our God has created; He formed them with knowledge, insight and reason. Strength and power has He placed in them, that they may have dominion throughout the world.

Full of luster and radiating brightness, beautiful is their luster throughout the universe. Joyous in their rising and exultant in their setting, they perform with awe the will of their possessor.

Glory and honor they give to His Name, jubilation and song to the mention of His sovereignty. He called to the sun and light shined; He observed and ordained the form of the moon.

This is an allusion to *Psalms* 19:6 which compares the joy of the sun to that of a bridegroom. Just as the bridegroom goes forth with joy but is glad to return to his bride, so does the sun rise with gladness but is happy to return at the close of the day. See *Radak, Psalms* 19:6.

פְּאֵר וְכָבוֹד נוֹתְנִים לִשְׁמוֹ — *Glory and honor they give to His Name.*

As stated in *Psalms* 19:2: הַשָּׁמַיִם מְסַפְּרִים כְּבוֹד אֵל, *The heavens recount the glory of God.* The regularity of the celestial movements redounds to the glory and honor of God. The immutability of their motion is testimony to the wisdom and omnipotence of God.

קָרָא לַשֶּׁמֶשׁ וַיִּזְרַח אוֹר — *He called to the sun and light shined.*

As stated in *Genesis* 1:5: וַיִּקְרָא אֱלֹהִים לָאוֹר יוֹם, *And God called the light day.*

רָאָה וְהִתְקִין צוּרַת הַלְּבָנָה — *He observed and ordained the form of the moon.*

Since the moon possesses no independent illumination, God ordained the moon as a body which reflects light. The Midrash, *Bereishis Rabbah* 6:1, declares that upon creating the sun God recognized that it would be worshiped as a god. Accordingly, He immediately created the moon since discerning persons will readily recognize that there cannot be a plurality of deities. Indeed, the Midrash reports that God recognized that both the sun and the moon would be deified by some individuals. However, God created both rather than the sun alone because creation of a single luminary would have resulted in an even larger number of sun worshipers.

וְהִתְקִין צוּרַת הַלְּבָנָה — *And ordained the form of the moon.*

The *Tur* cites a variant version

שֶׁבַח נוֹתְנִים לוֹ כָּל צְבָא מָרוֹם, תִּפְאֶרֶת
וּגְדֻלָּה, שְׂרָפִים וְאוֹפַנִּים וְחַיּוֹת הַקֹּדֶשׁ.

שִׁמְךָ יהוה אֱלֹהֵינוּ יִתְקַדַּשׁ, וְזִכְרְךָ מַלְכֵּנוּ יִתְפָּאַר,
בַּשָּׁמַיִם מִמַּעַל וְעַל הָאָרֶץ מִתָּחַת. תִּתְבָּרַךְ
מוֹשִׁיעֵנוּ עַל שֶׁבַח מַעֲשֵׂה יָדֶיךָ, וְעַל מְאוֹרֵי אוֹר
שֶׁעָשִׂיתָ, יְפָאֲרוּךָ סֶּלָה [נ״א. וְעַל מְאוֹרֵי אוֹר שֶׁיָּצַרְתָּ,
הֵמָּה יְפָאֲרוּךָ סֶּלָה].

[ברוב קהילות אין אומרים]

תהלים לג רַנְּנוּ צַדִּיקִים בַּיהוה, לַיְשָׁרִים נָאוָה תְהִלָּה. הוֹדוּ לַיהוה בְּכִנּוֹר,
בְּנֵבֶל עָשׂוֹר זַמְּרוּ לוֹ. שִׁירוּ לוֹ שִׁיר חָדָשׁ, הֵיטִיבוּ נַגֵּן
בִּתְרוּעָה. כִּי־יָשָׁר דְּבַר־יהוה, וְכָל מַעֲשֵׂהוּ בֶּאֱמוּנָה. אֹהֵב צְדָקָה
וּמִשְׁפָּט, חֶסֶד יהוה מָלְאָה הָאָרֶץ. בִּדְבַר יהוה שָׁמַיִם נַעֲשׂוּ,
וּבְרוּחַ פִּיו כָּל־צְבָאָם. כֹּנֵס כַּנֵּד מֵי הַיָּם, נֹתֵן בְּאֹצָרוֹת תְּהוֹמוֹת.
יִירְאוּ מֵיהוה כָּל־הָאָרֶץ, מִמֶּנּוּ יָגוּרוּ כָּל־יֹשְׁבֵי תֵבֵל. כִּי הוּא אָמַר
וַיֶּהִי, הוּא־צִוָּה וַיַּעֲמֹד. יהוה הֵפִיר עֲצַת גּוֹיִם, הֵנִיא מַחְשְׁבוֹת
עַמִּים. עֲצַת יהוה לְעוֹלָם תַּעֲמֹד, מַחְשְׁבוֹת לִבּוֹ לְדֹר וָדֹר. אַשְׁרֵי
הַגּוֹי אֲשֶׁר יהוה אֱלֹהָיו, הָעָם בָּחַר לְנַחֲלָה לוֹ. מִשָּׁמַיִם הִבִּיט
יהוה, רָאָה אֶת־כָּל־בְּנֵי הָאָדָם. מִמְּכוֹן שִׁבְתּוֹ הִשְׁגִּיחַ, אֶל כָּל־
יֹשְׁבֵי הָאָרֶץ. הַיֹּצֵר יַחַד לִבָּם, הַמֵּבִין אֶל כָּל־מַעֲשֵׂיהֶם. אֵין־
הַמֶּלֶךְ נוֹשָׁע בְּרָב חָיִל, גִּבּוֹר לֹא יִנָּצֵל בְּרָב־כֹּחַ. שֶׁקֶר הַסּוּס

וְהִקְטִין צוּרַת הַלְּבָנָה, "He reduced the size of the moon." This reading is based upon *Chullin* 60b which states, "The moon said to God, 'Sovereign of the universe, can two rulers [the sun and the moon] reign together as equals?' And God gave heed to the words of the moon and therefore reduced it in size."

שִׁמְךָ ה׳ אֱלֹהֵינוּ יִתְקַדַּשׁ ... וְעַל מְאוֹרֵי אוֹר שֶׁעָשִׂיתָ — *Your Name, O HASHEM, our God, shall be hallowed ... and for the luminaries of light which You have made.*

This passage was incorporated in the *Seder Bircas haChammah* by the author of *Pesach haDvir*. It expresses the concept that God alone is to be praised and that the sun is but an instrument of God through which He exercises providence. The intention is to deny the pagan notion that the sun exercises independent power.

◆§ רַנְּנוּ — **Psalm 33**

This psalm speaks in detail of God's providence as exercised on behalf of the individual in contrast to providence which is exercised on behalf of mankind in general through the operation of the laws of nature.

All the hosts on high render praise unto Him; the Seraphim and Ophanim and holy beings render glory and greatness.

Y*our Name, O* HASHEM, *our God, shall be hallowed and Your mention, O our King, shall be glorified in the heavens above and on the earth beneath. You shall be blessed, O our Deliverer, for the excellence of Your handiwork and for the luminaries of light which You have made; they shall glorify You. Selah.*

[In most communities the following psalm is not recited.]

Psalms 33 *¹* **S***ing joyfully, O righteous, because of* HASHEM; *for the upright, praise is fitting.* ²*Give thanks to* HASHEM *with a harp, with a ten-stringed lyre make music to Him.* ³*Sing Him a new song, play well with sounds of deep emotion.* ⁴*For the word of* HASHEM *is upright, and all His deeds [are done] with faithfulness.* ⁵*He loves righteousness and justice; the kindness of* HASHEM *fills the earth.* ⁶*By the word of* HASHEM *the heavens were made, and by the breath of His mouth all their host.* ⁷*He assembles the waters of the sea like a mound, He places the deep waters in vaults.* ⁸*Fear* HASHEM, *all the earth; be in dread of Him all inhabitants of the world.* ⁹*For He spoke and it came to be, He commanded and it stood firm.* ¹⁰HASHEM *annuls the counsel of nations, he thwarts the designs of peoples.* ¹¹*The counsel of* HASHEM *will endure forever, the designs of His heart from generation to generation.* ¹²*Praiseworthy is the nation that* HASHEM *is their God, the people He chose for His own heritage.* ¹³*From heaven* HASHEM *looks down, He sees all mankind.* ¹⁴*From His dwelling place He oversees all inhabitants of the earth,* ¹⁵*He Who fashions their hearts together, Who comprehends all their deeds.* ¹⁶*A king is not saved by a great army, nor is a hero rescued by great strength.*

Although not recited in most communities, this psalm may have been interpolated in the *Seder Bircas haChammah* in order to affirm that, while divine providence is manifest in the wonders of creation, providence is exercised in a personal manner as well. The psalm also refers to God as the Creator by whose word *the heavens were made.*

לִתְשׁוּעָה, וּבְרֹב חֵילוֹ לֹא יְמַלֵּט. הִנֵּה עֵין יהוה אֶל יְרֵאָיו,
לַמְיַחֲלִים לְחַסְדּוֹ. לְהַצִּיל מִמָּוֶת נַפְשָׁם, וּלְחַיּוֹתָם בָּרָעָב. נַפְשֵׁנוּ
חִכְּתָה לַיהוה עֶזְרֵנוּ וּמָגִנֵּנוּ הוּא. כִּי בוֹ יִשְׂמַח לִבֵּנוּ, כִּי בְשֵׁם
קָדְשׁוֹ בָטָחְנוּ. יְהִי חַסְדְּךָ יהוה עָלֵינוּ, כַּאֲשֶׁר יִחַלְנוּ לָךְ.

עָלֵינוּ לְשַׁבֵּחַ לַאֲדוֹן הַכֹּל, לָתֵת גְּדֻלָּה לְיוֹצֵר
בְּרֵאשִׁית, שֶׁלֹּא עָשָׂנוּ כְּגוֹיֵי הָאֲרָצוֹת,
וְלֹא שָׂמָנוּ כְּמִשְׁפְּחוֹת הָאֲדָמָה. שֶׁלֹּא שָׂם חֶלְקֵנוּ
כָּהֶם, וְגוֹרָלֵנוּ כְּכָל הֲמוֹנָם. שֶׁהֵם מִשְׁתַּחֲוִים
לְהֶבֶל וָרִיק, וּמִתְפַּלְּלִים אֶל אֵל לֹא יוֹשִׁיעַ.

‎§− עָלֵינוּ **— Aleinu**

R. Chaim Yosef David Azulai (*Chida*), in his *Moreh beEtzba*, no. 6, sec. 190, decries the practice of reciting the *Aleinu* prayer at the conclusion of *Kiddush Levanah* and describes this practice as a custom which arose "without thought" in some cities. *Chida* is most vehement in his opposition to recitation of *Aleinu* lest it appear that the moon is an object of veneration. The consideration which prompted *Chida's* opposition to recitation of *Aleinu* in conjunction with *Kiddush Levanah* would augur against its recitation in conjunction with *Bircas haChammah*.

The opinion of *Chida* notwithstanding, the custom to recite *Aleinu* at the conclusion of *Kiddush Levanah* has become widespread. R. Chaim haKohen Rapoport, *Teshuvos Mayim Chaim*, no. 22, declares that since *Aleinu* is recited in praise of God following *Kiddush Levanah*, it should, *a fortiori*, be recited in conjunction with *Bircas haChammah* in praise of God

who has preserved us to celebrate an event which occurs with such rarity. Recitation of *Aleinu* was also prescribed by *Teshuvos Chasam Sofer*, *Orach Chaim*, no. 56. Despite the view of *Chida*, subsequent Sephardic authorities, including *Pesach haDvir*, *Sedei Chemed* and *Ben Ish Chai* all include *Aleinu* in their order of *Bircas haChammah*.[1]

Pesach haDvir, III, p. 316a, expresses the opinion that there is even more reason to recite *Aleinu* in conjunction with *Bircas HaChammah* than as part of *Kiddush Levanah*. The *Tosefta*, *Berachos* 6:11, records the opinion of R. Judah who declares, "One who pronounces the blessing upon the sun, this is the way of heresy." R. Judah expresses a dissident opinion in opposition to the institution of *Bircas haChammah* on the grounds that the ignorant may erroneously believe that the sun is the object of worship.[2] However, *Minchas Bikkurim*, one of the commentaries on the *Tosefta*, and *Machazik*

---

1. The view of *Chida* is, however, endorsed by R. Chaim Palaggi, *Ruach Chaim*, *Orach Chaim* 229:9 and R. Yaakov Chaim Sofer, *Kaf haChaim* 229:18.

2. For additional considerations distinguishing *Bircas haChammah* from *Kiddush Levanah*, see *Kuntres Omer HaSadeh*, appended to *Yizrach Or*, p. 14a.

¹⁷ Illusory is the horse for salvation; despite its great strength it provides no escape. ¹⁸ Behold, the eye of HASHEM is on those who fear Him, upon those who await His kindness. ¹⁹ To rescue their soul from death, and to sustain them in famine. ²⁰ Our soul longed for HASHEM; He is our help and our shield. ²¹ For in Him will our hearts be glad; for in His Holy Name we trusted. ²² May Your kindness, HASHEM, be upon us, just as we awaited You.

It is our duty to praise the Master of all, to ascribe greatness to the Molder of primeval creation, for He has not made us like the nations of the lands and has not emplaced us like the families of the earth; for He has not assigned our portion like theirs nor our lot like all their multitudes. For they bow to vanity and emptiness and pray to a god which helps not.

Berachah 229:9, explain that R. Judah decries, not the recitation of the blessing every twenty-eight years, but the practice of reciting the blessing indiscriminately whenever one sees the sun.[3] Since ordinary mortals are not emotionally or intellectually aroused by usual events in a manner which would evoke a blessing of thanksgiving,[4] a blessing upon the sun other than on the unique occasion of *Bircas haChammah* might be interpreted, particularly by the ignorant, as an act of sun worship. It is therefore appropriate, declares *Pesach haDvir*, that *Aleinu*, which decries idol-worship, be recited on the occasion of *Bircas haChammah* in order to underscore the fact that our worship is directed to God alone.

Yet another symbolic reason for the recitation of *Aleinu* is advanced by *Pesach HaDvir* in the name of his son R. Shmuel. Authorship of *Aleinu* is traditionally ascribed to Joshua, who composed this prayer as an expression of thanksgiving at the time of his victory at Jericho. One midrashic source states that the days of creation, in which the world was created out of emptiness and void, symbolically represent seven barren women in Jewish history. The fourth day of creation corresponds to Rachel, who was the fourth of these women. In the dream of Joseph, the son of Rachel, the sun and the moon, which were created on the fourth day in the merit of Rachel, bowed down before him. *Midrash Talpiyos*, s.v. *chammah*, points out that Joshua was a descendant of Rachel and that it was because the sun was created in Rachel's merit that Joshua, as her

---

3. *Beis Efrayim, Orach Chaim*, no. 7. cites one authority who explains that R. Judah refers only to one who recites the blessing each year on the occasion of *Tekufas Nisan*. Another interpretation is that R. Judah refers to a person who recites the blessing in the form of *al hachammah* instead of *oseh ma'aseh bereishis*. See *Sedei Chemed, Pe'as haSadeh, ma'areches berachos*, no. 33, s.v. *ubeperush*, and *Me'orei Or*, p. 9a.

4. See above, chapter one.

וַאֲנַחְנוּ כּוֹרְעִים וּמִשְׁתַּחֲוִים וּמוֹדִים, לִפְנֵי
מֶלֶךְ מַלְכֵי הַמְּלָכִים הַקָּדוֹשׁ בָּרוּךְ הוּא.
שֶׁהוּא נוֹטֶה שָׁמַיִם וְיֹסֵד אָרֶץ, וּמוֹשַׁב יְקָרוֹ
בַּשָּׁמַיִם מִמַּעַל, וּשְׁכִינַת עֻזּוֹ בְּגָבְהֵי מְרוֹמִים.
הוּא אֱלֹהֵינוּ, אֵין עוֹד. אֱמֶת מַלְכֵּנוּ, אֶפֶס זוּלָתוֹ,
כַּכָּתוּב בְּתוֹרָתוֹ: וְיָדַעְתָּ הַיּוֹם וַהֲשֵׁבֹתָ אֶל לְבָבֶךָ,
כִּי יהוה הוּא הָאֱלֹהִים בַּשָּׁמַיִם מִמַּעַל וְעַל הָאָרֶץ
מִתָּחַת, אֵין עוֹד.

descendant, was privileged to halt the sun at Gibeon. Accordingly, concludes *Pesach haDvir*, it is appropriate to recite the prayer of thanksgiving composed by Joshua on the occasion of *Bircas HaChammah* which commemorates the creation of the sun.

The primary function of the *Aleinu* prayer is its role in the *Musaf shemoneh esreh* recited on *Rosh HaShanah* where it constitutes the prologue to *Malchiyos*, the blessing acknowledging and proclaiming the kingship of God, which is included in the *Musaf* of *Rosh HaShanah*. During the Middle Ages it became customary to conclude each of the three daily prayers with *Aleinu*. The earliest mention of this practice is in two thirteenth-century works, *Rokeach*, chap. 324 and the commentary of *Meiri* on *Berachos* (*Machon haTalmud haYerushalmi haShalem*), p. 118. Subsequently, *Aleinu* was incorporated as the conclusion of other worship services as well, e.g., as the concluding prayer of *Kiddush Levanah* and as the final prayer recited at a *Bris Milah*.

Numerous sources ascribe authorship of *Aleinu* to Joshua, who is reported to have composed it as a hymn of thanksgiving upon the conquest of Jericho. The initial letters of what may be regarded as the first four

sentences, עָלֵינוּ ... שֶׁלֹּא ... וַאֲנַחְנוּ ... הוּא ... אֱלֹהֵינוּ, when read backwards, form the word הוֹשֵׁעַ which was the name of Joshua before it was changed by Moshe to יְהוֹשֻׁעַ.

Others attribute authorship of *Aleinu* to Rav, the Babylonian *Amora* who is described in the *Yerushalmi*, *Rosh HaShanah* 1:5, as the author of various sections of the *Musaf* service of *Rosh HaShanah*. It has been suggested that Rav may have adapted the prayer originally composed by Joshua.

Aleinu expresses fundamental concepts of Judaism with clarity and beauty. It constitutes one of the most eloquent statements of the meaning of the election of Israel: שֶׁלֹּא עָשָׂנוּ כְּגוֹיֵי הָאֲרָצוֹת ... שֶׁלֹּא שָׂם חֶלְקֵנוּ כָּהֶם ... וַאֲנַחְנוּ כּוֹרְעִים וּמִשְׁתַּחֲוִים וּמוֹדִים לִפְנֵי מֶלֶךְ מַלְכֵי הַמְּלָכִים הַקָּדוֹשׁ בָּרוּךְ הוּא — *For He has not made us like the nations of the lands ... for He has not assigned our portion like theirs ... But we bend our knees, bow and acknowledge our thanks before the King Who reigns over kings, the Holy One, Blessed is He.* While the first section emphasizes our profound gratitude for this election, the second section underscores Judaism's universal commitment and its concern for the perfection of mankind through the reign of the Almighty לְתַקֵּן עוֹלָם בְּמַלְכוּת שַׁדַּי.

But we bend our knees, bow, and acknowledge our thanks before the King Who reigns over kings, the Holy One, Blessed is He. He stretches out heaven and establishes earth's foundation, the seat of His homage is in the heavens above and His powerful Presence is in the loftiest heights. He is our God and there is none other. True is our King, there is nothing beside Him, as it is written in His Torah: "You are to know this day and take to your heart that HASHEM is the only God — in heaven above and on the earth below — there is none other" (Deuteronomy 4:39).

שֶׁהֵם מִשְׁתַּחֲוִים לְהֶבֶל וָרִיק וּמִתְפַּלְלִים אֶל אֵל לֹא־יוֹשִׁיעַ — *For they bow to vanity and emptiness and pray to a god which helps not.*

This phrase is based upon *Isaiah* 30:7 and 45:20. Since the composition of *Aleinu* predates the Christian era, this phrase could hardly have been directed against Christianity. Nevertheless, these words became the excuse for repeated attacks upon Jewish practices. In 1399 an apostate Jew sought to demonstrate that this phrase is intended as an attack upon Christianity by showing that the numerical value of the letters spelling the word וָרִיק (316) equals that of the letters of the name of the founder of Christianity (יֵשׁוּ). R. Menashe ben Israel, in his noted *Vindiciae Judaeorum*, devoted an entire chapter to a refutation of this accusation — but to no avail. Therefore, censors frequently expunged the phrase. An edict issued in Prussia in 1703 decreed that the offending words be eliminated and further directed that the *Aleinu* prayer be recited aloud and in unison by the congregation in order to prevent worshipers from uttering the phrase in a manner which might go undetected by government agents. As a result of persistent government harassment the phrase was removed

and remains absent in most prayer-books used by Ashkenazic Jews. However, it is found in *siddurim* utilized by Oriental Jews since in their countries of residence censors did not tamper with the *Aleinu* prayer.

The editor of *Siddur Ishei Yisrael* (Jerusalem, 5695), p. 394, reports that Maharil Diskin insisted upon inclusion of this phrase in *Aleinu* when recited as part of the *Musaf Shemoneh Esreh* on *Rosh HaShanah*. Maharil Diskin regarded its omission as an unacceptable alteration of the liturgical form of the blessing ordained by the Sages (מַשְׁנֶה מִמַּטְבֵּעַ שֶׁטָּבְעוּ חֲכָמִים בִּבְרָכוֹת). This writer recalls using the *siddur* of R. Reuven Grozovsky זצ״ל, during the latter's illness and noting that the phrase was written into the *siddur* in the Rosh Yeshivah's own handwriting.

וַאֲנַחְנוּ כּוֹרְעִים וּמִשְׁתַּחֲוִים — *But we bend our knees, bow.*

When bowing upon uttering these words, care should be taken not to bow in the direction of the sun, but rather to the north or to the south, lest the bowing be construed as an act of obeisance to the sun. See *Tekufas haChammah uBirchosah*, p. 79. Cf. also *Mishnah Berurah* 426:14.

עַל כֵּן נְקַוֶּה לְּךָ יהוה אֱלֹהֵינוּ לִרְאוֹת מְהֵרָה בְּתִפְאֶרֶת עֻזֶּךָ, לְהַעֲבִיר גִּלּוּלִים מִן הָאָרֶץ, וְהָאֱלִילִים כָּרוֹת יִכָּרֵתוּן, לְתַקֵּן עוֹלָם בְּמַלְכוּת שַׁדַּי. וְכָל בְּנֵי בָשָׂר יִקְרְאוּ בִשְׁמֶךָ, לְהַפְנוֹת אֵלֶיךָ כָּל רִשְׁעֵי אָרֶץ. יַכִּירוּ וְיֵדְעוּ כָּל יוֹשְׁבֵי תֵבֵל, כִּי לְךָ תִּכְרַע כָּל בֶּרֶךְ, תִּשָּׁבַע כָּל לָשׁוֹן. לְפָנֶיךָ יהוה אֱלֹהֵינוּ יִכְרְעוּ וְיִפֹּלוּ, וְלִכְבוֹד שִׁמְךָ יְקָר יִתֵּנוּ. וִיקַבְּלוּ כֻלָּם אֶת עוֹל מַלְכוּתֶךָ, וְתִמְלֹךְ עֲלֵיהֶם מְהֵרָה לְעוֹלָם וָעֶד. כִּי הַמַּלְכוּת שֶׁלְּךָ הִיא וּלְעוֹלְמֵי עַד תִּמְלוֹךְ בְּכָבוֹד, כַּכָּתוּב בְּתוֹרָתֶךָ. יהוה יִמְלֹךְ לְעֹלָם וָעֶד. וְנֶאֱמַר. וְהָיָה יהוה לְמֶלֶךְ עַל כָּל הָאָרֶץ, בַּיּוֹם הַהוּא יִהְיֶה יהוה אֶחָד וּשְׁמוֹ אֶחָד.

[ברוב קהילות אין אומרים]

תהלים עד **מַשְׂכִּיל** לְאָסָף, לָמָה אֱלֹהִים זָנַחְתָּ לָנֶצַח, יֶעְשַׁן אַפְּךָ בְּצֹאן מַרְעִיתֶךָ. זְכֹר עֲדָתְךָ קָנִיתָ קֶּדֶם, גָּאַלְתָּ שֵׁבֶט נַחֲלָתֶךָ; הַר־צִיּוֹן, זֶה שָׁכַנְתָּ בּוֹ. הָרִימָה פְעָמֶיךָ לְמַשֻּׁאוֹת נֶצַח, כָּל־הֵרַע אוֹיֵב בַּקֹּדֶשׁ. שָׁאֲגוּ צֹרְרֶיךָ בְּקֶרֶב מוֹעֲדֶךָ, שָׂמוּ אוֹתֹתָם אֹתוֹת. יִוָּדַע כְּמֵבִיא לְמָעְלָה, בִּסְבָךְ עֵץ קַרְדֻּמּוֹת. וְעַתָּה [כתיב וְעַתּ] פִּתּוּחֶיהָ יָּחַד, בְּכַשִּׁיל וְכֵילַפֹּת יַהֲלֹמוּן. שִׁלְחוּ בָאֵשׁ מִקְדָּשֶׁךָ, לָאָרֶץ חִלְּלוּ מִשְׁכַּן־שְׁמֶךָ. אָמְרוּ בְלִבָּם, נִינָם יָחַד, שָׂרְפוּ כָל־מוֹעֲדֵי אֵל בָּאָרֶץ. אוֹתֹתֵינוּ לֹא רָאִינוּ; אֵין עוֹד נָבִיא, וְלֹא אִתָּנוּ יֹדֵעַ עַד מָה. עַד מָתַי אֱלֹהִים יְחָרֶף צָר, יְנָאֵץ אוֹיֵב שִׁמְךָ לָנֶצַח. לָמָה תָשִׁיב יָדְךָ וִימִינֶךָ, מִקֶּרֶב חֵיקְךָ כַלֵּה. וֵאלֹהִים מַלְכִּי מִקֶּדֶם, פֹּעֵל יְשׁוּעוֹת

◆§ **מַשְׂכִּיל לְאָסָף** — Psalm 74

This psalm laments the pain and bitterness of exile and expresses a prayer to God to redeem His people. In particular, God is described as the Creator of "the luminaries and the sun" which accounts for the inclusion, by some, of this psalm in the *Seder Bircas haChammah.*

A nd therefore we put our hope in You, HASHEM, our God, that we may soon see Your mighty splendor, to remove detestable idolatry from the earth, and false gods will be utterly cut off, to perfect the universe through the Almighty's sovereignty. Then all humanity will call upon Your Name, to turn all the earth's wicked toward You. All the world's inhabitants will recognize and know that to You every knee should bend, every tongue should swear. Before You, HASHEM, our God, they will bend every knee and cast themselves down, and to the glory of Your Name they will render homage, and they will all accept upon themselves the yoke of Your kingship that You may reign over them soon and eternally. For the kingdom is Yours and You will reign for all eternity in glory, as it is written in Your Torah: "HASHEM shall reign for all eternity" (Exodus 15:18). And it is said: "HASHEM will be King over all the world — on that day HASHEM will be One and His Name will be One" (Zechariah 14:9).

[In most communities the following psalm is not recited.]

Psalm 74

A maskil by Asaph. Why, O God, have You abandoned [us] for an eternity? [Why] does Your wrath smolder against the sheep of Your pasture? [2] Remember Your congregation, which You acquired long ago, You redeemed the tribe of Your heritage; the mountain of Zion, the one where You rested Your Presence. [3] Lift Your footsteps to wreak eternal ruin, [to avenge] everything that the enemy has harmed in the Sanctuary. [4] Your enemies have roared amidst Your meeting place, they made their signs for signs. [5] It had been regarded as bringing [a gift] to the One Above, the axes in the thicket of trees; [6] and now all its ornaments together, they beat down with hammer and chisels. [7] They have sent Your Sanctuary up in flames; to the ground have they desecrated the Abode of Your Name. [8] In their heart, they said — their rulers all together — they have burned all of God's meeting places on earth. [9] Our signs we have not seen; there is no longer a prophet, and there is none among us who knows for how long. [10] Until when, O God, will the tormentor revile, will the foe blaspheme Your Name forever? [11] Why do You withdraw Your hand, even Your right hand? Remove [it] from within Your bosom! [12] For God is my King from days of old, working salvations

בְּקֶרֶב הָאָרֶץ. אַתָּה פוֹרַרְתָּ בְעָזְּךָ יָם, שִׁבַּרְתָּ רָאשֵׁי תַנִּינִים עַל הַמָּיִם.
אַתָּה רִצַּצְתָּ רָאשֵׁי לִוְיָתָן, תִּתְּנֶנּוּ מַאֲכָל לְעָם לְצִיִּים. אַתָּה בָקַעְתָּ
מַעְיָן וָנָחַל, אַתָּה הוֹבַשְׁתָּ נַהֲרוֹת אֵיתָן. לְךָ יוֹם אַף לְךָ לָיְלָה, אַתָּה
הֲכִינוֹתָ מָאוֹר וָשָׁמֶשׁ. אַתָּה הִצַּבְתָּ כָּל־גְּבוּלוֹת אָרֶץ קַיִץ וָחֹרֶף
אַתָּה יְצַרְתָּם. זְכָר זֹאת אוֹיֵב חֵרֵף יהוה, וְעַם נָבָל נִאֲצוּ שְׁמֶךָ. אַל
תִּתֵּן לְחַיַּת נֶפֶשׁ תּוֹרֶךָ, חַיַּת עֲנִיֶּיךָ אַל תִּשְׁכַּח לָנֶצַח. הַבֵּט לַבְּרִית,
כִּי מָלְאוּ מַחֲשַׁכֵּי אֶרֶץ נְאוֹת חָמָס. אַל־יָשֹׁב דַּךְ נִכְלָם, עָנִי וְאֶבְיוֹן
יְהַלְלוּ שְׁמֶךָ. קוּמָה אֱלֹהִים רִיבָה רִיבֶךָ, זְכֹר חֶרְפָּתְךָ מִנִּי נָבָל כָּל
הַיּוֹם. אַל תִּשְׁכַּח קוֹל צֹרְרֶיךָ, שְׁאוֹן קָמֶיךָ עֹלֶה תָמִיד.

[בְּרוֹב קְהִלּוֹת אֵין אוֹמְרִים]

אֵין כֵּאלֹהֵינוּ, אֵין כַּאדוֹנֵינוּ, אֵין כְּמַלְכֵּנוּ, אֵין כְּמוֹשִׁיעֵנוּ. מִי
כֵאלֹהֵינוּ, מִי כַאדוֹנֵינוּ, מִי כְמַלְכֵּנוּ, מִי כְמוֹשִׁיעֵנוּ. נוֹדֶה
לֵאלֹהֵינוּ, נוֹדֶה לַאדוֹנֵינוּ, נוֹדֶה לְמַלְכֵּנוּ, נוֹדֶה לְמוֹשִׁיעֵנוּ. בָּרוּךְ
אֱלֹהֵינוּ, בָּרוּךְ אֲדוֹנֵינוּ, בָּרוּךְ מַלְכֵּנוּ, בָּרוּךְ מוֹשִׁיעֵנוּ. אַתָּה
הוּא אֱלֹהֵינוּ, אַתָּה הוּא אֲדוֹנֵינוּ, אַתָּה הוּא מַלְכֵּנוּ, אַתָּה הוּא
מוֹשִׁיעֵנוּ.

רַבִּי חֲנַנְיָא בֶּן עֲקַשְׁיָא אוֹמֵר. רָצָה הַקָּדוֹשׁ
בָּרוּךְ הוּא לְזַכּוֹת אֶת יִשְׂרָאֵל, לְפִיכָךְ
הִרְבָּה לָהֶם תּוֹרָה וּמִצְוֹת, שֶׁנֶּאֱמַר. יהוה חָפֵץ
לְמַעַן צִדְקוֹ, יַגְדִּיל תּוֹרָה וְיַאְדִּיר.

---

§ אֵין כֵּאלֹהֵינוּ **— Ein Keilokeinu**

The *Ein Keilokeinu* prayer dates to the Geonic period. It is recited on *Shabbos* and *Yom Tov*. As noted, *Ein Keilokeinu* is a late addition to the *Seder Bircas haChammah* and is not recited in most communities.

In the first three stanzas the letters spelling אָמֵן are repeated four times. In the last two stanzas, corresponding to the four times אָמֵן occurs in the acrostic, each of these twelve letters which form the four occurrences of אָמֵן appears in conjunction with a divine appellation. *Ein Keilokeinu* was composed for recitation on *Shabbos* and *Yom Tov* when the *Shemoneh Esreh* prayer contains only seven blessings instead of the usual nineteen. The twelve invocations of God's Name in a manner alluding to the formula of a *berachah* symbolize the twelve blessings which are absent in the Sabbath and Holy Day prayers (*Etz Yosef*).

§ רַבִּי חֲנַנְיָא **— R. Chananya**

The dictum of R. Chananya ben Akashya, which is found in the concluding Mishnah of *Makkos*, is said prior to the recitation of the *Kaddish deRabbanan* subsequent to Torah study. This practice is in conformity with the opinion which maintains that the *Kaddish deRabbanan* is recited only after Torah study which includes *aggadah*, or homiletical texts,

in the midst of the earth. [13] You shattered the sea with Your might; You smashed the heads of sea serpents upon the water. [14] You crushed the head of Leviathan; You will serve him as food to the people destined for the desolate wilderness. [15] You split open fountain and stream; You dried the mighty rivers. [16] Yours is the day, Yours is the night; You prepared the luminary and the sun. [17] You established all the boundaries of earth; summer and winter, You fashioned them. [18] Remember this: The foe reviled HASHEM, and the degenerate people blasphemed Your Name. [19] Do not deliver the soul of Your turtledove to the wild beast, do not forget the life of Your poor forever. [20] Look upon the covenant, for the earth's dark places [of Israel's exile] are filled with habitations of violence. [21] Let not the oppressed turn back in shame; let the poor and destitute praise Your Name. [22] Arise, O God, champion Your cause! Remember Your disgrace from the degenerate all day long. [23] Forget not the voice of Your enemies, the tumult of Your opponents which always rises.

[In most communities the following hymn is not recited.]

There is none like our God; there is none like our Master; there is none like our King; there is none like our Savior. Who is like our God? Who is like our Master? Who is like our King? Who is like our Savior? Let us thank our God; let us thank our Master; let us thank our King; let us thank our Savior. Blessed is our God; blessed is our Master; blessed is our King; blessed is our Savior. It is You Who is our God; it is You Who is our Master; it is You Who is our King; it is You Who is our Savior. You will save us. You will arise and show Zion mercy, for it will be the time to favor her, for the appointed time will have come.

Rabbi Chanania ben Akashia says: The Holy One, Blessed is He, wished to confer merit upon Israel; therefore He gave them Torah and mitzvos in abundance, as it is said: "HASHEM desired, for the sake of its [Israel's] righteousness, that the Torah be made great and glorious" (Isaiah 42:21).

---

rather than purely halachic ones. See *Rashi, Sotah* 49a, s.v., *akedusha desidra,* and compare the seemingly contradictory statements of *Rambam* cited by *Magen Avraham* 54:3. In the *Seder Bircas haChammah,* this saying of R. Chanania ben Akashia was

originally placed after the *Beraisa, Berachos* 59b. With the inclusion of later interpolations, it is recited after *Aleinu* at the end of the service.

לְזַכּוֹת אֶת־יִשְׂרָאֵל — *To confer merit upon Israel.*

Mitzvos are given, not as an

יִתְגַּדַּל וְיִתְקַדֵּשׁ שְׁמֵהּ רַבָּא. (.Cong– אָמֵן)
בְּעָלְמָא דִּי בְרָא כִרְעוּתֵהּ. וְיַמְלִיךְ
מַלְכוּתֵהּ, [וְיַצְמַח פֻּרְקָנֵהּ וִיקָרֵב מְשִׁיחֵהּ.
(.Cong– אָמֵן)] בְּחַיֵּיכוֹן וּבְיוֹמֵיכוֹן וּבְחַיֵּי דְכָל בֵּית
יִשְׂרָאֵל, בַּעֲגָלָא וּבִזְמַן קָרִיב. וְאִמְרוּ: אָמֵן.
(.Cong– אָמֵן. יְהֵא שְׁמֵהּ רַבָּא מְבָרַךְ לְעָלַם וּלְעָלְמֵי
עָלְמַיָּא.)

יְהֵא שְׁמֵהּ רַבָּא מְבָרַךְ לְעָלַם וּלְעָלְמֵי עָלְמַיָּא.
יִתְבָּרַךְ וְיִשְׁתַּבַּח וְיִתְפָּאַר וְיִתְרוֹמַם וְיִתְנַשֵּׂא
וְיִתְהַדָּר וְיִתְעַלֶּה וְיִתְהַלָּל שְׁמֵהּ דְּקֻדְשָׁא, בְּרִיךְ
הוּא. (.Cong– בְּרִיךְ הוּא.) — לְעֵלָּא מִן כָּל בִּרְכָתָא
וְשִׁירָתָא תֻּשְׁבְּחָתָא וְנֶחֱמָתָא דַּאֲמִירָן בְּעָלְמָא.
וְאִמְרוּ: אָמֵן. (.Cong– אָמֵן)

עַל יִשְׂרָאֵל וְעַל רַבָּנָן, וְעַל תַּלְמִידֵיהוֹן וְעַל
כָּל תַּלְמִידֵי תַלְמִידֵיהוֹן, וְעַל כָּל מָאן דְּעָסְקִין
בְּאוֹרַיְתָא, דִּי בְאַתְרָא הָדֵין וְדִי בְכָל אֲתַר וַאֲתַר.
יְהֵא לְהוֹן וּלְכוֹן שְׁלָמָא רַבָּא, חִנָּא וְחִסְדָּא
וְרַחֲמִין, וְחַיִּין אֲרִיכִין, וּמְזוֹנֵי רְוִיחֵי, וּפֻרְקָנָא מִן
קֳדָם אֲבוּהוֹן דִּי בִשְׁמַיָּא וְאַרְעָא. וְאִמְרוּ: אָמֵן.
(.Cong– אָמֵן)

---

obstacle course to entrap the violator, but as a means of acquiring merit. As a result of the sheer number of *mitzvos* given to Israel, every Jew is accorded the opportunity of acquiring great reward. *Rashi* observes that the *mitzvos* encompass many areas of human activity in which proper conduct is mandated by reason and inclination. Yet, by virtue of the status of such actions as the object of divine commandments, they are endowed with sanctity and lead to acquisition of merit.

In his commentary on this Mishnah, *Rambam* declares, "It is a principle of belief in the Torah that if a person fulfills one of the 613 *mitzvos* as is right and proper and does not in any manner introduce any mundane intention but performs [the *mitzvah*] for its own sake out of

May His great Name grow exalted and sanctified (Cong.— Amen.) in the world that He created as He willed. May He give reign to His kingship [and cause His salvation to sprout, and bring near His Messiah (Cong.— Amen.)], in your lifetimes and in your days, and in the lifetimes of the entire Family of Israel, swiftly and soon. Now respond: Amen.

(Cong.— Amen. May His great Name be blessed forever and ever.)

May His great Name be blessed forever and ever.

Blessed, praised, glorified, exalted, extolled, mighty, upraised, and lauded be the Name of the Holy One, Blessed is He (Cong.— Blessed is He) — beyond any blessing and song, praise and consolation that are uttered in the world. Now respond: Amen. (Cong.— Amen.)

Upon Israel, upon the teachers, their disciples and all of their disciples, and upon all those who engage in the study of Torah, who are here or anywhere else; may they and you have abundant peace, grace, kindness, long life, ample nourishment, and salvation from before their Father Who is in Heaven and on earth. Now respond: Amen. (Cong.— Amen.)

---

love ... he has thereby acquired life in the world-to-come." *Rambam* then explains the dictum of R. Chanania ben Akashia as stating that God gave Israel numerous *mitzvos* so that in the course of a lifetime it is virtually impossible for an individual not to perform at least one *mitzvah* in the optimal manner. (Cf., however, *Maharal, Tiferes Yisrael*, chap. 5, who disputes *Rambam's* view.)

Maharal cites the midrashic source (*Bereishis Rabbah* 44:1) which declares that *mitzvos* are designed for the moral and spiritual purification of Israel. A few *mitzvos* alone would not suffice for this purpose; in order to achieve this goal in the optimum manner the entire corpus of *mitzvos* is necessary. Therefore, the plethora

of *mitzvos* is a source of benefit to Israel. *Maharal* further comments that although an individual Jew may be remiss in fulfillment of *mitzvos* and incur punishment for violation of each *mitzvah*, nevertheless, Israel as a people is predisposed to fulfill God's commandments and hence the enhanced number of *mitzvos* is a source of merit to the people of Israel (*Tiferes Yisrael*, chap. 5).

◄§ קַדִּישׁ — **Kaddish**

The *Kaddish*, proclaiming the sanctification of God, is customarily recited following public worship or study. It is recited only when a *minyan*, a quorum of ten, is present. When recited following the study of rabbinic texts the paragraph עַל יִשְׂרָאֵל

יְהֵא שְׁלָמָא רַבָּא מִן שְׁמַיָּא, וְחַיִּים (טוֹבִים)
עָלֵינוּ וְעַל כָּל יִשְׂרָאֵל. וְאִמְרוּ: אָמֵן. (.אָמֵן –Cong.)

עֹשֶׂה שָׁלוֹם בִּמְרוֹמָיו, הוּא (בְּרַחֲמָיו) יַעֲשֶׂה
שָׁלוֹם עָלֵינוּ, וְעַל כָּל יִשְׂרָאֵל. וְאִמְרוּ. אָמֵן.
(.אָמֵן –Cong.)

מוֹדִים אֲנַחְנוּ לָךְ, וּמְהַלְּלִים לְשֵׁם תִּפְאַרְתֶּךָ. בְּרָכוֹת
וְהוֹדָאוֹת לְשִׁמְךָ הַגָּדוֹל וְהַקָּדוֹשׁ, עַל־שֶׁהֶחֱיִיתָנוּ
וְקִיַּמְתָּנוּ וְהִגַּעְתָּנוּ עַד־הַיּוֹם הַזֶּה לְבָרֵךְ בִּרְכַּת הוֹדָאָה זוֹ
לְפָנֶיךָ.

וִיהִי רָצוֹן מִלְּפָנֶיךָ, יהוה אֱלֹהֵינוּ וֵאלֹהֵי אֲבוֹתֵינוּ,
שֶׁכְּשֵׁם שֶׁזִּכִּיתָנוּ לְבָרֵךְ בִּרְכַּת הַחַמָּה
בַּיּוֹם הַזֶּה, כֵּן הָאֵל הַחַי הַטּוֹב וְהַמֵּטִיב לְכָל־
בְּרוּאָיו, כֵּן תְּחַיֵּנוּ וּתְקַיְּמֵנוּ וּתְחָנֵּנוּ וּתְזַכֵּנוּ לְבָרֵךְ
בְּרָכָה זוֹ לִתְקוּפוֹת הַחַמָּה הָאֲחֵרוֹת הַבָּאוֹת עָלֵינוּ
לְשָׁלוֹם, שְׂמֵחִים בְּבִנְיַן עִירֶךָ וְשָׂשִׂים בַּעֲבוֹדָתֶךָ.
וְתֵן לָנוּ חַיִּים אֲרוּכִים, חַיִּים שֶׁל שָׁלוֹם, חַיִּים שֶׁל
טוֹבָה, חַיִּים שֶׁל בְּרָכָה, חַיִּים שֶׁל פַּרְנָסָה טוֹבָה,
חַיִּים שֶׁל חִלּוּץ עֲצָמוֹת, חַיִּים שֶׁיֵּשׁ בָּהֶם יִרְאַת
חֵטְא, חַיִּים שֶׁאֵין בָּהֶם בּוּשָׁה וּכְלִמָּה, חַיִּים
שֶׁל עֹשֶׁר וְכָבוֹד לַעֲבוֹדָתֶךָ וּלְיִרְאָתֶךָ, חַיִּים
שֶׁתְּהֵא בָנוּ אַהֲבַת תּוֹרָה וְיִרְאַת שָׁמַיִם לִשְׁמָהּ,
חַיִּים שֶׁתְּמַלֵּא מִשְׁאֲלוֹת לִבֵּנוּ לְטוֹבָה לַעֲבוֹדָתֶךָ
וּלְיִרְאָתֶךָ, וּתְזַכֵּנוּ לִרְאוֹת פְּנֵי מְשִׁיחֶךָ וּתְקַיֶּם בָּנוּ
מִקְרָא שֶׁכָּתוּב עַל־יַד־נְבִיאָךְ, כָּאָמוּר. וְהָיָה אוֹר

וְעַל רַבָּנָן — *Upon Israel, upon the teachers* ... is inserted as a prayer on behalf of scholars and their students.

Modim — מוֹדִים ﻉ؟

Pesach haDvir, the author of this prayer, composed this formula

May there be abundant peace from Heaven, and good life, upon us and upon all Israel. Now respond: Amen. (Cong.— Amen.)

He Who makes peace in His heights, may He, in His compassion, make peace upon us, and upon all Israel. Now respond: Amen. (Cong.— Amen.)

We give thanks unto You and praise Your glorious Name. *Blessings and thanksgiving to Your great and holy Name for having sustained us in life, for having preserved us and for having caused us to reach this day to pronounce this blessing of thanksgiving before You.*

May it be Your will, O HASHEM our God and God of *our fathers, that, just as You have privileged us to recite Bircas haChammah on this day, so also O living God, Who is good and beneficent to all His creatures, sustain us in life, preserve us and grant us the privilege of pronouncing this blessing upon other equinoxes of the sun, may they come upon us in peace, happy in the building of Your city and joyous in Your service. Bestow upon us long life, a life of peace, a life of goodness, a life of blessing, a life of ample sustenance, a life of bodily vigor, a life in which there is fear of sin, a life in which there is no shame or embarrassment, a life of wealth and honor for Your service and for Your fear, a life in which we will have love of Torah for its own sake and fear of heaven, a life in which You will fulfill the requests of our heart for good, for Your service and for Your fear. Privilege us to behold the face of Your Messiah and fulfill through us the verse that was written by Your prophet as it is said: "And the light*

---

to be recited prior to the יְהִי רָצוֹן in lieu of the *shehechiyanu* blessing which is not part of the *Seder Bircas haChammah.*

וִיהִי רָצוֹן — Vihi Ratzon

This supplication reflects joy in the performance of the infrequent

mitzvah of *Bircas haChammah* and expresses a yearning that we be privileged to perform this *mitzvah* on future occasions and to dedicate our lives to the service of God. Coupled with this prayer is an entreaty that the advent of the Messiah be hastened and we be privileged to behold

הַלְּבָנָה כְּאוֹר הַחַמָּה. וְאוֹר הַחַמָּה יִהְיֶה שִׁבְעָתַיִם כְּאוֹר שִׁבְעַת הַיָּמִים. בְּיוֹם חֲבֹשׁ יהוה אֶת שֶׁבֶר עַמּוֹ וּמַחַץ מַכָּתוֹ יִרְפָּא. כֵּן יְהִי רָצוֹן.

[בְּרֹב קְהִלּוֹת אֵין אוֹמְרִים]

בְּטֶרֶם כָּל־יְצִיר נִבְרָא.	**אֲדוֹן** עוֹלָם אֲשֶׁר מָלַךְ,
אֲזַי מֶלֶךְ שְׁמוֹ נִקְרָא.	לְעֵת נַעֲשָׂה בְחֶפְצוֹ כֹּל,
לְבַדּוֹ יִמְלוֹךְ נוֹרָא.	וְאַחֲרֵי כִּכְלוֹת הַכֹּל,
וְהוּא יִהְיֶה בְּתִפְאָרָה.	וְהוּא הָיָה וְהוּא הֹוֶה,
לְהַמְשִׁיל לוֹ לְהַחְבִּירָה.	וְהוּא אֶחָד וְאֵין שֵׁנִי,
וְלוֹ הָעֹז וְהַמִּשְׂרָה.	בְּלִי רֵאשִׁית בְּלִי תַכְלִית,
בְּלִי שִׁנּוּי וּתְמוּרָה.	[בְּלִי עֵרֶךְ בְּלִי דִמְיוֹן,
גָּדוֹל כֹּחַ וּגְבוּרָה.]	בְּלִי חִבּוּר בְּלִי פֵרוּד,
וְצוּר חֶבְלִי בְּעֵת צָרָה.	וְהוּא אֵלִי וְחַי גֹּאֲלִי,
מְנָת כּוֹסִי בְּיוֹם אֶקְרָא.	וְהוּא נִסִּי וּמָנוֹס לִי,
[וְהוּא צוֹפֶה וְהוּא עֶזְרָה.]	[וְהוּא רוֹפֵא וְהוּא מַרְפֵּא
בְּעֵת אִישַׁן וְאָעֵירָה.	בְּיָדוֹ אַפְקִיד רוּחִי,
יהוה לִי וְלֹא אִירָא.	וְעִם רוּחִי גְּוִיָּתִי,
מְשִׁיחֵנוּ יִשְׁלַח מְהֵרָה.	[בְּמִקְדָּשׁוֹ תָּגֵל נַפְשִׁי,
אָמֵן אָמֵן שֵׁם הַנּוֹרָא.]	וְאָז נָשִׁיר בְּבֵית קָדְשִׁי,

---

speaks of the majesty, omnipotence and providence of God serves as a prefatory hymn to the morning service. Frequently, it is also sung at the conclusion of services and, the fulfillment of the prophecies regarding the Messianic era.

אֲדוֹן עוֹלָם — Adon Olam

The *Adon Olam* hymn which

of the moon shall be as the light of the sun, and the light of the sun shall be seven times seven as the light of the seven days, in the day that HASHEM binds up the breach of His people and heals the wound of their blow" (Isaiah 30:26). May so be Your will.

[In most communities the following hymn is not recited.]

M*aster of the universe, Who reigned*
before any form was created,
At the time when His will brought all into being —
then as "King" was His Name proclaimed.
After all has ceased to be,
He, the Awesome One, will reign alone.
It is He Who was, He Who is,
and He Who shall remain, in splendor.
He is One — there is no second to compare to Him,
to declare as His equal.
Without beginning, without conclusion —
His is the power and dominion.
[Without assessment, without comparison; without change or substitute.
Without composition, without separation, great in strength and in might.]
He is my God, my living Redeemer,
Rock of my pain in time of distress.
He is my banner, a refuge for me,
the portion in my cup on the day I call.
[He is the healer and He is the cure;
He is the prognosticator and He is the aid.]
Into His hand I shall entrust my spirit
when I go to sleep — and I shall awaken!
With my spirit shall my body remain.
HASHEM is with me, I shall not fear.
[In His Temple let my soul rejoice; may He speedily send our Messiah.
Then we will sing in my Holy House — Amen, Amen, O awesome Name.]

hence, its inclusion by *Ben Ish Chai* as the final hymn of the *Seder Bircas haChammah.*

The bracketed stanzas form part of the *Adon Olam* as sung in many Sephardic communities.

[The following is an expanded version of the concluding supplication composed by Rabbi Eliezer Chaim Deutsch, author of Teshuvos *Pri HaSadeh*, on the occasion of *Bircas HaChammah* in the year 5657, which marked the beginning of the two hundred and third solar cycle.]

רִבּוֹנוֹ שֶׁל עוֹלָם מוֹדִים אֲנַחְנוּ לְפָנֶיךָ עַל כָּל הַטּוֹבוֹת וְהַחֲסָדִים אֲשֶׁר עָשִׂיתָ עִמָּנוּ וְהֶחֱיִיתָנוּ
וְקִיַּמְתָּנוּ לַזְּמַן הַזֶּה לַתְּקוּפָה הַחֲדָשָׁה הַבָּאָה עָלֵינוּ לְטוֹבָה וְהִגַּעְתָּנוּ לִתְחִלַּת
הַמַּחֲזוֹר הַזֶּה, שֶׁהוּא מָאתַיִם וּשְׁלֹשָׁה מַחֲזוֹרִים שֶׁל שְׁמֹנֶה וְעֶשְׂרִים שָׁנָה מֵעֵת עָלָה בִּרְצוֹנְךָ
הַפָּשׁוּט לִבְרֹא הָעוֹלָם וְהִתְקַנְתָּ עוֹלָמְךָ לְטוֹבַת יְצִירֶיךָ.
וְאַתָּה בְּעִין חֶמְלָתְךָ מַשְׁגִּיחַ עַל־כָּל־הַנִּבְרָאִים מִקָּטָן וְעַד גָּדוֹל לְהַשְׁפִּיעַ לְכָל נִבְרָא שֶׁבָּעוֹלָם
דֵּי מַחְסוֹרוֹ לְכָל אֶחָד וְאֶחָד כְּפִי טִבְעוֹ. וּמִכָּל מִינֵי הַנִּבְרָאִים בָּחַרְתָּ בְּמִין הָאֱנוֹשִׁי וְעַל כָּל
אוֹתוֹ נִשֵּׂאתָ, כְּמוֹ שֶׁכָּתַב דָּוִד הַמֶּלֶךְ עָלָיו הַשָּׁלוֹם. "כֹּל שַׁתָּה תַחַת רַגְלָיו צֹנֶה וַאֲלָפִים כֻּלָּם
וְגַם בַּהֲמוֹת שָׂדָי". וּמִכָּל מִין הָאֱנוֹשִׁי בָּחַרְתָּ בְּעַמְּךָ יִשְׂרָאֵל לְסְגֻלָּתֶךָ. וּכְמוֹ שֶׁקָּבַעְתָּ מְאוֹרוֹת
בַּשָּׁמַיִם חַמָּה וּלְבָנָה לְהָאִיר פְּנֵי תֵבֵל וּלְהַשְׁפִּיעַ מֵכֹּחָם עַל יְבוּלָם וְצִמְחֵי הָאֲדָמָה, כְּמוֹ שֶׁכָּתַבְתָּ
בְּתוֹרָתְךָ הַקְּדוֹשָׁה. "מִמֶּגֶד תְּבוּאֹת שָׁמֶשׁ וּמִמֶּגֶד גֶּרֶשׁ יְרָחִים", כְּמוֹ כֵן הִשְׁפַּעְתָּ בְּכָל דּוֹר וָדוֹר
מֵרוּחַ חָכְמָתְךָ עַל חַכְמֵי הַדּוֹרוֹת וְהוֹפַעְתָּ עֲלֵיהֶם מֵרוּחַ קָדְשְׁךָ וְנָתַתָּ לָהֶם חָכְמָה לְנַהֵל אֶת אַנְשֵׁי
דוֹרָם לְהַדְרִיךְ אוֹתָם לַעֲשׂוֹת תָּמִיד רְצוֹנֶךָ.
וּבְכֵן עַל פִּי תַּקָּנַת חֲכָמֵינוּ הַקְּדוֹשִׁים נֶאֱסַפְנוּ בָּעֵת וּבָעוֹנָה הַזֹּאת לְבָרֵךְ לְךָ עַל בְּרִיאַת עוֹלָמְךָ.
בָּרוּךְ עוֹשֶׂה מַעֲשֵׂה בְרֵאשִׁית. וּבְכֵן אָנוּ מִתְפַּלְּלִים לְפָנֶיךָ. אָנָּא יהוה הָאֵל הַגָּדוֹל הַגִּבּוֹר וְהַנּוֹרָא
יְהִי רָצוֹן מִלְּפָנֶיךָ שֶׁיִּתַּמּוּ הַמְּאוֹרוֹת אֲשֶׁר בָּרֵאתָ וְהִתְקַנְתָּ בְּעוֹלָמְךָ לֹא נִבְרְאוּ לָרִיק, כִּי אֵינָם מְשַׁגִּים
אֶת־תַּפְקִידָם לָעוֹלָם וּמְאִירִים עַל פְּנֵי תֵבֵל כִּרְצוֹנְךָ הַטּוֹב, כֵּן בְּרַחֲמֶיךָ הָרַבִּים עָזְרֵנוּ עַל דְּבַר כְּבוֹד
שְׁמֶךָ שֶׁלֹּא תִהְיֶה יְגִיעָתֵנוּ לָרִיק חַס וְשָׁלוֹם, וְנִזְכֶּה לִהְיוֹת כָּל יְמֵי חַיֵּינוּ מְעוֹשֵׂי רְצוֹנֶךָ, שֶׁיִּקַיֵּם בָּנוּ
מִקְרָא שֶׁכָּתוּב. "וַיֹּאמֶר לִי עַבְדִּי אָתָּה יִשְׂרָאֵל אֲשֶׁר בְּךָ אֶתְפָּאָר". וְהָסֵר מִמֶּנּוּ כָּל טְרָדוֹת וְסִבּוֹת
הַמּוֹנְעִים אוֹתָנוּ מִתּוֹרָתְךָ וּמֵעֲבוֹדָתְךָ הַקְּדוֹשָׁה, וְתֵן בָּנוּ כֹּחַ שָׁנוּכַל לִכְבּוֹשׁ תַּאֲוֹתֵינוּ הַגּוּפָנִיּוֹת,
וְהַרְחִיקֵנוּ מִכָּל מִדּוֹת רָעוֹת הַמַּפְסִידוֹת עֲבוֹדָתְךָ הַקְּדוֹשָׁה.
וְאִם אָמְנָם נָמַס לִבֵּנוּ בְּקִרְבֵּנוּ עַל בְּהַעֲלוֹתֵנוּ עַל לְבָבֵנוּ גֹּדֶל קִצּוּרֵנוּ בַּעֲבוֹדָתֶךָ וְיָדַעְנוּ כִּי אֵין אָנוּ יוֹצְאִים
יְדֵי חוֹבָתֵנוּ נֶגְדֶּךָ, מֶלֶךְ מַלְכֵי הַמְּלָכִים הַקָּדוֹשׁ בָּרוּךְ הוּא, אֲפִילוּ אַחַת מֵאָלֶף, מָה אָנוּ מֶה חַיֵּינוּ,
וְעוֹמְדִים לְפָנֶיךָ בְּבֹשֶׁת פָּנִים. אִם נַחְפְּשָׂה דְרָכֵינוּ, כַּמָּה קִצַּרְנוּ בַּעֲבוֹדָתֶךָ בַּתְּקוּפָה וּבַמַּחֲזוֹר אֲשֶׁר
עָבַר עָלֵינוּ זֶה שְׁמֹנֶה וְעֶשְׂרִים שָׁנָה, כִּסַּתָּה כְלִמָּה פָנֵינוּ. מֶה הָיְתָה לָנוּ כִּי לֹא שָׁמַעְנוּ אֶל לִבֵּנוּ לְהֵיטִיב
דַּרְכֵּנוּ. אָמְנָם גָּלוּי וְיָדוּעַ לְפָנֶיךָ כִּי לֹא בְּמֶרֶד וּבְמַעַל חָלִילָה וְחָלִילָה מָרִינוּ אֶת פִּיךָ, רַק מִטִּרְדַת
הַיֵּצֶר וּשְׁאָר עִנְיָנִים הַמְבַלְבְּלִים שִׂכְלֵנוּ, וְכָשַׁל כֹּחֵנוּ לַעֲמֹד נֶגֶד טְרָדוֹת הַזְּמַן הֵן מֶחְסַר פַּרְנָסָה
בַּעֲוֹנוֹתֵינוּ הָרַבִּים וְהֵן מִשְּׁאָר סִבּוֹת אֲשֶׁר עָבְרוּ עַל נַפְשֵׁנוּ, רַבַּת צְרָרוּנִי וְרַב שָׂבְעָנוּ בוּז. כָּל אֵלֶּה הָיוּ
בַּעֲוֹנֵנוּ אֲשֶׁר לֹא הָיָה בָּנוּ כֹּחַ לְהַשְׁלִים אֲשֶׁר תְּכַלִּיתֵנוּ בְּרָאתָנוּ, אֵל הַטּוֹב וּמֵטִיב לַכֹּל, לְטוֹבָתֵנוּ.
וְעַתָּה בָּאנוּ לְפָנֶיךָ בִּתְפִלָּה וּבְבַקָּשָׁה, כִּי כָל אֵלֶּה גָּלוּי וְיָדוּעַ לִפְנֵי כִסֵּא כְבוֹדֶךָ, מַה נֹּאמַר לְפָנֶיךָ
וּמַה נְּסַפֵּר לְפָנֶיךָ, הֲלֹא כָל צְפוּן לִבֵּנוּ וּמַחְשְׁבוֹתֵינוּ לְפָנֶיךָ הֵם גְּלוּיִים וִידוּעִים. עָזְרֵנוּ בְּכָל עִנְיָנֵינוּ
עַל דְּבַר כְּבוֹד שְׁמֶךָ שֶׁנִּהְיֶה מֵהַיּוֹם וָהָלְאָה מֵעוֹשֵׂי מַעֲשֵׂי רְצוֹנֶךָ, שֶׁיּוּשְׁלַם עַל־יָדֵינוּ תַּכְלִית הַבְּרִיאָה.
וְתַצִּילֵנוּ בַּתְּקוּפָה הַזֹּאת הַבָּאָה עָלֵינוּ לְטוֹבָה מִכָּל צַעַר וָנֶזֶק, וּמִכָּל מִכְשׁוֹל וְתַקָּלָה חַס וְשָׁלוֹם,
וּמִכָּל הֶפְסֵד וַעֲנִיּוֹת וְדַלּוּת וְחֶסְרוֹן כִּיס, וּמִכָּל מִינֵי פֻּרְעָנִיּוֹת וַחֳלָאִים רָעִים וּמִכָּל גְּזֵרוֹת קָשׁוֹת
וְרָעוֹת הַמִּתְרַגְּשׁוֹת וְיוֹצְאוֹת בָּעוֹלָם. עֲשֵׂה עִמָּנוּ עַל דְּבַר כְּבוֹד שְׁמֶךָ כִּי שִׁמְךָ נִקְרָא עָלֵינוּ וּבִכְבוֹדֵנוּ
הוּא כְבוֹדֶךָ. וְתֵן בְּרַחֲמֶיךָ הָרַבִּים לָנוּ וּלְכָל הַגּוֹלִים אֵלֵינוּ וּלְכָל הַחֲפֵצִים בַּחֲבוּרָתֵנוּ וּלְכָל אַנְשֵׁי
מִשְׁפְּחוֹתֵינוּ חַיִּים אֲרֻכִּים, חַיִּים שֶׁל שָׁלוֹם, חַיִּים שֶׁל טוֹבָה, חַיִּים שֶׁל בְּרָכָה, חַיִּים שֶׁל חִלּוּץ
עֲצָמוֹת, חַיִּים שֶׁיֵּשׁ בָּהֶם יִרְאַת שָׁמַיִם וְיִרְאַת חֵטְא, חַיִּים שֶׁאֵין בָּהֶם בּוּשָׁה וּכְלִמָּה, חַיִּים שֶׁל עֹשֶׁר
וְכָבוֹד, חַיִּים שֶׁתְּהֵא בָנוּ אַהֲבַת תּוֹרָה וְיִרְאַת שָׁמַיִם, חַיִּים שֶׁתְּמַלֵּא לָנוּ כָּל מִשְׁאֲלוֹת לִבֵּנוּ לְטוֹבָה.

Sovereign of the universe! We give thanks before You for all the benefits and mercies which You have performed on our behalf and for having sustained us in life and preserved us to this season, to the new tekufah, may it come upon us for good, and for having caused us to reach the beginning of this cycle, which is the two hundred and [seventh] cycle of twenty-eight years from the time that it was Your desire to create the universe and from when You established Your world for the benefit of Your creatures.

You, with Your merciful eye, exercise providence over all creatures, from the smallest to the greatest, to provide every created being in the world with its needs, to each and every one in accordance with their nature. Of all the species of creatures, You chose the human species and elevated man above all others as King David, may he rest in peace, wrote: "You have placed everything under his feet, flocks and oxen all of them, and also beasts of the field" (Psalms 8:7-8). And of the entire human species You have chosen Your people Israel as Your own possession. Just as You have established luminaries in the heaven, the sun and the moon to illuminate the face of the earth and to provide of their powers unto the produce and vegetation of the earth, as it is written in Your holy Torah: "with choice fruits of the sun and the rich yield of the months" (Deuteronomy 33:14), so also, in each generation, have You given of the spirit of Your wisdom to the wise men of the generations and have appeared to them with Your holy spirit and have given them wisdom to lead the people of their generation and to guide them always to do Your will.

Therefore, in accordance with the edict of our holy Sages, we have assembled at this time and at this season to bless You for the creation of Your world: Blessed are You who makes the work of creation. And, accordingly, we pray before You, we beseech You, O HASHEM the great, powerful and awesome God, may it be Your will that, just as the luminaries which You have created and established in Your world were not created for naught — for unto eternity they will not change their task and they illuminate the face of the earth in accordance with Your gracious will — so also help us in Your great mercy, for the sake of the glory of Your Name, that our travail be not for naught, Heaven forfend. May we be privileged to be among those who fulfill Your will all the days of our life so that the verse, "And He said to me, You are My servant, O Israel, in whom I shall be glorified" (Isaiah 49:3) may be fulfilled through us. Remove from us all distractions and considerations which impede us from Your Torah and Your holy service. Give us the strength that we be able to conquer our corporeal desires and distance us from all evil traits which mar Your holy service.

Indeed, our heart becomes faint in us when we consider the vastness of our deficiencies in Your service. We are aware that we do not fulfill even one thousandth part of our obligations with regard to You, King of Kings, the Holy One, blessed is He. What are we? What is our life? We stand before You with shame. If we examine our ways, how remiss we have been in Your service these past twenty-eight years, in the tekufah and cycle which has passed. Shame covers our faces. What has happened to us, for we have not taken to heart to better our ways. However, it is revealed and known before You that we did not disobey You because of rebellion and intention, Heaven forbid, but because of the distractions of the evil inclination and other matters which confuse our minds. We were too weak to withstand the distractions of the moment because of lack of sustenance on account of our many sins, and because of other causes, for we have experienced great oppression and have suffered much contempt. All this has bespoiled us so that we did not have the strength to fulfill the purpose for which You created us, O beneficent God, who is kind to all for our benefit.

Now we come before You in prayer and supplication for all this is revealed and known before Your holy throne. What can we say and what can we recount before You? For all the hidden secrets of our hearts and thoughts are revealed and known to You. Help us in all our affairs, for the sake of Your holy name, that from this day forth we may be among those who perform Your will, so that the purpose of creation be completed through us.

During this tekufah, may it come upon us for good, preserve us from all pain and harm, from every stumbling-block and impediment, Heaven forfend, from all loss, poverty, destitution and financial reversal, from all manner of misfortune and dread illness, and from all severe and evil decrees which come upon the world. Do for us on account of Your Name, for by Your Name are we called and Our honor is Your honor. In Your great mercy grant to us and to all who join us, to all who desire our company and to all members of our families, long life, a life of peace, a life of good, a life of blessing, a life of bodily vigor, a life in which there is fear of Heaven and fear of sin, a life in which there is no shame or embarrassment, a life of prosperity and honor, a life in which we will have love of Torah and fear of Heaven, a life in which You will fulfill for us all the desires of our hearts for good. Cause us to hear good, true and proper tidings. May our children and

וְתַשְׁמִיעֵנוּ בְּשׂוֹרוֹת טוֹבוֹת אֲמִתִּיּוֹת וּכְשֵׁרוֹת וְיִהְיוּ זַרְעֵנוּ וְזֶרַע זַרְעֵנוּ עַד סוֹף כָּל הַדּוֹרוֹת צַדִּיקִים וַחֲסִידִים אֲהוּבִים לְמַעְלָה וְנֶחֱמָדִים לְמַטָּה.

רַחֵם נָא עַל עַנְיֵי עַמְּךָ בֵּית יִשְׂרָאֵל. אִם כְּבָר נִגְזַר עֲלֵיהֶם עֹנִי בְּכָל זֹאת אַל נָא תִּמְנַע הַשְׁגָּחָתְךָ מֵעֲלֵיהֶם וְהַרְוִיחַ לָהֶם מְדֻחְקָם. וְתֵן בָּהֶם כֹּחַ לִסְבֹּל עָנְיָם וּמְרוּדָם עַד אֲשֶׁר תְּרַחֵם עֲלֵיהֶם, וְאַל יַעֲבִיר אוֹתָם הָעֲנִיּוּת עַל דַּעְתְּךָ חַס וְשָׁלוֹם, וְאַל בְּאַפְּךָ תְיַסְּרֵם. וְאַתָּה בְּרַחֲמֶיךָ הָרַבִּים רַחֵם עֲלֵיהֶם בְּכָל מִינֵי רַחֲמָנוּת, עַד אֲשֶׁר נִזְכֶּה הָעֵת שֶׁיָּבוֹא הַזְּמַן שֶׁיְּקֻיַּם בָּנוּ מִקְרָא שֶׁכָּתוּב "אֶפֶס כִּי לֹא יִהְיֶה בְּךָ אֶבְיוֹן כִּי בָרֵךְ יְבָרֶכְךָ יְהוָה".

רִבּוֹנוֹ שֶׁל עוֹלָם גָּלוּי וְיָדוּעַ לְפָנֶיךָ, מֵעֵת אֲשֶׁר עָבְרוּ שְׁמוֹנֶה וְעֶשְׂרִים שָׁנָה מֵהַמַּחֲזוֹר הַתְּקוּפָה שֶׁעָבְרָה כַּמָּה אַלְפֵי נְפָשׁוֹת אֲשֶׁר חָלְפוּ מִזֶּה הָעוֹלָם לִשְׁכֹּן בְּאֶרֶץ הַחַיִּים, וְהַחֹדֶשׁ הַזֶּה אֲשֶׁר הוּא חֹדֶשׁ הָאָבִיב מְסֻגָּל וּמֻכְשָׁר לְהִתְפַּלֵּל גַּם עַל נַפְשׁוֹת הַמֵּתִים אֲשֶׁר בְּאֶרֶץ הַחַיִּים הֵמָּה וְנִשְׁמָתָם תִּתְלוֹנַן בְּצֵל שַׁדָּי. אָנָּא בְּרַחֲמֶיךָ הָרַבִּים רַחֵם עַל הָאַלְמָנוֹת וְהַיְתוֹמִים אֲשֶׁר נִשְׁאֲרוּ מֵהֶם כִּי אַתָּה אֲבִי יְתוֹמִים וְדַיָּן אַלְמָנוֹת.

וְאִם יֵשׁ מֵהֶם אֲשֶׁר לֹא קִבֵּל עוֹד עָנְשׁוֹ וְדִינוֹ בָּעוֹלָם הָעֶלְיוֹן, הָקֵל מֵעָלָיו דִּינוֹ וְהַצִּילֵהוּ מִבּוֹר שַׁחַת מְדִינָה שֶׁל גֵּיהִנֹּם וּמֵהַמַּלְאָךְ הָאַכְזָרִי אֲשֶׁר מְמֻנֶּה לַעֲנוֹשׁ הַנְּשָׁמוֹת וְיֵרָאוּ לְפָנֶיךָ זְכִיּוֹתֵיהֶם וְצִדְקוֹתֵיהֶם אֲשֶׁר עָשׂוּ בְּחַיֵּיהֶם וַאֲשֶׁר עָלוּ בְּמַחְשַׁבְתָּם לַעֲשׂוֹת.

וְעָלֵינוּ תְּרַחֵם לְהַאֲרִיךְ יָמֵינוּ בְּטוֹב וּשְׁנוֹתֵינוּ בַּנְּעִימִים, וְתִשְׁלַח רְפוּאָה שְׁלֵמָה לְחוֹלֵי עַמְּךָ בֵּית יִשְׂרָאֵל, וְהַבְּרִיאִים מֵעַמְּךָ בֵּית יִשְׂרָאֵל תִּשְׁמְרֵם שֶׁלֹּא יָבוֹאוּ לִידֵי חֳלִי חַס וְשָׁלוֹם. וְהַצִּילֵנוּ מִכָּל עֲלִילָה וְהֶפְסֵד וּמִכָּל מִינֵי פְגָעִים, וְלֹא יִשָּׁמַע עוֹד בְּכִי וּזְעָקָה בְּבָתֵּינוּ וְלֹא שֹׁד וָשֶׁבֶר בִּגְבוּלֵנוּ וְנִהְיֶה שְׁלֵמִים, שְׁקֵטִים, דְּשֵׁנִים וְרַעֲנַנִּים, בְּחַצְרוֹת קָדְשְׁךָ שְׁתוּלִים. וְיִהְיוּ כָל מַחְשְׁבוֹתֵינוּ דְּבֵקוֹת בְּךָ תָּמִיד כָּל יְמֵי חַיֵּינוּ.

וְהִנֵּה אֲנַחְנוּ בְּטוּחִים וּמְחַכִּים לִישׁוּעָתֶךָ, כִּי עוֹד טֶרֶם תַּגִּיעַ הַתְּקוּפָה הַבָּאָה עָלֵינוּ לְשָׁלוֹם וּלְשִׂמְחָה יִבָּנֶה בֵּית קָדְשֵׁנוּ עַל מְכוֹנוֹ וּגְבוּלוֹ, וְנִדְחֵי יִשְׂרָאֵל תְּקַבֵּץ, וְאַרְמוֹן עַל מִשְׁפָּטוֹ יֵשֵׁב, וְתַחֲזוֹר הַמֶּמְשָׁלָה הָרִאשׁוֹנָה לְבַת יְרוּשָׁלַיִם. עַל כֵּן אֲנַחְנוּ עוֹמְדִים בִּתְפִלָּה לְפָנֶיךָ שֶׁתְּזַכֵּנוּ כֻּלָּנוּ לִהְיוֹת חַיִּים וְקַיָּמִים עַד הַזְּמַן הַהוּא. וְתַצִּילֵנוּ מֵחֶבְלוֹ שֶׁל מָשִׁיחַ וּמִמִּלְחֶמֶת גּוֹג וּמָגוֹג, וּתְזַכֵּנוּ לִרְאוֹת פְּנֵי מָשִׁיחַ מַלְכֵּנוּ בְּאוֹפֶן שֶׁנּוּכַל לִסְבֹּל אֲנַחְנוּ וְכָל עַמְּךָ בֵּית יִשְׂרָאֵל.

וְהִנֵּה גָּלוּי וְיָדוּעַ לְפָנֶיךָ אָבִינוּ מַלְכֵּנוּ כִּי יֵשׁ לָנוּ עוֹד הַרְבֵּה דְּבָרִים אֲשֶׁר רָאוּי לְהִתְפַּלֵּל עֲלֵיהֶם לְפָנֶיךָ. אָמְנָם קְצָרָה לְשׁוֹנֵנוּ מִלְּהַבִּיעַ רִגְשׁוֹתֵינוּ וְעָמְקֵי מַחְשְׁבוֹת לִבֵּנוּ. רַק אַתָּה יָדַעְתָּ צְפוּן לִבֵּנוּ וְאַתָּה חוֹקֵר לֵב וּבוֹחֵן כְּלָיוֹת, וְנִשְׁעָנִים אֲנַחְנוּ בְּמִדַּת טוּבְךָ שֶׁאֵין לָהּ גְּבוּל וְתִכְלָה, כִּי אַף עַל אֲשֶׁר לֹא הִתְפַּלַּלְנוּ לְפָנֶיךָ תְּרַחֵם עָלֵינוּ לְהוֹשִׁיעֵנוּ בִּימִין צִדְקֶךָ, וְיִגָּלוּ רַחֲמֶיךָ עַל מִדּוֹתֶיךָ, וְתִזְכֹּר לָנוּ בְּרִית אֲבוֹתֵינוּ, וִיקֻיְּמוּ בָנוּ כָּל הַהַבְטָחוֹת שֶׁהִבְטַחְתָּנוּ עַל יְדֵי נְבִיאֶיךָ הַקְּדוֹשִׁים. וְיַעֲלֶה וְיָבֹא וְיַגִּיעַ וְיֵרָאֶה וְיֵרָצֶה לִפְנֵי כִסֵּא כְבוֹדֶךָ כָּל מַחְשְׁבוֹתֵינוּ וְהֶגְיוֹנֵינוּ לְפָנֶיךָ, וְתִשְׁמַע קוֹל שַׁוְעָתֵנוּ בִּזְכוּת שְׁמוֹתֶיךָ הַקְּדוֹשִׁים. שַׁוְעָתֵנוּ קַבֵּל וּשְׁמַע צַעֲקָתֵנוּ יוֹדֵעַ תַּעֲלוּמוֹת.

אַחֲלַי יִכֹּנוּ דְרָכָי לִשְׁמֹר חֻקֶּיךָ. לְךָ אֲנִי הוֹשִׁיעֵנִי כִּי פִקּוּדֶיךָ דָרָשְׁתִּי. יְבֹאוּנִי רַחֲמֶיךָ וְאֶחְיֶה כִּי תוֹרָתְךָ שַׁעֲשֻׁעָי. עֲשֵׂה עִם עַבְדְּךָ כְחַסְדֶּךָ וְחֻקֶּיךָ לַמְּדֵנִי. זָכַרְתִּי בַלַּיְלָה שִׁמְךָ יְהוָה וָאֶשְׁמְרָה תוֹרָתֶךָ. רְאֵה כִּי פִקּוּדֶיךָ אָהָבְתִּי יְהוָה כְּחַסְדְּךָ חַיֵּנִי.

הַזְכֵּנִי וְאַמְּצֵנִי לְמַעַן כְּבוֹד שְׁמֶךָ, וּתְקַבֵּל תְּפִלָּתֵנוּ כְּרֵיחַ נִיחוֹחִים לִהְיוֹת אִמְרֵי פִינוּ נַחַת רוּחַ לִפְנֵי כִסֵּא כְבוֹדֶךָ, וְיַעֲלֶה שִׂיחַ שִׂפְתוֹתֵינוּ לִהְיוֹת עֲטָרָה לְרֹאשֶׁךָ. וַאֲנִי תְפִלָּתִי לְךָ יְהוָה עֵת רָצוֹן אֱלֹהִים בְּרָב חַסְדֶּךָ עֲנֵנִי בֶּאֱמֶת יִשְׁעֶךָ. יִהְיוּ לְרָצוֹן אִמְרֵי פִי וְהֶגְיוֹן לִבִּי לְפָנֶיךָ יְהוָה צוּרִי וְגֹאֲלִי. בָּרוּךְ יְהוָה לְעוֹלָם אָמֵן וְאָמֵן וְכֵן יְהִי רָצוֹן וְנֹאמַר אָמֵן.

children's children until the end of generations be righteous and pious, beloved on high and a source of delight below.

Have mercy, we beseech You, upon the poor of Your people, the house of Israel. If poverty has already been decreed upon them, nevertheless, do not withhold Your providence from them and relieve them in their need. Instill in them the fortitude to bear their poverty and oppression until You have mercy upon them. Let not their poverty cause them to forsake You, Heaven forfend, and do not afflict them in Your anger. May You, in Your great mercy, have all manner of mercy upon them until we shall merit that the time and season arrive in which the verse "But there will be no poor among you for HASHEM will surely bless you" (Deuteronomy 15:4) will be fulfilled among us.

Sovereign of the universe! It is revealed and known before You how many thousands of souls have departed from this world to dwell in the land of the living during the course of the twenty-eight year cycle of the past tekufah. During this month, which is the month of Aviv, it is propitious to pray also on behalf of the souls of the deceased, who are in the land of the living, and whose souls rest in the shade of God. We beseech You, in Your great mercy, have compassion upon the bereft widows and orphans for You are the Father of orphans and the Judge on behalf of widows.

If there are among the departed souls any which has as yet not received his judgment and punishment in the world on high, mitigate his judgment and save him from the pit of destruction, from the judgment of purgatory and from the cruel angel who is appointed to punish the souls. May there appear before You their meritorious and righteous deeds which they performed in their lifetime as well as those good deeds which they intended to perform.

Have mercy upon us to prolong our lives in good and our years in pleasantness. Send a complete cure to the sick among Your people, the house of Israel. Watch over the healthy among Your people, that they shall not experience illness, Heaven forfend. Preserve us from every plot and loss and from all manner of plague. Let there not again be heard either weeping or outcry in our homes, nor let there be plunder and destruction within our borders. May we be peaceful, tranquil, satisfied and flourishing and planted in Your holy courtyards. May all our thoughts cleave to You constantly all the days of our lives.

Behold we are confident and await Your salvation that You shall rebuild our holy Temple on its site, gather in the exiles of Israel, cause the palace to sit upon its rightful place and restore the original sovereignty to the daughter of Jerusalem, yet before the next tekufah. We stand before You in prayer that You may privilege all of us to live and be sustained until that time. Preserve us from the birthpangs of the Messiah and from the war of Gog and Magog and privilege us and Your entire people, the house of Israel, to behold the face of the Messiah, our king, in a manner which we shall be able to sustain.

Behold it is revealed and known before You, our Father, our King, that we have yet many things for which it would be proper to pray unto You. Yet our tongues fall short of expressing our emotions and the depths of the thoughts of our heart. But You know that which is hidden in our heart; You examine the heart and test the kidneys. We rely upon Your attribute of beneficence which has no bounds or limits that You will have mercy upon us to aid us with Your right hand of righteousness even with regard to that which we have not prayed unto You. May Your mercy overwhelm Your attributes, and may You remember the covenant of our fathers that there be fulfilled through us all the promises which You have vouchsafed through Your holy prophets. May all our thoughts and meditations ascend, come, reach, appear and be acceptable before Your holy throne and may You hear the voice of our supplication in the merit of Your holy Name. Accept our supplications and hear our cries, O You who knows hidden things.

I pray, establish my path to observe Your law. I am Yours, save me because I seek Your commands. May Your mercy come to me that I may live, for Your Torah is my delight. Do unto Your servant in accordance with Your lovingkindness and teach me Your statutes. I remember Your Name at night, O Lord, and I will observe Your teachings. Behold that I love Your commandments, O Lord; preserve me in life in accordance with Your lovingkindness.

Strengthen me and give me courage for the sake of the glory of Your Name; accept our prayers as sweet and odorous burnt-offerings so that the words of our mouths may be pleasurable before the throne of Your glory. May the speech of our lips ascend to become a crown for Your head." And as for me, may my prayer unto You, HASHEM be at an opportune time; O God, in the abundance of Your lovingkindness, answer me with the truth of Your salvation" (Psalms 69:14). May the words of my mouth and the meditation of my heart be acceptable before You, HASHEM, my Rock and my Redeemer. Blessed is HASHEM forever, Amen and Amen. May it so be His will; and let us say, Amen.

❧ Appendices

Charts of *Zemanei Bircas haChammah*

Determination of correct *zemanim* or times as related to various *mitzvos* is an extremely complex area of Halachah. The principles governing the calculation of times presented in these tables are, of course, of significance not only with regard to *Bircas haChammah* but also with regard to determining the period during which *Shema* may be recited, the termination of *Shabbos* and *Yom Tov*, as well as manifold other aspects of Halachah.

The tables presented here were prepared by Vaad L'Chizuk Kiyum Hamitzvoth. Comprehensive daily halachic time charts for any city in the world are available from Vaad L'Chizuk Kiyum Hamitzvoth, Brooklyn, N.Y. (718)851-1314.

Zemanei Bircas haChammah

All times for cities in North America, Europe and Israel are given in Daylight Saving Time. Times for all other cities are given in Standard Time.

TABLE A

I. Sunrise is the earliest time at which *Bircas haChammah* may be recited. The times here given represent the first appearance of the crest of the sun over the horizon. [According to *Tekufas haChammah uBirchosah* sunrise for purposes of *Bircas haChammah* is the earliest time at which the full circumference of the sun is visible. This occurs approximately 2 ½ minutes later than sunrise as here indicated.]

II. According to many, the blessing must be recited before the close of a three-hour period following sunrise. Most authorities maintain that this period is calculated on the basis of *sha'os zemaniyos*, or temporary (and hence variable) hours. One such hour is calculated by dividing the period between sunrise and sunset by twelve. The times given in column II are determined by multiplying the length of a single temporary hour by three and adding that period to the time of sunrise.

III. According to R. Meir David Hertzberg, Or *haChammah*, the three-hour period is calculated in usual clock hours.

IV. Many authorities maintain that the blessing may be recited until midday, i.e., the time at which the sun is directly overhead. This time is determined by dividing the period between sunrise and sunset by one half. [Cf., however; *Iggros Moshe, Orach Chaim*, II, no. 20, for a somewhat different method of calculation.]

Zemanei Bircas haChammah — April 8, 2009

	I. הנץ החמה SUNRISE	II. ג שעות זמניות 3 TEMPORARY HOURS AFTER SUNRISE	III. ג שעות שוות 3 CLOCK HOURS AFTER SUNRISE	IV. חצות היום MIDDAY
UNITED STATES				
Albany, NY	6:25	9:41	9:25	12:57
Anchorage, AK	7:28	10:54	10:28	2:21
Ann Arbor, MI	7:05	10:21	10:05	1:37
Atlanta, GA	7:15	10:27	10:15	1:39
Austin, TX	7:12	10:22	10:12	1:33
Baltimore, MD	6:40	9:55	9:40	1:09
Bangor, ME	6:03	9:20	9:03	12:37
Binghamton, NY	6:34	9:50	9:34	1:06
Birmingham, AL	6:26	9:38	9:26	12:50
Boca Raton, FL	7:04	10:13	10:04	1:23
Boston, MA	6:14	9:30	9:14	12:46
Boulder, CO	6:34	9:48	9:34	1:03
Bridgeport, CT	6:24	9:40	9:24	12:55
Brookline, MA	6:15	9:31	9:15	12:47
Brooklyn, NY	6:28	9:43	9:28	12:58
Buffalo, NY	6:45	10:01	9:45	1:17
Chapel Hill, NC	6:52	10:05	9:52	1:18
Charleston, SC	6:59	10:10	9:59	1:22
Charlotte, NC	7:00	10:13	10:00	1:25
Chicago, IL	6:21	9:37	9:21	12:53
Cincinnati, OH	7:11	10:26	10:11	1:40
Cleveland, OH	6:57	10:13	9:57	1:28
Columbus, OH	7:04	10:19	10:04	1:34
Dallas, TX	7:06	10:18	10:06	1:29
Deal, NJ	6:28	9:43	9:28	12:58
Denver, CO	6:33	9:47	9:33	1:02
Des Moines, IA	6:45	10:01	9:45	1:17
Detroit, MI	7:02	10:18	10:02	1:34
Englewood, NJ	6:28	9:43	9:28	12:58
Far Rockaway, NY	6:27	9:42	9:27	12:57
Fort Lauderdale, FL	7:04	10:13	10:04	1:22
Harrisburg, PA	6:39	9:54	9:39	1:09
Honolulu, HI	7:18	10:26	10:18	1:33
Houston, TX	7:03	10:13	10:03	1:24
Indianapolis, IN	7:17	10:32	10:17	1:47
Irvine, CA	6:38	9:55	9:38	1:13
Ithaca, NY	6:36	9:52	9:36	1:08
Jackson, MI	7:08	10:24	10:08	1:40
Jacksonville, FL	7:07	10:18	10:07	1:29
Kansas City, KS	6:52	10:07	9:52	1:21
La Jolla, CA	6:28	9:39	9:28	12:51
Lakewood, NJ	6:29	9:44	9:29	12:59
Lancaster, PA	6:38	9:53	9:38	1:07
Las Vegas, NV	6:16	9:29	9:16	12:43
Louisville, KY	6:16	9:29	9:16	12:43
Los Angeles, CA	6:31	9:43	9:31	12:55
Madison, WI	6:27	9:44	9:27	1:00
Memphis, TN	6:36	9:49	9:36	1:01

Zemanei Bircas haChammah — April 8, 2009

	I. הנץ החמה SUNRISE	II. ג שעות זמניות 3 TEMPORARY HOURS AFTER SUNRISE	III. ג שעות שוות 3 CLOCK HOURS AFTER SUNRISE	IV. חצות היום MIDDAY
UNITED STATES				
Miami, FL	7:05	10:14	10:05	1:23
Milwaukee, WI	6:21	9:38	9:21	12:54
Minneapolis, MN	6:41	9:58	9:41	1:16
Monsey, NY	6:28	9:43	9:28	12:58
Monticello, NY	6:30	9:45	9:30	1:01
Nashville, TN	6:23	9:36	9:23	12:49
New Haven, CT	6:23	9:39	9:23	12:54
New York, NY	6:28	9:43	9:28	12:58
Norfolk, VA	6:41	9:54	9:41	1:07
Norman, OK	7:07	10:19	10:07	1:32
Oak Park, MI	7:03	10:19	10:03	1:35
Oakland, CA	6:43	9:57	9:43	1:11
Omaha, NE	6:55	10:11	9:55	1:26
Palm Beach, FL	7:03	10:13	10:03	1:22
Palo Alto, CA	6:43	9:57	9:43	1:11
Passaic, NJ	6:28	9:43	9:28	12:59
Philadelphia, PA	6:33	9:48	9:33	1:03
Phoenix, AZ	6:06	9:18	9:06	12:30
Pittsburg, PA	6:52	10:07	9:52	1:22
Portland, OR	6:37	9:55	9:37	1:13
Postville, IA	6:36	9:52	9:36	1:08
Richmond, VA	6:45	9:59	9:45	1:12
Rochester, MN	6:38	9:55	9:38	1:12
Rochester, NY	6:40	9:56	9:40	1:13
San Antonio, TX	7:15	10:26	10:15	1:36
San Diego, CA	6:27	9:38	9:27	12:50
San Francisco, CA	6:44	9:58	9:44	1:12
San Jose, CA	6:42	9:56	9:42	1:09
Savannah, GA	7:03	10:15	10:03	1:26
Scranton, PA	6:34	9:49	9:34	1:05
Seattle, WA	6:33	9:52	9:33	1:11
Silver Spring, MD	6:42	9:56	9:42	1:10
South Bend, IN	7:16	10:32	10:16	1:47
Springfield, MA	6:21	9:37	9:21	12:52
St Louis, MO	6:35	9:49	9:35	1:03
St Paul, MN	6:39	9:57	9:39	1:14
Sunnyvale, CA	6:43	9:57	9:43	1:10
Syracuse, NY	6:34	9:51	9:34	1:07
Tampa Bay, FL	7:12	10:22	10:12	1:32
Teaneck, NJ	6:28	9:43	9:28	12:58
Toledo, OH	7:05	10:21	10:05	1:36
Tucson, AZ	6:03	9:14	9:03	12:26
Washington, DC	6:42	9:56	9:42	1:10
Waterbury, CT	6:23	9:39	9:23	12:54
West Hartford, CT	6:22	9:37	9:22	12:53
West Palm Beach, FL	7:03	10:13	10:03	1:22
Yardley, PA	6:32	9:46	9:32	1:01

Zemanei Bircas haChammah — April 8, 2009

	I. הנץ החמה SUNRISE	II. ג שעות זמניות 3 TEMPORARY HOURS AFTER SUNRISE	III. ג שעות שוות 3 CLOCK HOURS AFTER SUNRISE	IV. חצות היום MIDDAY
FOREIGN COUNTRIES				
Amsterdam, Neth.	6:59	10:21	9:59	1:43
Antwerp, Belgium	7:02	10:24	10:02	1:45
Be'er Sheva, Israel	6:21	9:32	9:21	12:43
Berlin, Germany	6:25	9:47	9:25	1:09
Birmingham, England	6:26	9:48	9:26	1:10
Budapest, Hungary	6:09	9:27	9:09	12:46
Buenos Aires, Arg.	7:13	10:04	10:13	12:56
Calgary, AB	6:56	10:17	9:56	1:39
Cape Town, S.A.	7:04	9:56	10:04	12:48
Caracas, Venezuela	6:21	9:25	9:21	12:30
Curacao Neth., Antilles	6:28	9:33	9:28	12:38
Edmonton, AB	6:50	10:13	9:50	1:36
Eilat, Israel	6:22	9:32	9:22	12:42
Gateshead, UK	6:21	9:45	9:21	1:09
Geneva, Switzerland	7:02	10:20	10:02	1:38
Gibraltar, Spain	6:58	10:11	9:58	1:24
Glasgow, Scotland	6:30	9:54	9:30	1:19
Haifa, Israel	6:19	9:31	9:19	12:42
Halifax, NS	6:42	9:59	9:42	1:17
Hong Kong, China	6:10	9:18	9:10	12:25
Jerusalem, Israel	6:19	9:30	9:19	12:41
Johannesburg, S.A.	6:21	9:15	9:21	12:10
Kiev, Ukraine	6:19	9:40	9:19	1:00
Leningrad, USSR	6:03	9:32	9:03	1:01
Liverpool, UK	6:29	9:52	9:29	1:14
London, UK	6:20	9:41	9:20	1:02
Lugano, Switzerland	6:51	10:09	9:51	1:26
Manchester, UK	6:26	9:48	9:26	1:11
Marseiles, France	7:08	10:24	10:08	1:41
Melbourne, Australia	6:40	9:31	9:40	12:22
Mexico City, Mexico	7:24	10:31	10:24	1:38
Milan, Italy	6:40	9:56	9:40	1:12
Montreal, QC	6:21	9:39	9:21	12:57
Montreux, Switzerland	6:59	10:17	9:59	1:35
Moscow, USSR	6:42	10:07	9:42	1:32
Ottawa, QC	6:30	9:47	9:30	1:05
Paris, France	7:14	10:33	10:14	1:53
Perth, Australia	7:34	10:24	10:34	1:13
Rome, Italy	6:41	9:57	9:41	1:12
Santiago, Chile	7:00	9:52	10:00	12:44
Sao Paulo, Brazil	6:17	9:13	9:17	12:08
Strassbourg, France	6:53	10:12	9:53	1:31
Sydney, Australia	6:12	9:05	9:12	11:57
Tel Aviv, Israel	6:21	9:32	9:21	12:43
Toronto, ON	6:47	10:03	9:47	1:20
Vancouver, BC	6:34	9:55	9:34	1:15
Vienna, Austria	6:19	9:38	9:19	12:57
Vilnius, Lithuania	6:33	9:57	9:33	1:21
Warsaw, Poland	5:55	9:16	8:55	12:38
Winnipeg, MB	6:50	10:10	9:50	1:31
Zurich, Switzerland	6:51	10:10	9:51	1:28

TABLE B

V. Dawn, or the "rise of the morning star" (*alos hashachar*), occurs a certain period of time before sunrise. This period is reckoned as the time required to traverse a distance of 4 *mil*. The conventional practice, which reflects the view of *Terumas haDeshen,* no. 123 and *Shulchan Aruch, Orach Chaim* 459:2, is to reckon the time required to traverse a distance of a *mil* as 18 minutes. Accordingly, the 4-*mil* period between *alos hashachar* and sunrise equals 72 minutes.

VI. Some authorities maintain that the three-hour period described in II must be reckoned by dividing the period between *alos hashachar* and night (*tzeis hakochavim*) into twelve *sha'os zemaniyos* and then adding three such hours to the time of dawn. According to the conventional practice, night is also reckoned as occurring 72 minutes after sunset. [Those who reckon the three-hour period as clock hours beginning with *alos hashachar* would simply add three hours to the times listed in column V.]

VII. Most authorities agree that the period between dawn and sunrise and the period between sunset and night vary with distance from the equator and season of the year. They maintain that the 4-*mil* or 72-minute period refers only to the time between dawn and sunrise (and sunset and night) in *Eretz Yisrael* and Babylonia at the time of the equinox. At those places and on those dates the sun is 16.1° below the horizon 72 minutes before sunrise. Hence, for other dates and other locales dawn (and night) must be calculated as the time at which the sun is 16.1° below the horizon.

VIII. The times in this column are calculated on the basis of *sha'os zemaniyos* as in VI, but reckon dawn and night as described in VII. [Those who reckon the three-hour period as clock hours beginning with *alos hashachar* and calculate *alos hashachar* as in VII would add three hours to the times listed in column VII.]

IX. All authorities agree that *alos hashachar* is calculated on the basis of a 4-*mil* period prior to sunrise. [See R. Tucatzinsky, *Bein haShemoshos,* pp. 7-10.] However, many maintain that night is calculated by adding the time required to traverse ¾ of a *mil* to the time of sunset. According to the authorities who maintain that the time required to traverse a *mil* is 18 minutes in duration, ¾ of a *mil* equals 13 ½ minutes. This corresponds to the descent of the sun to a position 3.70° below the horizon in *Eretz Yisrael* and Babylonia at the time of the equinox. The times here given are based upon calculation of dawn as occurring when the sun is 16.1° below the horizon and night when the sun is 3.70° below the horizon. The intervening period is divided by twelve to determine a single *sha'ah zemanis*. [Cf., however, R. Tucatzinsky, *Bein haShemoshos*, p.98.]

X. The times in this column are calculated in the same manner as in column VII but are based upon reckoning the time required to traverse a single *mil* as being equal to 22 ½ minutes in accordance with the view of *Biur haGra, Orach Chaim* 459:10. [See also *Mishnah Berurah* 459:2.] According to this view, *alos hashachar* occurs 90 minutes before sunrise in *Eretz Yisrael* and Babylonia on the day of the equinox at which time the sun is 19.8° below the horizon.

XI. The times in this column are calculated in the same manner as in column IX but are based upon reckoning the time required to traverse a distance of a single *mil* as being equal to 22 ½ minutes and the time required to traverse a distance of 4 *mil* as being equal to 90 minutes as in column X. Accordingly, the ¾-*mil* period between sunset and night is equal to 16.875 minutes at which time the sun is 4.42° below the horizon in *Eretz Yisrael* and Babylonia on the day of the equinox.

XII. The times in this column are calculated in the same manner as in columns VII and X but are based upon reckoning the time required to traverse a single *mil* as being equal to 24 minutes in accordance with the view of *Rambam* and R. Ovadia of Bartenura in their respective commentaries on the Mishnah, *Pesachim* 3:2. According to this view, *alos hashachar* occurs 96 minutes before sunrise in *Eretz Yisrael* and Babylonia on the day of the equinox at which time the sun is 21° below the horizon.

XIII. The times in this column are calculated in the same manner as in columns IX and XI but are based upon reckoning the time required to traverse a distance of a single *mil* as being equal to 24 minutes and the time required to traverse a distance of 4 *mil* as being equal to 96 minutes as in column XII. Accordingly, the ¾-*mil* period between sunset and night is equal to 18 minutes at which time the sun is 4.61° below the horizon in *Eretz Yisrael* and Babylonia on the day of the equinox. [Dr. Leo Levi, *Halakhic Times*, 3rd edition (Jerusalem, 2000), p. 311, states that according to this view the calculation of *tzeis hakochavim* should be made on the basis of the time at which the sun reaches 4.81° below the horizon. That calculation is based upon a minor variation in postulating the length of a *mil*.]

Alternate *Zemanei Bircas haChammah* According to Some Authorities

	V. עלות השחר DAWN 72 MINUTES BEFORE SUNRISE	VI. ג שעות זמניות 3 TEMPORARY HOURS AFTER DAWN	VII. עלות השחר DAWN 16.1	VIII. ג שעות זמניות 3 TEMPORARY HOURS AFTER 16.1	IX. ג שעות זמניות 3 TEMPORARY HOURS DAWN 16.1 NIGHT 3.70
UNITED STATES					
Albany, NY	5:13	9:05	4:57	8:57	8:39
Anchorage, AK	6:16	10:18	5:21	9:51	9:24
Ann Arbor, MI	5:53	9:45	5:38	9:38	9:20
Atlanta, GA	6:03	9:51	5:59	9:49	9:34
Austin, TX	6:00	9:46	5:59	9:46	9:31
Baltimore, MD	5:28	9:19	5:17	9:13	8:56
Bangor, ME	4:51	8:44	4:31	8:34	8:16
Binghamton, NY	5:22	9:14	5:07	9:07	8:49
Birmingham, AL	5:14	9:02	5:10	9:00	8:44
Boca Raton, FL	5:52	9:37	5:54	9:38	9:24
Boston, MA	5:02	8:54	4:47	8:47	8:29
Boulder, CO	5:22	9:12	5:10	9:07	8:49
Bridgeport, CT	5:12	9:04	4:59	8:57	8:40
Brookline, MA	5:03	8:55	4:48	8:47	8:29
Brooklyn, NY	5:16	9:07	5:03	9:01	8:44
Buffalo, NY	5:33	9:25	5:17	9:17	8:59
Chapel Hill, NC	5:40	9:29	5:34	9:26	9:10
Charleston, SC	5:47	9:34	5:44	9:33	9:18
Charlotte, NC	5:48	9:37	5:43	9:34	9:18
Chicago, IL	5:09	9:01	4:55	8:54	8:36
Cincinnati, OH	5:59	9:50	5:49	9:44	9:27
Cleveland, OH	5:45	9:37	5:31	9:30	9:12
Columbus, OH	5:52	9:43	5:41	9:37	9:20
Dallas, TX	5:54	9:42	5:51	9:40	9:25
Deal, NJ	5:16	9:07	5:04	9:01	8:44
Denver, CO	5:21	9:11	5:10	9:06	8:49
Des Moines, IA	5:33	9:25	5:19	9:18	9:00
Detroit, MI	5:50	9:42	5:35	9:35	9:17
Englewood, NJ	5:16	9:07	5:03	9:00	8:43
Far Rockaway, NY	5:15	9:06	5:03	9:00	8:43
Fort Lauderdale, FL	5:52	9:37	5:54	9:38	9:24
Harrisburg, PA	5:27	9:18	5:15	9:12	8:55
Honolulu, HI	6:06	9:50	6:11	9:52	9:39
Houston, TX	5:51	9:37	5:50	9:37	9:22
Indianapolis, IN	6:05	9:56	5:54	9:50	9:33
Irvine, CA	5:26	9:19	5:04	9:09	8:50
Ithaca, NY	5:24	9:16	5:09	9:09	8:51
Jackson, MI	5:56	9:48	5:41	9:40	9:23
Jacksonville, FL	5:55	9:42	5:55	9:42	9:27
Kansas City, KS	5:40	9:31	5:30	9:26	9:09
La Jolla, CA	5:16	9:03	5:13	9:02	8:46
Lakewood, NJ	5:17	9:08	5:06	9:02	8:45
Lancaster, PA	5:26	9:17	5:14	9:11	8:54
Las Vegas, NV	5:04	8:53	4:58	8:50	8:34
Louisville, KY	5:04	8:53	4:58	8:50	8:34
Los Angeles, CA	5:19	9:07	5:15	9:05	8:49
Madison, WI	5:15	9:08	4:59	9:00	8:41
Memphis, TN	5:24	9:13	5:19	9:10	8:54

Alternate *Zemanei Bircas haChammah* According to Some Authorities

	V. עלות השחר DAWN 72 MINUTES BEFORE SUNRISE	VI. ג שעות זמניות 3 TEMPORARY HOURS AFTER DAWN	VII. עלות השחר DAWN 16.1	VIII. ג שעות זמניות 3 TEMPORARY HOURS AFTER 16.1	IX. ג שעות זמניות 3 TEMPORARY HOURS DAWN 16.1 NIGHT 3.70
UNITED STATES					
Miami, FL	5:53	9:38	5:56	9:39	9:25
Milwaukee, WI	5:09	9:02	4:53	8:54	8:35
Minneapolis, MN	5:29	9:22	5:09	9:12	8:53
Monsey, NY	5:16	9:07	5:03	9:01	8:43
Monticello, NY	5:18	9:09	5:04	9:02	8:45
Nashville, TN	5:11	9:00	5:04	8:57	8:41
New Haven, CT	5:11	9:03	4:58	8:56	8:38
New York, NY	5:16	9:07	5:03	9:01	8:43
Norfolk, VA	5:29	9:18	5:21	9:14	8:58
Norman, OK	5:55	9:43	5:49	9:41	9:25
Oak Park, MI	5:51	9:43	5:35	9:35	9:17
Oakland, CA	5:31	9:21	5:23	9:17	9:00
Omaha, NE	5:43	9:35	5:30	9:28	9:11
Palm Beach, FL	5:51	9:37	5:53	9:38	9:23
Palo Alto, CA	5:31	9:21	5:23	9:17	9:00
Passaic, NJ	5:16	9:07	5:03	9:01	8:44
Philadelphia, PA	5:21	9:12	5:10	9:06	8:49
Phoenix, AZ	4:54	8:42	4:50	8:40	8:25
Pittsburg, PA	5:40	9:31	5:28	9:25	9:08
Portland, OR	5:25	9:19	5:04	9:09	8:50
Postville, IA	5:24	9:16	5:07	9:08	8:50
Richmond, VA	5:33	9:23	5:25	9:19	9:02
Rochester, MN	5:26	9:19	5:08	9:10	8:52
Rochester, NY	5:28	9:20	5:11	9:12	8:54
San Antonio, TX	6:03	9:50	6:03	9:50	9:35
San Diego, CA	5:15	9:02	5:12	9:01	8:46
San Francisco, CA	5:32	9:22	5:23	9:18	9:01
San Jose, CA	5:30	9:20	5:22	9:16	8:59
Savannah, GA	5:51	9:39	5:49	9:38	9:22
Scranton, PA	5:22	9:13	5:08	9:06	8:49
Seattle, WA	5:21	9:16	4:56	9:04	8:44
Silver Spring, MD	5:30	9:20	5:19	9:15	8:58
South Bend, IN	6:04	9:56	5:50	9:49	9:31
Springfield, MA	5:09	9:01	4:54	8:53	8:36
St Louis, MO	5:23	9:13	5:13	9:08	8:52
St Paul, MN	5:27	9:21	5:07	9:11	8:52
Sunnyvale, CA	5:31	9:21	5:23	9:17	9:00
Syracuse, NY	5:22	9:15	5:06	9:06	8:48
Tampa Bay, FL	6:00	9:46	6:01	9:46	9:32
Teaneck, NJ	5:16	9:07	5:03	9:01	8:43
Toledo, OH	5:53	9:45	5:39	9:38	9:20
Tucson, AZ	4:51	8:38	4:48	8:37	8:22
Washington, DC	5:30	9:20	5:20	9:15	8:58
Waterbury, CT	5:11	9:03	4:57	8:56	8:38
West Hartford, CT	5:10	9:01	4:56	8:54	8:37
West Palm Beach, FL	5:51	9:37	5:53	9:38	9:24
Yardley, PA	5:20	9:10	5:08	9:04	8:47

Alternate *Zemanei Bircas haChammah* According to Some Authorities

	X. עלות השחר DAWN 19.8	XI. ג שעות זמניות 3 TEMPORARY HOURS DAWN 19.8 NIGHT 4.42	XII. עלות השחר DAWN 21	XIII. ג שעות זמניות 3 TEMPORARY HOURS DAWN 21 NIGHT 4.61
UNITED STATES				
Albany, NY	4:34	8:23	4:27	8:18
Anchorage, AK	4:41	8:56	4:26	8:45
Ann Arbor, MI	5:16	9:04	5:08	8:58
Atlanta, GA	5:40	9:20	5:34	9:16
Austin, TX	5:40	9:18	5:34	9:14
Baltimore, MD	4:56	8:41	4:49	8:36
Bangor, ME	4:07	7:58	3:59	7:53
Binghamton, NY	4:45	8:33	4:37	8:27
Birmingham, AL	4:51	8:31	4:45	8:27
Boca Raton, FL	5:37	9:12	5:31	9:08
Boston, MA	4:24	8:13	4:17	8:07
Boulder, CO	4:48	8:34	4:41	8:29
Bridgeport, CT	4:37	8:24	4:29	8:19
Brookline, MA	4:25	8:13	4:18	8:08
Brooklyn, NY	4:42	8:28	4:34	8:23
Buffalo, NY	4:54	8:43	4:46	8:38
Chapel Hill, NC	5:14	8:56	5:08	8:51
Charleston, SC	5:25	9:04	5:18	9:00
Charlotte, NC	5:23	9:04	5:16	9:00
Chicago, IL	4:32	8:20	4:25	8:15
Cincinnati, OH	5:27	9:12	5:20	9:07
Cleveland, OH	5:09	8:57	5:02	8:51
Columbus, OH	5:19	9:05	5:12	9:00
Dallas, TX	5:32	9:11	5:25	9:07
Deal, NJ	4:43	8:29	4:36	8:24
Denver, CO	4:48	8:34	4:41	8:29
Des Moines, IA	4:57	8:45	4:50	8:39
Detroit, MI	5:12	9:01	5:05	8:55
Englewood, NJ	4:41	8:27	4:33	8:22
Far Rockaway, NY	4:41	8:27	4:33	8:22
Fort Lauderdale, FL	5:37	9:12	5:31	9:08
Harrisburg, PA	4:54	8:40	4:46	8:35
Honolulu, HI	5:55	9:27	5:49	9:23
Houston, TX	5:32	9:10	5:26	9:05
Indianapolis, IN	5:32	9:18	5:25	9:13
Irvine, CA	4:40	8:32	4:31	8:26
Ithaca, NY	4:46	8:35	4:38	8:29
Jackson, MI	5:18	9:07	5:11	9:01
Jacksonville, FL	5:36	9:14	5:30	9:10
Kansas City, KS	5:09	8:54	5:02	8:49
La Jolla, CA	4:54	8:33	4:47	8:29
Lakewood, NJ	4:44	8:30	4:37	8:25
Lancaster, PA	4:53	8:39	4:45	8:33
Las Vegas, NV	4:38	8:20	4:31	8:15
Louisville, KY	4:38	8:20	4:31	8:15
Los Angeles, CA	4:55	8:36	4:49	8:31
Madison, WI	4:36	8:25	4:28	8:20
Memphis, TN	4:59	8:40	4:53	8:36

Alternate *Zemanei Bircas haChammah* According to Some Authorities

	X. עלות השחר DAWN 19.8	XI. ג שעות זמניות 3 TEMPORARY HOURS DAWN 19.8 NIGHT 4.42	XII. עלות השחר DAWN 21	XIII. ג שעות זמניות 3 TEMPORARY HOURS DAWN 21 NIGHT 4.61
UNITED STATES				
Miami, FL	5:38	9:13	5:33	9:09
Milwaukee, WI	4:30	8:19	4:22	8:13
Minneapolis, MN	4:45	8:36	4:36	8:30
Monsey, NY	4:40	8:27	4:33	8:22
Monticello, NY	4:41	8:29	4:34	8:24
Nashville, TN	4:44	8:27	4:38	8:22
New Haven, CT	4:35	8:23	4:28	8:17
New York, NY	4:41	8:28	4:34	8:23
Norfolk, VA	5:01	8:44	4:54	8:39
Norman, OK	5:29	9:11	5:23	9:06
Oak Park, MI	5:13	9:01	5:05	8:56
Oakland, CA	5:02	8:46	4:55	8:41
Omaha, NE	5:08	8:55	5:01	8:50
Palm Beach, FL	5:36	9:11	5:30	9:07
Palo Alto, CA	5:03	8:46	4:56	8:41
Passaic, NJ	4:41	8:28	4:34	8:23
Philadelphia, PA	4:48	8:34	4:41	8:29
Phoenix, AZ	4:31	8:11	4:25	8:07
Pittsburg, PA	5:06	8:52	4:59	8:47
Portland, OR	4:40	8:32	4:31	8:26
Postville, IA	4:44	8:33	4:36	8:28
Richmond, VA	5:04	8:48	4:57	8:43
Rochester, MN	4:44	8:35	4:36	8:29
Rochester, NY	4:48	8:37	4:40	8:32
San Antonio, TX	5:45	9:22	5:40	9:18
San Diego, CA	4:53	8:32	4:46	8:28
San Francisco, CA	5:03	8:46	4:56	8:42
San Jose, CA	5:02	8:45	4:55	8:40
Savannah, GA	5:30	9:09	5:24	9:05
Scranton, PA	4:46	8:33	4:38	8:28
Seattle, WA	4:30	8:25	4:21	8:19
Silver Spring, MD	4:58	8:43	4:51	8:38
South Bend, IN	5:28	9:15	5:20	9:10
Springfield, MA	4:31	8:20	4:24	8:14
St Louis, MO	4:52	8:37	4:45	8:32
St Paul, MN	4:43	8:34	4:34	8:29
Sunnyvale, CA	5:02	8:46	4:56	8:41
Syracuse, NY	4:43	8:32	4:35	8:26
Tampa Bay, FL	5:43	9:20	5:38	9:15
Teaneck, NJ	4:41	8:28	4:34	8:22
Toledo, OH	5:17	9:04	5:09	8:59
Tucson, AZ	4:29	8:09	4:23	8:04
Washington, DC	4:59	8:43	4:52	8:38
Waterbury, CT	4:35	8:22	4:27	8:17
West Hartford, CT	4:33	8:21	4:26	8:15
West Palm Beach, FL	5:36	9:11	5:30	9:07
Yardley, PA	4:46	8:32	4:39	8:27

Alternate *Zemanei Bircas haChammah* According to Some Authorities

	V. עלות השחר DAWN 72 MINUTES BEFORE SUNRISE	VI. ג שעות זמניות 3 TEMPORARY HOURS AFTER DAWN	VII. עלות השחר DAWN 16.1	VIII. ג שעות זמניות 3 TEMPORARY HOURS AFTER 16.1	IX. ג שעות זמניות 3 TEMPORARY HOURS DAWN 16.1 NIGHT 3.70
FOREIGN COUNTRIES					
Amsterdam, Neth.	5:47	9:45	5:09	9:26	9:03
Antwerp, Belgium	5:50	9:48	5:16	9:30	9:08
Be'er Sheva, Israel	5:09	8:56	5:08	8:55	8:40
Berlin, Germany	5:13	9:11	4:34	8:51	8:28
Birmingham, England	5:14	9:12	4:35	8:53	8:30
Budapest, Hungary	4:57	8:51	4:32	8:39	8:19
Buenos Aires, Arg.	6:01	9:28	5:58	9:27	9:12
Calgary, AB	5:44	9:41	5:09	9:24	9:02
Cape Town, S.A.	5:52	9:20	5:50	9:19	9:04
Caracas, Venezuela	5:09	8:49	5:18	8:54	8:41
Curacao Neth., Antilles	5:16	8:57	5:25	9:01	8:48
Edmonton, AB	5:38	9:37	4:55	9:16	8:52
Eilat, Israel	5:10	8:56	5:10	8:56	8:41
Gateshead, UK	5:09	9:09	4:21	8:45	8:20
Geneva, Switzerland	5:50	9:44	5:28	9:33	9:13
Gibraltar, Spain	5:46	9:35	5:39	9:31	9:15
Glasgow, Scotland	5:18	9:18	4:26	8:53	8:27
Haifa, Israel	5:07	8:55	5:04	8:53	8:38
Halifax, NS	5:30	9:23	5:11	9:14	8:55
Hong Kong, China	4:58	8:42	5:03	8:44	8:30
Jerusalem, Israel	5:07	8:54	5:05	8:53	8:38
Johannesburg, S.A.	5:09	8:39	5:12	8:41	8:27
Kiev, Ukraine	5:07	9:04	4:35	8:48	8:26
Leningrad, USSR	4:51	8:56	3:37	8:20	7:49
Liverpool, UK	5:17	9:16	4:35	8:55	8:31
London, UK	5:08	9:05	4:32	8:47	8:25
Lugano, Switzerland	5:39	9:33	5:17	9:22	9:03
Manchester, UK	5:14	9:12	4:31	8:52	8:28
Marseiles, France	5:56	9:48	5:39	9:40	9:22
Melbourne, Australia	5:28	8:55	5:22	8:52	8:36
Mexico City, Mexico	6:12	9:55	6:18	9:58	9:45
Milan, Italy	5:28	9:20	5:12	9:12	8:54
Montreal, QC	5:09	9:03	4:48	8:53	8:34
Montreux, Switzerland	5:47	9:41	5:24	9:29	9:10
Moscow, USSR	5:30	9:31	4:39	9:06	8:40
Ottawa, QC	5:18	9:11	4:57	9:01	8:42
Paris, France	6:02	9:57	5:34	9:43	9:23
Perth, Australia	6:22	9:48	6:12	9:43	9:26
Rome, Italy	5:29	9:21	5:15	9:14	8:56
Santiago, Chile	5:48	9:16	5:47	9:15	9:00
Sao Paulo, Brazil	5:05	8:37	5:11	8:39	8:26
Strassbourg, France	5:41	9:36	5:13	9:22	9:02
Sydney, Australia	5:00	8:29	4:59	8:28	8:13
Tel Aviv, Israel	5:09	8:56	5:06	8:55	8:40
Toronto, ON	5:35	9:27	5:17	9:18	9:00
Vancouver, BC	5:22	9:19	4:53	9:04	8:43
Vienna, Austria	5:07	9:02	4:40	8:49	8:28
Vilnius, Lithuania	5:21	9:21	4:35	8:58	8:34
Warsaw, Poland	4:43	8:40	4:05	8:22	7:59
Winnipeg, MB	5:38	9:34	5:07	9:19	8:58
Zurich, Switzerland	5:39	9:34	5:14	9:21	9:01

Alternate *Zemanei Bircas haChammah* According to Some Authorities

	X. עלות השחר DAWN 19.8	XI. ג שעות זמניות 3 TEMPORARY HOURS DAWN 19.8 NIGHT 4.42	XII. עלות השחר DAWN 21	XIII. ג שעות זמניות 3 TEMPORARY HOURS DAWN 21 NIGHT 4.61
FOREIGN COUNTRIES				
Amsterdam, Neth.	4:37	8:41	4:26	8:33
Antwerp, Belgium	4:46	8:47	4:35	8:40
Be'er Sheva, Israel	4:49	8:27	4:43	8:23
Berlin, Germany	4:02	8:06	3:51	7:58
Birmingham, England	4:04	8:07	3:53	7:59
Budapest, Hungary	4:06	8:00	3:57	7:54
Buenos Aires, Arg.	5:40	9:00	5:34	8:55
Calgary, AB	4:39	8:41	4:29	8:33
Cape Town, S.A.	5:32	8:52	5:26	8:48
Caracas, Venezuela	5:02	8:30	4:57	8:27
Curacao Neth., Antilles	5:09	8:38	5:04	8:34
Edmonton, AB	4:22	8:28	4:10	8:20
Eilat, Israel	4:51	8:29	4:46	8:24
Gateshead, UK	3:45	7:55	3:32	7:45
Geneva, Switzerland	5:02	8:56	4:54	8:49
Gibraltar, Spain	5:19	9:01	5:13	8:57
Glasgow, Scotland	3:48	8:00	3:35	7:50
Haifa, Israel	4:45	8:24	4:39	8:20
Halifax, NS	4:47	8:38	4:39	8:32
Hong Kong, China	4:46	8:19	4:41	8:15
Jerusalem, Israel	4:46	8:25	4:40	8:21
Johannesburg, S.A.	4:56	8:15	4:50	8:12
Kiev, Ukraine	4:06	8:06	3:56	7:58
Leningrad, USSR	2:45	7:11	2:22	6:54
Liverpool, UK	4:02	8:08	3:50	7:59
London, UK	4:01	8:03	3:51	7:56
Lugano, Switzerland	4:52	8:45	4:44	8:39
Manchester, UK	3:58	8:04	3:46	7:56
Marseiles, France	5:16	9:06	5:08	9:00
Melbourne, Australia	5:04	8:23	4:57	8:19
Mexico City, Mexico	6:02	9:34	5:57	9:30
Milan, Italy	4:49	8:38	4:41	8:32
Montreal, QC	4:24	8:16	4:15	8:10
Montreux, Switzerland	4:58	8:52	4:50	8:46
Moscow, USSR	4:02	8:13	3:48	8:04
Ottawa, QC	4:32	8:25	4:24	8:19
Paris, France	5:06	9:03	4:57	8:57
Perth, Australia	5:52	9:12	5:46	9:07
Rome, Italy	4:52	8:40	4:45	8:35
Santiago, Chile	5:29	8:48	5:23	8:44
Sao Paulo, Brazil	4:54	8:14	4:49	8:11
Strassbourg, France	4:46	8:42	4:37	8:36
Sydney, Australia	4:41	8:00	4:35	7:56
Tel Aviv, Israel	4:48	8:26	4:41	8:22
Toronto, ON	4:53	8:43	4:46	8:38
Vancouver, BC	4:25	8:23	4:15	8:16
Vienna, Austria	4:13	8:09	4:04	8:03
Vilnius, Lithuania	4:00	8:09	3:47	7:59
Warsaw, Poland	3:33	7:37	3:23	7:29
Winnipeg, MB	4:38	8:37	4:29	8:30
Zurich, Switzerland	4:48	8:43	4:39	8:36

Dates and Times of the *Tekufah* of Shmuel
5741-5769 (1981-2009)

מחזור גדול	YEAR	TEKUFAH	DAY	TIME
28	5741	ניסן	Tuesday, April 7, 1981	6:00 PM
28	5741	תמוז	Wednesday, July 8, 1981	1:30 AM
28	5742	תשרי	Wednesday, October 7, 1981	9:00 AM
28	5742	טבת	Wednesday, January 6, 1982	4:30 PM
1	5742	ניסן	Thursday, April 8, 1982	12:00 AM
1	5742	תמוז	Thursday, July 8, 1982	7:30 AM
1	5743	תשרי	Thursday, October 7, 1982	3:00 PM
1	5743	טבת	Thursday, January 6, 1983	10:30 PM
2	5743	ניסן	Friday, April 8, 1983	6:00 AM
2	5743	תמוז	Friday, July 8, 1983	1:30 PM
2	5744	תשרי	Friday, October 7, 1983	9:00 PM
2	5744	טבת	Saturday, January 7, 1984	4:30 AM
3	5744	ניסן	Saturday, April 7, 1984	12:00 AM
3	5744	תמוז	Saturday, July 7, 1984	7:30 PM
3	5745	תשרי	Sunday, October 7, 1984	3:00 AM
3	5745	טבת	Sunday, January 6, 1985	10:30 AM
4	5745	ניסן	Sunday, April 7, 1985	6:00 PM
4	5745	תמוז	Monday, July 8, 1985	1:30 AM
4	5746	תשרי	Monday, October 7, 1985	9:00 AM
4	5746	טבת	Monday, January 6, 1986	4:30 PM
5	5746	ניסן	Tuesday, April 8, 1986	12:00 AM
5	5746	תמוז	Tuesday, July 8, 1986	7:30 AM
5	5747	תשרי	Tuesday, October 7, 1986	3:00 PM
5	5747	טבת	Tuesday, January 6, 1987	10:30 PM
6	5747	ניסן	Wednesday, April 8, 1987	6:00 AM
6	5747	תמוז	Wednesday, July 8, 1987	1:30 PM
6	5748	תשרי	Wednesday, October 7, 1987	9:00 PM
6	5748	טבת	Thursday, January 7, 1988	4:30 AM
7	5748	ניסן	Thursday, April 7, 1988	12:00 PM
7	5748	תמוז	Thursday, July 7, 1988	7:30 PM
7	5749	תשרי	Friday, October 7, 1988	3:00 AM
7	5749	טבת	Friday, January 6, 1989	10:30 AM
8	5749	ניסן	Friday, April 7, 1989	6:00 PM
8	5749	תמוז	Saturday, July 8, 1989	1:30 AM
8	5750	תשרי	Saturday, October 7, 1989	9:00 AM
8	5750	טבת	Saturday, January 6, 1990	4:30 PM
9	5750	ניסן	Sunday, April 8, 1990	12:00 AM
9	5750	תמוז	Sunday, July 8, 1990	7:30 AM
9	5751	תשרי	Sunday, October 7, 1990	3:00 PM
9	5751	טבת	Sunday, January 6, 1991	10:30 PM
10	5751	ניסן	Monday, April 8, 1991	6:00 AM
10	5751	תמוז	Monday, July 8, 1991	1:30 PM
10	5752	תשרי	Monday, October 7, 1991	9:00 PM
10	5752	טבת	Tuesday, January 7, 1992	4:30 AM
11	5752	ניסן	Tuesday, April 7, 1992	12:00 PM

מחזור גדול	YEAR	TEKUFAH	DAY	TIME
11	5752	תמוז	Tuesday, July 7, 1992	7:30 PM
11	5753	תשרי	Wednesday, October 7, 1992	3:00 AM
11	5753	טבת	Wednesday, January 6, 1993	10:30 AM
12	5753	ניסן	Wednesday, April 7, 1993	6:00 PM
12	5753	תמוז	Thursday, July 8, 1993	1:30 AM
12	5754	תשרי	Thursday, October 7, 1993	9:00 AM
12	5754	טבת	Thursday, January 6, 1994	4:30 PM
13	5754	ניסן	Friday, April 8, 1994	12:00 AM
13	5754	תמוז	Friday, July 8, 1994	7:30 AM
13	5755	תשרי	Friday, October 7, 1994	3:00 PM
13	5755	טבת	Friday, January 6, 1995	10:30 PM
14	5755	ניסן	Saturday, April 8, 1995	6:00 AM
14	5755	תמוז	Saturday, July 8, 1995	1:30 PM
14	5756	תשרי	Saturday, October 7, 1995	9:00 PM
14	5756	טבת	Sunday, January 7, 1996	4:30 AM
15	5756	ניסן	Sunday, April 7, 1996	12:00 PM
15	5756	תמוז	Sunday, July 7, 1996	7:30 PM
15	5757	תשרי	Monday, October 7, 1996	3:00 AM
15	5757	טבת	Monday, January 6, 1997	10:30 AM
16	5757	ניסן	Monday, April 7, 1997	6:00 PM
16	5757	תמוז	Tuesday, July 8, 1997	1:30 AM
16	5758	תשרי	Tuesday, October 7, 1997	9:00 AM
16	5758	טבת	Tuesday, January 6, 1998	4:30 PM
17	5758	ניסן	Wednesday, April 8, 1998	12:00 AM
17	5758	תמוז	Wednesday, July 8, 1998	7:30 AM
17	5759	תשרי	Wednesday, October 7, 1998	3:00 PM
17	5759	טבת	Wednesday, January 6, 1999	10:30 PM
18	5759	ניסן	Thursday, April 8, 1999	6:00 AM
18	5759	תמוז	Thursday, July 8, 1999	1:30 PM
18	5760	תשרי	Thursday, October 7, 1999	9:00 PM
18	5760	טבת	Friday, January 7, 2000	4:30 AM
19	5760	ניסן	Friday, April 7, 2000	12:00 PM
19	5760	תמוז	Friday, July 7, 2000	7:30 PM
19	5761	תשרי	Saturday, October 7, 2000	3:00 AM
19	5761	טבת	Saturday, January 6, 2001	10:30 AM
20	5761	ניסן	Saturday, April 7, 2001	6:00 PM
20	5761	תמוז	Sunday, July 8, 2001	1:30 AM
20	5762	תשרי	Sunday, October 7, 2001	9:00 AM
20	5762	טבת	Sunday, January 6, 2002	4:30 PM
21	5762	ניסן	Monday, April 8, 2002	12:00 AM
21	5762	תמוז	Monday, July 8, 2002	7:30 AM
21	5763	תשרי	Monday, October 7, 2002	3:00 PM
21	5763	טבת	Monday, January 6, 2003	10:30 PM
22	5763	ניסן	Tuesday, April 8, 2003	6:00 AM
22	5763	תמוז	Tuesday, July 8, 2003	1:30 PM
22	5764	תשרי	Tuesday, October 7, 2003	9:00 PM
22	5764	טבת	Wednesday, January 7, 2004	4:30 AM
23	5764	ניסן	Wednesday, April 7, 2004	12:00 PM
23	5764	תמוז	Wednesday, July 7, 2004	7:30 PM
23	5765	תשרי	Thursday, October 7, 2004	3:00 AM
23	5765	טבת	Thursday, January 6, 2005	10:30 AM

מחזור גדול	YEAR	TEKUFAH	DAY	TIME
24	5765	ניסן	Thursday, April 7, 2005	6:00 PM
24	5765	תמוז	Friday, July 8, 2005	1:30 AM
24	5766	תשרי	Friday, October 7, 2005	9:00 AM
24	5766	טבת	Friday, January 6, 2006	4:30 PM
25	5766	ניסן	Saturday, April 8, 2006	12:00 AM
25	5766	תמוז	Saturday, July 8, 2006	7:30 AM
25	5767	תשרי	Saturday, October 7, 2006	3:00 PM
25	5767	טבת	Saturday, January 6, 2007	10:30 PM
26	5767	ניסן	Sunday, April 8, 2007	6:00 AM
26	5767	תמוז	Sunday, July 8, 2007	1:30 PM
26	5768	תשרי	Sunday, October 7, 2007	9:00 PM
26	5768	טבת	Monday, January 7, 2008	4:30 AM
27	5768	ניסן	Monday, April 7, 2008	12:00 PM
27	5768	תמוז	Monday, July 7, 2008	7:30 PM
27	5769	תשרי	Tuesday, October 7, 2008	3:00 AM
27	5769	טבת	Tuesday, January 6, 2009	10:30 AM
28	5769	ניסן	Tuesday, April 7, 2009	6:00 PM

Commencement of *Tal uMatar*
5743-5966 (1981-2205)

YEAR	TEKUFAH	DAY	TIME	ADJUSTMENT FOR TEKUFAH COMMENCING AFTER SUNSET	TAL UMUTAR BEGINS THE EVE OF
5742	תשרי	Wednesday, October 7, 1981	9:00 AM		December 5, 1981
5743	תשרי	Thursday, October 7, 1982	3:00 PM		December 5, 1982
5744	תשרי	Friday, October 7, 1983	9:00 PM	Saturday, October 8, 1983	December 6, 1983
5745	תשרי	Sunday, October 7, 1984	3:00 AM		December 5, 1984
5746	תשרי	Monday, October 7, 1985	9:00 AM		December 5, 1985
5747	תשרי	Tuesday, October 7, 1986	3:00 PM		December 5, 1986
5748	תשרי	Wednesday, October 7, 1987	9:00 PM	Thursday, October 8, 1987	December 6, 1987
5749	תשרי	Friday, October 7, 1988	3:00 AM		December 5, 1988
5750	תשרי	Saturday, October 7, 1989	9:00 AM		December 5, 1989
5751	תשרי	Sunday, October 7, 1990	3:00 PM		December 5, 1990
5752	תשרי	Monday, October 7, 1991	9:00 PM	Tuesday, October 8, 1991	December 6, 1991
5753	תשרי	Wednesday, October 7, 1992	3:00 AM		December 5, 1992
5754	תשרי	Thursday, October 7, 1993	9:00 AM		December 5, 1993
5755	תשרי	Friday, October 7, 1994	3:00 PM		December 5, 1994
5756	תשרי	Saturday, October 7, 1995	9:00 PM	Sunday, October 8, 1995	December 6, 1995
5757	תשרי	Monday, October 7, 1996	3:00 AM		December 5, 1996
5758	תשרי	Tuesday, October 7, 1997	9:00 AM		December 5, 1997
5759	תשרי	Wednesday, October 7, 1998	3:00 PM		December 5, 1998
5760	תשרי	Thursday, October 7, 1999	9:00 PM	Friday, October 8, 1999	December 6, 1999
5761	תשרי	Saturday, October 7, 2000	3:00 AM		December 5, 2000
5762	תשרי	Sunday, October 7, 2001	9:00 AM		December 5, 2001
5763	תשרי	Monday, October 7, 2002	3:00 PM		December 5, 2002
5764	תשרי	Tuesday, October 7, 2003	9:00 PM	Wednesday, October 8, 2003	December 6, 2003
5765	תשרי	Thursday, October 7, 2004	3:00 AM		December 5, 2004
5766	תשרי	Friday, October 7, 2005	9:00 AM		December 5, 2005
5767	תשרי	Saturday, October 7, 2006	3:00 PM		December 5, 2006
5768	תשרי	Sunday, October 7, 2007	9:00 PM	Monday, October 8, 2007	December 6, 2007
5769	תשרי	Tuesday, October 7, 2008	3:00 AM		December 5, 2008
5770	תשרי	Wednesday, October 7, 2009	9:00 AM		December 5, 2009
5771	תשרי	Thursday, October 7, 2010	3:00 PM		December 5, 2010
5772	תשרי	Friday, October 7, 2011	9:00 PM	Saturday, October 8, 2011	December 6, 2011
5773	תשרי	Sunday, October 7, 2012	3:00 AM		December 5, 2012
5774	תשרי	Monday, October 7, 2013	9:00 AM		December 5, 2013
5775	תשרי	Tuesday, October 7, 2014	3:00 PM		December 5, 2014
5776	תשרי	Wednesday, October 7, 2015	9:00 PM	Thursday, October 8, 2015	December 6, 2015
5777	תשרי	Friday, October 7, 2016	3:00 AM		December 5, 2016
5778	תשרי	Saturday, October 7, 2017	9:00 AM		December 5, 2017
5779	תשרי	Sunday, October 7, 2018	3:00 PM		December 5, 2018
5780	תשרי	Monday, October 7, 2019	9:00 PM	Tuesday, October 8, 2019	December 6, 2019
5781	תשרי	Wednesday, October 7, 2020	3:00 AM		December 5, 2020
5782	תשרי	Thursday, October 7, 2021	9:00 AM		December 5, 2021
5783	תשרי	Friday, October 7, 2022	3:00 PM		December 5, 2022
5784	תשרי	Saturday, October 7, 2023	9:00 PM	Sunday, October 8, 2023	December 6, 2023

YEAR	TEKUFAH	DAY	TIME	ADJUSTMENT FOR TEKUFAH COMMENCING AFTER SUNSET	TAL UMUTAR BEGINS THE EVE OF
5785	תשרי	Monday, October 7, 2024	3:00 AM		December 5, 2024
5786	תשרי	Tuesday, October 7, 2025	9:00 AM		December 5, 2025
5787	תשרי	Wednesday, October 7, 2026	3:00 PM		December 5, 2026
5788	תשרי	Thursday, October 7, 2027	9:00 PM	Friday, October 8, 2027	December 6, 2027
5789	תשרי	Saturday, October 7, 2028	3:00 AM		December 5, 2028
5790	תשרי	Sunday, October 7, 2029	9:00 AM		December 5, 2029
5791	תשרי	Monday, October 7, 2030	3:00 PM		December 5, 2030
5792	תשרי	Tuesday, October 7, 2031	9:00 PM	Wednesday, October 8, 2031	December 6, 2031
5793	תשרי	Thursday, October 7, 2032	3:00 AM		December 5, 2032
5794	תשרי	Friday, October 7, 2033	9:00 AM		December 5, 2033
5795	תשרי	Saturday, October 7, 2034	3:00 PM		December 5, 2034
5796	תשרי	Sunday, October 7, 2035	9:00 PM	Monday, October 8, 2035	December 6, 2035
5797	תשרי	Tuesday, October 7, 2036	3:00 AM		December 5, 2036
5798	תשרי	Wednesday, October 7, 2037	9:00 AM		December 5, 2037
5799	תשרי	Thursday, October 7, 2038	3:00 PM		December 5, 2038
5800	תשרי	Friday, October 7, 2039	9:00 PM	Saturday, October 8, 2039	December 6, 2039
5801	תשרי	Sunday, October 7, 2040	3:00 AM		December 5, 2040
5802	תשרי	Monday, October 7, 2041	9:00 AM		December 5, 2041
5803	תשרי	Tuesday, October 7, 2042	3:00 PM		December 5, 2042
5804	תשרי	Wednesday, October 7, 2043	9:00 PM	Thursday, October 8, 2043	December 6, 2043
5805	תשרי	Friday, October 7, 2044	3:00 AM		December 5, 2044
5806	תשרי	Saturday, October 7, 2045	9:00 AM		December 5, 2045
5807	תשרי	Sunday, October 7, 2046	3:00 PM		December 5, 2046
5808	תשרי	Monday, October 7, 2047	9:00 PM	Tuesday, October 8, 2047	December 6, 2047
5809	תשרי	Wednesday, October 7, 2048	3:00 AM		December 5, 2048
5810	תשרי	Thursday, October 7, 2049	9:00 AM		December 5, 2049
5811	תשרי	Friday, October 7, 2050	3:00 PM		December 5, 2050
5812	תשרי	Saturday, October 7, 2051	9:00 PM	Sunday, October 8, 2051	December 6, 2051
5813	תשרי	Monday, October 7, 2052	3:00 AM		December 5, 2052
5814	תשרי	Tuesday, October 7, 2053	9:00 AM		December 5, 2053
5815	תשרי	Wednesday, October 7, 2054	3:00 PM		December 5, 2054
5816	תשרי	Thursday, October 7, 2055	9:00 PM	Friday, October 8, 2055	December 6, 2055
5817	תשרי	Saturday, October 7, 2056	3:00 AM		December 5, 2056
5818	תשרי	Sunday, October 7, 2057	9:00 AM		December 5, 2057
5819	תשרי	Monday, October 7, 2058	3:00 PM		December 5, 2058
5820	תשרי	Tuesday, October 7, 2059	9:00 PM	Wednesday, October 8, 2059	December 6, 2059
5821	תשרי	Thursday, October 7, 2060	3:00 AM		December 5, 2060
5822	תשרי	Friday, October 7, 2061	9:00 AM		December 5, 2061
5823	תשרי	Saturday, October 7, 2062	3:00 PM		December 5, 2062
5824	תשרי	Sunday, October 7, 2063	9:00 PM	Monday, October 8, 2063	December 6, 2063
5825	תשרי	Tuesday, October 7, 2064	3:00 AM		December 5, 2064
5826	תשרי	Wednesday, October 7, 2065	9:00 AM		December 5, 2065
5827	תשרי	Thursday, October 7, 2066	3:00 PM		December 5, 2066
5828	תשרי	Friday, October 7, 2067	9:00 PM	Saturday, October 8, 2067	December 6, 2067
5829	תשרי	Sunday, October 7, 2068	3:00 AM		December 5, 2068
5830	תשרי	Monday, October 7, 2069	9:00 AM		December 5, 2069
5831	תשרי	Tuesday, October 7, 2070	3:00 PM		December 5, 2070
5832	תשרי	Wednesday, October 7, 2071	9:00 PM	Thursday, October 8, 2071	December 6, 2071

YEAR	TEKUFAH	DAY	TIME	ADJUSTMENT FOR TEKUFAH COMMENCING AFTER SUNSET	TAL UMUTAR BEGINS THE EVE OF
5833	תשרי	Friday, October 7, 2072	3:00 AM		December 5, 2072
5834	תשרי	Saturday, October 7, 2073	9:00 AM		December 5, 2073
5835	תשרי	Sunday, October 7, 2074	3:00 PM		December 5, 2074
5836	תשרי	Monday, October 7, 2075	9:00 PM	Tuesday, October 8, 2075	December 6, 2075
5837	תשרי	Wednesday, October 7, 2076	3:00 AM		December 5, 2076
5838	תשרי	Thursday, October 7, 2077	9:00 AM		December 5, 2077
5839	תשרי	Friday, October 7, 2078	3:00 PM		December 5, 2078
5840	תשרי	Saturday, October 7, 2079	9:00 PM	Sunday, October 8, 2079	December 6, 2079
5841	תשרי	Monday, October 7, 2080	3:00 AM		December 5, 2080
5842	תשרי	Tuesday, October 7, 2081	9:00 AM		December 5, 2081
5843	תשרי	Wednesday, October 7, 2082	3:00 PM		December 5, 2082
5844	תשרי	Thursday, October 7, 2083	9:00 PM	Friday, October 8, 2083	December 6, 2083
5845	תשרי	Saturday, October 7, 2084	3:00 AM		December 5, 2084
5846	תשרי	Sunday, October 7, 2085	9:00 AM		December 5, 2085
5847	תשרי	Monday, October 7, 2086	3:00 PM		December 5, 2086
5848	תשרי	Tuesday, October 7, 2087	9:00 PM	Wednesday, October 8, 2087	December 6, 2087
5849	תשרי	Thursday, October 7, 2088	3:00 AM		December 5, 2088
5850	תשרי	Friday, October 7, 2089	9:00 AM		December 5, 2089
5851	תשרי	Saturday, October 7, 2090	3:00 PM		December 5, 2090
5852	תשרי	Sunday, October 7, 2091	9:00 PM	Monday, October 8, 2091	December 6, 2091
5853	תשרי	Tuesday, October 7, 2092	3:00 AM		December 5, 2092
5854	תשרי	Wednesday, October 7, 2093	9:00 AM		December 5, 2093
5855	תשרי	Thursday, October 7, 2094	3:00 PM		December 5, 2094
5856	תשרי	Friday, October 7, 2095	9:00 PM	Saturday, October 8, 2095	December 6, 2095
5857	תשרי	Sunday, October 7, 2096	3:00 AM		December 5, 2096
5858	תשרי	Monday, October 7, 2097	9:00 AM		December 5, 2097
5859	תשרי	Tuesday, October 7, 2098	3:00 PM		December 5, 2098
5860	תשרי	Wednesday, October 7, 2099	9:00 PM	Thursday, October 8, 2099	December 6, 2099
5861	תשרי	Friday, October 8, 2100	3:00 AM		December 6, 2100
5862	תשרי	Saturday, October 8, 2101	9:00 AM		December 6, 2101
5863	תשרי	Sunday, October 8, 2102	3:00 PM		December 6, 2102
5864	תשרי	Monday, October 8, 2103	9:00 PM	Tuesday, October 9, 2103	December 7, 2103
5865	תשרי	Wednesday, October 8, 2104	3:00 AM		December 6, 2104
5866	תשרי	Thursday, October 8, 2105	9:00 AM		December 6, 2105
5867	תשרי	Friday, October 8, 2106	3:00 PM		December 6, 2106
5868	תשרי	Saturday, October 8, 2107	9:00 PM	Sunday, October 9, 2107	December 7, 2107
5869	תשרי	Monday, October 8, 2108	3:00 AM		December 6, 2108
5870	תשרי	Tuesday, October 8, 2109	9:00 AM		December 6, 2109
5871	תשרי	Wednesday, October 8, 2110	3:00 PM		December 6, 2110
5872	תשרי	Thursday, October 8, 2111	9:00 PM	Friday, October 9, 2111	December 7, 2111
5873	תשרי	Saturday, October 8, 2112	3:00 AM		December 6, 2112
5874	תשרי	Sunday, October 8, 2113	9:00 AM		December 6, 2113
5875	תשרי	Monday, October 8, 2114	3:00 PM		December 6, 2114
5876	תשרי	Tuesday, October 8, 2115	9:00 PM	Wednesday, October 9, 2115	December 7, 2115
5877	תשרי	Thursday, October 8, 2116	3:00 AM		December 6, 2116
5878	תשרי	Friday, October 8, 2117	9:00 AM		December 6, 2117
5879	תשרי	Saturday, October 8, 2118	3:00 PM		December 6, 2118
5880	תשרי	Sunday, October 8, 2119	9:00 PM	Monday, October 9, 2119	December 7, 2119

YEAR	TEKUFAH	DAY	TIME	ADJUSTMENT FOR TEKUFAH COMMENCING AFTER SUNSET	TAL UMUTAR BEGINS THE EVE OF
5881	תשרי	Tuesday, October 8, 2120	3:00 AM		December 6, 2120
5882	תשרי	Wednesday, October 8, 2121	9:00 AM		December 6, 2121
5883	תשרי	Thursday, October 8, 2122	3:00 PM		December 6, 2122
5884	תשרי	Friday, October 8, 2123	9:00 PM	Saturday, October 9, 2123	December 7, 2123
5885	תשרי	Sunday, October 8, 2124	3:00 AM		December 6, 2124
5886	תשרי	Monday, October 8, 2125	9:00 AM		December 6, 2125
5887	תשרי	Tuesday, October 8, 2126	3:00 PM		December 6, 2126
5888	תשרי	Wednesday, October 8, 2127	9:00 PM	Thursday, October 9, 2127	December 7, 2127
5889	תשרי	Friday, October 8, 2128	3:00 AM		December 6, 2128
5890	תשרי	Saturday, October 8, 2129	9:00 AM		December 6, 2129
5891	תשרי	Sunday, October 8, 2130	3:00 PM		December 6, 2130
5892	תשרי	Monday, October 8, 2131	9:00 PM	Tuesday, October 9, 2131	December 7, 2131
5893	תשרי	Wednesday, October 8, 2132	3:00 AM		December 6, 2132
5894	תשרי	Thursday, October 8, 2133	9:00 AM		December 6, 2133
5895	תשרי	Friday, October 8, 2134	3:00 PM		December 6, 2134
5896	תשרי	Saturday, October 8, 2135	9:00 PM	Sunday, October 9, 2135	December 7, 2135
5897	תשרי	Monday, October 8, 2136	3:00 AM		December 6, 2136
5898	תשרי	Tuesday, October 8, 2137	9:00 AM		December 6, 2137
5899	תשרי	Wednesday, October 8, 2138	3:00 PM		December 6, 2138
5900	תשרי	Thursday, October 8, 2139	9:00 PM	Friday, October 9, 2139	December 7, 2139
5901	תשרי	Saturday, October 8, 2140	3:00 AM		December 6, 2140
5902	תשרי	Sunday, October 8, 2141	9:00 AM		December 6, 2141
5903	תשרי	Monday, October 8, 2142	3:00 PM		December 6, 2142
5904	תשרי	Tuesday, October 8, 2143	9:00 PM	Wednesday, October 9, 2143	December 7, 2143
5905	תשרי	Thursday, October 8, 2144	3:00 AM		December 6, 2144
5906	תשרי	Friday, October 8, 2145	9:00 AM		December 6, 2145
5907	תשרי	Saturday, October 8, 2146	3:00 PM		December 6, 2146
5908	תשרי	Sunday, October 8, 2147	9:00 PM	Monday, October 9, 2147	December 7, 2147
5909	תשרי	Tuesday, October 8, 2148	3:00 AM		December 6, 2148
5910	תשרי	Wednesday, October 8, 2149	9:00 AM		December 6, 2149
5911	תשרי	Thursday, October 8, 2150	3:00 PM		December 6, 2150
5912	תשרי	Friday, October 8, 2151	9:00 PM	Saturday, October 9, 2151	December 7, 2151
5913	תשרי	Sunday, October 8, 2152	3:00 AM		December 6, 2152
5914	תשרי	Monday, October 8, 2153	9:00 AM		December 6, 2153
5915	תשרי	Tuesday, October 8, 2154	3:00 PM		December 6, 2154
5916	תשרי	Wednesday, October 8, 2155	9:00 PM	Thursday, October 9, 2155	December 7, 2155
5917	תשרי	Friday, October 8, 2156	3:00 AM		December 6, 2156
5918	תשרי	Saturday, October 8, 2157	9:00 AM		December 6, 2157
5919	תשרי	Sunday, October 8, 2158	3:00 PM		December 6, 2158
5920	תשרי	Monday, October 8, 2159	9:00 PM	Tuesday, October 9, 2159	December 7, 2159
5921	תשרי	Wednesday, October 8, 2160	3:00 AM		December 6, 2160
5922	תשרי	Thursday, October 8, 2161	9:00 AM		December 6, 2161
5923	תשרי	Friday, October 8, 2162	3:00 PM		December 6, 2162
5924	תשרי	Saturday, October 8, 2163	9:00 PM	Sunday, October 9, 2163	December 7, 2163
5925	תשרי	Monday, October 8, 2164	3:00 AM		December 6, 2164
5926	תשרי	Tuesday, October 8, 2165	9:00 AM		December 6, 2165
5927	תשרי	Wednesday, October 8, 2166	3:00 PM		December 6, 2166
5928	תשרי	Thursday, October 8, 2167	9:00 PM	Friday, October 9, 2167	December 7, 2167

YEAR	TEKUFAH	DAY	TIME	ADJUSTMENT FOR TEKUFAH COMMENCING AFTER SUNSET	TAL UMUTAR BEGINS THE EVE OF
5929	תשרי	Saturday, October 8, 2168	3:00 AM		December 6, 2168
5930	תשרי	Sunday, October 8, 2169	9:00 AM		December 6, 2169
5931	תשרי	Monday, October 8, 2170	3:00 PM		December 6, 2170
5932	תשרי	Tuesday, October 8, 2171	9:00 PM	Wednesday, October 9, 2171	December 7, 2171
5933	תשרי	Thursday, October 8, 2172	3:00 AM		December 6, 2172
5934	תשרי	Friday, October 8, 2173	9:00 AM		December 6, 2173
5935	תשרי	Saturday, October 8, 2174	3:00 PM		December 6, 2174
5936	תשרי	Sunday, October 8, 2175	9:00 PM	Monday, October 9, 2175	December 7, 2175
5937	תשרי	Tuesday, October 8, 2176	3:00 AM		December 6, 2176
5938	תשרי	Wednesday, October 8, 2177	9:00 AM		December 6, 2177
5939	תשרי	Thursday, October 8, 2178	3:00 PM		December 6, 2178
5940	תשרי	Friday, October 8, 2179	9:00 PM	Saturday, October 9, 2179	December 7, 2179
5941	תשרי	Sunday, October 8, 2180	3:00 AM		December 6, 2180
5942	תשרי	Monday, October 8, 2181	9:00 AM		December 6, 2181
5943	תשרי	Tuesday, October 8, 2182	3:00 PM		December 6, 2182
5944	תשרי	Wednesday, October 8, 2183	9:00 PM	Thursday, October 9, 2183	December 7, 2183
5945	תשרי	Friday, October 8, 2184	3:00 AM		December 6, 2184
5946	תשרי	Saturday, October 8, 2185	9:00 AM		December 6, 2185
5947	תשרי	Sunday, October 8, 2186	3:00 PM		December 6, 2186
5948	תשרי	Monday, October 8, 2187	9:00 PM	Tuesday, October 9, 2187	December 7, 2187
5949	תשרי	Wednesday, October 8, 2188	3:00 AM		December 6, 2188
5950	תשרי	Thursday, October 8, 2189	9:00 AM		December 6, 2189
5951	תשרי	Friday, October 8, 2190	3:00 PM		December 6, 2190
5952	תשרי	Saturday, October 8, 2191	9:00 PM	Sunday, October 9, 2191	December 7, 2191
5953	תשרי	Monday, October 8, 2192	3:00 AM		December 6, 2192
5954	תשרי	Tuesday, October 8, 2193	9:00 AM		December 6, 2193
5955	תשרי	Wednesday, October 8, 2194	3:00 PM		December 6, 2194
5956	תשרי	Thursday, October 8, 2195	9:00 PM	Friday, October 9, 2195	December 7, 2195
5957	תשרי	Saturday, October 8, 2196	3:00 AM		December 6, 2196
5958	תשרי	Sunday, October 8, 2197	9:00 AM		December 6, 2197
5959	תשרי	Monday, October 8, 2198	3:00 PM		December 6, 2198
5960	תשרי	Tuesday, October 8, 2199	9:00 PM	Wednesday, October 9, 2199	December 7, 2199
5961	תשרי	Thursday, October 9, 2200	3:00 AM		December 7, 2200
5962	תשרי	Friday, October 9, 2201	9:00 AM		December 7, 2201
5963	תשרי	Saturday, October 9, 2202	3:00 PM		December 7, 2202
5964	תשרי	Sunday, October 9, 2203	9:00 PM	Monday, October 10, 2203	December 8, 2203
5965	תשרי	Tuesday, October 9, 2204	3:00 AM		December 7, 2204
5966	תשרי	Wednesday, October 9, 2205	9:00 AM		December 7, 2205

Dates of Commencement of Each 28-Year Cycle
from Creation until 6049(2289)

JEWISH CALENDAR			CIVIL CALENDAR	
1	22	אדר	March 26	3760 B.C.E.
29	2	ניסן	March 26	3732 B.C.E.
57	12	אדר ב׳	March 26	3704 B.C.E.
85	20	אדר	March 26	3676 B.C.E.
113	2	ניסן	March 26	3648 B.C.E.
141	10	אדר ב׳	March 26	3620 B.C.E.
169	20	אדר ב׳	March 26	3592 B.C.E.
197	29	אדר	March 26	3564 B.C.E.
225	9	ניסן	March 26	3536 B.C.E.
253	17	אדר ב׳	March 26	3508 B.C.E.
281	27	אדר	March 26	3480 B.C.E.
309	9	ניסן	March 26	3452 B.C.E.
337	17	אדר ב׳	March 26	3424 B.C.E.
365	27	אדר	March 26	3396 B.C.E.
393	7	ניסן	March 26	3368 B.C.E.
421	15	אדר ב׳	March 26	3340 B.C.E.
449	24	אדר	March 26	3312 B.C.E.
477	5	ניסן	March 26	3284 B.C.E.
505	15	אדר ב׳	March 26	3256 B.C.E.
533	24	אדר	March 26	3228 B.C.E.
561	5	ניסן	March 26	3200 B.C.E.
589	13	אדר ב׳	March 26	3172 B.C.E.
617	22	אדר	March 26	3144 B.C.E.
645	2	ניסן	March 26	3116 B.C.E.
673	12	אדר ב׳	March 26	3088 B.C.E.
701	22	אדר ב׳	March 26	3060 B.C.E.
729	2	ניסן	March 26	3032 B.C.E.
757	12	ניסן	March 26	3004 B.C.E.
785	20	אדר ב׳	March 26	2976 B.C.E.
813	29	אדר	March 26	2948 B.C.E.
841	9	ניסן	March 26	2920 B.C.E.
869	19	אדר ב׳	March 26	2892 B.C.E.
897	29	אדר	March 26	2864 B.C.E.
925	9	ניסן	March 26	2836 B.C.E.
953	17	אדר ב׳	March 26	2808 B.C.E.
981	27	אדר	March 26	2780 B.C.E.
1009	7	ניסן	March 26	2752 B.C.E.
1037	17	אדר ב׳	March 26	2724 B.C.E.
1065	26	אדר	March 26	2696 B.C.E.
1093	5	ניסן	March 26	2668 B.C.E.
1121	15	אדר ב׳	March 26	2640 B.C.E.
1149	24	אדר	March 26	2612 B.C.E.
1177	5	ניסן	March 26	2584 B.C.E.
1205	13	אדר ב׳	March 26	2556 B.C.E.
1233	22	אדר ב׳	March 26	2528 B.C.E.

JEWISH CALENDAR			CIVIL CALENDAR	
1261	4	ניסן	March 26	2500 B.C.E.
1289	12	ניסן	March 26	2472 B.C.E.
1317	22	אדר ב'	March 26	2444 B.C.E.
1345	2	ניסן	March 26	2416 B.C.E.
1373	12	ניסן	March 26	2388 B.C.E.
1401	20	אדר ב'	March 26	2360 B.C.E.
1429	29	אדר	March 26	2332 B.C.E.
1457	11	ניסן	March 26	2304 B.C.E.
1485	20	אדר ב'	March 26	2276 B.C.E.
1513	29	אדר	March 26	2248 B.C.E.
1541	9	ניסן	March 26	2220 B.C.E.
1569	17	אדר ב'	March 26	2192 B.C.E.
1597	27	אדר	March 26	2164 B.C.E.
1625	7	ניסן	March 26	2136 B.C.E.
1653	17	אדר ב'	March 26	2108 B.C.E.
1681	26	אדר	March 26	2080 B.C.E.
1709	7	ניסן	March 26	2052 B.C.E.
1737	15	אדר ב'	March 26	2024 B.C.E.
1765	24	אדר ב'	March 26	1996 B.C.E.
1793	5	ניסן	March 26	1968 B.C.E.
1821	14	ניסן	March 26	1940 B.C.E.
1849	24	אדר ב'	March 26	1912 B.C.E.
1877	4	ניסן	March 26	1884 B.C.E.
1905	14	ניסן	March 26	1856 B.C.E.
1933	22	אדר ב'	March 26	1828 B.C.E.
1961	2	ניסן	March 26	1800 B.C.E.
1989	12	ניסן	March 26	1772 B.C.E.
2017	20	אדר ב'	March 26	1744 B.C.E.
2045	2	ניסן	March 26	1716 B.C.E.
2073	11	ניסן	March 26	1688 B.C.E.
2101	20	אדר ב'	March 26	1660 B.C.E.
2129	29	אדר	March 26	1632 B.C.E.
2157	9	ניסן	March 26	1604 B.C.E.
2185	17	אדר ב'	March 26	1576 B.C.E.
2213	27	אדר	March 26	1548 B.C.E.
2241	9	ניסן	March 26	1520 B.C.E.
2269	17	אדר ב'	March 26	1492 B.C.E.
2297	27	אדר ב'	March 26	1464 B.C.E.
2325	7	ניסן	March 26	1436 B.C.E.
2353	16	ניסן	March 26	1408 B.C.E.
2381	24	אדר ב'	March 26	1380 B.C.E.
2409	5	ניסן	March 26	1352 B.C.E.
2437	14	ניסן	March 26	1324 B.C.E.
2465	24	אדר ב'	March 26	1296 B.C.E.
2493	5	ניסן	March 26	1268 B.C.E.
2521	14	ניסן	March 26	1240 B.C.E.
2549	22	אדר ב'	March 26	1212 B.C.E.
2577	2	ניסן	March 26	1184 B.C.E.
2605	12	ניסן	March 26	1156 B.C.E.
2633	22	אדר ב'	March 26	1128 B.C.E.
2661	2	ניסן	March 26	1100 B.C.E.

JEWISH CALENDAR			CIVIL CALENDAR	
2689	12	ניסן	March 26	1072 B.C.E.
2717	20	אדר ב'	March 26	1044 B.C.E.
2745	29	אדר	March 26	1016 B.C.E.
2773	9	ניסן	March 26	988 B.C.E.
2801	19	אדר ב'	March 26	960 B.C.E.
2829	29	אדר ב'	March 26	932 B.C.E.
2857	9	ניסן	March 26	904 B.C.E.
2885	18	ניסן	March 26	876 B.C.E.
2913	27	אדר ב'	March 26	848 B.C.E.
2941	7	ניסן	March 26	820 B.C.E.
2969	16	ניסן	March 26	792 B.C.E.
2997	26	אדר ב'	March 26	764 B.C.E.
3025	5	ניסן	March 26	736 B.C.E.
3053	16	ניסן	March 26	708 B.C.E.
3081	24	אדר ב'	March 26	680 B.C.E.
3109	5	ניסן	March 26	652 B.C.E.
3137	14	ניסן	March 26	624 B.C.E.
3165	22	אדר ב'	March 26	596 B.C.E.
3193	2	ניסן	March 26	568 B.C.E.
3221	12	ניסן	March 26	540 B.C.E.
3249	22	אדר ב'	March 26	512 B.C.E.
3277	2	ניסן	March 26	484 B.C.E.
3305	12	ניסן	March 26	456 B.C.E.
3333	20	אדר ב'	March 26	428 B.C.E.
3361	29	אדר ב'	March 26	400 B.C.E.
3389	11	ניסן	March 26	372 B.C.E.
3417	19	ניסן	March 26	344 B.C.E.
3445	29	אדר ב'	March 26	316 B.C.E.
3473	9	ניסן	March 26	288 B.C.E.
3501	19	ניסן	March 26	260 B.C.E.
3529	27	אדר ב'	March 26	232 B.C.E.
3557	7	ניסן	March 26	204 B.C.E.
3585	16	ניסן	March 26	176 B.C.E.
3613	26	אדר ב'	March 26	148 B.C.E.
3641	7	ניסן	March 26	120 B.C.E.
3669	16	ניסן	March 26	92 B.C.E.
3697	24	אדר ב'	March 26	64 B.C.E.
3725	5	ניסן	March 26	36 B.C.E.
3753	14	ניסן	March 26	8 B.C.E.
3781	24	אדר ב'	March 26	21 C.E.
3809	4	ניסן	March 26	49 C.E.
3837	14	ניסן	March 26	77 C.E.
3865	22	אדר ב'	March 26	105 C.E.
3893	2	ניסן	March 26	133 C.E.
3921	12	ניסן	March 26	161 C.E.
3949	21	ניסן	March 26	189 C.E.
3977	2	ניסן	March 26	217 C.E.
4005	11	ניסן	March 26	245 C.E.
4033	19	ניסן	March 26	273 C.E.
4061	29	אדר ב'	March 26	301 C.E.
4089	9	ניסן	March 26	329 C.E.

JEWISH CALENDAR			CIVIL CALENDAR	
4117	19	ניסן	March 26	357 C.E.
4145	27	אדר ב׳	March 26	385 C.E.
4173	7	ניסן	March 26	413 C.E.
4201	18	ניסן	March 26	441 C.E.
4229	27	אדר ב׳	March 26	469 C.E.
4257	7	ניסן	March 26	497 C.E.
4285	16	ניסן	March 26	525 C.E.
4313	24	אדר ב׳	March 26	553 C.E.
4341	5	ניסן	March 26	581 C.E.
4369	14	ניסן	March 26	609 C.E.
4397	24	אדר ב׳	March 26	637 C.E.
4425	5	ניסן	March 26	665 C.E.
4453	14	ניסן	March 26	693 C.E.
4481	23	ניסן	March 26	721 C.E.
4509	2	ניסן	March 26	749 C.E.
4537	12	ניסן	March 26	777 C.E.
4565	21	ניסן	March 26	805 C.E.
4593	2	ניסן	March 26	833 C.E.
4621	11	ניסן	March 26	861 C.E.
4649	21	ניסן	March 26	889 C.E.
4677	29	אדר ב׳	March 26	917 C.E.
4705	9	ניסן	March 26	945 C.E.
4733	19	ניסן	March 26	973 C.E.
4761	27	אדר ב׳	March 26	1001 C.E.
4789	9	ניסן	March 26	1029 C.E.
4817	18	ניסן	March 26	1057 C.E.
4845	27	אדר ב׳	March 26	1085 C.E.
4873	7	ניסן	March 26	1113 C.E.
4901	16	ניסן	March 26	1141 C.E.
4929	26	אדר ב׳	March 26	1169 C.E.
4957	5	ניסן	March 26	1197 C.E.
4985	16	ניסן	March 26	1225 C.E.
5013	25	ניסן	March 26	1253 C.E.
5041	5	ניסן	March 26	1281 C.E.
5069	14	ניסן	March 26	1309 C.E.
5097	23	ניסן	March 26	1337 C.E.
5125	2	ניסן	March 26	1365 C.E.
5153	12	ניסן	March 26	1393 C.E.
5181	23	ניסן	March 26	1421 C.E.
5209	2	ניסן	March 26	1449 C.E.
5237	12	ניסן	March 26	1477 C.E.
5265	21	ניסן	March 26	1505 C.E.
5293	29	אדר ב׳	March 26	1533 C.E.
5321	9	ניסן	March 26	1561 C.E.
5349	19	ניסן	April 5	1589 C.E.
5377	29	אדר ב׳	April 5	1617 C.E.
5405	9	ניסן	April 5	1645 C.E.
5433	19	ניסן	April 5	1673 C.E.
5461	27	אדר ב׳	April 6	1701 C.E.
5489	7	ניסן	April 6	1729 C.E.
5517	16	ניסן	April 6	1757 C.E.

JEWISH CALENDAR			CIVIL CALENDAR	
5545	26	ניסן	April 6	1785 C.E.
5573	7	ניסן	April 7	1813 C.E.
5601	16	ניסן	April 7	1841 C.E.
5629	26	ניסן	April 7	1869 C.E.
5657	5	ניסן	April 7	1897 C.E.
5685	14	ניסן	April 8	1925 C.E.
5713	23	ניסן	April 8	1953 C.E.
5741	4	ניסן	April 8	1981 C.E.
5769	14	ניסן	April 8	2009 C.E.
5797	23	ניסן	April 8	2037 C.E.
5825	2	ניסן	April 8	2065 C.E.
5853	12	ניסן	April 8	2093 C.E.
5881	21	ניסן	April 9	2121 C.E.
5909	2	ניסן	April 9	2149 C.E.
5937	11	ניסן	April 9	2177 C.E.
5965	19	ניסן	April 10	2205 C.E.
5993	29	אדר ב'	April 10	2233 C.E.
6021	9	ניסן	April 10	2261 C.E.
6049	19	ניסן	April 10	2289 C.E.

עיונים בעניני ברכת החמה ℘

א. בענין הרקיע בטהרתה וברכת החמה

גרסינן בברכות דף נ"ט. אריב"ל הרואה רקיע בטהרתה אומר ברוך עושה בראשית אימתי אמר אביי כי אתא מטרא כולי ליליא ובצפרא אתא אסתנא ומגליא להו לשמיא. ושם בירושלמי פרק ט' הל' ב' נשנית באופן אחר, הרואה את החמה בתקופתה ואת הלבנה בתקופתה ואת הרקיע בטיהרו אומר ברוך עושה בראשית אמר רב הונא הדא דתימר בימות הגשמים בלבד לאחר שלשה ימים הה"ד ועתה לא ראו אור בהיר הוא בשחקים ורוח עברה ותטהרם.

וכפי הנראה הירושלמי וגמ' דידן מחולקים הם בשיעור מטר שעל ידו בא טוהר הרקיע שבדינו לחייב ברכת מעשה בראשית, שהרי בסוגיא דברכות מבואר שצריכים לברך במקרה שירדו גשמים משך כל שעות הלילה אפילו של לילה אחד כשבאה רוח צפונית בבקר ומגליא להו לשמיא, ואילו להירושלמי מברך רק כשיורד מטר כל ג' ימים רצופים. אמנם נראה שהמחלוקת בעיקרה אינה בשיעור המטר שע"י בא חיוב ברכה אלא ביסוד המחלוקת בין הירושלמי ובין גמ' דידן הוא בעצם המחייב של ברכה זו, דלגמ' דידן המחייב הוא עצם טוהר הרקיע וכל הרואה הרקיע בטהרתה מחויב להודות על מעשה בראשית כמו שמחויב להודות כשרואה הרים גבוהים וכדומה שכולם הם מנפלאות הבריאה, וכל שירדו גשמים כל הלילה די בזה שאז כשנושבת רוח צפונית נראה הרקיע בטהרתה כבתחילת בריאתו, וכן כתב רש"י וז"ל, אומר ברוך עושה בראשית שכך היתה בריאתו ואחר כך כסוהו עננים עכ"ל, אמנם לדעת הירושלמי טוהר הרקיע מצד עצמו אינו מחייב שום ברכה אלא טוהר הרקיע המחייב ברכת מעשה בראשית הוא שכשנזדכך הרקיע וטוהרו הוא כעין טוהר הרקיע כמו שהיה בשעת הבריאה אז חייב לא מצד הפלא אלא מצד שהוי כתחילת הבריאה, ועל זה בא רב הונא לפרש דרק לאחר שלשה ימים מברך מפני שרק כשהיה השמש מכוסה משך ג' ימים הוי דומה לתחילת יצירת השמש שאז בזמן הבריאה לא האיר משך ג' ימים הראשונים ורק בתחילת יום ד' נתלו המאורות. נמצא דלדעת הירושלמי הברכה היא לא על טוהר הרקיע מצד עצם הטוהר אלא מצד שע"י טוהר הרקיע והעדר השמש משך ג' ימים נראה לעינינו כעין דוגמת תחילת יצירת השמש שבשבעת תלייתו היתה גם כן הרקיע בטהרתה, ע' תשו' חת"ס או"ח סי' נ"ו.

ועוד כתב שם החת"ס לפרש שאולי הגירסא הנכונה בדברי רב הונא היא שלשים יום במקום שלשה ימים, ולדבריו אף לרב הונא הברכה היא בגדר אותו חיוב ברכה שתיקנו כשרואה ים הגדול או כשרואה הרים גבוהים וכדומה שכשרואה אותם לפרקים משלשים יום לשלשים יום מברך על

ראיתו ודכוותי׳ כשכיסו העבים את החמה והחמה לא היתה נראית שלשים
יום ולא פעל השמש פעולתו כראוי אז כשחוזר השמש לפעולתו חייב לברך
על ראייתו.

ונראה להסביר שבאמת ישנם ג׳ סוגי ברכות הראייה, ואע״פ שבכולם
מברכים עושה מעשה בראשית מ״מ לא הרי זה כהרי זה. והנה בנוגע להלל
ג״כ ישנם עכ״פ ב׳ סוגי הלל, ע׳ ספר עמק ברכה של הרה״ג ר׳ ארי׳ פומרנצ׳יק
זצ״ל שכתב דכל מה שאנו אומרים הלל אינו אלא תקנת חכמים לזכרון הנס
חוץ מהלל של ליל פסח שאינו משום הנס שנעשה לאבותינו אלא משום
הנס שנעשה לנו, שהרי בכל דור ודור חייב אדם לראות את עצמו כאילו הוא
יצא ממצרים, שלא את אבותינו בלבד גאל אלא אף אותנו גאל, ועיין רמב״ם
פ״ז מהל׳ חו״מ הל׳ ו׳ שכתב ועל דבר זה צוה הקב״ה בתורה וזכרת כי עבד
היית כלומר כאילו אתה בעצמך היית עבד ויצאת לחירות ונפדית וזהו מה
שהוקבע בנוסח ההגדה לפיכך אנחנו חייבים להודות פי׳ כיון שאנו בעצמינו
יצאנו זה עתה לחירות וכל הנסים של גאולת מצרים עשה גם לנו לפיכך אנו
חייבים לומר שירה על הנס שלנו, והיינו שהלל של ליל פסח הוא הלל על
הנס ולא הלל על זכרון הנס.

והנה פשוט שהחיוב ברכה על ההרים ועל הגבעות ועל הימים ועל הנהרות
ועל המדברות בא מפני שע״י שרואה אותם הדברים שא״א לו לאדם לעשות
כמותם מרגיש הרואה וחוזר ונתאמת אצלו שנבראו ע״י הקב״ה בששת ימי
בראשית ומברך על אותה הבריאה, הרי כשמברך על ההרים הגבוהים וכדומה
הברכה היא כעין זכרון הבריאה שנבראה מקדם בששת ימי בראשית ומברך
על פעולתו של הקב״ה בששת ימי בראשית. אמנם המברך עושה מעשה
בראשית על הזיקים ועל הברקים נראה שהברכה אינה על בריאה שנבראה
מכבר אלא על בריאה שנתחדשה עכשיו, שאילו היינו עומדים בשעת יצירת
שמים וארץ פשיטא שהיינו מברכים עושה מעשה בראשית, וזהו מה שתיקנו
לנו חז״ל שכשיזדמן שאנו עומדים מול יצירה חדשה חייבים לברך עליה
עושה מעשה בראשית, והזיקים והברקים הם כעין בריאה חדשה שברגע
מקודם לא היו זיקים וברקים ועכשיו פתאום נבראו. ובזה מובן למה תיקנו
לברך על הים הגדול ועל ההרים הגבוהים וכדומה רק לפרקים מל׳ יום לל׳
יום אבל על הברקים חוזרים ומברכים כל שנתפזרו העבים כמבואר באו״ח
סי׳ רכ״ז סעיף ב׳, והיינו מפני שכשמברכים על הים הגדול או על ההרים
הגבוהים הברכה היא על הימים ועל ההרים שנבראו מכבר שהרי ההרים
הגבוהים וים הגדול במקומם הם עומדים משעת יצירתם וכל אימת שרוצה
יכול לבוא ולראותם והרואה אותם לפרקים שמחויב לברך חיובו הוא רק מצד
שנתחדש בעיניו ולכן מברך רק אם לא ראה אותם משך ל׳ יום, אמנם על

הברקים מברכים על מה שנברא זה עתה וא"כ כל שבאמת יש יצירה חדשה לפנינו מברכים עליה.

ונראה דלגירסת החת"ס בדברי הירושלמי שלפי גירסתו בא רב הונא לומר דמברכים על הרקיע בטיהרו רק מל' יום ולל' יום צריך לפרש שהברכה באמת מיוסדת היא על עצם הפלא של הרקיע בטיהרו, היינו על מה שברא הקב"ה רקיע בטיהרו בתחילת הבריאה, כדומה ממש לברכה על הרים גבוהים ולכן מברך רק מל' יום ולל' יום כמו שמברך על ההרים הגבוהים ועל הים הגדול וכדומה רק כשרואה אותם לפרקים, אמנם לדברי הגמ' דידן מברך כל שירד מטר משך לילה אחד ונשבה רוח צפונית ונתגלה לנו הרקיע בטהרתה, ובזה לא נשנית ההלכה שמברכים מל' יום ולל' יום אלא אדרבה כל אימת דאתא מטרא כולי ליליא ובצפרא אתא אסתנא ומגליא להו לשמיא מברכים, והנראה דזהו מטעם דגלוי הרקיע בטהרתה הוי כמו בריאה שנתהוה בפנינו והיינו כשרואים איך הרוח הצפונית מפזרת העבים וע"י זה מתגלה לנו השמש והרקיע בטהרתה הרי זה אצלנו כעין בריאה חדשה הנוצרת לפנינו שברגע מקודם לא היה אפשר לראותה, כמו זיקים וברקים שלא היה אפשר לראותם מקודם זה עכשיו נברא. נמצא דלרב הונא הברכה היא ברכת הודאה הבאה על ידי זכרון תחילת הבריאה משא"כ לריב"ל הברכה היא ברכת הודאה על בריאה חדשה.

ונראה לומר שבאמת יש לנו גם סוג שלישי של ברכה בברכת עושה מעשה בראשית והיינו ששם ברכות דף נ"ט: איתא תנו רבנן הרואה חמה בתקופתה לבנה בגבורתה וכו' אומר ברוך עושה בראשית ואימת הוי ואמר אביי כל כ"ח שנין והדר מחזור ונפלה תקופת ניסן בשבתאי באורתא דתלת נגהי ארבע, וקשה דמה שייכות ישנה לברכת עושה מעשה בראשית למאורע כזה, הרי כשרואה את החמה ביום תקופת ניסן בתחילת מחזור הגדול של כ"ח שנה הרי אינו רואה שום שינוי או פלא אלא רואה אותו השמש ממש שראה אתמול והשמש עומד באותו מקום שעמד בו ביום התקופה בשנה שעברה ולא נתחדש בו שום דבר, וע"כ צ"ל שאינו מברך על שום חידוש במעשה בראשית ולא על שום פלא מנפלאות הבורא, אלא מאחר שבכל כ"ח שנה מתחיל מחזור חדש קבעו חז"ל ברכה כדי שיתאמת אצל המברך שהקב"ה מחדש בכל יום תמיד מעשה בראשית כמו שכתב הרמב"ם בהקדמתו לפרק חלק ובפרק א' מהל' יסודי התורה שהקב"ה מהוה את העולם תמיד, וקבעו ברכה זו בתחילת המחזור בעת שהחמה חוזרת למקומה הראשון ומתחלת סיבובה עוד הפעם מפני שמאורע זה מסמל עצם חידושה של הבריאה כולה והיינו שכמו שהחמה התחילת הילוכה עוד הפעם מנקודתה הראשונה ברקיע באותו יום ובאותה שעה שבהם נבראה כמו כן כל הבריאה מתחדשת בכל רגע ורגע.

ועפ"ז שפיר מובנים דברי הירושלמי כפי גירסת הספרים שלנו והיינו שרב הונא בא לומר שמברך עושה מעשה בראשית לא על עצם טוהר הרקיע אלא כשטוהר הרקיע בא אחר העדר השמש משך ג' ימים, וברכה זה לדעת רב הונא היא כעין הברכה על החמה בתוקפתה לדעת אביי בגמרא דידן, ובפרט לאותם הסוברים שהירושלמי חולק על אביי אז צריך לומר שלא בא רב הונא לפרש הביטוי „רקיע בטיהרו" אלא לפלוג על אביי ולפרש מובנו של „החמה בתקופתה" המוזכר בדברי הברייתא, ועכ"פ לפי דברי רב הונא הברכה היא דוגמת ברכת עושה מעשה בראשית שמברכים על החמה בתקופתה לדעת אביי, והיינו שבאמת ס"ל שע"י הגשמים לא נתחדש שום דבר לא בהחמה ולא בהרקיע אלא שהמאורע הוא דוגמת סדר הבריאה שהחמה בתחילת זריחתה התחילה פעולתה ושמשה אחרי העדרה ג' ימים, וכמו כן תיקנו שכל שלא זרח השמש משך ג' ימים רצופים שיברך על תחילת זריחתו והיינו מפני שהתחלת זריחתו אחר ג' ימים הוי כעין תחילת זריחתו בששת ימי בראשית ואז מתחדש סדר זריחתו עוד הפעם כמו בתחילת הבריאה ולזה תיקנו ברכה מיוחדת לאמת שהקב"ה מחדש בכל יום תמיד מעשה בראשית. נמצאנו למדים שבין לאביי ובין לרב הונא תיקנו ברכה על התחדשות הבריאה בכל רגע דבר שמסומל הוא באיזה אופן בזריחת השמש, אלא שלאביי נתקנה הברכה בתחילת מחזור החמה ולרב הונא נתקנה הברכה גם על חידוש הזריחה אחר העדרה משך ג' ימים שיש בזה ג"כ חידוש בזריחת השמש כעין תחילת הבריאה, ולאותם שס"ל שהירושלמי חולק על הבבלי ס"ל שלרב הונה נתקנה הברכה רק על מאורע זה ולא על תחילת מחזור החמה בכל כ"ח שנה.

ובזה מאד מובנים דברי הג' ר' יהושע הורוויץ בהסכמתו לקונטרס בקר יזרח שכתב שם לפרש כונת רב הונא שבא לפרש מובנו של חמה בתקופתה אבל לא בא לחלוק לגמרי על ש"ס דידן, והיינו שלא בא לומר דחמה בתקופתה לא תליא כלל בתקופת ניסן שאין הכונה דבכל פעם שיהיו ג' ימים מעוננים ואח"כ נזדכך הרקיע חייב לברך אלא שרב הונא דעתו לומר דמברך רק בעת תקופת ניסן אבל רק כשאירע שהיו ג' ימים מעוננים ואח"כ כשנראית החמה והוא ג"כ יום התקופה חיים לברך אבל בשאר ימות השנה אף אם היו ג' ימים מעוננים ואח"כ נראית החמה אינו מברך, ועי' בדברי הרה"ג ר' מאיר דוד הערצבערג בקונטרס אור החמה דף י' שהרבה לתמוה עליו דבשלמא אם נאמר שכונת הירושלמי לחייב ברכה בכל פעם שיהיו ג' ימים מעוננים שפיר שייך לומר שתיקנו ברכה על טוהר הרקיע מפני שהחמה נראית אחר שהיתה מכוסה בעננים ג' ימים רצופים והוי דוגמת הלבנה בחידושה שתיקנו לה ברכה מיוחדת, אבל אם נאמר שחיוב ברכה שייך רק בתקופת ניסן מפני

דאז נתלו המאורות א"כ מאיזה סברא בא רב הונה להוסיף שמברכים רק
לאחר ג' ימים מעוננים, ולפי הנ"ל ניחא דלדעת הירושלמי הברכה אינה על
תלויית המאורות אלא על חידוש הבריאה ולזה ס"ל להירושלמי כפי פירושו
של הגאון הנ"ל שהברכה לא נתקנה על זמן התקופה שבו נתלו המאורות
שהרי במאורע זה בלבד ס"ל שעדיין לא ניכר לנו חידוש הבריאה אלא נתקנה
הברכה רק במאורע שהתקופה חלה לאחר ג' ימים מעוננים שאז כשנראית
החמה ביום התקופה רואים דוגמת מעשה בראשית שהחמה עומדת ברקיע
בנקודתה הראשונה וזורחת לאחר ג' ימים של העדר זריחה ופעולה ובזה
מסמלת היא חידוש הבריאה בכל רגע ורגע.

ב. ברב עם הדרת מלך וזריזין מקדימין למצות

הנה במשאת בנימין סי' ק"א בענין ברכת החמה כתב וז"ל בשחרית
כשיוצאים מבהכנ"ס מתאספין הקהל יחד ומברכין ברכה זו ואחריו נמשכו
החת"ס בתשובותיו או"ח סי' נ"ו ובעל שו"ת מים חיים סי' כ"ב ויוסף אומץ
סי' שע"ח, אולם החיד"א בספרו מחזיק ברכה סי' רכ"ט סע' ז' כתב ע"ז
וז"ל ונ"ל דהזריז לברך כשרואה הנץ החמה ש"ד לברך ביחיד מלאחר עד
אחר התפלה בעשרה דאין זה אלא מנהג שרצו לנהוג רבנן בתראי משום ברב
עם וכו', ומוכח בש"ס בראש השנה דף ל"ב: דטעם דזריזין דחי לטעם ברב
עם וכו' ע"כ, ועי' קונטרס שערי מזרח בספר בקר יזרח פרק ג' להרה"ג ר'
יקותיאל אריה קאמעלהאר והרה"ג ר' יצחק זינגר בקונטרס זהרי חמה דף
י"ד וקונטרס אור החמה להרה"ג ר' מאיר דוד הערצבערג שכולם חיזקו דבריו
וכן נפסק בכף החיים אור החיים סי' רכ"ט ס"ק י"ד ובספר רוח חיים להרה"ג
ר' חיים פאלאגי או"ח סי' רכ"ט ס"ק ג' וכנראה כן היא דעת החיי אדם סי'
ס"ג כלל ה' וכן כתב בפירושו סי' ס"ח כלל ו' לענין שאר דברים שאין לאחר
משום ברב עם הדרת מלך, וכנראה זאת היתה ג"כ דעתו של הלקוטי מהרי"ל
כפי מה שהובאו דבריו בספר בקר יזרח להרה"ג ר' דוד מילדולה, עי' אור
החמה מאורי אור דף י':.

והנה ראייתו של החיד"א בספרו מחזיק ברכה מסוגיא דר"ה דף ל"ב:
כנראה שהיא ראיה חזקה שהרי שם במשנה איתא העובר לפני התיבה ביו"ט
של ר"ה השני מתקיע ובשעת ההלל הראשון מקריא את ההלל ושם בגמ'
מה שנא שני מתקיע משום דברב עם הדרת מלך אי הכי הלל נמי נימא בשני
משום דברב עם הדרת מלך אלא מאי שנא הלל דבראשון משום דזריזין
מקדימין למצוות תקיעה נמי נעביד בראשון משום דזריזין למצוות אמר רבי
יוחנן בשעת גזירת המלכות שנו ע"כ, הרי שכל המשא ומתן של הסוגיא

סובב על שאלה דידן ממש דהיינו האם יש להעדיף ברב עם הדרת מלך על זריזין מקדימין למצות או להיפך ומסקנת הסוגיא היא שהשני מתקיע, אבל טעמא דמילתא הוא מפני גזירת המלכות הא בלאו הכי על הראשון לתקוע משום זריזין מקדימין למצות ואין להמתין על רב עם, ואף שהרה"ג ר' יחיאל מיכל טוקצינסקי בספרו תקופת החמה וברכתה כתב לדחות ראיה זו מ"מ כך מוכח מפשטות הסוגיא.

ועי' בטורי אבן בפירושו לסוגיא דר"ה שנתקשה בענין רב עם הדרת מלך דמאי נ"מ אם הראשון מתקיע או השני מתקיע לגבי רב עם וכתב שם שכל מה שמאחרין לתקוע הוא מפני שבכל שעה יותר באים בני אדם לבהכ"נ ואיכא רב עם, ואין להקשות דלפי דבריו נמצא שאין הטעם שמאחרים משום מעלת רב עם אלא כדי שהכל יצאו ידי חובתם במצות תקיעת שופר שאם לא ימתינו אז נמצא שהמאחרים לא יצאו ידי חובתם כלל, וזה אינו שהרי אף המאחרים יכולים לצאת ידי חובתם ע"י תקיעות שעל סדר הברכות וא"כ נשאר רק מעלת ברב עם הדרת מלך בנוגע לתקיעות דמיושב, וע"ע שם בקונטרס אחרון שהביא הטורי אבן את דברי הירושלמי שם בסוגיא דמפורש להדיא הטעם שמאחרים משום דכתיב ואותי יום יום ידרשון זו תקיעה וערבה ופירש שם הקרבן עדה שהכל שומעין תקיעת שופר והכל נוטלין הערבה הלכך תקנו במוסף כשגם הקטנים הם בבית הכנסת משא"כ בשחרית עדיין ישנים הקטנים כדתנן דקטן פטור מק"ש לפי שאינו מצוי אז בשעת ק"ש ע"ש הרי יצא לנו חידוש שמעלת ברב עם הדרת מלך נתקיים גם ע"י קטנים.

אמנם אף שהראיה מסוגיא דר"ה שיש להעדיף זריזין מקדימין על מעלת ברב עם הדרת מלך ראיה חזקה היא מ"מ לכאורה יש בזה סתירה להאי כללא שנקטינן בקיום המצות המותר שמותר וגם מצוה לאחר המצוה כדי לקיימה בהידור מלקיים המצוה בלא הידור ע"י זריזין מקדימין למצוות, הרי שמעלת זריזין מקדימין נדחית מפני הידור מצוה. וכלל זה מפורש בכמה מקומות, עיין בתרומת הדשן סי' ל"ה שכתב שיש לאחר לקדש את הלבנה כשהוא מבוסם ולבוש בגדי שבת ולא להקדימה בחול משום זריזין מקדימין למצות וכן נפסק להלכה בשו"ע או"ח סי' תכ"ו סע"י ב', ועי' שו"ת שבות יעקב ח"א סי' ל"ד שבמקום שלאחר זמן יהיה לו אתרוג הדר שיש לאחר נטילת לולב עד שישיג אתרוג הדר ולא לקיים מצות ד' מינים מיד משום זריזין מקדימין, וכן לענין תפלה מבואר מדברי הספר חסידים (הוצאת מקיצי נרדמים) סי' תנ"ד שיש לאחר בכדי להתפלל בציבור כל שאין חשש שבינתים יעבור זמן תפלה, וא"כ קשה מאי שנה הא דלפי שורת הדין הראשון מתקיע לולי טעם גזרת המלכות ולמה לא יאחר מצות תקיעת שופר כדי לקיימה ברב עם

הדרת מלך ולמה דוקא נגד רב עם הדרת מלך נקטינן שזריזין מקדימין עדיף טפי ולא לענין שאר הידורים.

והנראה בזה הוא דבענין רב עם הדרת מלך מצינו במשנה פסחים דף ס״ד. שחט ישראל וקבל הכהן נותנו לחבירו וחבירו לחבירו וכו׳, ושם בגמ׳ דף ס״ד. מבואר שהטעם הוא משום ברב עם הדרת מלך וכן ביומא דף כ״ו. במשנה הפייס הרביעי מי מעלה אברים מן הכבש למזבח והיינו שהכהנים שהעלו את האברים על גבי הכבש לא העלו את האברים של התמיד מהכבש למזבח להקטירם אלא כהנים אחרים העלו מכבש למזבח משום רב עם הדרת מלך וכן לענין חילוק האברים מצינו בסוכה דף נ״ב: שהקטרתם היתה ע״י כהנים הרבה דוקא וכמו כן בנוגע לתנופת חזה ושוק כמבואר במנחות דף ס״ב. משום רב עם הדרת מלך, והנה בכל הני דינא דברב עם הדרת מלך נאמר בנוגע להעדיף קיום מצוה מהמצות ע״י הרבה בני אדם מע״י אדם אחד. אמנם אף כשאין המצוה מתחלקת בין הרבה בני אדם אלא כל אחד ואחד עושה בעצמו יש עדיפות כשכולם עושים ביחד בכנופיא וכנמצינו בפ״ג דבכורים משנה ב׳ שכל העיירות של מעמד מתכנסות לעירו של מעמד כדי שלא יעלו יחידים משום רב עם הדרת מלך. ועוד מצינו דין שלישי של רב עם בברכות דף נ״ג. ת״ר היו יושבין בבית המדרש והביאו אור לפניהם בש״א כל אחד ואחד מברך לעצמו ובה״א אחד מברך לכולן משום שנא׳ ברב עם הדרת מלך, הרי מבואר שנוסף למה שיש חשיבות של ברב עם כשהכל מקיימים המצוה בבת אחת יש עוד מעלה של ברב עם אם אחד מוציא את הרבים ידי חובתם וע״י זה נעשה עצם המצוה למצוה של הרבים, ואמנם עכ״פ בכל הני מצינו חשיבות של ברב עם הוא רק כשכל אחד מהרב עם בעצמו יש לו קיום של מצוה.

אמנם מסוגיא דיומא דף ע. יצא לנו סוג אחר של ברב עם הדרת מלך שהוא שונה לגמרי מכל הנ״ל, שם במשנה דף ס״ח: איתא הרואה כהן גדול כשהוא קורא אינו רואה פר ושעיר הנשרפין והרואה פר ושעיר הנשרפין אינו רואה כ״ג כשהוא קורא ולא מפני שאינו רשאי אלא מפני שהיתה דרך רחוקה ומלאכת שניהן שוה כאחת ושם בגמ׳ פריך פשיטא ומתרץ מהו דתימא כדריש לקיש דאמר ריש לקיש אין מעבירין על המצות ומאי מצוה ברב עם הדרת מלך קמ״ל, והרי שם פשיטא דהעומד ורואה שריפת פר ושעיר הנשרפין אינו מקיים שום מצוה ואעפ״כ יש בזה מעלה וחשיבות של ברב עם הדרת מלך, ולכן נראה שברב עם אינו מעלה והידור בקיום המצוה אלא שברב עם הוא מצוה מיוחדת בפני עצמה והיינו שע״י שמתאספים יחד נתרבה כבודו של מלך מלכי המלכים וזה גופא מצוה היא, נמצא שמי שעומד אצל שריפת פר ושעיר הנשרפים באמת יש לו קיום של מצות ברב עם לבד אבל מי שעוסק במצוה אחרת ברב עם יש לו קיום של ב׳ מצות דהיינו עצם המצוה שעוסק בה וגם קיום של מצוה

אחרת לגמרי דהיינו מצות ברב עם הדרת מלך.

ונראה להביא סעד לדברים אלו מדברי רש״י ביומא דף ע. שהרי מסוגיא
דיומא שם יוצא לנו שבנוגע למצות ברב עם ליתא להאי דינא של אין מעבירין
על המצות ומי שעומד במקום שמקיימים מצוה אחת מותר לו לילך למקום
שמקיימים מצוה אחרת וזהו חידושו של המשנה דאין בזה משום דאין מעבירין
על המצות, ובשלמה אם נאמר שמעלת ברב עם אינה מצוה בפני עצמה אלא
הידור בקיום המצוה יש לפרש חידוש זה, היינו דלא שייך לגבי הרב עם האי
דינא דאין מעבירין על המצות, באופן פשוט והיינו דהיה לנו לומר דאין ברב
עם מצוה בפני עצמה אלא הידור וחשיבות בקיום מצוה ממצות התורה וכללא
דאין מעבירין על המצות נאמרה רק על קיומן של מצות נפרדות שאין להניח
מצוה אחת כדי לעסוק במצוה אחרת, אמנם רש״י שם לא פירש כן אלא שם
בדה״מ קמ״ל כתב לבאר למה אין שייך בזה אין מעבירין וז״ל דלאו מעבר
הוא מאחר שאינו עסוק בה עכ״ל, הרי שכתב דלא שייך בה אין מעבירין לא
מפני שאינה מצוה אלא מפני ״שאינו עסוק בה״ ובפשטות כוונתו לומר שדינא
דאין מעבירין על המצות הוא מטעם שע״י שמניח את המצוה נראה שמואס
בה ומזניח אותה משא״כ כשהמצוה מתקיימת ממילא בלא עסק אינו נראה
כמואס בה ולכן מותר לעזוב מקום שהכ״ג קורא ולילך למקום ששורפין פר
ושעיר או להיפר. אמנם יש בפירוש זה מן הדוחק שהרי מי שמניח מצוה אחת
להיות נוכח בעשיית מצוה אחרת ג״כ נראה כאילו מואס במצוה הראשונה,
אלא נראה לפרש בכוונת דברי רש״י שבא להדגיש שמי שהולך ממקום אחד
למקום שני אינו נקרא שמניח קריאת התורה משום שריפת פר ושעיר או
להיפר שהרי אינו עוסק בשום אחת ממצות אלו ובין כך ובין כך אין לו קיום
של אף אחת משתי מצות אלו אבל יש לו קיום של מצות ברב עם הדרת מלך,
אמנם במה שנוגע למצות ברב עם הרי אותה המצוה אחת היא בין אם עומד
נוכח בשעת קריאת התורה ע״י כ״ג או אם עומד אצל שריפת פר ושעיר או
אצל מצוה אחרת, זאת אומרת שאין לנו מצות שונות של רב עם הדרת מלך,
ז״א מצוה אחת ברב עם בקריאת התורה ומצוה אחרת ברב עם בשריפת פר
ושעיר ומצוה אחרת ברב עם בהולכת הדם או העלאת אברים, אלא מצות
ברב עם הדרת מלך שוה היא בכל מצוה ומצוה, שהרי בקיומה של כל מצוה
ומצוה יש בה כבוד של מלך וכבודו מתרבה באותה האיכות ע״י רב עם
מבלי להתחשב עם דרגת המצוה שנתקיים באותו רב עם, ולכן שפיר מובן
למה לא שייך בזה אין מעבירין על המצות שהרי מי שהולך משריפת פר
ושעיר לשמוע קריאת התורה של כ״ג או להיפר הרי אינו מניח שום מצוה
בשביל מצוה אחרת אלא עומד והולך בקיומו של אותה מצוה ממש
דהיינו מצות ברב עם הדרת מלך שמצוה אחת היא ודו״ק.

והנה אף שלא נאמר כללא דזריזין מקדימין למצוות במקום שמניח קיום המצוה כדי לקיימה אח״כ בהידור מ״מ אינו מן החיוב וגם אסור הוא לאחר קיום המצוה כדי לקיים ג״כ מצוה אחרת אף אם ע״י זה תתבטל מצוה השניה לגמרי, עי׳ או״ח סי׳ רמ״ח ושם מבואר שלדבר מצוה מותר להפליג בספינה ושיירא אע״פ שיודע בודאי שיתבטל ממצות עונג שבת וגם יצטרך לחלל שבת מ״מ אין לו לאחר קיום המצוה מטעם זה, עיין נשמת אדם כלל ס״ח, וגם מבואר בפסחים דף ק״ה. כבוד יום וכבוד לילה וכבוד יום קודם ואם אין לו אלא כוס אחד אומר עליו קידוש היום מפני שקידוש היום קודם לכבוד היום והקשה שם הגמ׳ לישבקיה עד למחר וליעביד ביה תרתי ומתרץ שם חביבה מצוה בשעתה, הרי שאין לאחר שום מצוה אפילו כדי לקיים אותה מצוה לאחר זמן בהדי מצוה נוספת אף אם ע״י זה תתבטל מצוה השניה לגמרי, וכן מבואר להדיא בדברי הריטב״א בפירושו לסוכה דף כ״ה. לענין עוסק במצוה פטור מן המצוה וז״ל דהא קמ״ל דאפילו בעי להניח מצוה זו לעשות מצוה אחרת גדולה הימנה אין הרשות בידו סד״א איפטורי הוא דמיפטר מינה אבל אי בעי למשבק הא ולמיעבד אידך הרשות בידו קמ״ל דכיון דפטור מן האחרת׳ הרי היא אצלו עכשיו כדבר של רשות ואסור להניח מצותו מפני דבר שהוא של רשות ועוד למדנו הכתוב דאע״ג דאיכא עליה מצוה קבועה לזמן ודאי כגון ק״ש ושחיטת הפסח וקודם לכן באת לו מצוה אחרת שתבטלנו מן האחרת אם יתחיל בה רשאי הוא להתחיל בזו שבא לידו עכשיו ואם יבטל מן האחרת יבטל ואינו חשוב עצמו פורק ממנה כשפורקה מעליו מחמת דבר מצוה שאין חיוב המצוה עליו עד שיגיע זמנה וראשונה קודמת כנ״ל עכ״ל. נמצאנו למדים טעם הדבר שאין לאחר קיום המצוה בשביל קיום מצוה נוספת, אע״ג שמותר לותר על זריזין מקדימין למצוות ולאחר קיומה של אותה מצוה עצמה בכדי לקיימה בהידורה, הוא מפני שמצוה השניה זמנה עדיין לא בא וכשעוסק במצוה ראשונה אין שום טעם או מעליותא לאחרה כדי לקיים גם מצוה שניה מפני שבאותה עת המצוה השניה נחשבת אצלו כדבר של רשות.

ולפי״ז שפיר מובן למה אין לותר על מעלת זריזין מקדימין בכדי לקיים מצות תקיעת שופר ברב עם הדרת מלך והיינו שברב עם אינה מעלה וחשיבות במצות תקיעת שופר אלא נחשבת למצוה אחרת לגמרי ולכן אם אין רב עם עכשיו לפנינו אין להמתין על קיום מצוה הב׳ אלא צריך לקיים אותה המצוה המוטלת עליו עכשיו והיינו תקיעת שופר וצריך לקיימה בהקדם האפשרי משום זריזין מקדימין למצוות כמו בכל מצות שאין מניחין אותן בשביל קיום מצוה אחרת.

ובזה מיושב ג״כ מה שנתקשו האחרונים בדברי הרמ״א והמ״א באו״ח ריש

סימן כ״ה שכתב שם הרמ״א וז״ל מיהו אם תפילין מזומנים בידו ואין לו
ציצית אין צריך להמתין על ציצית אלא מניח תפילין וכשמביאים טלית
מעטפו וכתב שם המ״א אע״פ שי״ל שיעשה אח״כ המצוה יותר מן המובחר
וכי׳ חביבה מצוה בשעתה, והנה לפום רהיטא זהו בניגוד לכללא הנ״ל שהרי
כתב המ״א שלא לאחר קיום מצות תפילין משום הידור בניגוד לכל המקובל
לנו, אמנם לפי הנ״ל ניחא דרק בכה״ג שציצית ותפילין שתי מצות נינהו
בזה דייק בלשונו חביבה מצוה בשעתה כלשון הגמ׳ פסחים דף ק״ה: והיינו
שההידור הוא להתעטף בטלית מקודם מפני שהיא חביבה או מפני ששקולה
היא כנגד כל המצות אבל בשביל זה אין לאחר קיומה של מצוה אחרת שהרי
אין מאחרים קיומה של מצוה מן המצות בשביל מצוה אחרת אף אם תתבטל
האחרת לגמרי וכ״ש שאין מאחרין אותה משום הידורה של השניה.

נמצא שלענין ברכת החמה ג״כ פשיטא שיש לברך מיד בהנץ החמה משום
זריזין מקדימין למצות ואין להמתין עד שיתאספו בבית הכנסת בכדי לברך
ברב עם שהרי ברב עם הדרת מלך היא מצוה אחרת לגמרי ולא סתם ענין של
הידור וחשיבות.

ובזה ג״כ מיושב בפשטות מה שהקשו כמה מהאחרונים למה כתבו כל הני
פוסקים שיש לברך מיד בהנץ החמה ולא להתפלל תפילת שחרית מקודם
שהרי תדיר ואינו תדיר תדיר קודם ואין לך תדיר יותר מתפילת שחרית שהיא
בכל יום משא״כ ברכת החמה שהיא אחת לכ״ח שנה, ולפי הנ״ל יש לתרץ
שהרי פשוט שמי שבדעתו להתפלל בציבור בודאי שמותר לו לאחר תפילתו
כדי להתפלל בציבור ואין לו להיות מהזריזין המקדימין ולהתפלל ביחידות
משום שתפלה בציבור ודאי חשוב הידור בתפלה וא״כ מי שמאחר להתפלל
משום תפלה בציבור חשיב שמצות תפלה עדיין אינה לפניו וממילא מותר
לברך ברכת החמה מקודם שהרי האי כללא דתדיר ואינו תדיר תדיר קודם
הוא דוקא כששניהן עומדין לפניו משא״כ בזה מאחר שמותר לו להמתין
להתפלל עם הציבור אז אינה מונחת לפניו אלא ברכת החמה ושפיר מקדימה
לתפילת שחרית.

אמנם היוצא מן הנ״ל הוא שמי שיכול להתפלל בעשרה אין לו לאחר
להתפלל בציבור יותר גדול מטעם ברב עם הדרת מלך אלא מוטל עליו
להיות מהזריזין המקדימין למצות מאחר שיכול לקיים מצות תפלה בציבור
מיד, ואף שבשו״ת יד אליהו ובמ״א סי׳ צ׳ ס״ק ט׳ו לא משמע הכי מ״מ כן
נראה להדיא מדברי החיי אדם סי׳ ס״ח כלל ו׳ וכן נראה מוכח מסוגיא דר״ה
כמו שהביא החיי אדם בעצמו ראיה מסוגיא זו. ע״ע תורה תמימה, בראשית
י״ז-כ״ו אות נ״ג, והשוה ערוך השלחן, או״ח סי׳ רס״ח סע״י ח׳.

ג. ברכת החמה ע"י סומא וביום המעונן

הנה בענין סומא אם יברך ברכת החמה מובא בהקדמה לקונטרס בקר יזרח
שהוציא לאור החכם דוד מילדולה בשם ר' יעקב ן' נאים וז"ל נראה דתליא
בפלוגתא דהמהרש"ל והרדב"ז בברכת הלבנה דשניהם בדיבור אחד נאמרו
הרואה לבנה בחדושה הרואה חמה חמה בתקופתה וכו', אמנם דבריו תמוהים שהרי
המהרש"ל בתשובותיו סי' ע"ז כתב הטעם למה סומא מברך ברכת מחדש
חדשים הוא מאותו הטעם שיכול לברך יוצר המאורות כמבואר במגילה דף
כ"ב: דרבנן דס"ל דסומא פורס על השמע היינו משום דגם סומא אית ליה
הנאה מן המאורות ומייתי שם ראיה מר' יוסי דתניא א"ר יוסי כל ימי הייתי
מצטער על מקרא זה והייתי ממשש בצהרים כאשר ימשש העור באפלה וכי
מה איכפת ליה לעור בין אפילה לאורה עד שבא מעשה לידי פעם אחת הייתי
מהלך באישון לילה ואפלה וראיתי סומא שהיה מהלך בדרך ואבוקה בידו
אמרתי לו בני אבוקה זו למה לך אמר לי כל זמן שאבוקה בידי בני אדם רואין
אותי ומצילין אותי מן הפחתין ומן הקוצין ומן הברקנין, הרי מבואר להדיא
שברכת יוצר המאורות נתקנה על הנאת האור וכמו כן לדעת המהרש"ל
ברכת הלבנה ג"כ נתקנה על הנאת אור הלבנה, משא"כ ברכת החמה נתקנה
על חזרת השמש למקום שבו נברא כשחוזרת למקומה באותו יום ובאותה
שעה שנבראה. וכשרואה מאורע זה חייב לברך כלשון הברייתא הרואה חמה
בתקופתה וכו' משא"כ סומא שאינו יכול לראות מנא לן שנתחייב בברכה
זו, וכ"כ קשה על דברי הבעל זרע אמת ח"ג סי' כ"ד שכתב שסומא מחויב
לברך משום שנהנה מאור החמה שהרי ברכה זו אינה מברכות הנהנין אלא
ברכת הודאה התלויה בראיה וסומא א"י לראות, וכן מש"כ ר' יעקב ן' נאים
שלדעת הרדב"ז שסומא אינו מברך ברכת מחדש חדשים כמו כן אינו מברך
ברכת החמה, הרי ברכת הלבנה בודאי תליא בראיה ואם מכוסה היא בעננים
אינו מברך כמבואר ברמ"א או"ח סי' תכ"ו סעי' א' שאין לקדש אלא בעת
שהלבנה זורחת ונהנין מאורה, אבל בנוגע לברכת החמה כתב הפנים מאירות

---

1) אגב יש להעיר שלכאורה שלא בדקדוק נאמרו דברים אלו שהרי דינא דלבנה בחידושה
היא בסנהדרין דף מ"ב. לענין ברכת מחדש חדשים שעליה דנו המהרש"ל והרדב"ז לענין
סומא אם יברך או לא וברייתא דתקופת החמה שנויה בברכות דף נ"ט. ושם איתא הרואה
חמה בתקופתה לבנה בגבורתה וכוכבים במסילותם ומזלות כסדרן וכי' ושם בירושלמי קצת
בסגנון אחר הרואה את החמה בתקופתה ואת הלבנה בתקופתה וכו', ושם בברכות המדובר
לא על ראית הלבנה בחידושה אלא על המאורע של חזרת הלבנה לראש מזל טלה הרי
מבואר שברכת הלבנה דהיינו על חזרת הלבנה בחידושה וברכת החמה לאו בדבור אחד נאמרו, וכן מן
התימה על הגי' ר' שלמה קלוגר בחכמת שלמה או"ח סי' תכ"ט סע' ב' שכנראה ג"כ ערבב את
הדברים, אמנם עיין דברי הבעל מתא דירושלים שהובאו דבריו בקונטרס יזרח אור דף ט'.

ח"ב סי' ל"ח וז"ל ואע"פ שעננים מכסים אותה מ"מ אנו יודעים שהיא בעת
ההיא בנקודה ראשונה והיא מאירה לנו באור היום ראוי לברך ושם בתחילת
דבריו כתב שראוי לברך אף שמכוסה בעננים מפני ש"נהנה ממנה ביום שנתלה
במרכז הראשון" הרי שלדעתו ברכת החמה אינה תלויה בראיה דוקא, הרי
אף לדעת הרדב"ז שסומא פטור מברכת הלבנה מפני שהיא ברכת הראיה
מ"מ יש מקום לומר שברכת החמה אינה תלויה בראיה דוקא. וכ"כ בשו"ת
כתב סופר או"ח סי' ל"ד דיומא דעיבא כולה שמשא וענין לאורה.

ובאמת ק"ק גם על דברי הפנים מאירות איזו נפקותא היא שננינן לאורה
מאחר שמה שמברכין על חמה בתקופתה ברכת הודאה היא ולא ברכת
הנהנין שהרי באותה ברייתא נשנה ג"כ כוכבים במסילותם ומזלות כסדרן
ובהם לא שייך שום הנאה וע"כ שברכת החמה ברכת הודאה היא וא"כ איזו
שייכות בזה לטעם שכתב הפנים מאירות שנהנה מאורה הרי ברכת הראיה
היא ותלויה בראיה ולא בהנאה, עיין דברי הגרי"מ טוקצינסקי בספרו תקופת
החמה וברכתה (ירושלים, תש"ג) בהערה סע' ל"ו שכתב דהברכה שמברכים
בכל חודש על חידוש הלבנה הרי היא ברכת הנהנין על הנאת חידוש מאור
הלבנה כמו שמברכין בכל יום יוצר המאורות על הנאת אור השמש ואילו
הברכה לתקופת הלבנה וכו' היא על מחזור הלבנה בזמן תליית המאורות
ושם ע' ס"א כתב דלא דמי כלל ברכת החמה לברכת הלבנה דבברכת הלבנה
הברכה היא על הנאת האור ע"ז שמחדש אורה וזוהי מעין ברכה שמברכין כל
בקר על השמש יוצר המאורות ואילו ברכת החמה בתקופתה אין בה ממהות
ברכת הנהנין דלא נתחדש דבר בהנאתה ושם ע' ל"ד כתב לשלול חיוב ברכה
מסומא וז"ל דכאן לא על הנאת החמה מברך עכשיו אלא רק על ראייתה ומה
לנו שהסומא נהנה מאורה ע"ש.

והנראה בזה דהנה יש לנו ג' סוגי ברכות, והיינו ברכות הנהנין ברכות
המצוות וברכות הודאה, ולא הרי זה כהרי זה, ובנוגע לברכות הודאה הרי
נתקנו לא על שום הנאה מיוחדת אלא על הכרת גדלות ורוממות השם ית'
אלא אעפ"כ בכל ברכת הודאה יש לנו סיבה או מאורע המחייבת הברכה,
למשל ברכות השחר נתקנו על הטובות המתחדשות בכל בקר ובברכות
הראיה נתקנו שיברך אותן באותה שעה ואותו זמן שרואה נפלאות הבריאה
ואף שברכת הודאה שונה היא מברכת המצוה מ"מ מצינו ג"כ שקיומה של
מצוה מחייבת לא רק ברכת המצוה אלא גם ברכת הודאה שהרי על המילה
מברך האב להכניסו בבריתו של אברהם אבינו שהיא ברכה נוספת על ברכת
המצוה דהיינו ברכת על מצות מילה, ולפעמים תיקנו חז"ל רק ברכת הודאה
בגלל קיום המצוה ולא תיקנו ברכת המצוה בכלל, עי' ט"ז יו"ד סי' א' ס"ק
י"ז שכתב לפרש דברי הרא"ש דאית ליה שהשומע ואינו מדבר שוחט אפילו

לכתחילה אם אחר מברך וכדבריו פסק השו"ע שם סע' ז', והקשה הב"י מאי
שנא מהא דאלם וערום לא יתרומו וכתב הט"ז דאף דבברכת המצות אין
לחלק המצוה לזה והברכה לזה מ"מ הרא"ש ס"ל דברכת השחיטה אינה
באה על השחיטה עצמה דהא אין חיוב לשחיטה אם אינו רוצה לאכול אלא
עיקר הכוונה לתת שבח למקו' ב"ה על שאסר לנו אכילת בשר בלא שחיטה
ובזה ודאי כל ישראל שייך באותה ברכה שהרי על כולם יש איסור אלא שאין
מקום לברך שבח זה אלא בשעת שחיטת שום בהמה וכו', וכ"כ כתב שם
הט"ז שברכת אירוסין ג"כ ברכת הודאה חשיבא ולא ברכת המצות ומשום
הכי ניחא שהחתן מארס והרב מברך דגם שם מברך על איסור עריות שאסר
לכל ישראל, וכ"כ כתב הערוך השלחן סי' כ"ה סע' י' לענין ברכת על מצות
תפילין והיינו שברכת להניח תפילין היא ברכת המצוה וברכת על מצות
תפילין היא ברכת הודאה שזכנו ה' לעשות אות בינו ובינינו וזה שייך לשל
ראש כמו שדרשו על קרא דראו כל עמי הארץ כי שם ה' נקרא עליך ויראו
ממך אלו תפילין שבראש.

והנה יש מקום לפרש שכמו שלפעמים תקנו חז"ל ברכת הודאה נוסף
לברכת המצוה בשעת קיום המצוה ולפעמים לא תיקנו אלא ברכת הודאה
בעת קיום המצוה כ"כ יש לומר שלפעמים על הנאה מסוימת תיקנו ברכת
הודאה ולא תיקנו כלל ברכת הנהנין, וביאור הדבר הוא שאף שעל האדם
להרגיש טובותיו של הקב"ה תמיד ולהתעורר לשבח והודאה בכל עת מ"מ
לא תיקנו ברכה אלא על מקרה מסוים כש"כ הט"ז לענין ברכת השחיטה
שאין מקום לשבח זה אלא בשעת שחיטה, והיינו דלדעת הזרע אמת דאית
ליה שסומא מברך ברכת החמה שהרי נהנה מאורה וכן לדעת הפנים מאירות
מברך אף אם מכוסה בעננים מפני שנהנה מאורה אין הכוונה שחשובה ברכת
הנהנין כמו שתפס בדעתם הגרי"מ טוקצינסקי זצ"ל אלא יש לפרש בכונתם
שברכה זו ברכת הודאה היא רק שאין מברכין ברכת הודאה על ידיעה לבד
היינו שאין מברכין על גדולתו ורוממותו של הקב"ה אלא כשנרגש ונתאמת
הדבר אצל המברך ע"י מאורע מסוים, שהרי חז"ל תיקנו ברכות רק על
מאורעות מסוימות המעוררות שבח והודאה בלב האדם, ולכן לא תיקנו שיברך
ברכת החמה בלילה בשעת התקופה ממש שהיא בתחילת הלילה באורתא
דתלת נגהי ארבע כדאיתא שם בברכות דף נ"ט: מאחר שבאותה העת שום
דבר אינו מורגש ולכן קבעו הברכה בבקר בשעה שנהנה מאורה, אבל אין
זה ברכת הנהנין שהרי לא נתחדש שום דבר בהנאתה ביום זה יותר מבשאר
ימים וגם הנאה זו הרי היא הנאה הבאה מאליה ול"ש בזה ברכת הנהנין,
אלא ברכת החמה ברכת הודאה היא שלדעת הפנים מאירות והזרע אמת
הוקבעה לא בשעת ראיה דוקא אלא בשעת הנאה. וכן מדויק בלשון הפנים

מאירות שכתב וז"ל דעיקר הברכה שזכינו לראות השמש בנקודה הראשונה
בשעה שנתלו המאורות ושומשא אביב נייחי ואע"פ שעננים מכסים אותה
מ"מ אנו יודעים שהיא בעת ההיא בנקודה ראשונה והיא מאירה לנו באור
היום ע"כ, הרי הברכה על מה שהחמה עומדת בנקודה ראשונה אבל מ"מ אין
מקום לברכה אלא מפני שמאירה לנו ונהנין ממנה. וכן נראה מוכרח מדברי
הכתב סופר שהסכים לדברי הפנים מאירות, ושם באותה התשובה עצמה
כתב לפטור וגם לאסור לנשים לברך ברכת החמה, ואתתמהא אם ברכת
החמה חשובה ברכת הנהנין איך יש לנו לפטור נשים מברכה זו שהרי אנשים
ונשים שוים בכל ברכות הנהנין אלא ע"כ שברכת החמה להני רבוותא חשובה
ג"כ ברכת הודאה, אלא המאורע שעליו קבועה אינו ראייתה של החמה כמו
בשאר ברכות הראיה אלא הנאת אורה היא המאורע שעליו קבעו ברכה זו.

ובאמת נראה שאף ברכת מחדש חדשים היא ברכת הודאה ולא ברכת
הנהנין ודלא כמש"כ הגרי"מ טוקצינסקי שהרי נשים פטורות מברכת הלבנה
ואף שכתב השל"ה שהן גרמו לפגימת הלבנה מ"מ טעם זה יפה כחו רק
לפטור מברכת הודאה והיינו שאין לנשים להודות על חידוש אור הלבנה
שמאחר שגרמו שאורה נתקטן אין מקום אצלן להודאה זו, משא"כ אם
הברכה היא ברכת הנהנין מה בכך שגרמו למיעוטה של הלבנה הא מ"מ נהנות
מאותו האור שיש לה עכשיו אלא ע"כ ברכת הודאה היא על חידוש האור
אחר העדרו.

ועכשיו שנחתינן להכי נראה שמוכח כן לגבי ברכת יוצר המאורות ג"כ אף
שבסוגיא דמגילה מפורש שסומא חייב לברך משום דאית ליה הנאה מ"מ
נראה שאין ברכת יוצר המאורות בכלל ברכת הנהנין דא"כ למה נפטרו נשים
מברכות קריאת שמע [זולת ברכת גאל ישראל לדעת המ"א או"ח סי' ע' ס"ק
א', שיש בה זכירת יציאת מצרים] אם ברכת יוצר המאורות חשיבא ברכת
הנהנין שהרי נשים אינן פטורות משום ברכת הנהנין אלא ע"כ הטעם כמש"כ
שברכת יוצר המאורות ברכת הודאה היא על זריחת השמש בבקר, אלא
שאין מקום לקבוע הודאה על דבר שנרגש רק בשכל ואינו מבוסס על מאורע
מסוים או הנאה מסוימת ומבואר שם במגילה שקבעו ברכה זו לא על ראיית
השמש שא"כ סומא לא היה יכול להיות פורס על השמע אלא על ההנאה
של זריחתה ויש בהנאה זו ג"כ בכדי לחייב סומא בברכת יוצר המאורות.

ונראה שהדבר מפורש הוא בדברי המהרש"ל שברכת הלבנה היא ברכת
הודאה ולא ברכת הנהנין וכ"כ ברכת יוצר המאורות ברכת הודאה היא שהרי
כתב לגבי סומא וז"ל אבל ברכת הלבנה נ"ל דיכול שפיר לברך אף שאמרו
ג"כ בה עד שיאותו לאורה מ"מ לא אמרו שהוא יראה לאורה אלא שהעולם
יאותו לאורה **כי ברכה זו על בריאת עולמו וחידושו קאי** ודומה לסומא שיכול

לברך יוצר המאורות ע"כ, הרי שעצם החיוב הוא על בריאת העולם וחידושו אלא הא דבעינן שיאותו לאורו זהו תנאי בחיוב ברכת הודאה שנתקנה רק על מאורע מסוים וגם כתב שם לדמות ברכת הלבנה לברכת יוצר המאורות הרי שברכת יוצר המאורות ג"כ ברכת הודאה היא.

ובזה מבוארים דברי ר' יעקב ו' נאים על בורים שכתב לדמות דינו של סומא בנוגע לברכת החמה לדינו של סומא בנוגע לברכת הלבנה וכתב לומר שהלכה זו תלויה במחלוקת המהרש"ל והרדב"ז והיינו דס"ל דברכת החמה ברכת הודאה היא אך בנוגע לשאלה אם נתקנה במקרה של ראיה ממש או אם די בהנאה לבד כמו ברכת יוצר המאורות ס"ל שדבר זה תלוי במחלוקת המהרש"ל והרדב"ז דלדעת המהרש"ל תיקנו ברכת הלבנה באותה הצורה של ברכת יוצר המאורות וא"כ מן הסברא שאף ברכת החמה נתקנה בצורה זו ג"כ, אמנם לדעת הרדב"ז תיקנו ברכת הלבנה רק בתור ברכת הראיה ממש וא"כ כ"ש שהרואה חמה בתקופתה דייקא וחשובה ג"כ ברכת הראיה, ולפי"ז לדעתו של ר' יעקב ו' נאים מסתבר שחיוב ברכה ביום המעונן תלוי ג"כ בפלוגתא של המהרש"ל והרדב"ז, אמנם כנראה שהחכם ר' דוד מילדולה לא הרגיש בזה שהרי שם הביא דברי הפנים מאירות בנוגע לברכת החמה ביום המעונן בסתמא מבלי להזכיר שדינו של סומא ודין ברכת החמה ביום המעונן שייכים להדדי.

ד. זמן ברכת החמה באירופה ובאמריקה

הגאון האדר"ת בס' עובר אורח הנספח לספר אורחות חיים להג' מספינקא סי' רכ"ט כתב וז"ל בשנת תרכ"ט כתבתי בס"ד שי"ל דעיקר הברכה לשעה שנתלית וע"כ תשתנה שעת הברכה לפי המקומות ובמדינותינו הנוטות לצפון י"ל שהשעה מכוונת ליום השלישי לעת ערב בשעה השישית בעוד שלא שקעה חמה וכן כל מקום לפי אופקו, והרבה הסכימו לי אז, במה שלא קדמני אדם עכ"ל. והנה ראיתי מאמר מידידי הרה"ג ר' משה נחום שפירא שליט"א ראש כולל רב אחא בירושלים נדפס בספר ברכת החמה כהלכתה להרב מנחם מענדיל גערליץ ונשנו הדברים בירחון מוריה שבט תשמ"א, שבו יצא לחדש על פי דברי האדר"ת שאנו בני הגולה יושבי אירופה ואמריקה מחויבים לברך ביום ג' וע"כ לחוש לדעתו של האדר"ת שלא לברך ביום ד' בבקר בשם ומלכות, ומפני שנוגע לדינא ולענ"ד אגב חורפיה שגה בדברי האדר"ת מוכרח אני להאריך בדבריו, והיינו שהרה"ג ר' משה נחום שפירא כתב בביאור דברי האדר"ת וז"ל דכל חשבונות המולדות והתקופות בנוים על אופק ירושלים כמ"ש הרמב"ם (סוף פי"א מה' קה"ח) ושאר חכמי העיבור

אשר לפ"ז אותן המדינות השוכנות למערב ירושלים, ולהם מתאחר היום
לבוא, ובעת אשר בירושלים הוא תחילת ליל ד', והיא שעת התקופה, עדיין
חמה זורחת והיא עת ערב של יום שלישי בארצות שהן למערב ירושלים
כגון אירופה וביבשת אמריקה אשר שם מתאחר היום מירושלים עם שש
שבע שעות, ובעת שבירושלים הוא תחילת יום ד' אצלם עדיין חצות יום
ג' יש להם לברך על החמה, כי זאת שעת התקופה וכו' ע"כ, ושוב מסיק
לומר וז"ל אמנם כד נעיין במילתא דא יוצא לנו חידוש יותר גדול מזה, דלא
זו בלבד שיש לברך על החמה אז ביום ג' משום זריזות מצוה, אלא דבאלו
הארצות שהם למערב ירושלים והיום מתאחר שם בכדי שש או שבע שעות,
כגון ביבשת אמריקה, אם לא יברכו ביום ג' מחצות היום שהוא תחילת ליל
ד' בירושלים, שוב לא יוכלו לברך למחרת ביום ד' לא מיבעיא לדעת המג"א
דס"ל עד ג' שעות של היום יכול לברך, שהוא ט"ז שעות מתחילת ליל ד',
אלא אפילו לדעת הדגול מרבבה וסיעתו דס"ל עד חצות יכול לברך, שהיא
י"ח שעה מתחילת ליל ד', לא יוכל לברך למחרת ביום ד' אפילו בבוקר
שהוא כבר אחר י"ח שעה מתחילת התקופה, וכבר עברה חמה מן המקום
שהיתה בעת תלייתה במעשה בראשית עכ"ל.

הנה הוציא לנו המבחר הנ"ל שני דברים שאינם נמצאים בדברי האדר"ת:
א) שיש לברך אפילו מחצות היום לפי השעון המקומי במקום שהיום מתאחר
לבוא ערך שש שעות, ב) שסוף זמן הברכה תלוי ג"כ לפי האופק ושיעורו
לעולם ט"ו או י"ח שעות אחר תחילת זמנו על פי החשבון הנ"ל, ועוד כתב
לחדש דין ג' והיינו שלפי דעת האדר"ת סוף זמן ברכת החמה אינו סוף
שעה שלישית או חצות היום בדיוק אלא בהקדם קצת בסוף ט"ו או י"ח
שעות מעת התקופה. ולענ"ד ג' חידושים אלו אינם נכונים ומעולם לא נתכוון
האדר"ת לדברים אלו כלל וכלל, ואפרש מילי:

הנה בנוגע לקידוש החודש החודש פשוט וברור הוא שזמן קידוש לבנה הוא כפי
אופק ירושלים, זאת אומרת שבין הזמן שבו ראוי לקדש ובין סוף זמן קידוש
לבנה הם ברגע אחד בכל העולם, וזהו מפני שמולד הלבנה הוא מאורע
טבעי חד פעמי בכל חודש ואף שאין מולד הלבנה נראה ברגע אחד בכל
העולם מ"מ המאורע אחד לכל העולם, והזמן שמחשבין ומכריזין בתור זמן
המולד הוא זמנו של המאורע כפי השעון של ירושלים וזמן קידוש לבנה
נקבע לפי כללא דשית שעי מיכסי סיהרא ואינה ראויה לקדש עד שיעברו
עליה שש שעות, וע"י בפירוש הרמב"ם לר"ה שכתב דגם כשמקדשים את
החודש ע"י חשבון ג"כ אין מקדשין אותו עד אחר שש שעות מהמולד וזמן
קידוש לבנה הוא רק עד חצי הזמן של כ"ט י"ב ותשצ"ג, והזמנים שעליהם
מחשבים הם כפי אופק ירושלים אבל הזמן כפי שעות השעון משתנה לפי

האופק ולכן העיר לנכון הגרי"א הענקין זצ"ל בספרו עדות לישראל בכללים לקביעות החודש והשנה אות ט"ו דכדי לחשב סוף זמן קידוש לבנה בארצות שהן למערב א"י צריכים לנכות מזמן הנדפס בלוח כפי שינוי השעון משעון א"י, וכ"ז לענין מה שתלוי במולד שהוא מאורע טבעי אחד לכל העולם, ולכן אף שזמן קידוש לבנה משתנה לפי שינוי השעון מ"מ עצם העובדא אחד הוא ואינו משתנה לפי האופק אלא זמנו אחד הוא בכל העולם.

וכנראה שהבין המחבר הנ"ל שברכת החמה זמנה ג"כ שוה בכל העולם מאחר שנתקנה על תליית השמש ברקיע ומאחר שזמנה תלויה היא בתקופה שהיא ג"כ מאורע טבעי השוה בכל העולם, והיינו שבאמת רגע התקופה שוה הוא בכל העולם, ולכן מן הדין לברך באותו הרגע בכל אופק ואופן שעת הברכה תהי' שוה בכל העולם והשינוי יהי' רק לפי שעות השעון. אמנם באמת זמנה של ברכת הלבנה וזמנה של ברכת החמה אינם דומין להדדי שהרי בנוגע לברכת החמה לא תיקנו חז"ל לברך בשעת התקופה דוקא אלא כלשון הרמב"ם בפ' י' מהל' ברכות הל' י"ח הרואה הל' י"ח הרואה את החמה ביום תקופת ניסן של תחלת המחזור של שמונה ועשרים שנה שהתקופה בתחילת ליל רביעי **כשרואה אותה ביום רביעי בבקר** מברך ברוך עושה בראשית, היינו שהברכה שהיא ברכת הראיה נתקנה לא על שעת התקופה אלא כשרואה החמה בתקופתה ואף שאינו רואה את החמה ברגע התקופה ממש מ"מ די במה שרואה השמש במקום הסמוך למקומה בשעת שנתילת ברקיע והטעם שתקנו באופן זה הוא מפני שבאותו הרגע שהחמה נמצאת ברקיע בנקודה שבה נבראה, שהיא עת התקופה, עת ערב היא וא"א לראות את החמה באותו זמן ולכן תקנו לברך למחר בבקר אמנם כשמתאחר יותר מדי אין מברכים וכלשונו של המ"א שכתב שאין לברך אחר ג' שעות של היום **שכבר עברה ממקומה**, והיינו שבזמן שהחמה כבר אינה אפילו סמוך לנקודה שבה עמדה בשעה שנתלה ברקיע אין לברך.

הרי שאין הברכה על עצם הגעת השמש למקום שנתלה ברקיע אלא על מה **שרואה** החמה באותו המקום, ולכן שפיר מובן מה שלא נמצא בשום פוסק ראשון או אחרון (גם לרבות האדר"ת) שזמן החיוב שוה הוא בכל העולם ואינו משתנה לפי האופק, והיינו שבאמת פשוט הדבר שזמן החיוב באמת משתנה לפי האופק והיינו שאף שהתקופה היא מאורע אחד שוה בכל העולם אמנם ראית התקופה אינה שוה בכל העולם, זאת אומרת שתקופת החמה בתחילת המחזור של כ"ח שנה היא בשעה ששית והיינו שמגיע לנקודה מסוימת ברקיע ונראית שם באותה הנקודה באופק ירושלים בשעה ששית (או במלים יותר מדויקות: ראויה היתה לראות שם אילו לא שקעה חמה), אמנם במקומות שהם למערבה של ירושלים עדיין אין החמה נראית באותה נקודה ברקיע

ואין מקום לברכה זו לאותם השוכנים למערב ירושלים אלא כשיראו החמה כשהגיעה לאותה נקודה. נמצא שמבקומות שהיום מתאחר לבוא בכמו שש שעות אמת הדבר שכשהגיעה עת התקופה, שהיא שעה ששית בירושלים, באותו רגע השעון עומד בחצות היום במקום שהיום מתאחר לבוא ערך שש שעות אבל מ"מ היושב באותו מקום עדיין אינו רואה את השמש במקומה ברקיע במקום שנבראה ולא יראה מאורע זה עד אשר יעברו עוד שש שעות, ולכן אין מקום לחייבו בברכה זו עד שתגיע שעה ששית במקומו, וזהו גופא דוגמא למעשה בראשית שעליו מברכים עושה מעשה בראשית. הנה בעצמך בשעת בריאת השמש לו כבר היה קיים איזה נברא בעולם וויושב בירושלים היה רואה את השמש בשעה ששית בלילה (ואף אם נאמר שנבראה החמה בתחילת היום אבל לא נתלו המאורות עד שעה ג' בבקר של יום ד' מ"מ הדברים מכוונים לעת הבריאה), אמנם לו היה קיים איזה נברא ויושב באופק אירופה או באופק אמריקה באותה העת הרי לא היה רואה שום דבר עד יעבור, למשל, שש שעות, ואז היה רואה אותו ממש הדבר שראה יושב ירושלים בעת בריאת השמש, ואילו לא היה יודע לו למי שישב בארצות המערב ענין מהלך השמש היה נדמה לו שבאותו הרגע שהוא רואה השמש שבאותו רגע נברא, ולכן תקנו חז"ל הברכה לא על העובדא האסטרונומית של התקופה אלא על **ראיית** חזרת השמש לנקודה שעמדה בה בתחילת בריאתה וזהו לעולם בשעה ששית (כפי שהיא משתנית) לכל יושבי כדור הארץ בכל מקום לפי האופק, וכן מוכח בעליל מעצם דברי האדר"ת שכתב ובמדינותינו הנוטות לצפון י"ל שהשעה מכוונת ליום שלישי **לעת ערב בשעה הששית בעוד שלא שקעה החמה**, היינו שבמדינותינו קבע הזמן בשעה המכוונת, בשעה ששית בלילה, ולפי דברי הגרמ"ן שפירא היה לו להאדר"ת לקבוע זמנו של ברכת החמה בשעה מוקדמת, שבמדינתו, מדינת רוסיא, היום מתאחר ב' שעות מא"י, ולכן בשעה שהיא שעה ששית בירושלים היא שעה ד' אחה"צ במתא מיר ששם היה מושבו.

אלא פשוט וברור בכוונתו שגם בא"י היה ראוי בעצם לתקן שיברכו ברכת החמה בשעה ששית בעת התקופה דוקא אי לו משום שאז כבר שקעה חמה ואינה נראית ולכן הוצרכו לתקן לברך שיברכו בבקר בשעה שהחמה נראית אבל בעצם עיקר זמנה הוא בלילה, ומטעם זה קבע הגאון האדר"ת שבמדינות שעדיין לא שקעה חמה ביום ג' בערב בשעה ששית, שבאותה עת נראית החמה כעומדת באותה הנקודה שבה עמדה בשעה ששית בירושלים אלא שבירושלים אינה נראית בפועל מפני שכבר שקעה, שפיר יכולים לברך בשעה ששית בזמן המכוון מאחר שבאותן מדינות נראית החמה באותו הזמן, והיינו בשעה ששית דוקא אבל לא מקודם. וגם מה שנוגע לסוף זמן ברכת החמה

הדין הוא ג"כ כמו בירושלים שיכול לברך גם למחר עד ג' שעות לדעת
המ"א או עד חצות כדעת הדגול מרבבה שהרי זמן הברכה בכל העולם הוא
בדיוק כזמנה של ירושלים אלא שמשתנה כפי האופק.

והנה אף שכתב הגאון האדר"ת "והרבה הסכימו לי" מ"מ כנראה לא
נתקבלו דבריו להלכה אצל גדולי ההוראה, והטעם נראה פשוט שהרי לפי
האמת למשל בשנת תשמ"א שקיעת החמה בירושלים היתה כמו י"א דק'
אחר זמן התקופה שהרי התקופה היתה בשעה 5:39 [ואע"ג שתקופת ניסן היא
בשעה שש, היינו לפי שעות השמש, אמנם השעון הנהוג בירושלים מתאחר
הוא לשעות השמש בכמו 21 דק', עי' ספר בין השמשות להגרי"מ טוקצינסקי
עמוד ק"ה], ואילו שקיעת החמה בירושלים ביום התקופה היתה בערך 5:50,
והיינו בערך 11 דק' **אחרי** התקופה, וגם בזמנו של שמואל ואף בזמן המשנה
היתה תקופת ניסן נופלת לפני שקיעת החמה בירושלים, אבל מ"מ חז"ל
כשתיקנו ברכת החמה על המאורע של חזרת החמה למקום שבה עמדה
בשעת בריאתה תיקנו לפי חשבונו של שמואל, אף שאינו מדויק כל כך כמו
שהעירו האחרונים, ואילו תקופת ניסן האמיתית היא קודמת לתקופה כפי
חשבונו של שמואל ונופלת בזמן שהיום והלילה שוים הם באמת, ואף שהיום
והלילה אינם שוים ביום שהוא יום התקופה לפי חשבונו של שמואל זהו מפני
שאין התקופה האמיתית באותו היום שנתקבל אצלנו כיום התקופה כפי
חשבונו של שמואל, אבל מאחר שהלכה בנוגע לברכת החמה נקבעה כאילו
אותו היום הוא יום התקופה האמיתית, וביום התקופה היום והלילה שוים הם
כמבואר בירושלמי ברכות פרק א' הלכה א', ממילא אם היו מתקנים לברך
ברכת החמה בירושלים ביום ג' אחרי התקופה אבל לפני שקיעת החמה הוי
כמו תרתי דסתרי. ולכן נלע"ד כדבר פשוט שבירושלים א"א בשום אופן
לברך ברכת החמה ביום ג' לפנות ערב אחרי התקופה ולפני השקיעה, שברכת
החמה תיקנו רק בבקר כמבואר בפירוש בדברי הרמב"ם שהובאו לעיל וכן
נפסק בשו"ע או"ח סי' רכ"ט.

ומה שהוסיף ידידי הרה"ג ר' משה נחום שפירא לכתוב שאף בירושלים יש
לחשב סוף זמן ברכת החמה כט"ו או י"ח שעות מזמן התקופה ממש שהיא
מתקדמת לשעה ששית נראה נכון אף לפי הבנתו בדברי האדר"ת, שכל
דבריו של האדר"ת מכוונים לשאר אופקים, אבל בירושלים מעולם לא נתכוין
לומר שמחשבין לפי הקדם התקופה לפני השקיעה, ואף האדר"ת שכתב שיש
לברך ביום ג' בערב לא כיון אלא למדינות הנוטות מאופק ירושלים שידוע
שהזמנים משתנים משל א"י אבל בא"י לא הזכיר כלל שיש לברך ביום ג'
מאחר שביום התקופה האמיתית היום והלילה שוים הם, נמצא שמי שמחשב
התקופה כפי חשבונו של שמואל ומברך לפני השקיעה הרי יש בו משום

סתירה מיניה וביה דאילו הוי יום התקופה האמיתית אז הוי כבר אחר שקיעת החמה וכל עצמותו של ברכת החמה נתקנה על החשבון שהתקופה נופלת בעת השקיעה. ומיהו האדר"ת דעתו דכ"ז בא"י שיש סתירה מיניה וביה כשמברך ביום ג' משא"כ בשאר ארצות שאין כאן סתירה מאחר שחשבונם של חז"ל שהיום והלילה שוים ביום התקופה נאמר רק על א"י, א"כ בשאר ארצות שפיר יכולים לברך אחר התקופה אם עדיין לא שקעה חמה, ואותם שחולקים על האדר"ת ס"ל שכמו שבא"י א"א לברך לפני השקיעה אף שכבר הגיעה התקופה כמו כן בשאר מקומות א"א לברך באותו זמן דעיקר הברכה נתקנה ביום ד' דוקא מטעם הנ"ל ונתקנה כן גם בשאר אופקים בדיוק כמו בא"י. ואולי גם האדר"ת לא הרגיש בזה שבירושלים באמת יש שהות לברך אחר התקופה לפני שקיעת החמה וא"כ נשאר אצלו שמה שאין מברכים בא"י ביום ג' הוא מפני שבמציאות החמה אינה נראית ולא מפני התקנה, וא"כ אצלו לא היה מקום לומר שזה גופא נכנס בתוך תקנת חז"ל שלא לברך ביום ג' אף בשאר ארצות, אבל מאחר שלפי האמת בטח כלול בתוך תקנת חז"ל שלא לברך בירושלים ביום ג' מאד מסתבר שלא חילקו בתקנתם בין א"י לשאר ארצות, ואולי אם היה ידוע להאדר"ת שמה שבירושלים אין מברכים ביום ג' מוכרח הדבר שהוא מצד התקנה ולא מצד המציאות לא היה מחלק בין א"י לשאר מדינות ודו"ק.

Bibliography

This bibliography is not a catalogue of all the works cited in this volume. *Bircas haChammah* is discussed in the basic codes of Jewish law including *Mishneh Torah, Tur, Shulchan Aruch* and the various commentaries on these works. Over the years the subject has been treated in numerous monographs, responsa and halachic compendia. The following is a selected list limited to texts which present the order of *Bircas haChammah*. Many of these sources also contain discussions of the pertinent *halachos*.

Castillo, R. Abraham Isaac. Ed. *Tefillah Zakkah*. Leghorn, 5549.

Cohen, R. Zevi. *Bircas haChammah: Halachos uMinhagim haShalem*. Jerusalem, 5741. Also published appended to his *Erev Pesach shechal beShabbos*. Jerusalem, 5741.

Gerlitz, R. Menachem. *Sefer Bircas haChammah keHilchosah*. Jerusalem, 5741.

Goldzweig, R. Jacob. *Sefer Kiddush Machzor haGadol*. Manchester, 5656.

Hertzberg, R. Meir David. *Or haChammah*. Przemysl, 5684. Selections republished by J. Hochhauser. *Kuntres Bircas Kiddush haChammah*. London, 5713.

R. Joseph Chaim b. Elijah of Bagdad. *Ben Ish Chai*. Jerusalem, 5658.

Kamelhar, R. Yekusiel Aryeh. *Boker Yizrach, Sha'arei Mizrach*. Cracow, 5656.

Knoller, R. Chaim. *Bircas haChammah*. Przemysl, 5684.

Lunz, R. Abraham Moshe. *Luach Eretz Yisrael*. Jerusalem, 5656.

Medini, R. Chaim Chizkiyahu. *Sedei Chemed*. New York, 5722. VII, 74-77. [In Kehot edition (New York, 5736), IX, 3850-3853.]

Meldola, R. David. *Boker Yizrach*. London, 5601. Republished, Czernowitz, 5627 and 5652.

Palaggi, R. Chaim. *Ateres haChaim*. Salonica, 5601.

Pontremoli, R. Chaim Binyamin. *Pesach haDvir*. Vol. III. Smyrna, 5633. *Hashmottos leOrach Chaim*.

Papo, R. Eliezer. *Chesed laAlafim*. Salonica, 5601.

Rapoport, R. Chaim haKohen. *Teshuvos Mayim Chaim*. Zhitomir, 5618. Responsum no. 22.

Schwartz, R. Pinchas Zelig. *Yizrach Or*. Nagyvarad, 5685. Republished, New York, 5712 and 5741.

Seder Bircas haChammah. Jerusalem, 5713.

Seder Bircas haChammah. Published by Eliyahu Volk. Warsaw, 5657.

Segner, R. Shlomo. *Or haChammah*. Munkacs, 5657.

Singer, R. Isaac. *Zoharei Chammah*. Cracow, 5656.

Sofer, R. Moshe. *Teshuvos Chasam Sofer. Orach Chaim*. Pressburg, 5615. Responsum no. 56.

Thayer, J. Ed. *Bircas Kiddush haChammah*. Frankfurt-am-Main, 5685.

Tucatzinsky, R. Yechiel Michel. *Tekufas haChammah uBirchosah*. Jerusalem, 5685. Revised second edition. Jerusalem, 5713. Revised third edition. Jerusalem, 5741.

Wissoker, B. *Sefer Bircas haChammah*. 5657.